Global Issues

Series Editors

Jim Whitman
Wakefield
West Yorkshire, UK

Paolo D. Farah
Department of Public Administration
West Virginia University
Morgantown, USA

The rapid pace of globalizing dynamics has brought in its wake a proliferation of crises, governance challenges and large-scale stresses, unprecedented in their range, seriousness and urgency. These emerging conditions and relations are variously global is their range, inclusiveness and impacts; and many of them are outpacing our legal, political and ethical systems of deliberation and control. Climate change, the ravages of contagious diseases and financial turmoil are all cases in point. Similarly, the transformative implications of new scientific and technological developments, from Big Data to gene editing, are already upon us. This book series is dedicated to providing insights into the complex interaction of human and natural systems; modes of cooperation and conflict; and the ways and degrees to which human values can be reconciled and more effectively enacted. The concentration throughout is on an integration of existing disciplines toward the clarification of political possibility as well as impending crises.

The series is published in cooperation with gLAWcal - Global Law Initiatives for Sustainable Development.

Martin Faix • Ondřej Svaček
Editors

ICC Jurisprudence and the Development of International Humanitarian Law

palgrave
macmillan

Editors
Martin Faix
Faculty of Law
Palacký University
Olomouc, Czech Republic

Ondřej Svaček
Faculty of Law
Palacký University
Olomouc, Czech Republic

ISSN 2947-8863 ISSN 2947-8871 (electronic)
Global Issues
ISBN 978-3-031-45993-1 ISBN 978-3-031-45994-8 (eBook)
https://doi.org/10.1007/978-3-031-45994-8

Published in cooperation with gLAWcal - Global Law Initiatives for Sustainable Development, Essex, UK

Cover credit: Bernt Ove Moss / EyeEm / Getty Images

This Palgrave Macmillan imprint is published by the registered company Springer Nature Switzerland AG.
The registered company address is: Gewerbestrasse 11, 6330 Cham, Switzerland

Paper in this product is recyclable.

Foreword

Twenty years have passed since the establishment of the International Criminal Court. During this period, political, current and scholarly interest in the functioning of the Court and in the Court's international criminal justice project have generated a voluminous body of knowledge, remarkable in both scope and diversity, given the Court's recent origins as a permanent institution for adjudicating international crimes. Even though international support for ending impunity and providing justice for the victims of war crimes, crimes against humanity, genocide and wars of aggression is indisputable, it couldn't shield the Court from the effects of adversarial developments in the course of time. Varied as these developments were, some attracted more media attention than others. On the one end we had theatrical attacks on the Court by some states, often coinciding with opportunistic claims to head of state immunity by states parties who, when ratifying the Rome Statute, accepted the irrelevance of such immunities. On the other end, inaction on the part of the Security Council and the Assembly of States Parties to attend timeously to member states' non-compliance with their Rome Statute obligations undermined the ability of the Court to close the impunity gap. In circles of less-discerning consideration of what really matters, developments of this kind are easily seized upon to substantiate claims that the Court is ineffective or even irrelevant.

However, despite these ramifications, the ICC's substantive work under its jurisdictional power within the framework of the Rome Statute, in particular its trial and appeal proceedings, is ongoing and constitutes the golden thread that determines the contents and scope of its jurisprudential contributions. It is this aspect that really matters for the Rome Statute phase of international criminal law development in the substantive sense of the word. This volume contributes commendably to this aspect of the Court's work through the choice of topics and the efforts of the contributing authors in applying their expert analyses in respect of the following: the involvement of the ICC in the Colombian transitional justice project; law-making by the international criminal tribunals; human rights principles in the Rome Statute's hierarchy of sources; the enlistment of child soldiers and their protection under international humanitarian law; conflict classification; comparative interpretative approaches; and war crimes jurisprudence in the case of sentences imposed by irregularly constituted tribunals. These contributions further enhance our understanding of how international humanitarian law has been enforced and developed in the jurisprudence and practice of the ICC within certain socio-political and historical contexts. The reader will also benefit from the two organizing ideas the editors have used in giving structure to the contents: the identification, interpretation and application of the law, and developments in respect of the substantive elements of international criminal law.

University of Johannesburg
Johannesburg, South Africa
May 2023

Hennie Strydom

The International Criminal Court (ICC) as a Mechanism for Global Justice and Rule of Law

Global Issues, Palgrave Macmillan/gLAWcal—Global Law Initiatives for Sustainable Development book series, tackles the numerous and critical global challenges our society confronts.[1] While globalization, with its mix of positive and negative externalities, has been extensively studied, this series provides fresh perspectives on how to deal and adapt to these challenges.[2] It also explores how humans and their institutions engage with and attempt to manage global issues such as environmental protection,[3]

[1] For some titles in the series dealing with global challenges, see: Oliver P Richmond, *Maintaining Order, Making Peace* (Palgrave Macmillan UK 2002) <http://link.springer.com/10.1057/9780230289048> accessed 26 June 2023; Svenja Gertheiss and others (eds), *Resistance and Change in World Politics* (Springer International Publishing 2017) <http://link.springer.com/10.1007/978-3-319-50,445-2> accessed 26 June 2023; Federico Lorenzo Ramaioli, *Juridical Perspectives between Islam and the West* <https://link.springer.com/book/9783031378430> accessed 9 August 2023.

[2] On the needs of crisscrossing between academic disciplines and adopt an interdisciplinary approach see, John N Clarke and Geoffrey R Edwards (eds), *Global Governance in the Twenty-First Century* (Palgrave Macmillan UK 2004) <http://link.springer.com/10.1057/9780230518698> accessed 26 June 2023; M Verweij and M Thompson (eds), *Clumsy Solutions for a Complex World: Governance, Politics and Plural Perceptions* (Palgrave Macmillan 2006).

[3] B Gleeson and N Low (eds), *Govering for the Environment: Global Problems, Ethics and Democracy* (2001st edition, Palgrave Macmillan 2001); For the relationship between law and the environment, see generally: R Boardman, *Governance of Earth Systems: Science and Its Uses* (2010th edition, Palgrave Macmillan 2010).

human rights,[4] peacebuilding.[5] Martin Faix and Ondřej Svaček's book aligns with the series' objectives and offers a detailed analysis of the intersection between the International Criminal Court (ICC) and broader challenges within international humanitarian law (IHL) and its interconnections and intertwinement with International Criminal Law (ICL) and International Human Rights Law (IHRL). ICC, a human-designed mechanism aimed at addressing and prosecuting individuals responsible for atrocities, is scrutinized for its interaction. The editors point out that while many studies focus on how treaty law shapes commitments under public international law, the 'law-making' aspects of the ICC remain understudied. IHL is not a separated or isolated discipline within public international law. The relevance of the mutual relationship can be demonstrated and witnessed in many ways, such as in the search for the definition of the term "armed conflict" as a fundamental term of IHL. Furthermore, the connections with ICL and IHRL continue to expand well beyond the initial conceptualization, as demonstrated in current debates on reparations for victims of serious violations of international humanitarian law. Throughout history, human institutions have been the chosen platforms for governing and regulating society. However, in the twenty-first century, with unprecedented connectivity and interdependence, working towards multilateral solutions for global challenges, whether in climate change through the UNFCCC or in trade via the World Trade Organization, has become increasingly complex. The rise in complexities within the human landscape has not been met with proportional attention to cooperation, conflict resolution, and harmonizing human values. Only recently have global governance institutions started transcending narrow perspectives to offer holistic approaches. The book underscores the potential of ethical considerations and legal institutions to act in the best interests of global society. The ICC plays a pivotal role in shaping the understanding of international humanitarian law, guiding the incorporation of excesses and atrocities into a legal framework that seeks global justice. The editors illustrate this through case studies that range from methodological queries about the ICC's operations and legal findings mechanisms to substantive

[4] Kurt Mills and David Jason Karp (eds), *Human Rights Protection in Global Politics* (Palgrave Macmillan UK 2015) <http://link.springer.com/10.1057/9781137463173> accessed 26 June 2023.

[5] Richmond (n 1); H Jeong, *Approaches to Peacebuilding* (2002nd edition, Palgrave Macmillan 2002).

matters like child soldiers and armed conflicts. The editors highlight how the ICC's practices serve as an additional means of defining the rule of law, its implications, and its scope. While not initially intended as a law-making body, the ICC increasingly assumes this role in practice. The book focuses on the ICC, but its reasoning applies to other international courts, especially those with adjudicative functions, which are integral to the evolution and reform of international humanitarian law. The ICC's enforcement and interpretation influence IHL development, adapting legal principles to societal transformations and needs. Although the ICC's enforcement is limited to Rome Statute parties or those accepting its jurisdiction, its impact transcends state boundaries, significantly influencing IHL development, particularly in relation to war crimes. The editors emphasize the often-overlooked symbiotic relationship between the ICC and IHL. Even within the constraints of non-party jurisdiction, the ICC has positively contributed to IHL development and the clarification of customary international law principles. Notably, the ICC's influence is pronounced in cases involving war crimes and child soldiers, enhancing clarity and adapting definitions to the evolving nature of conflicts, now involving non-state actors and asymmetrical warfare. The comprehensive analysis of the ICC sheds light on the intricate interplay among ethical considerations, global challenges, the rule of law, and the role of law and institutions. Bridging divergent worldviews within the global community is arduous, particularly with the growing criticism of Eurocentrism directed at global institutions. Nonetheless, the ICC has demonstrated its capacity as a capable forum, albeit within limitations, to intersect and expand boundaries in pursuit of international community coexistence.

This book is a great addition to the *Global Issues*, Palgrave Macmillan/gLAWcal—Global Law Initiatives for Sustainable Development book series. gLAWcal—Global Law Initiatives for Sustainable Development is an independent non-profit research organization and think tank (http://www.glawcal.org.uk/) that attempts to shed new light on global issues and non-trade concerns through research, policy analysis, and advocacy. Non-Trade Concerns include good and global governance, human rights, right to water, rights to food, social, economic and cultural rights, labor rights, access to knowledge, public health, social welfare, consumer interests and animal welfare, climate change, energy, environmental protection and sustainable development, product safety, food safety, and security. All of these values are directly affected by the global expansion of world trade and should be upheld to balance the excesses of globalization. *Global*

Issues, Palgrave Macmillan/gLAWcal—Global Law Initiatives for Sustainable Development book series aims to develop and analyze innovative, balanced, and sustainable solutions for addressing global challenges, explores many other relevant matters and provides insights into the complex interaction of human and natural systems; modes of cooperation and conflict; and the ways and degrees to which human values can be reconciled and more effectively enacted. The concentration throughout is on an integration of existing disciplines toward the clarification of political possibilities as well as impending crises. The rapid pace of globalizing dynamics has brought in its wake a proliferation of crises, governance challenges, and large-scale stresses, unprecedented in their range, seriousness, and urgency. These emerging conditions and relations are various, global is their range, inclusiveness and impacts, and many of them are outpacing our legal, political, and ethical systems of deliberation and control. Climate change, the ravages of contagious diseases and financial turmoil are all cases in point. Similarly, the transformative implications of new scientific and technological developments, from Big Data to gene editing, are already upon us.

The book fits within this broader discussion on how to relate and engage in dialogue with divergent worldviews and transnational issues; whether there can be an effective global instrument to guarantee peace and security within such a fragmented, multilayered, and multiscalar world that more broadly should address and deliver new ways to reach rule of law and global justice, in particular when atrocities and reparations for victims of serious violations of international humanitarian law, armed conflicts, or child soldiers are concerned. The edited collection by Faix and Svaček makes a timely and necessary addition to this effort. It also highlights how institutions evolve over time, adapting swiftly to evolving civil society sensitivities. While the prevalent paradigm has been cooperation versus conflict in addressing global challenges, the book emphasizes the need to transcend this dichotomy for enduring, sustainable solutions, all in the pursuit of global justice. Addressing global challenges typically occurs within specific disciplinary contexts, neglecting the fact that the transnational and transboundary nature of these issues demands a breadth of perspectives. The legal phenomenon here is not limited to the law of the treaties but is complemented by a rich analysis of how individuals perceive frame and explain the law in a context where atrocities and violence is dominant. Interpretation and the evolution of the ICC practices brings the reader closer to the social aspects of law and to how in this rapidly changing context core ethical questions are co-shaped and subsumed within the legal but also political system.

West Virginia University, Morgantown, WV
gLAWcal—Global Law Initiatives for Sustainable Development, Essex, UK

Paolo D. Farah Paolo Davide Farah, full professor, West Virginia University, Eberly College of Arts and Sciences, John D. Rockefeller IV School of Policy and Politics; founder and director of the West Virginia University, Energy Justice and Just Transition Lab; founder and coordinator of the Eberly College Interdisciplinary Research Collaborative on Global Challenges and Local Responses Initiatives; visiting professor, University of Pittsburgh, Law School; founder, president, director, principal investigator and senior research fellow, at gLAWcal—Global Law Initiatives for Sustainable Development (United Kingdom). Dual PhD in International Law from Aix-Marseille University (France) and University of Milan (Italy), LLM in European Legal Studies from the College of Europe in Bruges (Belgium), Maitrise (J.D.) in International and European Law from Paris Ouest La Defense Nanterre University (France)

Acknowledgements

The editors would like to thank all the authors for their patience and reviewers for their valuable comments. František Tóth and Charles Bird deserve gratitude for their accurate unification of contributions format and language proofreading. Last but not least, this book would not have been published without the kind support of prof Paolo D. Farah, the editor of the series "Global Issues".

Contents

Notes on Contributors

Walter Arévalo-Ramírez is a principal professor of Public International Law and director of the postgraduate program in International Law at the Universidad del Rosario (Colombia), Constitutional Law specialist, PhD in law from Universidad del Rosario. Diploma in Maritime Spaces and international watercourses of The Hague Academy of International Law. Tutor of The Hague Academy of International Law. Fellow of the international law Fellowship of the United Nations, Office of Legal Affairs, and visiting researcher at the University of Copenhagen (iCourts). Coeditor of the Colombian Yearbook of International Law. President of the Colombian Academy of International Law. Director of the Latin American Network of International Law Journals.

Martha M. Bradley is an associate professor of Public International Law and International Humanitarian Law at the Department of Public Law, Faculty of Law, University of Johannesburg, and associate researcher at the South African Research Chair for International Law at the University of Johannesburg. She also serves as an external expert at the Centre for International Humanitarian and Operational Law of the Palacký University Olomouc. She is the Recipient of the University of Johannesburg's 2019 Postdoctoral Research Fellows Excellence Award. Her research focuses on the law of non-international armed conflict and, in particular, the legal classification of non-international armed conflict.

Martin Faix is a senior lecturer in international law at the Faculty of Law, Palacký University Olomouc, where he also serves as the Head of the Centre of International Humanitarian and Operational Law. He obtained his law degree from the Justus Liebig University Giessen, Germany. In 2011, he completed his PhD on international law aspects of the EU's military operations at Charles University, Prague. Between 2015 and 2020, Martin served as an alternate member of the Management Board of the EU Agency for Fundamental Rights. Martin's research interests include general international law, international institutional law, international law on the use of force, international humanitarian law, and human rights.

Abhaya Ganashree holds an LLM in Public International Law from the London School of Economics and an LLB from the University of Leeds. She has previously worked at the Special Tribunal for Lebanon and is currently a research assistant at the Law Commission (for England and Wales) in the criminal law team. She has a keen interest in public international law and criminal justice.

Tamás Hoffmann is a senior research fellow at the Centre for Social Sciences Institute for Legal Studies (Hungarian Academy of Sciences Centre of Excellence) and associate professor at Corvinus University of Budapest. He obtained his law degree from the ELTE Budapest Faculty of Law and an LLM in Public International Law from King's College, London. He received his PhD in Public International Law from the ELTE Faculty of Law and a diploma in International Humanitarian Law from the International Committee of the Red Cross. His current research focuses on the impact of international criminal law on national criminal law norms.

Demetra Loizou is a lecturer in ICL and IHL at the University of Central Lancashire, Cyprus. Demetra holds an LLM in International Law from the University of Edinburgh and a PhD in law from the School of Oriental and African Studies, University of London. In her doctoral thesis, she explored the establishment and early jurisprudence of the ICC, focusing on the substantive law-making potential of the Court. Her main areas of expertise are ICL, IHL, and human rights law. Her current research interests include human trafficking and migration, sexual and gender-based violence and children in armed conflict.

Sergii Masol is a Humboldt postdoctoral research fellow at the University of Cologne. Sergii obtained his doctorate in law from the European

University Institute, where he also worked as a research assistant. Sergii was a visiting researcher at the University of Copenhagen and the Institute for Human Sciences in Vienna. Previously, he worked as a language assistant at the Organisation for Security and Co-operation in Europe and completed internships at the International Criminal Court, the European Court of Human Rights, the Office of the United Nations High Commissioner for Human Rights and the Raoul Wallenberg Institute of Human Rights and Humanitarian Law.

René Provost Ad.E. FRSC is James McGill Professor of Law at McGill University, where he was the founding director of the Centre for Human Rights and Legal Pluralism. His books include *Rebel Courts—the Administration of Justice by Armed Insurgents* (2021); *International Human Rights and Humanitarian Law* (2002); *State Responsibility in International Law* (2002); *Mapping the Boundaries of Belonging: Law between Religious Revival and Post-Multiculturalism* (2014); *Culture in the Domains of Law* (2017); *Confronting Genocide* (2011); *Dialogues on Human Rights and Legal Pluralism* (2013).

Ondřej Svaček is an associate professor at the Department of International and European Law, Faculty of Law, Palacký University Olomouc and the same department of Faculty of Law, Masaryk University, Brno. He also serves as an assistant to Justice of the Czech Constitutional Court, Vojtěch Šimíček. He regularly lectures abroad and completed long-term research stays at the T. M. C. Asser Instituut in The Hague and the Max Planck Institute in Heidelberg. He specializes in international criminal law, international human rights law, and general issues of public international law (e.g., law of State responsibility, jurisdictional immunities and creation of States).

Raghavi Viswanath is a doctoral researcher at the European University Institute in Florence. Raghavi holds postgraduate degrees from Leiden Law School and the University of Oxford. From September to December 2022, she was a visiting fellow at the Amsterdam Centre for International Law. Raghavi is a consultant for cultural rights collectives/ministries in India, Italy and Kenya, a research fellow at the Global Citizenship Observatory, and a senior research associate at Public International Law and Policy Group. Raghavi has taught at the National Law School of India University, the University of Salamanca, La Sapienza University and the University of East London.

Gus Waschefort is an associate professor at Essex Law School and Human Rights Centre, and barrister, at Guernica 37 Chambers, London. Gus holds a PhD from SOAS, University of London. His primary research and practice areas are international humanitarian law and international human rights law, with a focus on the protection of life and children's rights. Moreover, much of his work focuses regionally on the African continent.

CHAPTER 1

The Contribution of the International Criminal Court to the Development of International Humanitarian Law

Martin Faix and Ondřej Svaček

International courts have been significantly contributing to the formation and development of international law by, among else, providing evidence of international practice, helping in interpreting international treaties, and defining customary international law. This idea is ultimately recognized by Article 38 of the Statute of the International Court of Justice, which lists judicial decisions as one of the subsidiary means for the determination of rules of international law. As the only permanent international criminal judicial body, the International Criminal Court (ICC) contributes to the understanding of the fundamental questions of international humanitarian law (IHL), one of the oldest branches of international law, the rules of which aim at limiting the methods and means of warfare and protecting the victims of armed conflicts. Serious breaches of IHL constitute war

M. Faix (✉) • O. Svaček
Faculty of Law, Palacký University, Olomouc, Czech Republic
e-mail: martin.faix@upol.cz; ondrej.svacek@upol.cz

M. Faix, O. Svaček (eds.), *ICC Jurisprudence and the Development of International Humanitarian Law*, Global Issues,
https://doi.org/10.1007/978-3-031-45994-8_1

crimes, for which individuals may bear direct responsibility. Taking into account that the jurisdictional scope of the ICC also encompasses war crimes, the starting premise and consideration of the book is thus the extraordinary potential of the ICC in its normative relationship with IHL.

Even though the ICC was created only in 1998, the intertwinement between IHL and international criminal law (ICL) has existed since the beginning of modern IHL development in the second half of the nineteenth century. At the outset, the responsibility for breaches of these rules was to be borne only by states. However, in 1870, Gustave Moynier, in his commentary on the 1864 Geneva Convention for the Amelioration of the Condition of the Wounded in Armies in the Field, considered the idea of an international court for enforcement of the treaty. He rejected the idea at first, but further developments, including the Franco-Russian War, made him reconsider his position. Moynier proposed the establishment of an international tribunal at a meeting of the International Committee of the Red Cross on 3 January 1872. The proposal was published in the *Bulletin international des Sociétés de secours aux militaires blessés.*[1] His idea marks the point of time when rules of international law on individual criminal responsibility under international law started to develop, allowing for the prosecution of individuals for serious violations of IHL.[2] It might be difficult to assess the merits of Moynier's proposal.[3] Nevertheless, it highlights the specific intertwining between IHL and ICL, which has existed from the very beginning of the creation of modern IHL.

Despite this strong and longstanding bond between the IHL and ICL, international courts for a long time have played a relatively minor role in the development of IHL, whereas focus was placed on the development of treaty law (Geneva Conventions, 1977 Additional Protocols, etc.). Still, the adoption of Charters of the Nuremberg and Tokyo Tribunals constituted a significant step in the codification of IHL, as they were the first instruments defining crimes under international law for which individuals could be held responsible at the international level.

[1] G. Moynier, 'Note sur la creation d'une institution judiciaire internationale propre à prévenir et à réprimer les infractions à la convention de Genève', 3 *Bulletin International des Societes de Secours aux Militaires Blesses* (1872), at 122–131.

[2] On the war crimes under international law in general, see for example, Y. Dinstein, M. Tabory, *War Crimes in International Law* (The Hague/Boston/London: Martinus Nijhoff Publishers, 1996).

[3] Ch. K. Hall, 'The first proposal for a permanent international criminal court', 322 *International Review of the Red Cross* (1998), at 64.

In the period following the Nuremberg and Tokyo trials, the case law of national courts was scarce, whereas case law from international courts and tribunals was almost non-existent. The work of the non-permanent international criminal tribunals, established not by an agreement of sovereign states but as a collective measure by decisions of the UN Security Council, brought the change.[4] The International Criminal Tribunals for the former Yugoslavia (ICTY)[5] and Rwanda (ICTR)[6] began their work in the 1990s. Their judgements addressed fundamental questions of IHL, both the treaty-based and its customary counterpart.

In the post-Nuremberg era, one of the most important developments in ICL and IHL is associated with the ICC. The ICC, being the only permanent international criminal court/tribunal with the task to prosecute individuals for what the international community as a whole considers to be the most serious offences, including serious violations of IHL, has the potential to shape the normative relationship with IHL in a particularly significant way. A similar argument has been put forward in the context of the International Court of Justice's (ICJ) role in shaping IHL. Because of its institutional specificities, the ICJ shall have a normative interpretative power and a particular 'norm-making' capacity in identifying the rules of law and determining their character like customary rules, erga omnes, and jus cogens that exceed those powers that national courts, ad hoc

[4] See for example, M. Ch. Bassiouni, P. Manikas, *The Law of the International Criminal Tribunal for the Former Yugoslavia* (New York: Transnational Publishers, 1996); K. Lescure, *International Justice for Former Yugoslavia: The Workings of the International Criminal Tribunal of the Hague* (The Hague: Kluwer Law International, 1996).

[5] Resolution 808 (1993), this time in the application of the rules set forth in Chapter VII of the United Nations Charter, the Security Council decided to establish the International Criminal Tribunal for the prosecution of persons responsible for serious violations of international humanitarian law committed in the territory of the former Yugoslavia since 1991 (ICTY), which was given jurisdiction in respect of serious violations of the 1949 Geneva Conventions, violations of the laws and customs of war, genocide and crimes against humanity.

[6] Resolution 955 (1994). See for example, M. Mubiala, 'Le tribunal international pour le Rwanda: vraie ou fausse copie du tribunal pe´nal international pour l'ex Yugoslavie?', 99 *Revue Générale de droit International Public* (1995), 929; M. Mandiaye Niang, 'Le Tribunal Pénal International pour le Rwanda. Et si la contumace e´tait possible!', 103 *Revue Générale de droit International Public* (1999), 379; C. Cissé, 'The end of a culture of impunity in Rwanda?', *Yearbook of International Humanitarian Law* (1998) 161.

international criminal courts, or transitional scenarios may have in their jurisprudence.[7]

Can such a conclusion also be reached for the relationship between the ICC and IHL? Indeed, some aspects suggest that this is the case. The role of the ICC exceeds in certain respect the standard applicable to international courts in international law. Whereas the primary function of international courts, including the ICJ, is not law-making but the application of international law in respective proceedings, according to the Rome Statute [Article 21(2)], the ICC may 'apply principles and rules of law as interpreted in its previous decisions'.

This book provides a selective overview of the major impact and role of the ICC in developing new concepts, meanings, and enforcement mechanisms of IHL. By examining the groundwork laid by the Court that fosters greater development of IHL, the book efficiently explores how the Court's accomplishments successfully contribute to this legal area beyond its adjudicative mandate. It starts from the premise that the jurisprudence of international courts in general and the ICC in particular, although not an independent law-making process, is a particularly useful additional means of determining the existence of a rule of law, its meaning, and its scope. To put it in different terms: the phenomenon of law-making capacity of international judicial institutions, including the ICC, is taken for granted here.[8]

The book proposes an analysis of the collective 'legacy in making' of the ICC on the development of IHL by exploring how IHL has been enforced and developed in the jurisprudence and practice of the ICC. A partial focus is given here to the phenomenon of child soldiering, which became symptomatic for the early practice of the ICC. The book provides its readers with broad insight into the activity of the ICC as it covers a wide range of questions concerning ICL and IHL. In order to get a clearer and more systematic picture of how the ICC contributed (or continues to contribute) to the development of IHL, the chapters of the book are divided into two parts. The first part contains chapters focused on the

[7] W. Arévalo-Ramírez, 'The International Court of Justice and the international humanitarian law rules for armed conflicts', 20 *Revista Científica General José María Córdova* (2022) 38, at 425–442. See also C. Kress, 'The International Court of Justice and the Law of Armed Conflicts', in Ch. J. Tams and James Sloan (eds), *The Development of International Law by the International Court of Justice* (Oxford: Oxford University Press 2013).

[8] See for example, A. Von Bogdandy and I. Venzke, 'Beyond Dispute: International Judicial Institutions as Lawmakers', 12 *German Law Journal* (2011), 5, at 979–1003.

methodology of law-finding before the ICC, that is, identification, interpretation, and application of the law. The authors address complex issues concerning the mutual relationship between treaty law (Article 8 of the ICC Statute) and customary international law (customary IHL) and explore the relevance of IHRL in the application and interpretation of Article 8 of the Rome Statute. The second part, on the other hand, consists of chapters focused on *substantive international criminal law*. The authors address issues concerning contextual elements of war crimes (qualification of armed conflict), passive personal scope of applicability ratione personae of IHL (adversary element of war crimes), denying judicial guarantees as serious breach of IHL, forms of responsibility (here in the context of transitional justice), and circumstances precluding wrongfulness (namely mental incapacity and duress). Concerning the structure, editors of this book followed the idea that it is necessary firstly to define the method of law-finding before the law (i.e., substantive international criminal law) itself is being interpreted with respect to specific areas of ICL. The approach taken by editors is selective, the study does not have ambition to discover or comprehensively analyse all possible aspects of intersection between IHL and ICL. Still, the book makes up a 'self-contained' system which, after the presentation of general consideration on the identification of applicable legal framework focuses on the key aspects of substantive ICL, including, as already described, elements of war crimes in general, elements of particular war crimes that were already pronounced in the ICC's case law, forms of responsibility, and circumstances precluding wrongfulness. This study does not consider international criminal procedural issues (e.g., jurisdiction of the ICC, personal immunity, or cumulative charges).

The opening chapter by Tamás Hoffmann assesses A. Pellet's reflection on a reference in Article 8 of the ICC Statute to the established framework of international law as a 'veritable brainwashing operation led by criminal lawyers' that can eventually result in freezing the further evolution of customary law. The chapter aims to critically analyze this claim focusing on the practice of the ICC and determine whether customary international humanitarian law truly needs further development by international criminal courts. It examines the question of whether the institutional design of the Rome Statute has indeed restricted the development of international criminal law, focusing on the field of war crimes law. The chapter first analyses the relationship between international humanitarian law and international criminal law, then addresses the historical role of the

Nuremberg Tribunal and the International Criminal Tribunal for the Former Yugoslavia in the development of war crimes law. Finally, it zeroes in on the Rome Statute and investigates whether the crime definitions and the emphasis on the principle of legality have actually curbed the potential for judicial innovation.

The next chapter by Demetra Loizou focuses on the ICC's early jurisprudence and explores the chambers' approach to the interpretation of the applicable sources of law as set out in Article 21 of the Rome Statute. The purpose of this exercise is to identify specific instances and trends whereby the ICC's interpretation of Article 8 relied more heavily on the ICC's legal framework than the general framework of IHL when compared with the interpretative approach of its predecessors. Demetra Loizou argues that in order to understand the ICC's normative potential with respect to the development of IHL, an in-depth exploration of the Court's reliance on the Rome Statute legal regime vis-à-vis the wider IHL framework is both necessary and timely. The chapter examines the relationship between ICL and IHL before the establishment of the ICC, focusing on the work of the ad hoc tribunals. Secondly, it assesses how the relationship between ICL and IHL was redefined after the establishment of the ICC. The first comparison is necessary in order to make a distinction between the law-making potential of the ad hoc tribunals with that of the ICC. The second comparison aims at demonstrating how the formulation of the war crimes provision has a direct bearing on the normative potential of the ICC and the Chambers' interpretative approaches.

Chapter 4, by Raghavi Viswanath, tests the correctness of the interpretive approaches employed by the ad hoc tribunals and the ICC on questions of IHL. Given the multiplicity of interpretive approaches that are in circulation now, this chapter selects certain traditional and non-traditional rules that have been invoked in readings of both treaties and customary IHL. The chapter canvases the rules of treaty interpretation employed by the chosen tribunals, be it the International Criminal Tribunal for the former Yugoslavia, the International Criminal Tribunal for Rwanda, the Special Court of Sierra Leone, or the ICC. It draws comparisons between the interpretative trends emerging out of the practice of each tribunal and unpacks the more systemic and political causes underlying these trends.

In the final chapter concerning the methodology of law-finding before the ICC, Sergii Masol explores the place of human rights norms in the legal regime of the ICC by examining the relevant case law and explaining certain jurisprudential problems through the lens of Robert Alexy's

Theorie der Grundrechte. He argues that the super-legality approach to Article 21(3) of the Rome Statute, according to which internationally recognized human rights are superior to any other legal norms outlined in Article 21(1) of the Rome Statute, is—legally speaking—largely correct. Nevertheless, this approach is not omnipotent if examined in the light of Alexy's distinction between two types of norms: rules and principles.

The second part of the book, concerning issues of substantive ICL, opens with a chapter by Martha Bradley. The purpose of this chapter is to determine the intensity threshold expressed in Article 8(2)(f) of the Rome Statute in the wording 'protracted armed conflict'. In examining Article 8(2)(f) of the Statute, the ordinary meaning of the text, the context, the object, and purpose of the provisions is considered in accordance with the general principles of treaty interpretation. Martha Bradley concludes that the inclusion of the phrase 'protracted armed conflict' in the second sentence of Article 8(2)(f) possibly creates a requirement for a higher threshold of violence than the minimum intensity of violence associated with protracted armed violence and, in fact, could institute a new category of non-international armed conflict. Alternatively, it may be that the inclusion of the phrase 'protracted armed conflict' is superfluous and is merely the repetition of the intensity of violence requirement already inherent in a Common Article 3-type armed conflict which provides that the intensity threshold is fulfilled if violence is protracted in nature.

The following chapter by Gus Waschefort contributes to the recent debate on the question of whether children continue to enjoy special protection in terms of IHL once they are enlisted, conscripted, or used for active participation in hostilities, and whether such children enjoy protection against sexual violence on an intra-party basis, as a matter of law. It responds to arguments raised in the *Ntaganda* case before the ICC that the laws of armed conflict do not protect members of armed groups from acts of violence directed against them by their own forces. The focus of this chapter is to consider whether at the individual normative level the special protection afforded children during armed conflict continues to operate to provide protection to children against sexual violence even once they no longer belong to the categories of persons traditionally included in the passive personal scope of applicability ratione personae of IHL (i.e., persons who do not or no longer directly participate in hostilities: wounded, sick and shipwrecked, prisoners of war, and civilians).

In the next chapter, René Provost focuses on another substantive intersection between ICL and IHL with his analysis of the *Al-Hassan* case before the ICC, where for the first time in the history of international criminal justice, a defendant is being tried with—generally speaking—the charge of the war crime of denying judicial guarantees. René Provost inquires whether international law recognizes that non-state armed groups can lawfully establish their own regime of administration of justice in zones of armed conflict and challenges the validity of the Pre-Trial Chamber's conclusion and confusion between the concept of the 'regular constitution' of a court and its 'independence and impartiality'. The chapter first maps out the concept of a 'regularly constituted' court included in Common Article 3 and Article 8(2)(c)(iv) of the Rome Statute and then tackles the relationship of this concept to that of 'independence and impartiality' that appears as a substitute in Additional Protocol II, and also in the ICC's Elements of Crimes.

The chapter written by Walter Arévalo-Ramírez explores the interaction between national and international legal standards in the implementation of the Colombian Special Jurisdiction for Peace (SJP) and in its first indictment rendered in January 2021. Walter Arévalo-Ramírez refers to three elements of the SJP's normative framework that challenge international legal standards and—depending on their implementation—might provide grounds for the ICC's intervention in Colombia: restorative sanctions, the differentiated treatment for members of the armed forces, and command responsibility. Finally, the first indictment of the SJP (Order 019) is considered to demonstrate how its judges have drawn on international jurisprudence in attributing criminal responsibility to top leaders of the FARC-EP for war crimes and crimes against humanity.

In the final chapter, Abhaya Ganashree focuses on the case of Dominic Ongwen before the ICC, where the accused, recruited as a child soldier, was being tried for committing crimes during his adulthood. The chapter contributes to the debate on the possible dual status of child soldiers which blurs the line between victim and perpetrator. The question that this chapter deals with is the extent of the protection afforded to child soldiers and assesses whether ICL permits the consideration of the impact of the experiences as a child soldier on future conduct. Using this case as a starting point, the chapter addresses the core question of whether mental incapacity and duress can be treated as a defence under Article 31 of the Rome Statute and whether sociological and psychological circumstances could be considered by the ICC.

The book contributes to the ongoing debate on the mutual relationship between ICL and IHL, which is almost intimate. Enough is to remind words of Marco Sassòli that 'IHL [...] forms part of ICL [and] [t]he ICL of war crimes in turn forms part of IHL'.[9] It has been already stressed that this mutual relationship may be further developed through the case law of international criminal tribunals, and given its predominant position in the recent system of international criminal justice, particularly through the case law of the ICC. It goes without saying that this process, which should be acclaimed above all as it is indicative of the overall progressive development of the international legal system, has its limits and pitfalls. Concerning the limits, the possible contribution of the ICC to the development of IHL is excluded in areas where the ICC simply lacks jurisdiction ratione materiae, although (and despite the fact) respective regulation is laid down in customary international law.[10] Having in mind Article 21 of the Rome Statute, the ICC cannot step out from its own shadow here and must accept that without the adoption of amendments to the Rome Statute, customary IHL will be 'ahead of the game', at least in relation to treaty-based ICL. Next, possible pitfalls of the intertwinement between IHL and ICL have until recently been most accurately described and analysed by Rogier Bartels, who argues that 'viewing IHL through the lens of ICL also entails risks [because] [n]ot all "clarifications" by [international] courts and tribunals have simplified, or indeed clarified, IHL. Whilst certain rulings might be understandable from a criminal law point of view, the impact on IHL when applied on the battlefield, instead of in the courtroom, could actually lead to confusion and to a blurring of the (usually) clear and basic rules of IHL'.[11] The undesired effect would be that this 'clarified' form of IHL, once it gets back from courtrooms to battlefields, might eventually diminish the level of protection afforded to individuals in times of war.

It is the humble wish of the co-editors that this book will contribute to the ongoing debate over these complex issues of mutual relationship between IHL and ICL, including its benefits, limits, and pitfalls.

[9] M. Sassòli, 'Humanitarian Law and International Criminal Law', in Antonio Cassese (ed.), *The Oxford Companion to International Criminal Justice* (Oxford: Oxford University Press, 2009), at 111.

[10] See for example, A. Cassese, P. Gaeta et al. *Cassese's International Criminal Law* (3rd edn., Oxford: Oxford University Press, 2013), at 79–83. Cassese points out examples of legal regulation concerning prohibited means and methods of warfare in the Rome Statute, which is narrower than regulation in customary international law.

[11] R. J. Bartels, *From the battlefield to the courtroom (and back): The interplay between international humanitarian law and international criminal law* (PhD Thesis, Universiteit van Amsterdam: 2022), at 28.

PART I

Methodology of Law-finding Before the International Criminal Court

CHAPTER 2

Freezing or Consolidating the Development of War Crimes Law? The International Criminal Court and the Role of Judicial Innovation

Tamás Hoffmann

2.1 Introduction—A Blight in Disguise?

In 1998, the adoption of the Statute of the International Criminal Court (ICC) at the Rome Diplomatic Conference was universally hailed as a monumental milestone in the development of international criminal law. After over a century, the utopian dream of Gustave Moynier about the creation of a permanent international criminal court finally became

T. Hoffmann (✉)
Centre for Social Sciences Institute for Legal Studies (Hungarian Academy of Sciences Centre of Excellence) and Corvinus University, Budapest, Hungary

M. Faix, O. Svaček (eds.), *ICC Jurisprudence and the Development of International Humanitarian Law*, Global Issues,
https://doi.org/10.1007/978-3-031-45994-8_2

reality.[1] Amid the general elation, however, many scholars were unsatisfied with the institutional design of the court, which they perceived to be specifically devised to curtail judicial innovation following a period of exponential expansion led by the jurisprudence of the International Criminal Tribunal of the Former Yugoslavia (ICTY). The Rome Statute, they argued, with its reliance on the principle of legality (nullum crimen sine lege) and the exhaustive definition of crimes, unduly limited the judges' ability to engage in the development of international criminal law. One particularly vicious criticism was voiced by Alain Pellet, who accused the drafters of the statute that as a 'result of a veritable brainwashing operation led by criminal lawyers, with the self-interested support of the United States [...] have frozen customary definitions in a process of rapid evolution'.[2] In his view, this was a potentially fatal error as 'men's criminal imagination appears unlimited and, by enclosing the definition of the crimes in narrow, punctilious formulations, they have forbidden the judges in advance to suppress future malevolent inventions of the human spirit'.[3]

Other commentators and even prominent judges agreed that the 'veritable obsession' with the nullum crimen sine lege principle and the codification of crimes provisions[4] resulted in a 'jurisdictional fever'[5] that reflects the drafters' explicit resolve to marginalize the development of customary international law.[6] David Hunt, a former judge of the ICTY feared that

[1] Ch. K. Hall, 'The First Proposal for A Permanent International Criminal Court', 38 *International Review of the Red Cross* (1998) 57–74.

[2] A. Pellet, 'Applicable Law', in A. Cassese, P. Gaeta, J. R. W. D. Jones (eds) *The Rome Statute of the International Criminal Court: A Commentary*, Vol. II. (Oxford: Oxford University Press, 2002) 1051–1084, at 1056–1057.

[3] *Ibid*, at 1059.

[4] C. Kress, 'The International Criminal Court as a Turning Point in the History of International Criminal Justice', in A. Cassese (ed.), *The Oxford Companion to International Criminal Justice* (Oxford, New York: Oxford University Press, 2009), 143–159, at 146.

[5] H. Ascensio, 'La Cour pénale internationale et l'héritage des Tribunaux pénaux internationaux. Le point de vue de la doctrine', in P. Tavernier (ed.), *Actualité de la jurisprudence pénale internationale à l'heure de la mise en place de la Cour pénale internationale* (Bruxelles: Bruylant, 2004) 243–249, at 246.

[6] L. v. d. Herik, 'The Decline of Customary International Law as a Source of International Criminal Law' in C. A. Bradley (ed.), *Custom's Future—International Law in a Changing World* (Cambridge University Press, 2016) 230–252, at 231. Sivakumaran also cautioned that 'Resort to international criminal law in this manner may also have the unintended effect of freezing international humanitarian law. Developments in international humanitarian law may take place only when the ICC has an opportunity to pronounce on the matter, and, given the importance of the nullum crimen sine lege principle, opportunity for development may be limited'. S. Shivakumaran, *The Law of Non-international Armed Conflict* (New York: Oxford University Press, 2012) 81.

the codification 'may well have the effect of stultifying further growth in the law',[7] while Antonio Cassese, the first president of the Yugoslavia Tribunal was concerned about 'retrograde elements freezing legal development'.[8]

This chapter aims to further examine the question of whether the institutional design of the Rome Statute of the International Criminal Court has indeed restricted the development of international criminal law, focusing on the field of war crimes law. It first analyses the relationship between international humanitarian law[9] and international criminal law, then addresses the historical role of the Nuremberg Tribunal and the International Criminal Tribunal for the Former Yugoslavia in the development of war crimes law. Finally, it zeroes in on the Rome Statute and investigates whether the crime definitions and the emphasis on the principle of legality have actually curbed the potential for judicial innovation.

2.2 International Humanitarian Law and International Criminal Law—A Symbiotic but Separate Existence

Normative efforts to mitigate violence during armed conflicts have a long historical pedigree, and starting from the second half of the nineteenth century, the laws of war became subject to numerous international treaties, creating an inter-state regulatory framework.[10] Far from being 'at the vanishing point of law',[11] contemporary international humanitarian law is arguably the most extensively codified area of public international law.[12]

[7] D. Hunt, 'High Hopes, "Creative Ambiguity" and an Unfortunate Mistrust in International Judges', 2 *Journal of International Criminal Justice* (2004) 56–70, at 59.

[8] A. Cassese, 'The Statute of the International Criminal Court: Some Preliminary Reflections', 10 *European Journal of International Law* (1999) 144–171, at 158.

[9] I use the terms international humanitarian law, law of armed conflicts, law of war and laws of war interchangeably in this chapter.

[10] See for example, M. E. O'Connell, 'Historical Development and Legal Basis', in D. Fleck (ed.), *The Handbook of International Humanitarian Law* (3rd edn., Oxford University Press, 2013) 1–42, at 15–42.; J. H. W. Verzijl, *International Law in a Historical Perspective, Vol. IX.: The Laws of War* (Brill, Nijhoff, 1979).

[11] H. Lauterpacht, 'The Problem of the Revision of the Law of War', 29 *British Yearbook of International Law* (1952) 360–382, at 382.

[12] As O'Donoghue pithily remarked, 'the sheer volume of IHL treaty law instils a sense of apprehension into many public international lawyers who do not feel comfortable engaging with a topic so heavily treaty-laden'. A. O'Donoghue, 'Splendid Isolation: International Humanitarian Law, Legal Theory and the International Legal Order', 14 *Yearbook of International Humanitarian Law* (2011) 107–131, at 113.

While the laws of war aim to create a delicate balance between military necessity and the considerations of humanity by the adoption of compromises as outcomes of negotiations,[13] its enforcement was ultimately ensured by extra-legal considerations such as resource management, the goal of avoiding retaliations, moral condemnation, or the re-establishment of post-war relations with the enemy nation.[14] International humanitarian law also has a salient role in ensuring military discipline and thus several of its rules originate in national military codes.[15] Consequently, pragmatism in the creation and application of the law of war was of paramount importance that often resulted in an anti-formalist ethos, putting emphasis on principles and standards instead of rules, especially concerning the regulation of methods and means of combat.[16] While IHL definitely aims to constrain violence, it also legitimizes it.[17]

In light of the above, one might agree with the statement that '[T]he movement for laws of war owes less to professors, statesmen[,] and moralists than to military commanders'.[18] In practice, most international humanitarian law experts belong either in the military or in the International Committee of the Red Cross (ICRC),[19] and even though the ICRC enjoys

[13] M. N. Schmitt, 'Military Necessity and International Humanitarian Law: Preserving the Delicate Balance', 50 *Virginia Journal of International Law* (2010) 795–839.

[14] Ch. af Jochnick, R. Normand, 'The Legitimation of Violence: Critical History of the Laws of War', 35 *Harvard International Law Journal* (1994) 49–95.

[15] R. Liivoja, 'Law and Honour—Normative Pluralism in the Regulation of Military Conduct' in J. Klabbers and T. Piiparinen (eds), *Normative Pluralism and International Law* (New York: Cambridge University Press, 2013) 143–166, at 150.

[16] D. Kennedy, 'War and International Law: Distinguishing Military and Humanitarian Professions', 82 *International Law Studies* (2007) 3–33, at 13–14.

[17] See more in detail Jochnick, Normand, *supra* note 14. In a recent book, Samuel Moyn argued that while the laws of war indeed manage to influence the belligerents' behaviour towards a more humane armed conflict, these less brutal conflicts eventually resulted in longer periods of fighting as resort to violence and prolonging the conflict became less difficult for political leaders. S. Moyn, *Humane: How the United States Abandoned Peace and Reinvented War* (New York: Farrar, Straus, and Giroux, 2021) 294–295. Nevertheless, Kaye rightly emphasizes that 'even minimal, uncertain constraints serve a useful function as "the best that could be achieved" under such circumstances'. D. Kaye, 'Complexity in the Law of War', in R. A. Miller and R. M. Bratspies (eds) *Progress in International Law* (Leiden, Boston: Martinus Nijhoff, 2008) 681–706, at 690.

[18] Summer Maine quoted in J. L. Kunz, 'The Chaotic Status of the Laws of War and the Urgent Necessity for Their Revision', 45 *American Journal of International Law* (1951) 37–61, at 61.

[19] O'Donoghue, *supra* note 12, at 109–112.

a unique legitimacy as the guardian of the 1949 Geneva Conventions, constantly working together with military lawyers on the battlefield, actively participating in international codifications and producing influential legal commentaries and studies, they also have to operate in an environment that is dominated by military lawyers.[20] This environment inevitably fosters deference to state authority.

However, a human rights-oriented approach denies the classical pragmatic and sovereignty-focused conception of the law of war. For instance, Lauterpacht passionately pleaded that 'We shall utterly fail to understand the true character of the law of war unless we are to realize that its purpose is almost entirely humanitarian in the literal sense of the word, namely[,]to prevent or mitigate suffering and, in some cases, to rescue life from the savagery of battle and passion. This, and not the regulation and direction of hostilities, is its essential purpose'.[21] Beyond the influence of human rights, this perspective foregrounds the significance of international criminal law and claims that the development of war crimes law by international criminal fora 'humanized humanitarian law',[22] leading from an inter-state to an individual-rights perspective, as also evidenced by the phrase 'international humanitarian law' increasingly supplanting other terms such as the 'law of war'.[23] Such an approach could significantly influence even the most fundamental rules of IHL.[24]

[20] On the role of the ICRC in the development of international humanitarian law, see more in detail L. Perna, *The Formation of the Treaty Law of Non-international Armed Conflicts* (Leiden: Martinus Nijhoff, 2006) 34–39.

[21] Lauterpacht, *supra* note 11, 363–4.

[22] T. Meron, 'The Humanization of Humanitarian Law', 94 *American Journal of International Law* (2000) 239–278.

[23] T. Meron, *The Humanization of International Law* (Leiden, Boston: Martinus Nijhoff, 2006). Solis rather sardonically remarks that human rights NGOs desire 'to avoid phrases like "law of war" in favour of more pacific terms, perhaps in the hope that battlefield actions may someday follow that description' and that [A] few scholars argue that both 'law of war' and 'law of armed conflict', are passé terms, replaced in the eyes of some internationalists by 'international humanitarian law', passing over the irony of how a body of law defining how noncombatants may lawfully be killed (i.e., collateral damage) is 'humanitarian'. G. D. Solis, *The Law of Armed Conflict: International Humanitarian Law in War* (Cambridge: Cambridge University Press, 2010), at 22.

[24] Goodman, for instance, argues that the law of armed conflict forbids the killing of enemy fighters in some circumstances when it is manifestly unnecessary—a view that is clearly at odds with the classical approach. R. Goodman, 'The Power to Kill or Capture Enemy Combatants', 24 *European Journal of International Law* (2013), 819–853.

In contrast to the fundamentally state-centric regulatory framework of international humanitarian law, international criminal law is premised on the concept of individual criminal responsibility, which requires the application of more precise norms. To meet this specificity requirement, war crimes law had to transform the underlying humanitarian law norms to effectively establish criminality, often making the underlying IHL rules more precise.[25]

Even though war crimes law is based on the rules and principles of the highly specialized field of international humanitarian law, it has a distinct epistemic community. International criminal law is claimed to have three dimensions: 'the "universalist" aspirations of public international law, the "humanist" dimension of human rights law and the legality and fairness-oriented foundations of criminal law'.[26] As elaborated below, modern international criminal law institutions are largely dominated by human rights sensitivities[27] that generally view sovereignty as a potential roadblock on the road to progress to international criminal justice.[28]

While international humanitarian law is indispensable for the existence of war crimes law, the opposite is not necessarily apparent. Even though it has been suggested that 'the rule of international humanitarian law depends on its enforcement through the prosecution and punishment of its offenders',[29] Sivakumaran rightly points out that criminal enforcement

[25] M. Sassòli, 'Humanitarian Law and International Criminal Law', in Cassese, *supra* note 4, 111–122, at 116–117.

[26] C. Stahn, L. v. d. Herik, '"Fragmentation", Diversification and "3D" Legal Pluralism: International Criminal Law as the Jack-in-the-Box?' in C. Stahn, L. v. d. Herik (eds) *The Diversification and Fragmentation of International Criminal Law* (Brill, 2012), 21–89, at 23. See also Clapham's witty description of the 'three tribes' of international criminal law composed of criminal lawyers (pénalistes), human rights advocates (droit de l'hommistes), and public international lawyers (internationalistes). A. Clapham, 'Three Tribes Engage on the Future of International Criminal Law', 9 *Journal of International Criminal Justice* (2011) 689–695. This reflects my own experiences as an LLM student at the University of London LLM-programme in 2002–2003, where I was surprised to see that very few people attended both the laws of armed conflict and the international criminal class.

[27] D. Robinson, 'The Identity Crisis of International Criminal Law', 21 *Leiden Journal of International Law* (2008), 925–963, at 925.

[28] As Cryer wryly observes, 'when sovereignty appears in [international criminal law] scholarship, it commonly comes clothed in hat and cape. A whiff of sulphur permeates the air'. R. Cryer, 'International Criminal Law vs. State Sovereignty: Another Round?', 16 *European Journal of International Law* (2005) 979–1000, at 980.

[29] A. Cassese, 'On the Current Trends towards Criminal Prosecution and Punishment of Breaches of International Humanitarian Law', 9 *European Journal of International Law* (1998) 2–17, at 17.

is limited as it necessarily relates to violations that have already taken place. As such, it can only act as a complement to other forms of enforcement and implementation.[30] Indeed, the laws of armed conflict were traditionally not enforced by criminal law norms and most international humanitarian law norms are even today not subject to criminal enforcement as that requires a customary norm criminalizing the underlying conduct.[31] Still, the development of war crimes law can potentially broaden the scope of application of IHL, such as in the case of the enlargement of the rules applicable to non-international armed conflicts.[32] However, war crimes norms can even restrict the application of the underlying humanitarian norm by creating the false impression that if a specific conduct is not a war crime, then it is lawful.[33] Blum poignantly refutes the latter view by reminding us that 'the lion's share of the human casualties and the property destruction of protected persons and objects on these battlefields can be traced to everyday combat missions carried out with no criminal intent, under resource constraints, conditions of uncertainty, and a general preference for the defense of one's own forces and civilians'.[34]

One example of the potential danger of restricting humanitarian protection by adopting international criminal law standards is the application of the proportionality standard during targeting decisions. International criminal law's more demanding proportionality assessment that requires 'excessive' civilian casualties during targeting already has an impact on the IHL interpretation, which arguably threatens the attainment of humanitarian values by allowing a much larger amount of collateral damage than the classic humanitarian law standard.[35] This, however, raises the question

[30] S. Sivakumaran, *The Law of Non-International Armed Conflict* (New York: Oxford University Press, 2012) 475.

[31] D. Akande, 'Sources of International Criminal Law', in A. Cassese (ed.) *Oxford Companion to International Criminal Justice* (New York: Oxford University Press, 2007) 41.

[32] See in detail, T. Hoffmann, 'The Gentle Humanizer of Humanitarian Law: Antonio Cassese and the Creation of the Customary Law of Non-International Armed Conflicts' in C. Stahn, L. v. d. Herik (eds) *Future Perspectives on International Criminal Justice* (Hagues: T.M.C. Asser Press, 2010) 58–80.

[33] Sassòli, *supra* note 25, at 118.

[34] G. Blum, 'The Shadow of Success: How International Criminal Law Has Come to Shape the Battlefield', 100 *International Law Studies* (2023) 133–185, at 137.

[35] *Ibid.*, at 160.

whether the engagement of international criminal fora in the development of war crimes law could occasionally threaten the integrity of the laws of armed conflict.

2.3 International Criminal Fora and the Development of War Crimes Law

The Application of War Crimes Law after the World Wars

The idea that international judicial institutions could have the power to apply international humanitarian law without clear jurisdictional limitations, have been controversial ever since its first appearance during the First World War. On 25 January 1919, the victorious Allied Powers established the Commission on the Responsibility of the Authors of the War and the Enforcement of Penalties that proposed the creation of an international criminal tribunal tasked with prosecuting alleged German war criminals.[36] The United States, however, flatly rejected the idea. It emphasized that '[T]he American representatives know of no international statute or convention making a violation of the laws and customs of war—not to speak of the laws of principles of humanity—an international crime, affixing a punishment to it, and declaring the court which has jurisdiction over the offence'.[37]

While the proposed High Tribunal never became operational, similar concerns were raised during the drafting process of the London Charter of the International Military Tribunal (IMT), when both the British and the US delegates argued that the judges are not supposed to determine what constitutes a violation of international law.[38] Nevertheless, eventually, the bench was provided with ample opportunity to determine applicable war crimes law as Article 6(b) of the charter defined war crimes broadly as 'violations of the laws or customs of war', listing a few prohibited acts, thus allowing judges to establish individual criminal responsibility by

[36] For more background, see H. M. Rhea, 'The Commission on the Responsibility of the Authors of the War and on Enforcement of Penalties and its Contribution to International Criminal Justice after World War II', 25 *Criminal Law Forum* (2014) 147–169.

[37] 'Commission on the Responsibility of the Authors of the War and on Enforcement of Penalties', 14 *American Journal of International Law* (1920) 95–154, at 145–46.

[38] S. Darcy, *Judges, Law and War—The Judicial Development of International Humanitarian Law* (Cambridge University Pres, 2014), at 55.

recourse to customary international law.[39] Even though this was criticized by the defence lawyers as inconsistent with the principle of legality,[40] the tribunal dismissed this argument. It emphasized that 'the maxim [nullum crimen sine lege] is not a limitation of sovereignty, but is in general a principle of justice. To assert that it is unjust to punish those who in defiance of treaties and assurances have attacked neighbouring states without warning is obviously untrue, for in such circumstances the attacker must know that he is doing wrong, and so far from it being unjust to punish him, it would be unjust if his wrong were allowed to go unpunished'.[41]

The Nuremberg Tribunal at the same time underlined that the definitions of crimes set out in its charter are based on extant rules of public international law.[42] However, it also explained that the laws of war 'are not static, but by continual adaptation follow the needs of a changing world',[43] justifying how violations of certain provisions of the IV Hague Convention of 1907 could give rise to criminal responsibility despite the lack of explicit statement to that effect.[44]

[39] Charter of the International Military Tribunal—Annex to the Agreement for the Prosecution and Punishment of the Major War Criminals of the European Axis, 8 August 1945, at Art. 6(b), which reads: 'War Crimes: namely, violations of the laws or customs of war. Such violations shall include, but not be limited to, murder, ill-treatment or deportation to slave labor or for any other purpose of civilian population of or in occupied territory, murder or ill-treatment of prisoners of war or persons on the seas, killing of hostages, plunder of public or private property, wanton destruction of cities, towns or villages, or devastation not justified by military necessity'. The Charter of the International Military Tribunal for the Far East did not even include a non-inclusive list of war crimes. Special Proclamation—Establishment of an International Military Tribunal for the Far East, 19 January 1946, at Art. 5(b), which reads: 'Conventional War Crimes: Namely, violations of the laws or customs of war'.

[40] K. S. Gallant, *The Principle of Legality in International and Comparative Criminal Law* (1st edn. New York: Cambridge University Press, 2009) 99–110.

[41] *Trial of the Major War Criminals before the International Military Tribunal, Nuremberg, 14 November 1945–1 October 1946, Volume I.* (Nuremberg, 1947) (hereafter Trial of the Major War Criminals), at 219.

[42] 'The Charter is not an arbitrary exercise of power on the part of the victorious nations, but in view of the Tribunal, as will be shown, it is the expression of International Law existing at the time of its creation; and to that extent is itself a contribution to International Law'. Trial of the Major War Criminals, *supra* note 42, at 218.

[43] *Ibid.*, at 221.

[44] *Trial of the Major War Criminals before the International Military Tribunal, Nuremberg, 14 November 1945–1 October 1946, Volume I* (Nuremberg, 1947), at 253.

Ultimately, the Nuremberg Tribunal played a significant role in the development of war crimes law. It created a precedent for the application of customary law to establish individual criminal responsibility while at the same time denying the innovative nature of its jurisprudence.[45]

The Open Revolution of the Yugoslavia Tribunal

In contrast to its predecessors, the ICTY has proudly acknowledged its prominent role in the development of international humanitarian law.[46] The drafters of its statute explicitly allowed direct recourse to customary international humanitarian law in Article 3 that provided a non-exhaustive list of violations of the laws or customs of war.[47] It has been described as a 'residual clause' designed to ensure that the jurisdiction of the tribunal over all serious violations of humanitarian law as the category of war crimes is 'watertight and inescapable'.[48] Utilizing this provision, the Yugoslavia Tribunal embarked on a quest to revolutionize war crimes law. In the 1995 *Tadić* Appeals Decision, the Appeals Chamber 'stunned international lawyers by issuing a broad and innovative reading of [...] war

[45] This strategy reaffirms Lauterpacht's observation that '[M]any an act of judicial legislation may in fact be accomplished under the guise of the ascertainment of customary law'. H. Lauterpacht, *The Development of International Law by the International Court* (Praeger, 1958), at 368.

[46] The Tribunal lists as one of its achievements that '[S]ince its establishment, the Tribunal has consistently and systematically developed international humanitarian law [...] The legal precedents set by the Tribunal have expanded the boundaries of international humanitarian and international criminal law, both in terms of substance and procedure', available online at: https://www.icty.org/en/about/tribunal/achievements (accessed 15 August 2022).

[47] Article 3 reads: 'The International Tribunal shall have the power to prosecute persons violating the laws or customs of war. Such violations shall include, but not be limited to: (a) employment of poisonous weapons or other weapons calculated to cause unnecessary suffering; (b) wanton destruction of cities, towns or villages, or devastation not justified by military necessity; (c) attack, or bombardment, by whatever means, of undefended towns, villages, dwellings, or buildings; (d) seizure of, destruction or wilful damage done to institutions dedicated to religion, charity and education, the arts and sciences, historic monuments and works of art and science; (e) plunder of public or private property'. Rome Statute of the International Criminal Court (adopted 17 July 1998, entered into force 1 July 2002), 2187 UNTS 90, at Art. 3.

[48] *See* Decision on the Defence Motion for Interlocutory Appeal on Jurisdiction, *Prosecutor v. Dusko Tadic aka 'Dule'* (IT-94-1-AR72), Appeals Chamber, 2 October 1995 (hereafter *Tadić*), § 91.

crimes',[49] in particular by claiming that the rules applicable in non-international armed conflicts are largely identical to the regulatory framework of international armed conflicts. Most commentators regarded this move as a clear example of judicial law-making.[50]

Officially, however, judges were not vested with law-making capacity at the ICTY. In this respect, the Secretary-General unequivocally stated that 'the application of nullum crimen sine lege requires that the international tribunal should apply rules of international humanitarian law which are beyond any doubt part of customary law so that the problem of adherence to some but not all [s]tates to specific conventions does not arise'.[51] This interpretation was later affirmed in the tribunal's jurisprudence.[52]

The formal requirement of strict legality led to extensive reliance on customary law, disguising the judicial revolution as a conservative ascertainment of customary law, ostensibly demonstrating the existence of the requisite state practice and opinio juris to prove the existence of a customary norm.[53] Nevertheless, in practice, the tribunal provided remarkably few instances of state practice,[54] and instead invoked humanitarian ideals as a form of opinio juris. The expansion of the rules applicable to international armed conflicts to the domain of non-international armed conflicts was primarily justified by the assertion that '[I]f international law, while of course duly safeguarding the legitimate interests of [s]tates, must gradually turn to the protection of human beings, it is only natural that the aforementioned dichotomy should gradually lose its weight'.[55] In this

[49] W. A. Schabas, *An Introduction to the International Criminal Court* (Cambridge University Press, 2016), at 119.

[50] See for example, J. Powderly, *Judges and the Making of International Criminal Law* (Brill, 2020) 375–394; Darcy, *supra* note 38, 59–67; A. M. Danner, 'When Courts Make Law: How the International Criminal Tribunals Recast the Laws of War', 59 *Vanderbilt Law Review* (2006) 1–65; Hoffmann, *supra* note 32, 58–80.

[51] *Report of the Secretary-General pursuant to Paragraph 2 of Security Council Resolution 808 (1993)* UN Doc. S/25704 (1993), § 34.

[52] See *Tadić*, *supra* note 48, § 143.

[53] This led Meron to state that '[T]he legality principle thus serves as a restraint on the tribunals' ability to be "progressive" in their contributions to the development of customary humanitarian law. The term "conservative" here suggests reluctance to contribute to an overly broad or rapid expansion of customary law offenses'. T. Meron, 'Revival of Customary Humanitarian Law', 99 *American Journal of International Law* (2005), 817–834, at 818.

[54] See for example, the prohibition of perfidy in non-international armed conflict, which was deemed to have a customary status citing a single Nigerian judicial decision, which in turn was based on the Nigerian Criminal Code. See *Tadić*, *supra* note 48, § 125.

[55] *Ibid*, § 97.

spirit, declaring that weapons prohibited in international armed conflicts are automatically prohibited in non-international armed conflicts was deemed obvious since 'elementary considerations of humanity and common sense make it preposterous that the use by [s]tates of weapons prohibited in armed conflicts between themselves be allowed when [s]tates try to put down rebellion by their own nationals on their own territory. What is inhumane, and consequently proscribed, in international wars, cannot but be inhumane and inadmissible in civil strife'.[56]

This approach reached its pinnacle in the *Kupreškić* Trial Judgment, which declared that the Martens Clause 'clearly shows that principles of humanitarian law may emerge through a customary process under the pressure of the demands of humanity or the dictates of the public conscience, even where [s]tate practice is scant or inconsistent'.[57] However, this radical reinterpretation of the formation of customary international law that would have practically equated morality with law ultimately failed.[58] Still, notwithstanding the criticism of certain scholars, who decried the potential impact of the ICTY's relaxed methodology in the ascertainment of customary international law,[59] most authors immediately espoused the findings of the tribunal.[60]

Even though most scholars analysing the judicial innovations of the Yugoslavia Tribunal focused on its methodology of ascertaining customary rules, the ICTY also attempted to expand the protective scope of international humanitarian law through progressive interpretation. In the *Aleksovski* judgement, the tribunal stated that the nullum crimen sine lege principle 'does not prevent a court, either at the national or international

[56] *Ibid*, § 119.

[57] *Prosecutor v. Kupreskić*, Judgment, (IT-95-16-T), 14 January 2000, § 527.

[58] Hoffmann, *supra* note 32, at 73.

[59] Rauter recently thoroughly criticized the Tribunal's approach of relying predominantly on opinio juris by noting that 'if customary international law is also merely based on opinio juris, the barriers separating customary international law and general principles of law become not only blurred, but non-existent'. T. Rauter, *Judicial Practice, Customary International Criminal Law and Nullum Crimen Sine Lege* (1st edn., Springer, 2017) 111. In similar fashion, Arajärvi expressed concerns that 'the implementation of political, social or moral considerations on the substantive law creates legal uncertainty and reduces the function of the law to a vehicle for the advancement of extra-legal norms and undermines the essence of the rule of law'. N. Arajärvi, *The Changing Nature of Customary International Law—Methods of Interpreting the Concept of Custom in International Criminal Tribunals* (1st edn., New York: Routledge, 2014), at 6.

[60] Hoffmann, *supra* note 32, 69 and accompanying footnotes.

level, from determining an issue through a process of interpretation and clarification as to the elements of a particular crime'.[61]

Interpretation, of course, is already inherent in the identification of customary norms as it is 'required to answer what general practice is and when this is accepted as law'.[62] The tribunal, however, aimed to radically reinterpret IHL treaties as well through the adoption of a 'victim-focused teleological reasoning' that conflated 'the "general justifying aim" of the criminal law system as a whole—which may be a utilitarian aim of protecting society—with the question of whether it is justified to punish a particular individual for a particular crime'.[63] The focus on the protection of individual rights of the potential victims led to a reliance on the object and purpose of treaties—a classical human rights court approach[64]—justifying generally broad interpretations of crimes fundamentally at odds with the classical criminal law approach that favours the strict construction of statutes.[65]

This expansive interpretation is amply demonstrated by the tribunal's jurisprudence concerning the nationality requirement in Article 4 of Geneva Convention IV that sets out the personal scope of application of the convention. It states that

[61] Judgment, *Prosecutor v Zlatko Aleksovski*, Appeals Chamber (IT-95-14/1-A), 24 March 2000 (hereafter Aleksovski), § 127. See also Judgment, *Prosecutor v. Zejnil Delalic, Zdravko Mucic, also known as 'Pavo', Hazim Delic Esad Landzo also known as 'Zenga'*, Appeals Chamber (IT-96-21-A), 20 February 2001, § 173.

[62] V. P. Tzvelekos, 'Juris Dicere: Custom as a Matrix, Custom as a Norm, and the Role of Judges and (Their) Ideology in Custom Making', in N. M. Rajkovic, T. E. Aalberts, T. Gammeltoft-Hansen (eds), *The Power of Legality: Practices of International Law and their Politics* (Cambridge University Press, 2016) 188–208, at 192.

[63] Robinson, *supra* note 27, at 938.

[64] See for example, F. Tulkens, 'Judicial Activism v Judicial Restraint: Practical Experience of This (False) Dilemma at the European Court of Human Rights', 3 *European Convention on Human Rights Law Review* (2022) 293–300; L. Lixinski, 'Treaty Interpretation by the Inter-American Court of Human Rights: Expansionism at the Service of the Unity of International Law', 21 *European Journal of International Law* (2010) 585–604.

[65] L. Grover, 'A Call to Arms: Fundamental Dilemmas Confronting the Interpretation of Crimes in the Rome Statute of the International Criminal Court', 21 *European Journal of International Law* (2010) 543–580, at 550. Danner and Martinez also agree that a human rights approach to interpretation, that favours broad and liberal constructions, is inapposite to international criminal law. A. M. Danner, J. S. Martinez, 'Guilty Associations: Joint Criminal Enterprise, Command Responsibility and the Development of International Criminal Law', 93 *California Law Review* (2005), 75–169, at 81–89.

> Persons protected by the Convention are those who, at a given moment and in any manner whatsoever, find themselves, in case of a conflict or occupation, in the hands of a Party to the conflict or Occupying Power of which they are not nationals.
>
> Nationals of a [s]tate which is not bound by the Convention are not protected by it. Nationals of a neutral [s]tate who find themselves in the territory of a belligerent [s]tate, and nationals of a co-belligerent [s]tate, shall not be regarded as protected persons while the [s]tate of which they are nationals has normal diplomatic representation in the [s]tate in whose hands they are.

A plain reading of the text clearly suggests that the states parties did not intend to extend the application of GCIV to their own nationals when they are on opposing sides of an armed conflict. Nevertheless, the ICTY proposed a radically different approach: in a string of decisions, it claimed that beyond the formal category of nationality, even those persons should be protected by the convention who have the same nationality as the state in whose 'hands' they find themselves if they have ethnic allegiance to the foreign party participating in the conflict.[66] The tribunal emphasized that its interpretation was based 'not only the text and the drafting history of the Convention but also, and more importantly, the Convention's object and purpose'.[67]

Even though in the *Čelebići* case this approach was challenged by the defence as an effective re-writing of the Geneva Conventions, the Appeals Chamber reasserted that the nationality requirement in Article 4 of Geneva Convention IV should be ascertained within the context of the object and purpose of humanitarian law, which 'is directed to the protection of civilians to the maximum extent possible', taking into account the changing nature of the armed conflicts since 1945, and in particular the development of conflicts based on ethnic or religious grounds.[68]

[66] Judgment, *Tadić*, Appeals Chamber (IT-94-1-A), 15 July 1999, §§ 166–168; Aleksovski, *supra* note 61, §§ 151–152; Judgment, *Prosecutor v Blaskić*, Appeals Chamber (IT-95-14), 29 July 2004, § 182.

[67] Judgment, *Tadić*, *supra* note 66, §§ 166–168.

[68] *Prosecutor v. Zejnil Delalic, Zdravko Mucic, also known as 'Pavo', Hazim Delic Esad Landzo also known as 'Zenga'*, Appeals Chamber (IT-96-21-A), 20 February 2001 (hereafter Čelebići), § 73.

While this extensive interpretation was generally espoused in legal doctrine[69] and by the International Criminal Court,[70] it is clearly contrary to both the plain text of the convention and the original intention of the drafters.[71] Similar to the progressive approach to the identification of customary norms, it also relies on an 'in dubio pro humanitate' approach where the court tries to create a generally applicable rule for the future with the intention of protecting future victims of conflicts, disregarding its impact on the defendants.[72] As the general 'humanization' doctrine, it also presumes that the 1949 Geneva Conventions 'have been drawn up first and foremost to protect individuals, and not to serve [s]tate interests'.[73] This, however, has not necessarily reflected historical reality. Contemporary

[69] See for example, W. J. Fenrick, 'The Application of the Geneva Conventions by the International Criminal Tribunal for the Former Yugoslavia', 81 *International Review of the Red Cross* (1999), at 326; J. J. Urbina, 'La Protection des Personnes Civiles au Pouvoir de L'Ennemi et L'Etablissement d'une Juridiction Pénale Internationale', 82 *International Review of the Red Cross* (2000), at 858; K. Rubenstein, 'Rethinking Nationality in International Humanitarian Law', in U. Dolgopol, J. Gardam (eds), *The Challenge of Conflict: International Law Responds* (1st edn., Brill, Nijhoff, 2006) 89–104, at 102–103; S. Reeves, 'The Expansive Definition of 'Protected Persons' in War Crimes Jurisprudence' 39 *The Army Lawyer* (2009) 23–27; D. Fleck, 'Shortcomings of the Grave Breaches Regime', 7 *Journal of International Criminal Justice* (2009) 842–3; K. Mačák, *Internationalized Armed Conflicts in International Law* (1st edn., New York: Oxford University Press, 2018) 234–237. While agreeing with the ICTY's interpretation, Salmón notes that it might be difficult to implement as it is virtually impossible to verify allegiance to the state. E. Salmón, 'Who is a Protected Civilian?' in A. Clapham, P. Gaeta, M. Sassòli (eds) *The 1949 Geneva Conventions—A Commentary* (New York: Oxford University Press, 2015) 1135–1154, at 1145.

[70] *The Prosecutor v Thomas Lubanga*, Judgment pursuant to Article 74 of the Statute (ICC-01/04-01/06), 14 March 2012, § 564.

[71] See T. Hoffmann, 'The Perils of Judicial Construction of Identity—A Critical Analysis of the International Criminal Tribunal for the Former Yugoslavia's Jurisprudence on Protected Persons' in Kim Rubenstein (ed.) *Connecting International Law with Public Law—Allegiance and Identity in a Globalised World* (Cambridge University Press, 2014) 497–521; M. G. Martínez, 'The 'Allegiance' Test: Judicial Legislation and Interpretation of GCIV', 27 *Journal of Conflict and Security Law* (2022) 21–51.

[72] In Garabian's words '[I]n interpreting their statutes, these judges claim that they are simply bringing to light a pre-existing, albeit hidden meaning intended by the 'international legislator' (in other words, sovereign [s]tates), made explicit by means of a purely cognitive activity which thereby guarantees that the principle of legality is respected'. S. Garibian, 'By Men, not Gods: The (Hidden) Evolutionary Interpretation of International Criminal Law in Light of Extrinsic Sources' in Georges Abi-Saab et al. (eds), *Evolutionary Interpretation and International Law* (Hart, 2019) 153–170, at 156.

[73] *Čelebići*, Sentencing Judgment, Trial Chamber (IT-96-21-T), 16 November 1998, § 263.

scholars generally agreed that the Geneva Conventions were 'based, as it should be, on practical and realistic considerations, striking [...] an equilibrium between the cruel necessities of war and humanitarian ideals',[74] and this balancing act between individual and state security is clearly revealed in the travaux préparatoires of the conventions.[75]

It seems that a number of consecutive factors explain the reasons for the undeniable success of the ICTY in judicial law-making. While the institutional design of the tribunal enabled the judges to invoke customary war crimes with reference to 'laws and customs of war' in Article 3 of the statute, that was in itself insufficient.[76] A much more significant aspect in its achievement was a unique combination of opportune time and the support of the international community and legal scholarship.

The Yugoslavia Tribunal was created after the collapse of the Cold War system, during a period of time of unprecedented cooperation between the permanent members of the Security Council addressing violations of a conflict receiving intense media coverage all over the world.[77] The ICTY was a 'safe' tribunal in the sense that it was unlikely to prosecute nationals of any of the major military powers[78] and its most important judicial innovations

[74] J. L. Kunz, 'The Chaotic Status of the Laws of War and the Urgent Necessity for their Revision', 45 *American Journal of International Law* (1951), 37–61, at 59.

[75] Danner, *supra* note 50, at 32. See more in detail B. v. Dijk, *Preparing for War—The Making of the Geneva Conventions* (Oxford University Press, 2022).

[76] Art. 4 of the Statute of the International Criminal Tribunal for Rwanda also included an open-ended reference to 'serious violations of Article 3 common to the Geneva Conventions of 12 August 1949 for the Protection of War Victims, and of Additional Protocol II thereto of 8 June 1977', emphasizing that these violations 'shall include, but shall not be limited to' the listed eight prohibited acts. Statute of the International Criminal Tribunal for Rwanda, S/RES/955, 8 November 1994, at Art. 4. Nevertheless, the ICTR failed to charge a single individual with a war crime not explicitly included in Art. 4 of the statute.

[77] A. Cassese, 'On the Current Trend Towards Criminal Prosecution and Punishment of Breaches of International Humanitarian Law', 9 *European Journal of International Law* (1998), at 7–8.

[78] See R. Cryer, *Prosecuting International Crimes—Selectivity and International Criminal Law Regime* (Cambridge University Press, 2005) at 233–88. In 1999, after the NATO intervention in Yugoslavia, the Prosecutor recommended not to investigate potential international crimes because 'either the law is not sufficiently clear or investigations are unlikely to result in the acquisition of sufficient evidence'. *Final Report to the Prosecutor by the Committee Established to Review the NATO Bombing Campaign Against the Federal Republic of Yugoslavia*, available online at: https://www.icty.org/en/press/final-report-prosecutor-committee-established-review-nato-bombing-campaign-against-federal (accessed 15 July 2022). For a critical view see P. Benvenuti, 'The ICTY Prosecutor and the Review of the Bombing Campaign against the Federal Republic of Yugoslavia', 12 *European Journal of International Law* (2001) 503–529.

concerned non-international armed conflicts that not only did not unduly concern the influential states but even allowed them to benefit from the newly created customary rules during the 'war on terror'.[79] This created an environment where the judges could act without fear of jeopardizing their institution or even the 'edifice of international law'[80] and facing accountability.[81] Moreover, certain judges, most notably the first president of the tribunal, the renowned international lawyer Antonio Cassese openly advocated judicial law-making, wondering 'whether one ought not to move beyond the strict legal parameters agreed upon by states, at least whenever the need to oppose glaring injustice would oblige one to do so'.[82]

Ultimately, the ICTY's success was cemented by the widespread scholarly acceptance of most of its jurisprudence.[83] While 'academic demolitions

[79] See Hoffmann, *supra* note 32, at 78. Unsurprisingly, when the ICTY tried to introduce the so-called 200-metre rule that could have potentially restricted targeting decisions during military operations, it caused a palpable fervour in the US military lawyer community. See *Prosecutor v Ante Gotovina, Ivan Čermak and Mladen Markač* (IT-01-45-T), 15 April 2011, §§ 1892–1945. For the US reaction see *Operational Law Experts Roundtable on the Gotovina Judgment: Military Operations, Battlefield Reality and the Judgment's Impact on Effective Implementation and Enforcement of International Humanitarian Law* (Emory Law School: International Humanitarian Law Clinic, 4 November 2011).

[80] Terris, Romano and Swigart comment that 'international judges who, knowingly or inadvertently, cross the line between interpreting the law as is and writing law, put at risk the future of the court itself, if not the whole edifice of international law. They are more likely to see themselves as compelled to break new ground by circumstance, rather than seeking opportunities to make their mark by developing new law'. D. Terris, C. P. Romano, L. Swigart, *The International Judge—An Introduction to the Men and Women Who Decide the World's Cases* (Oxford University Press, 2007), at 130.

[81] Judge Wald recounted her own experiences at the Tribunal with tangible consternation. 'There was no court above us and no legislature to change the law if it did not like our rulings. There was no public constituency in, or even enough coverage by, the media to act as much of a brake. We were independent indeed, but often I asked myself, how accountable were we and to whom?' P. M. Wald, 'International Criminal Courts: Some Kudos and Concerns', 150 *Proceedings of the American Philosophical Society* (2006) 241–260, at 244–245.

[82] A. Cassese, 'Soliloqui' in A. Cassese, P. Gaeta, S. Zappalà (eds), *The Human Dimension of International Law: Selected Papers of Antonio Cassese* (New York: Oxford University Press, 2008) lix–lxxxii, at lxiii.

[83] For instance, the ICRC Customary Law Study explicitly admits that not all international court decisions claiming to ascertain customary international law have relied on state practice and opinio juris but these decisions are still taken into account. The Study states that 'it appears that international courts and tribunals on occasion conclude that a rule of customary international law exists when that rule is a desirable one for international peace and security or for the protection of the human person provided there is no important contrary opinio juris'. J.-M. Henckaerts, L. Doswald-Beck (eds), *Customary International Humanitarian Law—Vol. I.: Rules.* (New York: Cambridge University Press, 2009), at xliii.

of the reasoning and results in cases can have a considerable effect on the reception of such decisions',[84] uniform support in the international legal scholarship practically elevates court decisions to the level of primary source of international law.[85]

2.4 The International Criminal Court—A Bulwark against Judicial Activism?

The 1998 Rome Diplomatic Conference has largely codified the judicial innovations of the ICTY in war crimes law. For instance, the definition of non-international armed conflict in Article (2)(f), which is almost a verbatim repetition of the definition set forth in the *Tadić* Jurisdiction Appeal Decision.[86] Philippe Kirsch, the chairperson of the Committee of the Whole at the Rome Diplomatic Conference and the ICC's first president, opined that states generally agreed that 'the definitions of crimes in the ICC Statute were to reflect existing customary international law, and not create new law'.[87] Correspondingly, in a recent judgment, the Appeals Chamber considered that 'the crimes under the Statute were intended to

[84] R. Cryer, 'Of Custom, Treaties, Scholars and the Gavel: The Influence of the International Criminal Tribunals on the ICRC Customary Law Study', 11 *Journal of Conflict and Security Law* (2002), 239–263, at 249.

[85] I. Bantekas, 'Reflections on Some Sources and Methods of International Criminal and Humanitarian Law', 6 *International Criminal Law Review* (2006), 121–136, at 129.

[86] The *Tadić* decision defined non-international armed conflict as 'protracted armed violence between governmental authorities and organized armed groups or between such groups within a [s]tate'. See *Tadić*, § 70. Art. 8(f) on the other hand, speaks about 'protracted armed conflict between governmental authorities and organized armed groups or between such groups'. It seems that the Sierra Leonean delegation proposed the definition based on the *Tadić* decision. See T. Graditzky, 'War Crime Issues before the Rome Diplomatic Conference on the Establishment of an International Criminal Court', 5 *U.C. Davis Journal of International Law and Policy* (1999) 199–218, at 209–10.

[87] P. Kirsch, 'Foreword', in K. Dörmann, et al. (eds) *Elements of War Crimes under the Rome Statute of the International Criminal Court* (Cambridge University Press, 2003), at xiii; See also D. Scheffer, 'The United States and the International Criminal Court', 93 *American Journal of International Law* (1999) 12–22, at 16.

be generally representative of the state of customary international law when the Statute was drafted'.[88]

However, the participating countries no longer seemed to be willing to provide an opportunity for judges to engage in judicial law-making. At the opening plenary of the conference, President Scalfaro of the host state Italy pronounced that '[C]riminal law should always precede crimes; it should be known that the crimes were punishable by law and what the penalties would be'.[89] This sentiment was echoed by the US that emphasized that '[T]he Court must have a clear, precise and well-established understanding of what conduct constituted a crime […] Vague formulas that left the Court to decide on the fundamental parameters of crimes should be avoided'.[90] To achieve this required level of precision, the United States had proposed the development of the Elements of Crimes,[91] and Article 8 of the ICC Statute aimed to provide for an exhaustive catalogue of prohibited acts and as a result, the definition of war crimes reached a level of unprecedented specificity.[92]

[88] *The Prosecutor v. Ali Muhammad Ali Abd-Al-Rahman* (Ali Kushayb), Judgment on the Appeal of Mr. Abd-Al-Rahman against the Pre-Trial Chamber II's 'Decision on the Defence "Exception d'incompétence", (ICC-02/05-01/20-302)', Appeals Chamber, 1 November 2021, No. ICC-02/05-01/20 0A8, § 89. However, this statement is questionable. As seen above, the customary status of war crimes committed during non-international armed conflicts was by no means conclusive and other crimes could also be seen innovative. Staiano points out that the inclusion of gender-based persecution within Article 7(1)(h) of the statute was an innovative development as in 1998; customary international law only prohibited persecution on the grounds on political, racial, or religious grounds. F. Staiano, 'Customary International Law as a Source of Individual Criminal Responsibility—Reflections in the Wake of the Abd-Al-Rahman Judgment', 20 *Journal of International Criminal Justice* (2022) 981–1000, at 989.

[89] S. Darcy, 'The Principle of Legality at the Crossroads of Human Rights and International Criminal Law', in M. M. deGuzman, D. Marie Amann (eds), *Arcs of Global Justice—Essays in Honour of William A. Schabas* (Oxford University Press, 2018) 203–226, at 206.

[90] United Nations Diplomatic Conference, Volume II, Summary Records of the Plenary Meetings, 5th Plenary Meeting, 17 June 1998, para. 61, 95.

[91] The Japanese delegate also emphasized the 'cardinal importance' of the principle of legality. Darcy, *supra* note 89, at 206.

[92] Schabas points out that whereas Article 6(b) of the 1945 London Agreement defined war crimes in 73 words, and Articles 2 and 3 of the statute of the ICTY in 239 words, Article 8 of the Rome Statute in devoted 1594 words to its regulation. W. Schabas, 'The Follow Up to Rome: Preparing for Entry into Force of the International Criminal Court Statute', 20 *Human Rights Law Journal* (1999) 157–166, at 163. Robinson suggests that this could have been partly due to concerns about the 'safeness' of the new court. 'The creators of the Rome Statute, who could not know whether the provisions would be applied to their foes, to strangers, to friends, or to themselves, opted for a complete codification with a closed list of defined crimes'. Robinson, 'The Identity Crisis', 958–959.

As further precaution against the 'Cassese approach',[93] the drafters adopted several provisions with the intention of curtailing judicial innovation and ensuring that the criminal lawyers' perspective prevails over the humanization narrative.[94] Article 21 of the ICC Statute created a hierarchy of applicable sources that obliged the Court to use its statute, Elements of Crimes and its Rules of Procedure and Evidence in the first place and every other potential source only if those are inadequate to come to a conclusion.[95] Moreover, Article 22 of the statute codified the nullum crimen sine lege principle prescribing strict construction of the definition of

[93] Cassese claimed that the drafters of the Rome Statute of the International Criminal Court 'feared the "Cassese approach", namely judges overdoing it, becoming dangerous by, say, producing judgments that can be innovative'. H. V. Stuart, M. Simons, *The Prosecutor and the Judge: Benjamin Ferencz and Antonio Cassese* (Amsterdam University Press, 2009) 52–53.

[94] Fletcher and Ohlin observe that in this perspective, 'the reason for legislation is to drive custom from the system and to create a regime based on rules and standards declared publicly, in advance, by a competent authority'. G. P. Fletcher, J. David Ohlin, 'Reclaiming Fundamental Principles of Criminal Law in the Darfur Case', 3 *Journal of International Criminal Justice* (2005) 539–561, at 559.

[95] 1. The Court shall apply:
   (a) In the first place, this Statute, Elements of Crimes and its Rules of Procedure and Evidence;
   (b) In the second place, where appropriate, applicable treaties and the principles and rules of international law, including the established principles of the international law of armed conflict;
   (c) Failing that, general principles of law derived by the Court from national laws of legal systems of the world including, as appropriate, the national laws of states that would normally exercise jurisdiction over the crime, provided that those principles are not inconsistent with this Statute and with international law and internationally recognized norms and standards.
2. The Court may apply principles and rules of law as interpreted in its previous decisions.
3. The application and interpretation of law pursuant to this article must be consistent with internationally recognized human rights and be without any adverse distinction founded on grounds such as gender as defined in Article 7, paragraph 3, age, race, colour, language, religion or belief, political or other opinion, national, ethnic or social origin, wealth, birth or other status.

crimes.[96] Schabas sardonically observed that 'the drafters of the ICC Statute decided that while they appreciated the results of judicial activism in the past, they were not anxious for it to be repeated'.[97]

A further sign of distrust in judges is the fact that the very term 'custom' has become 'something of taboo'.[98] The ICC Statute does not mention the term 'customary international law' but refers more generically to 'rules of international law'.[99] However, Article 21(1)(b) of the Rome Statute expressly refers to 'the established principles of the international law of armed conflict', and the introduction to War Crimes in the Elements of Crimes instructs its interpretation 'within the established framework of the international law of armed conflict'. Accordingly, the statute itself actually allows for recourse to custom in specific cases. However, as pointed out by Bufalini, 'the customary rule at issue must be coherent with the other provisions of the Statute and adequate to be part of its normative system'.[100]

This is supported by the Court's jurisprudence. In the *Katanga* case, the Pre-Trial Chamber (PTC) held that 'principles and rules of international law constitute a secondary source applicable only when the statutory material fails to prescribe a legal solution'.[101] In the Al Bashir case, the ICC concluded that customary rules and general principles of law 'can only be applied when the following two conditions are met: (i) there is a lacuna in the written law contained in the Statute, the Elements of Crimes and the Rules; and (ii) such lacuna cannot be filled by the application of

[96] 1. A person shall not be criminally responsible under this Statute unless the conduct in question constitutes, at the time it takes place, a crime within the jurisdiction of the Court.
2. The definition of a crime shall be strictly construed and shall not be extended by analogy. In case of ambiguity, the definition shall be interpreted in favour of the person being investigated, prosecuted or convicted.
3. This article shall not affect the characterization of any conduct as criminal under international law independently of this Statute.

[97] W. A Schabas, 'Prosecutorial Discretion v. Judicial Activism at the International Criminal Court', 6(4) *Journal of International Criminal Justice* (2008) 731–761, at 755.

[98] Pellet, *supra* note 2, at 1059.

[99] Herik, *supra* note 6, 230–252, at 240.

[100] A. Bufalini, 'The Principle of Legality and the Role of Customary International Law in the Interpretation of the ICC Statute', 14 *The Law and Practice of International Courts and Tribunals* (2015) 233–254, at 239.

[101] *Prosecutor v. Germain Katanga and Mathieu Chui, Decision on the Confirmation of Charges*, Pre-Trial Chamber I (ICC-01/04-01/07), 30 September 2008, § 508.

the criteria provided for in [A]rticles 31 and 32 of the Vienna Convention on the Law of the Treaties and [A]rticle 21(3) of the Statute'.[102]

However, as Powderly pointed out, Article 21(1)(b) and the Elements of Crimes 'invite recourse to customary rules and principles of international humanitarian law, regardless of whether or not a lacuna exists. There is significant creative potential in accepting this invitation'.[103] The ICC did not fail to capitalize on this potential. For instance, it discovered a 'glaring statutory gap' concerning the lack of a definition for international and non-international armed conflicts[104] and for the civilian population[105] in the statute.

The law-making potential of the Court was eventually exposed in the *Ntaganda* judgement that has been described as 'a problematic interpretation from the point of view of the principle of legality and the limits of judicial law-making',[106] and 'the most dramatic expansion in the scope of war crimes since the *Tadić* case'.[107] In *Ntaganda*, the ICC used different strategies to prove that war crimes—in this case, rape and sexual slavery—can be committed by members of armed forces on members of the same armed force, which radically refuted the prevailing orthodoxy that crimes committed between servicemen do not constitute war crimes.[108]

The Pre-Trial Chamber found that children under the age of 15 do not automatically become direct or active participants in hostilities by joining

[102] *Prosecutor v. Omar Hassan Ahmad Al Bashir, Decision on the Prosecution's Application for a Warrant of Arrest against Omar Hassan Ahmad Al Bashir*, Pre-Trial Chamber I (ICC-02/05-01/09-3), 4 March 2009, § 44.

[103] Powderly, *supra* note 50, at 500.

[104] *Prosecutor v Lubanga*, Decision on the Confirmation of Charges, Pre-Trial Chamber I (ICC-01/04-01/06), 29 January 2007, §§ 208–209.

[105] *Prosecutor v Bemba,* Decision Pursuant to Article 61(7)(a) and (b) of the Rome Statute on the Charges of the Prosecutor Against Jean-Pierre Bemba Gombo, Pre-Trial Chamber II (ICC-01/05-01/08-424), 15 June 2009, § 78, fn. 101.

[106] C. Kenny, Y. McDermott, 'The Expanding Protection of Members of a Party's Own Armed Forces under International Criminal Law', 68 *International and Comparative Law Quarterly* (2019) 943–976, at 953.

[107] Powderly, *supra* note 50, at 501.

[108] For instance, Cassese emphasized that 'crimes committed by combatants of one party to the conflict against members of their own armed forces do not constitute war crimes'. Antonio Cassese et al., *International Criminal Law* (3rd edn., Hampshire: Oxford University Press, 2013), at 67. The Special Court for Sierra Leone similarly held that 'the law of armed conflict does not protect members of armed groups from acts of violence directed against them by their own forces'. Judgment, *Prosecutor v Sesay, Kallon, Gbao (RUF Case)*, (SCSL-04-15-T), Trial Chamber, 2 March 2009 (hereafter Sesay), § 1451.

an armed group because that 'would contradict the very rationale underlying the protection afforded to such children against recruitment and use in hostilities'.[109] The PTC concluded that child soldiers under the age of 15 only lose their protected status afforded by IHL during direct/active participation in hostilities; however, '[T]he sexual character of these crimes, which involve elements of force/coercion or the exercise of rights of ownership, logically preclude active participation in hostilities at the same time'.[110] Even though the PTC's argumentation was innovative, it was not a radical reinterpretation of the existing normative framework. While the concept of protection for persons hors de combat is firmly established in both international and non-international armed conflicts,[111] it was originally not envisaged to include intra-party violence, as members of the same party are not a threat to each other under normal circumstances. Nevertheless, a broad reading to protect children under the age of 15 is certainly justifiable from a humanitarian perspective and does not create potential structural problems in the system of international humanitarian law.[112]

The Trial Chamber came to the same conclusion as the Pre-Trial Chamber, but relied on a completely different basis, combining textual interpretation of the Rome Statute and the requirements of humanity. The chamber first noted that even though Articles 8(2)(a) and (c) referred to

[109] *Prosecutor v Ntaganda, Decision Pursuant to Article 61(7)(a) and (b) of the Rome Statute on the Charges of the Prosecutor Against Bosco Ntaganda*, Case No ICC-01/04-02/06-309, 9 June 2014, § 78.

[110] *Ibid*, § 79.

[111] Art. 12 'Members of the armed forces and other *persons* mentioned in the following Article, who are wounded or sick, shall be respected and protected in all circumstances'. Convention (I) for the Amelioration of the Condition of the Wounded and Sick in Armed Forces in the Field. Geneva, 12 August 1949.

Art. 12 'Members of the armed forces and other persons mentioned in the following Article, who are at sea and who are wounded, sick or shipwrecked, shall be respected and protected in all circumstances'. Convention (II) for the Amelioration of the Condition of Wounded, Sick and Shipwrecked Members of Armed Forces at Sea. Geneva, 12 August 1949.

Common Art. 3(1) 'Persons taking no active part in the hostilities, including members of armed forces who have laid down their arms and those placed 'hors de combat' by sickness, wounds, detention, or any other cause, shall in all circumstances be treated humanely, without any adverse distinction founded on race, colour, religion or faith, sex, birth or wealth, or any other similar criteria'. Conventions (I)–(IV), Geneva, 12 August 1949.

[112] See T. Rodenhäuser, 'Squaring the Circle? Prosecuting Sexual Violence against Child Soldiers by their 'Own Forces', 14 *Journal of International Criminal Justice* (2016) 171–193, at 187–192.

specific victim status requirements in their chapeau, that is, that the person be protected by the relevant provisions of the Geneva Conventions under paragraph (a) or be taking no active part in hostilities under paragraph (c), no such limitations could be found in sub-paragraphs (b) and (e), the provisions under which Ntaganda had been charged.[113] It added that the widespread prohibition of rape and other forms of sexual violence and the reference of the Martens clause to 'the principles of humanity and [...] dictates of public conscience' support the contention that the protection against such acts should be widely applicable and any limitation of the scope of protection is contrary to the rationale of international humanitarian law.[114] This decision much more closely resembles the ICTY's revolutionary jurisprudence than the Pre-Trial Chamber's conclusions, as it explicitly invokes a humanizing rationale to expand the scope of application of humanitarian law. However, this approach seems positively restrained compared to the Appeals Chamber's analysis.

The Appeals Chamber stipulated that the reference to 'the established framework of international law' allows for the direct application of norms of custom in cases of crimes within Articles 8 (2) (b) and (e) and thus the introduction of additional elements to these crimes, even in the absence of a lacuna. The Court emphasized that

> If customary or conventional international law stipulates in respect of a given war crime set out in [A]rticle 8(2)(b) or (e) of the Statute an additional element of that crime, the Court cannot be precluded from applying it to ensure consistency of the provision with international humanitarian law, irrespective of whether this requires ascribing to a term in the provision a particular interpretation or reading an additional element into it.[115]

According to the Appeals Chambers, the war crimes under Articles 8(2) (b) and (e) did not require the victim to hold the status of civilian or person hors de combat under customary international law as 'international humanitarian law does not contain a general rule that categorically excludes members of an armed group from protection against crimes committed by members of the same armed group'.[116] The Appeals Chamber

[113] *Prosecutor v Ntaganda*, Second Decision on the Defence's Challenge to the Jurisdiction of the Court in Respect of Counts 6 and 9, (ICC-01/04-02/06-1707), 4 January 2017, § 40.

[114] *Ibid*, §§ 46–48.

[115] *Prosecutor v Ntaganda*, Judgment on the Appeal of Mr Ntaganda against the 'Second Decision on the Defence's Challenge to the Jurisdiction of the Court in respect of Counts 6 and 9' (ICC-01/04-02/06), 15 June 2017, § 53.

[116] *Ibid*, § 63.

claimed this approach is applicable even if the victims of the crimes do not meet the status requirements.[117] Moreover, in a potentially even more impactful statement, it pronounced that it is the 'nexus requirement, and not the purported Status Requirement, that sufficiently and appropriately delineates war crimes from ordinary crimes'.[118] Accepting this logic, every single crime that is committed in the context of an armed conflict could be deemed as a war crime.

The Court was fully mindful of the potential ramifications of its decision.[119] Instead of retaining the compromise solution of the Pre-Trial Chamber, it boldly employed a teleological interpretation underscored by an alleged lack of contrary custom to expand the protective scope of international humanitarian law in a manner that 'a war crime does not have to violate IHL'.[120] The Ntaganda case clearly demonstrates that the institutional design of the ICC Statute cannot prevent the judges from judicial law-making as the different chambers of the ICC all managed to find different methods to achieve their desired outcome, freely resorting to invoking customary law (or the lack thereof), teleological interpretation, or direct referral to humanitarian considerations. The ICC thus was prepared to embark on the path of judicial revolution, just like the ICTY, whose jurisprudential practice was supposed to be its antithesis.[121]

[117] *Ibid*, § 64.

[118] *Ibid*, § 68.

[119] 'The Appeals Chamber appreciates the seemingly unprecedented nature of this conclusion. The Appeals Chamber is also mindful of Mr Ntaganda's apprehension that this conclusion seems to result from a "wider application" of the Rome Statute through "judicial activism" or amounts to a "substantial and unjustified extension of the scope of war crimes law". However, as reasoned above, the conclusion is not only permissible under article 8(2)(b)(xxii) and 8(2)(e)(vi) of the statute, but is also aligned with the established framework of international law'. *Ibid*, § 67 (footnotes omitted).

[120] K. J. Heller: 'ICC Appeals Chamber Says a War Crime Does Not Have to Violate IHL', (15 June 2017) *Opinio Juris Blog*, available online at: http://opiniojuris.org/2017/06/15/icc-appeals-chamber-holds-a-war-crime-does-not-have-to-violate-ihl/ (accessed 15 September 2022).

[121] Interesting to contrast the Ntaganda decision(s) with Sierra Leone Special Court's approach, which rejected an expansive interpretation, alarmed by its potential ramifications. The Court declared that '[T]he law of international armed conflict was never intended to criminalise acts of violence committed by one member of an armed group against another, such conduct remaining first and foremost the province of the criminal law of the [s]tate of the armed group concerned and human rights law. In our view, a different approach would constitute an inappropriate reconceptualisation of a fundamental principle of international humanitarian law. We are not prepared to embark on such an exercise'. *Sesay, supra* note 108, § 1453.

2.5 Conclusion—Much Ado about Nothing?

Even in the early 2010s, several authors considered that the exhaustive codification of the Rome Statute and the central role of the principle of legality would restrict judicial creativity at the International Criminal Court. Darcy opined that 'the detailed, exhaustive approach of Article 8 of the Rome Statute and the "Elements of Crimes" may preclude its judges from straying too far from the letter of the written law',[122] while Schabas surmised that '[A]rguably, some of the broad interpretations of the definitions of crimes in the statutes of the ad hoc tribunals, such as [...] the expansion of "laws or customs of war" to crimes committed in non-international armed conflict [...] would be impermissible were [A]rticle 22(2) to be applied'.[123] In a recent writing, Pellet retained his earlier opinion and expressed his apprehension that 'by freezing it in a sometimes daring but often inadequate and regressive text, the authors of the Statute have limited the chances of making the Court an efficient instrument in the struggle against the crimes it is supposed to repress'.[124]

The more recent jurisprudence of the Court, however, seems to have allayed these fears. As Powderly observed, '[T]he bench has identified sufficient wriggle-room in order to allow them to breathe life into the law'.[125] Even though overt reference to customary law has significantly diminished compared to the Yugoslavia Tribunal's case law, the ICC was still free to develop new judicial interpretations that significantly expanded the scope of application of war crimes law. Ultimately, institutional design cannot prevent judges from (re)interpreting the law according to their personal

[122] S. Darcy, 'The Reinvention of War Crimes by the International Criminal Tribunals' in S. Darcy, J. Powderly (eds), Judicial Creativity at the International Criminal Tribunals (Oxford University Press, 2010) 106–128, at 127.

[123] W. A. Schabas, *The International Criminal Court: A Commentary on the Rome Statute* (Oxford University Press, 2011) 410–411.

[124] A. Pellet, 'Revisiting the Sources of Applicable of law before the ICC' in M. M. deGuzman, D. M. Amann (eds) *Arcs of Global Justice—Essays in Honour of William A. Schabas* (Oxford University Press, 2018) 227–256, at 232.

[125] J. Powderly, 'The Rome Statute and the Attempted Corseting of the Interpretative Judicial Function: Reflections on Sources of Law and Interpretative Technique' in C. Stahn (ed.), *The Law and Practice of the International Criminal Court* (Oxford University Press, 2015) 444–98, at 498.

preferences.[126] Paradoxically, the denial of the judges' law-making capacity is exactly what makes judges capable of creating new laws.[127]

Thus, Pellet's insight proved to be prophetic: 'One may, thus, predict that the judges will interpret the text, at least partially, so as to recover the powers inherent in all courts, of which the drafters of the Statute dearly wanted to deprive them'.[128] Still, the Court should be mindful of its responsibility when engaging in judicial law-making to avoid undermining the regulatory framework of the law of armed conflict through the undue expansion of war crimes law.[129]

[126] Tzvelekos pointed out that 'Be they impartial, judges still see law and the facts behind it from their own, subjective perspective. They do not adjudicate in a vacuum; they carry to the bench their personal system of values and ideology, their personal understanding of what law is or ought to be, and they evaluate and assess the law the way they perceive it through the lens of their personal experience in life'. Tzvelekos, *supra* note 62, at 196.

[127] Hart describes this phenomenon in the common law system as 'the courts often disclaim any such creative function and insist that the proper task of statutory interpretation and the use of precedents is, respectively, to search for the 'intention of the legislature' and the law that already exists'. H. L. A. Hart, *The Concept of Law* (Clarendon Press, 1994) 135–136.

[128] Pellet, *supra* note 2, at 1053.

[129] In this vein, Akhavan warns that 'utopian jurisprudence that disregards the imperatives of humanitarian law in the name of progress will only dissipate what remains of chivalry and professional pride among the world's armed forces'. P. Akhavan, 'Reconciling Crimes against Humanities with the Laws of War—Human Rights, Armed Conflict, and the Limits of Progressive Jurisprudence', 6 *Journal of International Criminal Justice* (2008) 21–37, at 37.

CHAPTER 3

The Development of International Humanitarian Law in the Jurisprudence of the International Criminal Court: Formulation and Interpretation of Article 8 of the Rome Statute

Demetra Loizou

3.1 Introduction

The contribution of the International Criminal Court (ICC) to the development of international humanitarian law (IHL) lies on two levels: the *formulation* of the war crimes' provision in Article 8 of the Rome Statute and the Court's ***interpretative approach*** with respect to war crimes to date. The exploration of these two issues will illustrate some important distinctive characteristics of the ICC's contribution to the development of IHL and how it may be distinguished from the earlier work of other international criminal courts and tribunals.

D. Loizou (✉)
University of Central Lancashire, Larnaka, Cyprus
e-mail: dloizou@uclan.ac.uk

M. Faix, O. Svaček (eds.), *ICC Jurisprudence and the Development of International Humanitarian Law*, Global Issues,
https://doi.org/10.1007/978-3-031-45994-8_3

First, this chapter will examine the relationship between international criminal law (ICL) and IHL *before* the establishment of the ICC, focusing on the work of the ad hoc tribunals. Second, it will assess how the relationship between ICL and IHL was redefined *after* the establishment of the ICC. The first comparison is necessary in order to make a distinction between the law-making potential of the ad hoc tribunals with that of the ICC. The second comparison aims at demonstrating how the formulation of the war crimes provision has a direct bearing on the normative potential of the ICC and its Chambers' interpretative approaches. The Court's evolving jurisprudence on child soldiers will inform the assessment of the ICC's work in practice. An overarching consideration will be the ICC's establishment as the first permanent tribunal of its kind, at a much more advanced stage in the development of ICL norms.

3.2 The Relationship between ICL and IHL Before the Establishment of the ICC

Despite their formal status as 'subsidiary means for the determination of rules of law',[1] the judicial decisions of international criminal courts and tribunals have long played a key role in the identification and clarification of ICL rules and in the advancement of IHL.[2] During the 1990s, the establishment of the ad hoc tribunals initiated a 'synergistic relationship' between their statutes, their case law and 'the growth of customary law'.[3] As early as 1998, Meron stated that the pace of development of IHL norms had been faster since the beginning of the conflict in former Yugoslavia than in the forty-five years since the Nuremberg Tribunals.[4]

Notably, in its first major ruling in the *Tadić* case, the International Criminal Tribunal for the former Yugoslavia (ICTY) interpreted the scope of its jurisdiction with reference to IHL to determine that it had the power to prosecute all serious violations of IHL. According to the Appeals Chamber (AC), the enumeration of the violations of the laws or customs

[1] Statute of the International Court of Justice (adopted 26 June 1945, entered into force 24 October 1945, hereafter Statute), at Art. 38

[2] A.Z. Borda, 'A Formal Approach to Article 38(1)(d) of the ICJ Statute from the Perspective of the International Criminal Courts and Tribunals', 24 *European Journal of International Law* (2013) 649, at 657.

[3] T. Meron, 'War Crimes Law Comes of Age', 92 *American Journal of International Law* (1998) 462, at 464.

[4] *Ibid*, at 463.

of war in Article 3 was 'merely illustrative'.[5] This interpretation was justified on the basis of a literal interpretation of Article 3 of the ICTY Statute, which stated that the violations 'shall include, but not limited to'. Further, the AC referred to Article 89 of Additional Protocol I (AP I), according to which the contracting parties undertake to act in situations of 'serious violations' of the Geneva Conventions (GCs) and AP I (thus, not being restricted to only grave breaches). On the basis of this interpretation, the ICTY proceeded to convict individuals for crimes not listed in its statute, such as 'unlawful attacks on civilians' when these were not justified by military necessity.[6] The non-exhaustive enumeration of the prescribed acts in Article 3 and the 'opening' in the system of IHL provided by AP I facilitated the dynamic reform of the conventional law of armed conflict in the context of both international armed conflicts (IAC) and non-international armed conflicts (NIAC). Most notably, the AC in *Tadić* confirmed the applicability of some provisions of the GCs to NIAC as well as the criminalisation of breaches of Common Article 3 (CA3).[7]

Prior to the ICC, international criminal courts and tribunals were faced with scant war crimes definitions which did not sufficiently define the prohibited conduct. Significantly, gaps were filled by means of judicial interpretation whereby the courts clarified the scope and content of war crimes by relying heavily on the relevant IHL treaties and rules of customary law. In this respect, greater emphasis was placed on opinio juris rather than state practice in ascertaining the existence of the prohibition.[8] According to the AC in *Tadić*, when ascertaining the formation of customary rules of armed conflict, it is difficult, if not impossible, to ascertain state practice. To this effect, because of 'the inherent nature of this subject-matter, reliance must primarily be placed on such elements as official pronouncements of states, military manuals and judicial decisions'.[9]

[5] Decision on defence motion for Interlocutory Appeal on Jurisdiction, *Tadić* (IT-94-1-AR72), Appeals Chamber, 2 October 1995, § 87.

[6] Judgment, *Kordić et al.* (IT-95-14/2-A), Appeals Chamber, 17 December 2004, § 40.

[7] *Tadić, supra* note 5, §§ 86–93.

[8] R. Cryer, 'International Criminal Tribunals and the Sources of International Law: Antonio Cassese's Contribution to the Canon', 10 *Journal of International Criminal Justice* (2012) 1045, at 1049. See also: F. Kirgis, 'Custom on a Sliding Scale', 81 *American Journal of International Law* (1987) 146.

[9] *Tadić supra* note 5, § 99; Judgment, *Prosecutor v. Zoran Kupreškić, Mirjan Kupreškić, Vlatko Kupreškić, Drago Josipović, Dragan Papić, Vladimir Santić, also known as "VLADO"* (IT-95-16-T), Trial Chamber, 14 January 2000, § 27.

The development of IHL by international courts and tribunals was inextricably linked with the wider IHL framework, which often extended beyond the strict parameters of the war crimes provisions. In this respect, the statutes of the ad hoc tribunals were jurisdictional in nature; the crimes were not enumerated as in a criminal code but simply as a specification of the jurisdictional authority of the relevant court.[10] Adherence to the principle of legality was assessed with reference to customary international law (CIL), especially as regards the ICTY.[11] The AC's reasoning in *Galić* is illustrative of this approach:

> [T]he Judges have consistently endeavoured to satisfy themselves that the crimes charged in the indictments before them were crimes under customary international law at the time of their commission and were sufficiently defined under that body of law. This is because in most cases, treaty provisions will only provide for the prohibition of a certain conduct, not for its criminalisation, or the treaty provision itself will not sufficiently define the elements of the prohibition they criminalise and customary international law must be looked at for the definition of those elements.[12]

In order to understand the contribution of the ad hoc tribunals, in particular the ICTY, to the development of war crimes, it is necessary to contrast how they perceived their jurisdiction ratione materiae vis-à-vis the statutory formulations of the crimes. The latter provided the starting point for determining the former. The statutory formulations were not the centrepiece in the development of war crimes; rather, the wider field of IHL provided the impetus. According to *Tadić*, 'as a general principle, provisions of the Statute defining the crimes within the jurisdiction of the Tribunal should always be interpreted as reflecting customary international law' unless there is a contrary intention.[13]

The situation has been reversed in relation to the ICC. In the case of the Rome Statute, there is no need to test the definitions of the crimes against the backdrop of CIL in order to determine compliance with the principle of legality. Notably, the ICC AC, in determining that CIL

[10] A. Cassese and P. Gaeta (eds), *Cassese's International Criminal Law* (3rd edn., Oxford: Oxford University Press, 2013), at 5.

[11] T. Meron, *The making of international criminal justice: The view from the bench: Selected Speeches* (1st edn., New York: Oxford University Press, 2011), at 32–33.

[12] Judgment, *Galić* (IT-98-29-A), Trial Chamber, 30 November 2006, § 83.

[13] Judgment, *Tadić* (IT-94-1-A), Appeals Chamber, 15 July 1999, § 296.

imports no status requirements for the offences of sexual slavery and rape against child soldiers, did not explicitly discuss its approach to the identification of custom.[14] Under the Rome Statute, the starting point and the main focus of any interpretative exercise is the crime's definition in Article 8 of the Statute, while the applicable law is elaborately set out in Article 21. As seen below, Article 21 supports the Rome Statute's substantive nature.

3.3 The Relationship between ICL and IHL Under the Rome Statute

Essentially, an exploration of the ICC's role in the development of IHL invites the question as to the extent to which the ICC is to be seen as a 'norm entrepreneur'[15] articulating and reinforcing norms of ICL under the Rome Statute, and more broadly under IHL and general international law.

The dynamism of this relationship has been fundamentally re-defined because of the extensive treaty-proper negotiations which took place during the adoption of the Rome Statute, the participants involved and the end result of this process. Significantly, it was the first time that war crimes, along with the other crimes within the Court's jurisdiction, were negotiated as part of a multilateral treaty-making for the purpose of setting up an international judicial institution to deal with individual criminal responsibility. Thus, the Statute's negotiating history and the crime definitions, as eventually adopted, are extremely important in reflecting the will of the drafters, the scope of the crimes and their status under CIL.[16]

In a sense, the ICC is in a much stronger position to influence the development of CIL than the ad hoc tribunals. The Rome Statute is the product of a multilateral convention whereby its terms were extensively discussed and amended in order to reach the final result. As indicated by the International Court of Justice, 'multilateral conventions may have an important role to play in recording and defining rules deriving from

[14] Y. Tan, 'The Identification of Customary Rules in International Criminal Law', 34 *Utrecht Journal of International and European Law* (2018) 92, at 101.

[15] C. Rudolph, 'Constructing an Atrocities Regime: The Politics of War Crimes Tribunals', 55 *International Organization* (2001) 655, at 681.

[16] *Third report on identification of customary international law by Michael Wood, Special Rapporteur*, UN. Doc. A/CN.4/682, 27 March 2015, § 33.

custom, or indeed in developing them'.[17] According to Oppenheim, factors such as 'extensive participation in a treaty, coupled with a subject matter of general significance and stipulations which accord with the general sense of the international community' give to a treaty a legislative character and 'assist the acceptance of the treaty's provisions as customary international law in addition to their contractual value for the parties'.[18] The aforementioned factors support the qualification of the Rome Statute as a 'law-making treaty', as opposed to being solely a 'contractual treaty' as between the states parties.[19]

During the drafting, several states supported the view that 'the Statute should codify customary international law and not extend to the progressive development of international law'.[20] At the same time, the process by which the crimes' definitions were negotiated and re-negotiated had an extensive effect on their final form and their normative potential. While the drafters proceeded on the premise that they were dealing with 'existing' rather than 'new' crimes, the highly legalised formulation of the crimes necessarily incorporated a significant element of progressive development. Moreover, on occasions the Rome Statute exceeded CIL. As regards war crimes, Article 8 of the Rome Statute developed the law in the areas of child soldiering and sexual offences.[21]

The legalised nature of the Rome Statute signifies that '[t]he ICC Statute more closely resembles a civil law code. Unlike pleadings in the ICTY, therefore, the gravamen of future pleadings in the ICC will be the interpretation of the Statute, not its customary law underpinnings'.[22] For example, in *Lubanga*, the first trial before the ICC, the Defence argued that the charges violated the principle of legality because child recruitment was not a crime under CIL when the offence was committed. The Pre-Trial Chamber (PTC) disagreed, finding that the crime had already

[17] *Continental Shelf case (Libyan Arab Jamahiriya v. Malta)*, Judgment of 3 June 1985 [1985] ICJ Rep. 13, at 29.

[18] R. Jennings and A.Watts (eds), *Oppenheim's International Law: Volume I Peace* (9th edn., Oxford University Press, 2008), at 1205, § 583.

[19] C. Brölmann, 'Law-Making Treaties: Form and Function in International Law', 74 *Nordic Journal of International Law* (2005) 383, at 388.

[20] *Report of the Preparatory Committee on the Establishment of an International Criminal Court, Volume I (Proceedings of the Preparatory Committee During March-April and August 1996)*, UN Doc. A/51/22, G.A. 51st Sess., Supp. No. 22, 1996, at 16.

[21] W. Schabas, *An Introduction to the International Criminal Court* (4th edn, Cambridge: Cambridge University Press, 2011), at 139.

[22] Meron, *supra* note 11, at 40.

attained customary status at the time. Most importantly, the PTC grounded its decision on the fact that there was sufficient evidence establishing substantial grounds to believe that the accused was aware that the crime of child recruitment 'entailed his criminal responsibility *under the Statute*', which the Democratic Republic of Congo had already ratified before the occurrence of the events contained in the charges.[23]

While judicial interpretation has played a particularly critical role in the development of ICL norms, it is not without its limits. Significantly, these limits have been changing alongside the concomitant gradual evolvement of ICL towards a more fully fledged body of law. The Rome Statute constitutes a significant leap forward both in terms of the elaborate definitions of the crimes but also as regards its unprecedented focus on the principle of legality. In assessing the ability of the ICC to develop the crimes within its jurisdiction, it is necessary to consider the principle of legality. Most importantly, the ICC is 'the first international tribunal to explicitly contain provisions relating to the different components of the principle of legality'.[24] The principle of legality in the ICC is found in Articles 22 (nullum crimen sine lege), 23 (nullum poena sine lege) and 24 (non-retroactivity ratione personae). Arguably, '[t]he ICC Statute constitutes in that respect, at least in theory, what appears to be a perfect embodiment of the principle of legality in its various components'.[25]

The pertinent question here is the extent to which the strict legalism that characterises the definitions of the crimes may hinder the development of the ICC crimes *via* judicial interpretation. The elaborate definitions of the crimes reflect the firm intention of the drafters that the ICC was not mandated to undertake the broad interpretative approaches pursued by the ad hoc tribunals. Moreover, the Court was established at a much more advanced stage in the development of ICL norms. *Lubanga* was never going to be *Tadić*, and this should have been obvious to start with. At first sight, the Chambers in *Lubanga* engaged in incremental

[23] Decision on the Confirmation of the Charges, *Situation in the Democratic Republic of the Congo in the Case of The Prosecutor v. Thomas Lubanga Dyilo* (ICC-01/04-01/06-803-tEN), Pre-Trial Chamber, 29 January 2007, § 306–307 (emphasis added).

[24] D. Jacobs, 'Positivism and International Criminal Law: The Principle of Legality as a Rule of Conflict of Theories', International Legal Positivism World, J. d´Aspremont and J. Kammerhofer (eds), Cambridge University Press, Forthcoming, 27 September 2012, available online at https://papers.ssrn.com/sol3/papers.cfm?abstract_id=2046311 (last visited 10 July 2021), at 16.

[25] *Ibid.*

development of ICL rather than prompting any groundbreaking developments.[26] However, as seen below, the Chambers' findings provided early indications of the ICC's novel understanding of the relationship between the law in the Rome Statute and the broader IHL framework.

One must not forget the nature of the ICC as a permanent penal institution involved simultaneously in a number of situations exhibiting different characteristics.[27] This aspect is expected to have an impact on the gradual development of the crimes by means of judicial interpretation whereby the ICC provides an authoritative reference point on the scope of the crimes within its jurisdiction. At the same time, although the Rome Statute is a highly legalised instrument, its nature is still dominated by substantive justice considerations. As a result, the Statute's strict legalism is in tension with the treaty's object and purpose, which at least from a substantive justice perspective, calls for a teleological interpretation of the crimes.[28] A teleological interpretation of the crimes is further supported by the Rome Statute's qualification as a law-making treaty,[29] that is a treaty whose influence can extend far beyond its contractual boundaries and effect changes under CIL, including IHL. As discussed below, the ICC's ability to develop the crimes within its jurisdiction, and to contribute to the development of IHL more broadly, is circumscribed by the formulation of the war crimes regime in the Rome Statute.

Formulation of War Crimes in Article 8

Aside from the crime of genocide, the drafting of crimes against humanity and war crimes on many occasions involved 'the *substantial alteration*, or the *complete reform*, of existing rules'.[30] This is especially obvious in relation to war crimes. The bulk of acts in Article 8 was based on widely rati-

[26] T.R. Liefländer, 'The Lubanga Judgment of the ICC: More than just the First Step?', 1 *Cambridge Journal of International and Comparative Law* (2012) 191, at 212.

[27] S.T. Deuitch, 'Putting the Spotlight on "The Terminator": How the ICC Prosecution of Bosco Ntaganda Could Reduce Sexual Violence During Conflict', 22 *William & Mary Journal of Women and Law* (2016) 655, at 687.

[28] C. Stahn, 'Justice Delivered or Justice Denied? The Legacy of the Katanga Judgment', 12 *Journal of International Criminal Justice* (2014) 809, at 815–816.

[29] Brölmann, *supra* note 19, at 393.

[30] M.E. Villiger M, *Customary international law and treaties: a manual on the theory and practice of the interrelation of sources* (Kluwer Law International, 1997), at 105 (emphasis in original).

fied conventions, many of which were considered to be part of CIL before their incorporation into the Statute. The added detail in relation to several crimes in Article 8 was to remedy the rather scant and vague wording of some of these primary rules of IHL. It entailed the effective transition of war crimes from rules of IHL, ill-fitted for the purpose of individual criminal responsibility, to a fully fledged modern war crimes definition.

Article 8 reflects to a much greater extent the ICC's nature as the first permanent tribunal of its kind with a non-conflict specific jurisdiction. The text agreed in Rome represents the first attempt to formulate a comprehensive, albeit not complete, war crimes provision. This involved an exercise by the drafters of choosing which rules of IHL were sufficiently important to be included or were not that controversial so as to endanger the successful outcome of the negotiations. Moreover, the drafters had to deal with the difficulty that the provisions of the GCs were not 'self-executing' but in need of elaboration and clarification.[31]

Article 8 of the Rome Statute is inextricably linked to the general IHL regime. Article 8(2)(a) criminalises violations of the grave breaches of the 1949 GCs. Article 8(2)(b) refers to serious violations of the laws and customs of war in IAC. Its provisions are drawn from both customary law (mainly the 1907 Hague Regulations) and widely accepted treaty law such as AP I. While Article 8(2)(b) is predominantly based on AP I and the Hague Regulations, none of the acts that are contained in this list explicitly refer to their origin, like Article 8(2)(a). Sometimes while an offence under Article 8(2)(b) is clearly based on these previous instrument(s), its adoption in the Statute was not done without changes. Moreover, Article 8(2)(b) has not incorporated all serious violations of AP I. Article 8(2)(c) deals with 'serious violations' of CA3 while Article 8(2)(e) refers to '[o]ther serious violations of the laws and customs applicable in armed conflicts not of an international character, within the established framework of international law'. Notably, the proscribed acts under Article 8(2)(e) rather than being based solely on Additional Protocol II (AP II), have been incorporated to the extent that they also appear in Article 8(2)(b).[32]

In this regard, the chapeau elements of Article 8(2) exemplify the relationship between ICL and IHL under the Rome Statute, and the

[31] M. Bothe, 'War Crimes' in A. Cassese, P. Gaeta, and R.W.D. Jones John (eds), *The Rome Statute of the International Criminal Court: A Commentary*, Volume 1A (Oxford University Press, 2002), at 392.

[32] *Ibid*, at 420.

relevance of IHL as an interpretative source of law in the jurisprudence of the ICC. The contours of this relationship are further clarified by situating the war crimes provision within the broader legal framework of the Rome Statute. Of particular relevance are the Elements of Crimes (EoC), as well as Articles 10 and 21 which are examined in turn below, before proceeding to the Court's evolving jurisprudence.

Article 9 Elements of Crimes

According to Article 9 of the Rome Statute, the EoC 'shall assist the Court in the interpretation and application' of the ICC crimes. The Introduction to Article 8 in the EoC provides for the interpretation of Article 8 'within the established framework of the international law of armed conflict'. The EoC were added at the insistence of the United States delegation, eager to prevent the type of judicial activism pursued by the judges of the ad hoc tribunals. The adoption of the EoC was particularly relevant with respect to the war crimes provision in view of its long-standing IHL pedigree, characterised by insufficiently precise prohibitions, outdated terminology and often duplicate offences.[33] Significantly, the EoC created 'a consistent framework with consistent and modern terminology'.[34] Terminologies from old treaties, such as 'declaring that no quarter will be given' are now explained in plain and clear language.[35]

Despite their non-binding character, the EoC seem to enjoy near-binding status.[36] Pursuant to Article 21, the EoC, together with the Rome Statute and the Rules of Procedure and Evidence (RPE) take precedence over CIL and are to be employed by the Court in the application and interpretation of crimes. Notably, the PTC majority in the *Al Bashir* case took the view that the EoC are to be applied by the Chambers unless there

[33] W.K. Lietzau, 'Checks and Balances and Elements of Proof: Structural Pillars for the International Criminal Court', 32 *Cornel International Law Journal* (1999) 477, at 480.

[34] P. Kirsch and V. Oosterveld, 'The Post-Rome Conference Preparatory Commission' in Cassese, Gaeta, and Jones John, *supra* note 31, at 97.

[35] Rome Statute of the International Criminal Court (adopted 17 July 1998, entered into force 1 July 2002) 2187 UNTS 90 (hereafter Rome Statute), at Art. 8(2)(b)(xii).

[36] R. Cryer, 'Royalism and the King: Article 21 of the Rome Statute and the Politics of Sources', 12 *New Criminal Law Review* (2009) 390, at 400.

is an 'irreconcilable contradiction' between the EoC and the Rome Statute. On such an occasion, the Rome Statute would prevail.[37]

Article 10

Article 10 of the Statute is a unique provision[38] in multilateral treaty-making and deserves attention because it attempts to define the relationship between ICC crimes and CIL.[39] The provision states that '[n]othing ... shall be interpreted as limiting or prejudicing in any way existing or developing rules of international law for purposes other than this Statute'. Notably, this provision was originally proposed during the negotiations on war crimes.[40] Article 10 was vehemently supported by the International Committee of the Red Cross ('ICRC'), which stated that '[i]t is essential that the Statute of the Court indicate that it in no way affects existing humanitarian law nor impede its development'. [41] The ICRC was particularly concerned that omissions from Article 8 should not be taken as evidence that they did not constitute war crimes.

It may be argued that Article 10 serves as an acknowledgement on the part of the drafters that the ICC Statute establishes minimum rules of conduct.[42] The successful outcome of the negotiation process necessitated significant compromises. Therefore, the provision attempts to prevent any developments which may occur in relation to the 'ICC law' from being considered a reflection of CIL. Despite the intended purpose of Article 10, the process by which the Rome Statute was adopted points towards a diametrically opposite result. The process by which the Rome Statute was adopted is a strong expression of opinio juris as to its material jurisdiction.

[37] *Al* Bashir, Decision on the Prosecution's Application for a Warrant of Arrest against Omar Al Bashir, ICC-02/05-01/09, Pre-Trial Chamber, 4 March 2009, § 128.

[38] L.N. Sadat, 'Custom, Codification and Some Thoughts About the Relationship Between the Two: Article 10 of the ICC Statute', 49 *De Paul Law Review* (2000) 909, at 917.

[39] L.N. Sadat, *The International Criminal Court and the Transformation of International Law: Justice for the New Millennium* (New York: Transnational Publishers, Inc. 2002), at 262.

[40] W. Schabas, *The International Criminal Court: A Commentary on the Rome Statute* (Oxford University Press, 2010), at 272.

[41] *International Committee of the Red Cross Statement of 8 July 2008 Relating to the Bureau Discussion Paper in Document A/CONF.183/C.1/L.53, United Nations Diplomatic Conference of Plenipotentiaries on the Establishment of an International Criminal Court*, UN Doc. A/CONF.183/INF/10, para.4, available online at http://legal.un.org/icc/rome/proceedings/E/Rome%20Proceedings_v3_e.pdf (visited 12 July 2021)

[42] Sadat, *supra* note 39, at 263.

This position is given further weight by the consideration that the categories of crimes included were largely considered to constitute jus cogens norms.[43] Despite its intended purpose, Article 10 constitutes an important acknowledgement on the part of the drafters as to the ICC's law-making potential. It supports the view that a paradigm shift took place at the Rome Conference, whereby for the first time, ICL came closer to a 'developed' legal system with adopted rules of conduct.[44] As the ICTY Trial Chamber (TC) stated, even before the Statute had entered into force, notwithstanding Article 10, 'the Rome Statute may be taken to restate, reflect or clarify customary rules or crystallise them, whereas in some areas it creates new law or modifies existing law'.[45] An examination of the Rome Statute's drafting history reveals that such considerations were particularly germane as regards developments under IHL.

Article 21 Applicable Law

Article 21 of the Rome Statute sets out the 'Applicable law' for the Court. The provision provides that the Chambers shall apply *in the first place* the Statute, the EoC and the RPE [Article 21(1)(a)]. The rules of international law, including 'the established rules of the international law of armed conflict' will only come into play *in the second place, where appropriate* [Article 21(1)(b)]. Lastly, failing the aforementioned, the Court will apply general principles of law [Article 21(1)(c)]. Based on the above arrangement, the starting point in any interpretative exercise concerning the crimes within the court's jurisdiction is the crime definitions, as set out in the Rome Statute and the EoC. This premise is unequivocally confirmed by the Court's evolving jurisprudence and its approach to the applicable sources of law. The ICC Chambers have consistently held that they will only resort to the sources of law included in paragraphs (1)(b) and 1(c) above, if there is a 'lacuna' in the Rome Statute, EoC and RPE and such a lacuna cannot be bridged by the application of the rules of interpretation contained in Articles 31 and 32 of the Vienna Convention

[43] M.C. Bassiouni, 'The Normative Framework of International Humanitarian Law: Overlaps, Gaps and Ambiguities', 8 *Transnational Law & Contemporary Problems* (1998) 199, at 201–2.

[44] Sadat, *supra* note 39, at 263.

[45] Judgment, *The Prosecutor v. Anto Furundzija* (IT-95-17/1-T), Trial Chamber, 10 December 1998, § 227.

on the Law of Treaties (VCLT) and Article 21(3) of the Statute.[46] In effect, rules of international law (including rules of CIL) and general principles of law are classified as 'subsidiary sources of law'.[47]

Article 21 of the Rome Statute provides for a hierarchical relationship between the sources of law, where the Court's founding texts are accorded primacy in the application of the law by the Chambers. This is in contrast to the long-standing non-hierarchical relationship pursuant to Article 38 of the ICJ Statute.[48] This arrangement provides for different methodological interpretation when compared to the ad hoc tribunals, which is inextricably linked to the ability of the ICC to effect developments under the Rome Statute and general IHL. Before proceeding to the court's evolving jurisprudence, it is necessary to locate the role played by the VCLT rules of interpretation. Irrespective of their appropriateness as tools of interpretation in the context of criminal proceedings, their relevance in the interpretative process is undeniable.

Vienna Convention on the Law of Treaties

The Court established early on that the interpretation of the Statute is governed by the VCLT. The General Rule of Interpretation in Article 31 of the VCLT prescribes that the various ingredients - the ordinary meaning, the context and the object and purpose - be considered together in good faith. Hence, the General Rule refers to a holistic approach, which

[46] Judgment on the Prosecutor's Application for Extraordinary Review of Pre-Trial Chamber I's 31 March 2006 Decision Denying Leave to Appeal, *Situation in the Democratic Republic of the Congo* (ICC-01/04-168), Appeals Chamber, 24 July 2006, §§ 22–24, 32–33 and 39, Judgment on the appeals of William Ruto and Mr Joshua Arap Sang against the decision of Trial Chamber V (A) of 17 April 2014 entitled 'Decision on Prosecutor's Application for Witness Summonses and resulting Request for State Party Cooperation', *The Prosecutor v. William Samoei Ruto and Joshua Arap Sang* (ICC-01/09-01/11-1598), Appeals Chamber, 9 October 2014, § 105.

[47] Judgment pursuant to Article 74 of the Statute, *Situation in the Central African Republic In the Case of the Prosecutor v. Jean-Pierre Bemba Gombo* (ICC-01/05-01/08-3343), Trial Chamber, 21 March 2016, § 79.

[48] Cryer, *supra* note 36, at 393–395. See also: L. Grover, 'A Call to Arms: Fundamental Dilemmas Confronting the Interpretation of Crimes in the Rome Statute of the International Criminal Court', 21 *European Journal of International Law* (2010) 543, at 553.

does not establish any hierarchical or chronological order in which those various ingredients are to be examined and then applied.[49]

Article 31 of the VCLT also provides that together with the context, consideration shall be given to 'any relevant rules of international law applicable in the relations between the parties'. In this respect, according to the TC in *Katanga*, the bench may rely on rules which are extraneous to the ICC's founding texts, where it is established that such rules apply between the states parties. Notably, where there is a gap in the founding texts, 'the Chamber must refer to treaty or customary humanitarian law and the general principles of law'.[50] The Court has discussed the extent to which the principle of legality can be reconciled with the General Rule of Interpretation. According to the Court, the interpretative method invited by the General Rule must always be consistent with the principle of legality, 'which constitutes a clear and explicit restriction on all interpretative activity'.[51]

The Chamber in *Katanga* referred to the tension between the principle of legality and the General Rule of Interpretation in the context of ICL, in particular where the object and purpose of the treaty appear critical for the interpretation of statutory provisions. In this regard, recourse to a teleological approach 'could be considered antithetical to the principle of legality'.[52] The TC attempts to reconcile the tension in the following way:

> It is self-evident that the aim of the Statute [...] to put an end to impunity for the perpetrators of the most serious crimes within the jurisdiction of the Court, can under no circumstance be used to create a body of law extraneous to the terms of the treaty or incompatible with a purely literal reading of its text. Nonetheless, the object and purpose of the Statute must always be borne in mind and fully considered during the interpretation of its provisions as they are one of the components which make it possible to establish its definitive meaning.[53]

[49] Judgment pursuant to article 74 of the Statute, *Situation in the Democratic Republic of the Congo in the Case of The Prosecutor v. Germain Katanga* (ICC-01/04-01/07-3436-tENG), Trial Chamber, 7 March 2014, § 44.

[50] *Ibid*, § 47.

[51] *Ibid*, § 51.

[52] *Ibid*, § 54.

[53] *Ibid*, § 55.

The formulation of Article 8 within the broader Rome Statute structure demonstrates the creation of a novel legal framework both in terms of substance and available interpretative tools. However, this novel state of affairs is still underscored by long-standing tensions between legal form and the quest for justice in the field of ICL. Thus, it is necessary to examine the work of Chambers in practice in order to understand the interpretative approach invited by the formulation of the war crimes regime.

3.4 Interpretation of Article 8 of the Rome Statute

A perusal of the Court's case law seeks to identify instances that demonstrate how the Chambers' interpretation of Article 8 will influence the development of war crimes and IHL more broadly. These are by no means exhaustive.

Child Soldiers

To date, the ICC has rendered a considerable jurisprudence in relation to the war crime of conscripting, enlisting and using child soldiers under the age of fifteen to participate actively in hostilities. The court's case law on this crime, and other crimes against children, namely sexual violence and rape against child soldiers, illustrate the Court's willingness to push the traditional boundaries of IHL.

The use of child soldiers in hostilities was considered by the ICC in *Lubanga*, the first case to come before the Court. Our discussion will focus on the court's interpretation of 'active participation in hostilities'. The war crime is based on Article 77(2) AP I and Article 4(3)(c) AP II, for IAC and NIAC, respectively. According to the ICRC Commentaries to AP I and II, the participation of children in hostilities encompasses both direct and indirect forms of participation.[54]

While IHL treats 'active' and 'direct' participation as synonymous terms to be interpreted interchangeably,[55] the ICC's interpretation of

[54] Y. Sandoz, Ch. Swinarski, and B. Zimmerman (eds), *Commentary to the Additional Protocols of 8 June 1977 to the Geneva Conventions of 12 August 1949* (1987), at § 3187 and 4557.

[55] N. Melzer, *ICRC Interpretative Guidance on the Notion of Direct Participation in Hostilities under International Humanitarian Law* (International Committee of the Red Cross, 2009), at 43.

'active' participation reflects a broader understanding of the term compared to its meaning and scope under IHL. According to the AC in *Lubanga*: '[T]he interpretation given to Common Article 3 of the Geneva Conventions in the context of the principle of distinction cannot be simply transposed to that of Article 8 (2)(e)(vii) of the Statute. Rather, the term 'participate actively in hostilities' must be given an interpretation that bears in mind that provision's purpose.[56]

The Court's view was that the term 'active' can encompass both direct and indirect participation.[57] The question which arises is how the court's interpretation fits within the broader IHL framework and principles, such as the principle of distinction, and the extent to which it may bring about normative changes under both ICL and IHL. Significantly, the Chambers' interpretation of using children to participate actively in hostilities, for the purpose of determining individual criminal responsibility, sits uneasily with one of the most fundamental tenets of IHL, the concept of direct participation in hostilities for the purpose of distinguishing between combatants and non-combatants.

The Court's interpretation gives rise to an interesting question. Does the court's approach solely pertain to the offence of child soldiering, which was brought within the sphere of ICL for the first time because of its incorporation in the Rome Statute? Or are the Chambers' willingness to push the traditional boundaries of IHL indicative of the ICC's potential role to develop the crimes within its jurisdiction, and as a consequence promote the further development of IHL? On the one hand, the ICC's reasoning has obvious benefits in terms of advancing accountability for all those responsible for the embroilment of children in armed conflict. At the same time, this approach must be reconciled and located within the wider IHL framework in order to understand how it may promote the development of IHL. Otherwise, children (and more broadly civilians) are more likely to become legitimate targets on the basis of a broader understanding of 'active' participation in hostilities.

[56] Judgment on the appeal of Mr Thomas Lubanga Dyilo against his conviction, *Lubanga* (ICC-01/04-01/06-3121-Red), Appeals Chamber, 1 December 2014, § 324.

[57] *Ibid*, § 340. See also: Judgment pursuant to Article 74 of the Statute, *Lubanga* (ICC-01/04-01/06-2842), Trial Chamber, 14 March 2012, §§ 535–538.

The Court's broad interpretative approach was followed in later cases that dealt with the same charge.[58] Significantly, in *Ntaganda*, the ICC took a step further and convicted the defendant for the commission of rape and sexual slavery against child soldiers by members of their own group.

Intra-party Violence Against Child Soldiers

Throughout the *Ntaganda* proceedings, the Defence had steadfastly argued that the Court could not exercise jurisdiction over the crimes of rape and sexual slavery against child soldiers by members of their own group. The Defence's objection was grounded on a clear premise that IHL does not protect participants in hostilities from crimes committed against them by members of their own side.[59]

There is merit in the Court's approach in that it seeks to address an obvious weakness in terms of protecting children from the perils of armed conflict. Sadly, sexual violence is an all-too-common feature of armed conflicts. It flies in the face of logic to argue that sexual violence did not take place 'in the context of and was associated with an armed conflict'. However, from an IHL perspective, active combatants, including children, are not protected from violence committed against them by members of their own side of the conflict.[60] The TC avoided this limitation, including finally tackling the question of whether sexual violence comes within the notion of *using* children to participate actively in hostilities, by stating that members of the same armed force are not per se excluded as victims of the war crimes of rape and slavery, under the Rome Statute,

[58] The protection of children is also a priority issue for the ICC Prosecutor. See: *Strategic Plan 2019–2021*, Office of the Prosecutor 17 July 2019, strategic goal 4 (at 5), available online at https://www.icc-cpi.int/itemsDocuments/20190726-strategic-plan-eng.pdf (visited 13 July 2021). See also: *Policy on Children*, Office of the Prosecutor, November 2016, available online at https://www.icc-cpi.int/iccdocs/otp/20161115_otp_icc_policy-on-children_eng.pdf (visited 14 July 2021).

[59] Decision Pursuant to Article 61(7)(a) and (b) of the Rome Statute on the Charges of the Prosecutor Against Bosco Ntaganda, *Situation in the Democratic Republic of the Congo. The Prosecutor v. Bosco Ntaganda* (ICC-01/04-02/06-309), Pre-Trial Chamber, 9 June 2014, § 76.

[60] Cassese, *supra* note 31, 67; K.J. Heller, 'ICC Appeals Chamber Says a War Crime Does Not Have to Violate IHL', Opinio Juris, 15 June 2017, available at http://opiniojuris.org/2017/06/15/icc-appeals-chamber-holds-a-war-crime-does-not-have-to-violate-ihl/ (visited 12 July 2021).

IHL or international law more generally.[61] The AC conclusively rejected the Defence's challenge as follows: '[I]n the absence of any general rule excluding members of armed forces from protection against violations by members of the same armed force, there is no ground for assuming the existence of such a rule specifically for the crimes of rape or sexual slavery'.[62]

The benefits of the above finding in terms of enhancing accountability and victim protection are undeniable. Nonetheless, the AC's reasoning could have rested on a firmer basis which better accords with the ability of the ICC to promote developments under IHL. Arguably, the AC subtracted an element of the crime—the status requirement—in order to reach the above conclusion.[63] According to Sellers, further reliance by the AC on Article 77 AP I and Article 4 AP II, respectively, would have strengthened the Court's reasoning.[64] The protection accorded to children under Article 77(1) AP I is not diminished by a child's status, and covers any form of indecent assault, including sexual violence. This reading is given further support by Article 77(3), which states that children under the age of fifteen who participate in hostilities and fall into the powers of the opposite party 'shall continue to benefit from the special protection accorded by this Article, whether or not they are prisoners of war'. Sellers argues that the scope of protection afforded by Article 77 together with the customary prohibition of sexual violence should have informed the court's reasoning in *Ntaganda*. While the said provision only applies with respect to IAC, Seller further points out that the AC should have accorded more attention to Article 4(3) AP II, which parallels the prohibition in Article 77(I) AP I. Notably, neither AP I or AP II nor the two ICRC Commentaries which accompany them specifically provide for the protection of children from sexual exploitation by members of their own group. The AC did refer to the updated ICRC commentary to GC

[61] *Ntaganda* (Second decision on the Defence's challenge to the jurisdiction of the Court in respect of Counts 6 and 9), (ICC-01/04-02/06-1710), Trial Chamber, 4 January 2017, § 54.

[62] *Ntaganda* (Judgment on the appeal of Mr Ntaganda against the 'Second Decision on the Defence's challenge to the jurisdiction of the Court in respect of Counts 6 and 9'), (ICC-01/04-02/06-1962), Appeals Chamber, 15 June 2017, § 65.

[63] S. K. Blank, '*Prosecutor v Ntaganda*—The International Criminal Court's dangerous foray into the shade of Lochner', 27 *Michigan State International Law Review* (2018) 1, at 22.

[64] P.V. Sellers, 'Ntaganda: Re-Alignment of a Paradigm', International Institute of Humanitarian Law 2018, available at https://iihl.org/wp-content/uploads/2018/04/Ntaganda-VI.pdf (visited 14 July 2021) at 12–16.

I. According to the commentary, the fact that the conduct is committed by one's own party should not preclude protection under CA3.[65] The AC admitted that the references on which the ICRC relies are limited; however, this in itself, was not an indication that the ICRC's conclusion was incorrect.[66] Notably, the court's reasoning does not deal with the sole but clear requirement conditioning the application of CA3, that the person concerned 'abstains from active participation in hostilities'.[67]

Despite its deficits, the Court's conclusion is both welcome and forward-looking. However, its long-term impact, and its ability to promote the further development of IHL, are contingent on the gradual clarification and refinement of the court's reasoning. Otherwise, its findings may be perceived as an unwarranted exercise of judicial activism, which clashes with the principle of legality.[68] Different proposals have been put forward to this effect. According to Prosperi, the AC should have placed greater emphasis on a teleological interpretation of Article 8(2)(e)(vi) pursuant to the Rome Statute's object and purpose as well as the methodological interpretation invited by Article 21(3), which provides that the application and interpretation of all applicable law 'must be consistent with internationally recognized human rights'. Considering that IHL does not 'generally and categorically' prohibit intra-group violence, 'it is the evolutionary nature of the Rome Statute, which should at any time be interpreted in light of international human rights law, to justify the adoption of the broadest possible interpretation of Article 8(2)(b)(xxii) and 8(2)(e)(vi)'.[69]

[65] *Commentary on the First Geneva Convention: Convention (I) for the Amelioration of the Condition of the Wounded and Sick in Armed Forces in the Field* (2nd edn., International Committee of the Red Cross, 2016), § 547.

[66] *Ntaganda* (Appeal Against Second Decision on Jurisdiction), *supra* note 62, § 61.

[67] J. K. Kleffner, 'The Beneficiaries of the Rights Stemming from Common Article 3' in A. Clapham, P. Gaeta, M. Sassoli (eds), *The 1949 Geneva Conventions: A Commentary* (Oxford: Oxford University Press, 2015), at 436.

[68] Heller, *supra* note 60; O. Svaček, 'Brothers and Sisters in Arms as Victims of War Crimes: Ntaganda Case Before the ICC', 8 *Czech Yearbook of International Law* (2017) 346; L.P. Rossetti, 'Intra-party sexual crimes against child soldiers as war crimes in *Ntaganda*: "Tadić moment" or unwarranted exercise of judicial activism?', *Questions of International Law 60* (2019) 49, at 60–62; Blank, *supra* note 63, 18–23.

[69] L. Prosperi, 'The Appeals Chamber Was Not Wrong (But Could Have Been More Right) in Ntaganda', Opinio Juris, 21 June 2017, available at http://opiniojuris.org/2017/06/27/33178/ (visited 14 July 2021).

Kenny and McDermott also propose improvements to the court's reasoning on the basis of an overarching approach which is based on an assessment of whether the victim at the material time was under the scope of protection of international law. They base their case on the concepts of hors de combat for NIAC and allegiance as regards IAC.[70] With respect to the former, the authors are more in agreement with the PTC's finding that child soldiers, as victims of sexual slavery and rape, could not be considered active combatants at the time of the commission of the sexual acts by reason of the coercive nature of these crimes.[71] At the time, the PTC failed to tackle the applicability of the continuous combat function and the 'revolving door' situation and their relevance to the case at hand.[72] By placing the focus on whether the victims are hors de combat, as opposed to fighters, the authors argue that the key consideration in determining whether a child is a victim of war crime in a NIAC is 'whether they were directly participating in hostilities at the time of their victimisation such that they are characterised as hors de combat'.[73] Such a determination would need to take place on a case-by-case basis taking into account the specific circumstances of a potential victim.[74] Alternatively, Svaček proposes a bifurcated standard of protection with respect to child soldiers, pursuant to which child combatants would enjoy protection from intra-group victimisation whilst remaining a lawful target for the adversary. Significantly, such an approach would not undermine the fundamental IHL concept of direct participation in hostilities and ensure compatibility with the principle of legality.[75]

Significantly, the AC was cognisant of the 'seemingly unprecedented nature' of its finding and made explicit reference to the Defence's argument that the court's conclusion rested on a 'wide application' of the Rome Statute pursued by way of 'judicial activism'.[76] The AC reasoned that the armed conflict nexus is the appropriate criterion for delimiting

[70] C. Kenny and Y. McDermott, 'The Expanding Protection of Members of a Party's Own Armed Forces under International Criminal Law', 68 *International and Comparative Law Quarterly* (2019) 943.

[71] *Ntaganda* (Decision Pursuant to Article 61(7)(a) and (b) of the Rome Statute on the Charges of the Prosecutor Against Bosco Ntaganda), *supra* note 59.

[72] Melzer, *supra* note 55, at 70–73.

[73] Kenny and McDermott, *supra* note 70, at 963.

[74] *Ibid*, at 975.

[75] Svaček, *supra* note 68, at 357.

[76] *Ntaganda* (Appeal Against Second Decision on Jurisdiction), *supra* note 62, § 67.

war crimes from ordinary crimes.[77] The AC agreed with the TC's determination that the war crimes of rape and sexual slavery do not import status requirements as to who can be a victim of these crimes under the Rome Statute and the 'established framework of international law'.[78]

To date, the ICC's case law on the participation of children in hostilities reveals a strong willingness on the part of both the prosecution and the judiciary to expand the boundaries of IHL. The Court's interpretative approach demonstrates a shift in the balance between ICL (in the form of Article 8 of the Rome Statute) and IHL (whether treaty-based and/or customary), as the driving force for effecting normative developments in the context of war crimes prosecutions. While the ICC was established at a much more advanced stage in the development of both IHL and ICL, the former has been less open to change than the latter. The early ICC jurisprudence reveals a fertile ground for the development of ICL in such a way as to ameliorate obvious shortcomings of IHL, including occasions intra-group sexual violence.

The key question is whether this is an omission, a gap in IHL that must be filled by extending the reach of the law, or whether this is a matter which does not belong to the ambit of IHL. Sexual offences have not traditionally been the focus of IHL or ICL. The Nuremberg and Tokyo Charters did not explicitly criminalise sexual violence and their case law dealt with them only incidentally, mainly in the context of rape.[79] Moreover, the GC regime characterised rape and other forms of sexual violence as attacks against the honour of women rather than violent crimes.[80] The atrocities committed in the former Yugoslavia provided the turning point for the shift from the implicit to the explicit criminalisation of sexual violence as a war crime. The adoption of the Rome Statute represented the culmination of this process; acts of sexual violence became a separate

[77] *Ibid*, § 68.

[78] *Ibid*, § 46–51 and 52–70.

[79] P.V. Sellers, *The Prosecution of Sexual Violence in conflict: The Importance of Human Rights as Means of Interpretation* (The United Nations High Commissioner for Human Rights, 2008) available online at www.ohchr.org/english/issues/women/docs/Paper_Prosecution_of_Sexual_Violence.pdf (visited 16 July 2021), at 7–8.

[80] Geneva Convention Relative to the Protection of Civilian Persons in Time of War of 12 August 1949 (adopted 12 August 1949, entered into force 21 August 1950), at Art. 27; Protocol Additional to the Geneva Conventions of 12 August 1949, and Relating to the Protection of Victims of International Armed Conflicts (Protocol I) (adopted 8 June 1977, entered into force 7 December 1978), at Art. 75(2)(b).

explicit category in its own right.[81] Despite this remarkable progress, the existing legal framework cannot effectively incorporate the plight of child soldiers by members of their own group. The decision tries to ameliorate the gender-blindness of both ICL and IHL. It remains to be seen whether a more gender-attuned approach would hold strong in the case law of the ICC, ultimately effecting changes under IHL.

The explicit listing in the Rome Statute of various forms of sexual violence as war crimes reflects changes in society in recent decades, in particular the demand for greater respect for and recognition of women. To date, Ntaganda has been convicted for the war crimes of rape and sexual slavery; in February 2021, Ongwen became the first person to be convicted by an international criminal tribunal for the war crime of enforced pregnancy.[82] The Chamber's interpretation of the legal elements of this crime is a valuable input to the Court's evolving case law. Significantly, he was convicted for an array of sexual and gender-based crimes, namely, forced marriage, torture, rape, sexual slavery, enslavement, forced pregnancy and outrages upon personal dignity. Ongwen's conviction demonstrates that the ICC could be moving beyond 'safer' categories of sexual crimes, such as rape and sexual slavery, in an attempt to secure higher confirmation and conviction rates, to other less popular types of sexual offences, such as enforced pregnancy.[83]

Looking into the future, the Court's case law on the participation of children in hostilities provides an indication as to the role of the ICC in the development of war crimes beyond the context of child soldiering and other crimes affecting children.[84] Children of all ages as well as adults of both sexes are also victimised by members of their own armed group.[85] Notably, the Office of the Prosecutor (OTP) referred to the potentially

[81] K. Ambos, 'Sexual Offences in International Criminal Law, With a Special Focus on the Rome Statute of the International Criminal Court' in M. Bergsmo, A.B. Skre, and E.J. Wood (eds), *Understanding and Proving International Sex Crimes* (Beijing: Torkel Opsahl Academic EPublisher, 2012), at 143–145.

[82] Judgment, *The Prosecutor v. Dominic Ongwen* (ICC-02/04-01/15-1762-Red), Trial Chamber, 4 February 2021.

[83] J. Tridgell, 'Prosecutor v Ntaganda: The End of Impunity for Sexual Violence against Child Soldiers', 23 *Australian International Law Journal* (2017) 153, at 159–160.

[84] R. Grey, 'Sexual Violence Against Child Soldiers', 16 *Feminist Journal of Politics* (2014) 601, at 612.

[85] D.M. Amann, 'The Policy on Children of the ICC Office of the Prosecutor: Towards greater accountability for crimes against and affecting children', 101 *International Review of the Red Cross* (2019) 537, at 546–547.

normative ramifications of *Ntaganda*. As stated in its Strategic Plan 2019–2021, the OTP considers that the judgement contributed to the Court's emerging jurisprudence by '*extending the protective embrace of international humanitarian law* to cover crimes committed by an armed group against members of their own group, including sexual violence against women and children'.[86]

By way of contrast, it is pertinent to consider the 'growth' of Article 8 from the Kampala Review Conference onwards. Article 8 is the only crime within the court's jurisdiction to have been amended since the adoption of the Rome Statute. The approach pursued to achieve the amendments is informative as to the best way forward in achieving amendments to the Court's jurisdiction ratione materiae. More specifically, it sheds light on the relationship between IHL and ICL in the framework of the Rome Statute through the work of the Assembly of States Parties (ASP).

3.5 Amendments to Article 8 of the Rome Statute

The ASP is a unique body in the context of international tribunals. Following the exercise of prescriptive jurisdiction in Rome, it is responsible for the further exercise of such jurisdiction. As a result, the Court's material jurisdiction is not a self-contained body of law but may be amended by a decision of the state's parties at a regular session of the ASP or a Review Conference.[87] At a minimum, the Court's first Review Conference demonstrated that the amendment route is a workable one in practice. To this effect, the crimes within the Court's jurisdiction could be amended and developed by the ASP. The question which arises is what kind of law-making might be expected via this avenue?

In preparing for the Review Conference, the ASP decided that proposals for amendments to the Rome Statute should 'focus on amendments likely to command very broad, preferably consensual support'.[88] Of particular relevance were the three amendment proposals put forward by Belgium.[89] Amendment 1 sought to expand the prohibition on poison or

[86] Strategic Plan 2019–2021, *supra* note 58, at 9 (emphasis added).

[87] Rome Statute, *supra* note 35, at Art. 121(3).

[88] *Report of the Bureau on the Review Conference, Eight Session*, ICC-ASP/8/43, 18–26 November 2009, at 3, §2, available online at http://www.icc-cpi.int/iccdocs/asp_docs/ASP8/ICC-ASP-8-43-ENG.pdf (visited 7 December 2022).

[89] *Report of the Working Group on the Review Conference, Eight Session*, ICC-ASP/8/20 volume I, annex II, at 59–63, available online at http://www.icc-cpi.int/iccdocs/asp_docs/RC2010/WGRC-ENG.pdf (visited 7 December 2022).

poisoned weapons; asphyxiating, poisonous or other gases; and all analogous liquids, materials or devices and bullets that expand or flatten easily in the human body to NIAC. Amendment 2 proposed prohibition on the use of biological, chemical and anti-personnel mines and Amendment 3 was intended to prohibit use of non-detectable fragments and blinding laser weapons. Both amendments, 2 and 3, sought to extend the Court's jurisdiction with respect to both IAC and NIAC. Belgium circulated the above amendment proposals more than two years before the Review Conference.[90] This enabled Belgium to assess the amount of support that these amendments would garner. While numerous delegations supported Amendment 1 or did not have strong views in this respect, this was not the case in relation to Amendments 2 and 3, where the general view was that 'they were not mature enough'.[91] To this effect, Belgium decided to withdraw Amendments 2 and 3 from the proposed Review Conference agenda.[92]

At the Rome Conference, Amendment 1, the Belgian proposal, was adopted by consensus.[93] This amendment prima facie demonstrated that it was possible for crimes over which the Court has jurisdiction to evolve. Moreover, the amendments that took place had the result of 'creating a symmetry between the texts governing non-international and international armed conflict with respect to three categories of prohibited weapons'.[94] Nevertheless, such an amendment has been hailed as 'symbolic', whose real importance lies in creating a 'procedural precedent' for future amendments to the Statute.[95]

Both in Rome and at the Review Conference, proposals for a broader provision were sacrificed for political expediency. The Review Conference demonstrated that long preparation, solid proposals, strong support and the ability to assuage the concerns of certain powerful states are necessary before a proposal is to be entertained as an agenda item at a future review conference. This is demonstrated not only by Belgium's methods and

[90] *Ibid*, at 53, § 27.

[91] *Ibid*, at 53, § 30.

[92] *Ibid*, at 53, § 33.

[93] RC/Res.5, Amendments to Article 8 of the Rome Statute, 10 June 2010, available online at http://www.icc-cpi.int/iccdocs/asp_docs/Resolutions/RC-Res.5-ENG.pdf.

[94] W.A. Schabas, *An Introduction to the International Criminal Court* (6th edn., Oxford University Press, 2020) at 139.

[95] A. Alamuddin and P. Webb, 'Expanding Jurisdiction over War Crimes under Article 8 of the ICC Statute', 8(5) *Journal of International Criminal Justice* (2010) 1219, at 1236–1237.

approach in amending Article 8 but also by the work behind the adoption of a definition for the crime of aggression. Both amendments reveal the role to be played by the ASP and its working groups in the development of ICC crimes. Of particular importance in this respect is the work of the Working Group on Amendments (WGA) created by the ASP in 2009 for the purpose of identifying amendments to be forwarded to the ASP for consideration.[96] Effectively, this development made the amendment procedure as a regular item at the ASP sessions 'more concrete'.[97]

The WGA's mandate provides that when examining proposals for a new crime, it will particularly consider 'whether the crime can be characterized as one of the most serious crimes of concern to the international community as a whole and whether the crime is based on an existing prohibition under international law'.[98] The fate of amendment proposals post Kampala demonstrates the continuing relevance of the broader framework of international law (beyond the Rome Statute) in affecting the ultimate fate of amendment proposals. The 2017 amendments proposed by Belgium extended the list of prohibited weapons as regards both IAC and NIAC and brought within the Court's jurisdiction microbial or other agents; toxins; weapons, the primary effect of which is to injure by fragments undetectable by x-rays in the human body; and blinding laser weapons.[99] There was widespread support for these amendments which concerned weapons prohibited by treaties which enjoyed broad ratification or acceptance. Interestingly, in the absence of unanimity amongst delegates as to the amendments' customary status, the ASP resolution that adopted the amendments was ultimately revised to exclude any reference to their existence as rules of CIL.[100] However, as aptly stated by Akande, 'including

[96] *Review Conference*, ICC-ASP/8/Res.6, 26 November 2009, § 4, available online at https://asp.icc-cpi.int/sites/asp/files/asp_docs/Resolutions/ICC-ASP-8-Res.6-ENG.pdf (visited 7 December 2022).

[97] Alamuddin and Webb, *supra* note 95.

[98] *Strengthening the International Criminal Court and the Assembly of States Parties*, 21 November 2012, ICC-ASP/11/Res.8, annex II, § 9, available online at https://asp.icc-cpi.int/sites/asp/files/asp_docs/Resolutions/ASP11/ICC-ASP-11-Res8-ENG.pdf (visited 7 December 2022).

[99] *Resolution on amendments to article 8 of the Rome Statute of the International Criminal Court*, ICC-ASP/16/Res.4,14 December 2017, available online at https://asp.icc-cpi.int/sites/asp/files/asp_docs/Resolutions/ASP16/ICC-ASP-16-Res4-ENG.pdf (visited 7 December 2022).

[100] *Report of the Working Group on Amendments, Sixteenth session*, ICC-ASP/16/22, 4–14 December 2017, at 12, available online at https://asp.icc-cpi.int/sites/asp/files/asp_docs/ASP16/ICC-ASP-16-22-ENG.pdf (visited 7 December 2022).

such a crime within the ICC Statute may be regarded not only as criminalization by treaty but also as a step in the direction of criminalization under customary international law'.[101] The 2019 amendment extended the war crime of starvation to NIAC.[102] Such criminalisation was already part of Article 8 as regards IAC, and its omission from the final package in Rome seems to have been an 'oversight'.[103]

Unlike Belgium's proposal, which had to be revised and refined over a number of years—including removing anti-personnel mines from the list of proposals 'in order to achieve a consensual outcome'[104]—the Swiss proposal was adopted far more swiftly. There was no justification for distinguishing the protection of civilians from starvation between IAC and NIAC. The WGA Report reveals no disagreement among delegates as to the amendment's customary status.[105] Moreover, the amendment was a step forward towards achieving harmonisation of the Court's jurisdiction as regards war crimes committed in IAC and NIAC.

A perusal of the work of the WGA confirms that the status of IHL norms under CIL remains a prevalent consideration in effecting changes to the ICC's material jurisdiction, which is further qualified by the need to adopt decisions by consensus and appease individual state parties. Recurrent concerns to have been put forward by delegations in the context of the WGA meetings include the negative impact of amendments on the universality of the Court and the risk of fragmenting the Rome Statute as a result of consecutive amendments.[106] The practical impact of the amendments is further restricted by the fact that according to Article

[101] D. Akande, 'Customary International Law and the Addition of New War Crimes to the Statute of the ICC', EJIJ: Talk! Blog of the European Journal of International Law, 2 January 2018, available online at https://www.ejiltalk.org/customary-international-law-and-the-addition-of-new-war-crimes-to-the-statute-of-the-icc (visited 7 December 2022).

[102] *Resolution on amendments to article 8 of the Rome Statute of the International Criminal Court*, ICC-ASP/18/Res.5,6 December 2019, available online at https://asp.icc-cpi.int/sites/asp/files/asp_docs/ASP18/ICC-ASP-18-Res5-ENG.pdf (visited 7 December 2022).

[103] *Report of the Working Group on Amendments, Eighteenth session*, ICC-ASP/18/32, 2–7 December 2017, §10, available online at https://asp.icc-cpi.int/sites/asp/files/asp_docs/ASP18/ICC-ASP-18-Res5-ENG.pdf (visited 7 December 2022).

[104] *Assembly of States Parties to the Rome Statute of the International Criminal Court*, Sixteenth session, ICC-ASP/16/20, 4–14 December 2017, at 79, §10, available online at https://asp.icc-cpi.int/sites/asp/files/asp_docs/ASP16/ICC-ASP-16-20-vol-I-ENG.pdf (visited 7 December 2022).

[105] ICC-ASP/18/32, *supra* note 105.

[106] For example, *ibid*, §10.

121(5) of the Rome Statute, the new crimes only apply to those state parties which ratify the amendments. The work of the ICC Chambers is not hampered by such a severe limitation. The ICC Chambers' law-making potential, and their capacity to influence normative developments of ICL norms and advance the evolution of IHL, is premised on the interpretative approaches pursued by the judges. The Court's case law on child soldiers has provided clear signals that such interpretation is at least expansive and potentially transformative, and less restricted by the general framework of the laws of armed conflict compared to the amendments avenue.

3.6 Concluding Remarks

The ICC Chambers' attempt to 'dilute' the normative connection between the primary rules of IHL and the secondary rules of ICL is undeniable.[107] Notwithstanding the intention of the drafters to curtail the law-making capacity of the bench, the early case law of the ICC indicates that they overestimated the elevated role accorded to the principle of legality and its ability to limit judicial creativity. According to d'Aspremont, what we have been witnessing is a shift from source-based expansionism (which informed the work of the post-war military tribunals and the *ad hoc* tribunals) to interpretation-based expansionism under the Rome Statute. Such expansive interpretation is enabled by the interpretative methodology invited by Article 21 of the Rome Statute.[108]

There is no question that the principle nullum crimen sine lege does not bar progressive development of the law through interpretation.[109] The issue is whether we are witnessing an unwarranted 'divorce' or a re-balancing of the normative relationship between ICL and IHL, with the ICC taking a leading role in effecting normative developments. The ICC's

[107] Rossetti, *supra* note 68, at 59.

[108] J. d'Aspremont, 'The Two Cultures of International Criminal Law' in K.J. Heller, F. Mégret, S. Nouwen, J.D. Ohlin, and D. Robinson (eds), *The Oxford Handbook of International Criminal Law* (New York, Oxford University Press, 2020), at 417. See also: B. Perrin, 'Searching the Law While Seeking Justice: The Difficulties of Enforcing International Humanitarian Law in International Criminal Trials', 39 *Ottawa Law Review* (2008) 367, at 398. For a comparison of the judicial activism displayed by the *ad hoc* tribunals and the ICC alike see: A. Appazov, 'Judicial Activism' and the International Criminal Court', iCourts Working Paper Series, No.17, 2015.

[109] See generally: M. Shahabuddeen, 'Does the Principle of Legality Stand in the Way of Progressive Development of Law?', 2 *Journal of International Criminal Justice* (2004) 1007.

case law on child soldiers is highly informative. Most importantly, *Ntaganda* was a case where both the statutory prohibition and the IHL rule were sufficiently clear. The Court *opted* to interpret the prohibition in the way that it did. However, its interpretative approach must be better placed within the ICC's jurisdiction ratione materiae, the broader legal framework of the Rome Statute, and the particularities of the ICC as the first international tribunal of its kind. All the aforementioned have a role to play in the ICC's ability to develop the law within its jurisdiction and promote the further development of IHL.

The adoption of the Rome Statute and the establishment of the ICC ushered a new era in the adjudication of war crimes, and ultimately, the development of IHL. Article 8 of the Rome Statute constitutes an effective transition of war crimes from decades-long vague and ill-defined formulations to full-fledged definitions. The question explored concerns the ICC's role in the further development of IHL. Article 21 of the Rome Statute, the chapeau elements of Article 8(2) and the EoC exemplify the relevance of IHL as an interpretative source of law in the jurisprudence of the ICC. At the same time, the ICC's contribution to the development of IHL is conditioned upon two interrelated factors. Firstly, the ICC was established at a much more advanced stage in the development of ICL norms. Essentially, the ICC case law builds upon existing jurisprudence. Thus, the kind of development that will take place as a result of the ICC's work is of a different quality and not comparable to the development that took place in the past. Secondly, the detailed elaboration of war crimes and the methodological interpretation invited by Article 21 has shifted the balance for the advancement of normative developments towards the legal framework established by the Rome Statute and away from the general framework of IHL, at least as regards the war crimes within the Court's jurisdiction. As discussed in section 3.5 above, the ICC's prescriptive jurisdiction via the ASP is more likely to rely on existing or widely accepted IHL norms than the ICC Chambers.

The Court's work in prima facie internal conflicts has meant that Article 8's jurisprudential advancement has unevenly shifted in favour of war crimes committed in NIAC. The ICC's focus on a particular segment of Article 8 highlights the normative role played by the Court itself *in action*. Importantly, such a development is taking place irrespective of the far greater level of protection afforded by Article 8 to war crimes committed in IAC. In sum, the ICC in action can modify the direction of a crime's development independently and in spite of its substantive law scope under the Statute. Given that the prosecutor, restrained among others by budgetary and workload issues, will necessarily select a limited number of situations and cases, the Court's establishment unavoidably promotes the asymmetrical development of the crimes within its jurisdiction.

Lastly, the ICC's non-situation-specific ambit is a unique factor that forms part of the Court's nature as a law-making institution. The diverse situations in which the Court is involved bring into play different considerations as regards the application and the interpretation of the law by the Chambers. Therefore, the Chambers will necessarily evolve and adapt their interpretation of the crimes. The ICC's establishment as a permanent institution is inextricably linked to the further and future development of the crimes within the Court's jurisdiction. The Court's law-making potential as the first permanent institution of its kind is founded on the *continuity* of its jurisprudence over the course of simultaneously ongoing diverse situations. The ICC's case law on child soldiers exemplifies this trend.

CHAPTER 4

Comparing International Criminal Tribunals' Interpretive Approaches to International Humanitarian Law

Raghavi Viswanath

4.1 Introduction

International humanitarian law (IHL) is conventionally described as a set of rules which seek, for humanitarian reasons, to limit the effects of armed conflict.[1] However, IHL finds its roots in a place of paradox. In Meurant's words, it prescribes a "legal system to regulate acts which are fundamentally opposed to the law".[2] With the setting up of the International Committee of the Red Cross, it was commonly accepted that IHL was not a promise to eliminate war but an endeavour to mitigate

[1] International Committee of the Red Cross, *The International Review of the Red Cross No 221* (March–April 1981), at 76.
[2] J. Meurant, "Inter Arma Caritas: Evolution and Nature of International Humanitarian Law", 24 (3) *Journal of Peace Research* (1987), at 237–249.

R. Viswanath (✉)
European University Institute, Florence, Italy
e-mail: raghavi.viswanath@eui.eu

M. Faix, O. Svaček (eds.), *ICC Jurisprudence and the Development of International Humanitarian Law*, Global Issues,
https://doi.org/10.1007/978-3-031-45994-8_4

and attenuate its hostilities.[3] This naturally leaves much to interpretation. There are two main understandings of the function of interpretation. To some scholars, interpretation is the process which releases the exact meaning of a legal norm.[4] To others, interpretation is an argumentative praxis that gives fresh meaning to a norm.[5] Grover has usefully deconstructed the interpretive exercise into parts—noting that the first step is to identify a primary interpretive principle, offer arguments to ground this principle, and canvas a list of aids in which this argument finds support.[6] In this chapter, I consider this latter understanding of interpretation as an exercise to give meaning to IHL norms. IHL relies on multiple interpreters—from the International Committee of the Red Cross (ICRC), members of armed forces, States, and more recently, international tribunals. As Blishchenko noted, IHL owes a great deal to decisions handed down by national and international courts.[7]

This chapter is particularly interested in studying and comparing the interpretive practices of international criminal tribunals. Established to "prosecute and prevent continuing violations of international humanitarian law", international criminal tribunals have assumed the primary role in articulating the interpretive framework for IHL.[8] Especially in a regime such as IHL, which is dominated by the lack of practice, international

[3] J. Pictet, *Development and Principles of International Humanitarian Law* (Dordrecht: Nijhoff, Henry Dunant Institute, 1985), at 23.

[4] J. M. Sorel and V. B. Eveno, "Article 31", in O. Corten and P. Klein (eds), *The Vienna Conventions on the Law of Treaties: A Commentary* (New York, Oxford University Press, 2011), 804–837, at 806.

[5] I. Venzke, "Sources in Interpretation Theories: The International Law-Making Process" in Besson and D'Aspremont (eds), *The Oxford Handbook of the Sources of International Law* (New York, Oxford University Press, 2017), at 402, 405.

[6] L. Grover, "A Call to Arms: Fundamental Dilemmas Confronting the Interpretation of Crimes in the Rome Statute of the International Criminal Court", 21(3) *European Journal of International Law* (2010), at 543–583. Grover references D.N. MacCormick and R.S. Summers (eds), *Interpreting Statutes: A Comparative Study* (London, Routledge, 1991) to support her point.

[7] I. P. Blischenko, "Judicial Decisions as a Source of International Humanitarian Law", in A. Cassese (ed.), *The New Humanitarian Law of Armed Conflict* (Napoli, Editoriale Scientifica, 1979), at 41, 51. For a modern appraisal, see G. Mettraux, *International Crimes and the ad Hoc Tribunals* (New York, Oxford University Press, 2005), at 13–18.

[8] *Report of the Secretary-General pursuant to paragraph 2 of Security Council Resolution 808(1993)*, U.N. Doc. S/25704, 3 May 1993 (hereafter ICTY Report); *Report of the Secretary-General pursuant to paragraph 5 of Security Council Resolution 955 (1994)*, U.N. Doc. S/1995/134, 13 February 1995 (hereafter ICTR Report), § 1.

tribunals command considerable weight due to the assertive and reasoned character of their decisions.[9] This chapter focuses on the interpretive approaches used by the *ad hoc* tribunals [the International Criminal Tribunal for the former Yugoslavia (ICTY) and International Criminal Tribunal for Rwanda (ICTR)], the International Criminal Court (ICC), and the Special Court of Sierra Leone (SCSL). Given the multiplicity of interpretive approaches that are in circulation now, this chapter selects certain traditional and non-traditional rules which have been invoked in readings of both treaties and customary IHL. As I will later explain, the chosen tribunals represent a healthy range in terms of formality, political context, judicial independence, and state of the art of IHL and international human rights law (IHRL). Sects. 4.2, 4.3, 4.4 and 4.5 of the chapter canvas the rules of treaty interpretation employed by the chosen tribunals. These sections also draw comparisons between the trends emerging out of the practice of each tribunal. Section 4.6 unpacks the more systemic and political causes underlying the aforementioned interpretive trends.

4.2 Literal Approach

Plain and Ordinary Meaning

The jurisprudence of the *ad hoc* tribunals is hard to ignore when taking stock of IHL. Created at a time when international criminal law was just beginning to take shape, the *ad hoc* tribunals had scant guidance to fall back on.[10] They were left to create rules of procedure for their own working and add legs to the substantive and procedural norms that they had the opportunity to adjudicate.[11]

While there are differences between domestic and international law-making,[12] both regimes mostly share the same interpretive toolboxes. In

[9] R. Cryer, "Of Custom, Treaties, Scholars and the Gavel: The Influence of the International Criminal Tribunals on the ICRC Customary Law Study", 11(2) *Journal of Conflict and Security Law* (2006), at 239–263; Sir G. Fitzmaurice, "Some Problems Regarding the Formal Sources of International Law", (1958) *Symbolae Verzijl*, at 153, 172.

[10] K. D. Askin "Reflections on Some of the Most Significant Achievements of the ICTY", 37 *New England Law Review* (2003), at 4, 903.

[11] Grover, *supra* note 6, at 550.

[12] O. Ammann, *Domestic Courts and the Interpretation of International Law* (Brill Nijhoff, 2020), 133–158, at 133.

both fields, arguably, one of the most commonly used interpretive tools is the literal approach.[13] The literal approach prods the interpreters to assign the ordinary meaning to the text of the statute.[14] Some argue that the literal approach commands the greatest weight because it is autonomous and greatly limits interpretive discretion and the politics that accompany it.[15] However, the text is not always a guarantee of clarity.[16] Contrary to the belief that the text mitigates the risk of politicization, the text by itself is the product of hegemonic legal structures and is invoked precisely to show the door to epistemologies which challenge its preferred narrative.[17]

Nonetheless, the early case law of the *ad hoc* tribunals reveals a recurring application of the literal rule.[18] The Report of the Secretary-General, constituting the ICTY and ICTR explicitly identifies the Statute of the Tribunal as the primary source/applicable law.[19]

Albeit difficult to believe based on the popular legacy of the *Tadić* case, conventional text was very much the anchor of various phases of the case. Case in point is the Appeals Chamber decision in *Tadić*. Here, the Chamber disagreed with the Trial Chamber's view that grave breaches of the Geneva Conventions could occur in non-international armed conflicts. The Chamber's sole reason was that Article 2 of the Statute placed a burden on the parties/the Court to establish the fact of an international armed conflict[20] and that the statute enjoyed precedence over customary law. The requirement of proving an international armed conflict led the

[13] A. Scalia and B. A. Garner, *Reading Law: The Interpretation of Legal Texts* (St. Paul, Thomson/West 2012), at 110.

[14] Vienna Convention on the Law of Treaties (adopted 23 May 1969, entered into force 27 January 1980), UNTS 1155, at Art. 31(1).

[15] Ammann, *supra* note 12, at 191, 194.

[16] S. Fish, *Is There a Text in This Class? The Authority of Interpretive Communities* (Cambridge, Massachusetts, Harvard University Press, 1980), at 5.

[17] S. Roy, "The Visual Culture of Law in India: A response to Rahela Khorakiwala" in Ballakrishnen and Dezaley (eds), *Invisible Institutionalisms: Collective Reflections on the Shadows of Legal Globalisation* (Hart Publishing, 2020), at 107, 108.

[18] Judgment, *Prosecutor v. Dusko Tadić* (ICTY-94-1-A), Appeals Chamber, 15 July 1999, para. 296 (hereafter—*Tadić*); Judgment, *Prosecutor v. Milorad Krnojelac* (ICTY-97-25-A), Separate Opinion of Judge Schomburg, Appeals Chamber, 17 Sept. 2003, para. 13; Decision, *The Prosecutor v Ferdinand Nahimana, Jean-Bosco Barayagwiza, Hassan Ngeze* (ICTR-97-19-AR72), Separate Opinion of Judge Shahabuddeen, Trial Chamber, 3 November 1999, at 4.

[19] ICTY Report, *supra* note 8, paras. 19, at 32.

[20] *Tadić* (Decision on the Defence Motion for Interlocutory Appeal on Jurisdiction), (IT-94-1-AR72), Appeals Chamber, 2 October 1995, §§ 71–78.

Chamber to also read the list of "protected persons" strictly. In so doing, the Chamber stressed that grave breaches had to be directed against victims of a nationality different from that of the perpetrator.[21]

Similarly, in the *Akayesu* case before the ICTR, the Appeals Chamber was tasked with giving meaning to the term 'instigation' when determining liability for IHL violations.[22] The Chamber looked at the thesaurus meaning of the word 'instigation' to conclude that instigation did not require the call to be direct *and* public.[23] Interestingly, despite its strong linguistic commitment, it did not give enough credit to the semantic difference between the English term 'instigation' and its French translation.[24]

Despite the regular recourse to the literal rule, *ad hoc* tribunals had little source material to work with given the glaring ambiguities and scantness of their constitutive statutes.[25] International criminal law itself was rather nascent at the time. The tribunals were left with no choice but to consult customary norms and general principles to bolster their reasoning.[26] Unsurprisingly, every instance of departure from the text by the tribunals was overwhelmingly written off as a rebellious act of judicial law-making.[27] An unexpected source of support was the Secretary-General of the UN whose report had forewarned that text would be an insufficient source of lawmaking for the tribunals.[28] Seeing this, when drafting the statute of the ICTY, the Secretary-General was particular to recommend a recourse to customary law. As the late Robert Cryer pertinently highlights, the same cannot be said of the ICTR statute whose drafting the Secretary-General did not partake in.[29] The Secretary-General famously remarked that the war crimes provision of the ICTR statute, in relying on Additional Protocol

[21] *Ibid*, §§ 81–84.

[22] Judgment, *Prosecutor v. Jean-Paul Akayesu* (ICTR-96-4-A), Appeals Chamber, 1 June 2001, fn 8, § 474.

[23] *Ibid*, § 478.

[24] *Ibid*.

[25] J. Wessel, "Judicial Policy-Making at the International Criminal Court: An Institutional Guide to Analyzing International Adjudication", 44 *Columbia Journal of International Law* (2006), at 377.

[26] Cryer, *supra* note 9, at 260.

[27] See discussion in M. Swart, "Tadić Revisited: Some Critical Comments on the Legacy and the Legitimacy of the ICTY", 3 *Goettingen Journal of International Law* (2011), at 985–1009.

[28] ICTY Report, *supra* note 8, §§ 33–34.

[29] D. Shraga and R. Zacklin, "The International Criminal Tribunal for Rwanda", 7 *European Journal of International Law* (1996), at 501, 504.

II, had moved beyond the realm of customary law.[30] This soon became the defining identity of the *ad hoc* tribunals. The turn to custom and the consequent pushing of the boundaries of IHL/ICL was not as well-received by States. The raging criticism of the practice of the *ad hoc* tribunals was the disregard of the principle of legality according to which offences must be clearly defined by the law and criminalized before the commission of the impugned conduct.[31]

The reprisals against the turn to custom prompted the inclusion of an applicable laws provision in the Rome Statute setting up the International Criminal Court (ICC).[32] Article 21 of the Statute now requires the ICC to first apply the principles prescribed by the Statute itself and then consult its previous decisions, general principles of international law, and such.[33] Article 21 was intended to be a codified instruction to the Court to prioritize the Statute over custom.[34] The enforced hierarchy has also led to greater application of text by the Court. In almost all cases before the Court, the judges first test out the literal approach, before moving to other approaches. Illustratively, in *Lubanga*, the Trial Chamber differentiated between "enlistment" and "conscription" using their thesaurus meanings.[35] In the *Katanga* admissibility decision where the Court was posed with unravelling the meaning of the term 'commencement of the trial' under Article 19(4) of the Rome Statute, the Court emphasized on the primacy of the literal approach.[36] Here too, the literal approach was the first resort, with the Court rushing

[30] ICTR Report, *supra* note 8, § 12.

[31] D. Jacobs, "International Criminal Law" in J. Kammerhofer and J. D'Aspremont (eds), *International Legal Positivism in a Post-Modern World* (Cambridge, Cambridge University Press, 2015), at 451, 458–66.

[32] M. M. Deguzman, "Article 21, Applicable Law" in O. Triffterer and K. Ambos (eds), *The Rome Statute of the International Criminal Court: A Commentary* (3rd edn., München: C.H. Beck, 2016), at 933, para. 2.

[33] Rome Statute of the International Criminal Court (adopted 17 July 1998, entered into force 1 July 2002), 2187 UNTS 90, Art. 21; A. Kumar, "Custom as a Source Under Article 21 of the Rome Statute", *Asian Journal of International Law* (2021), at 1–13.

[34] J. Powderly, "The Rome Statute and the Attempted Corseting of the Interpretative Judicial Function: Reflections on Sources of Law and Interpretative Technique" in C. Stahn, ed., *The Law and Practice of the International Criminal Court* (1st edn., New York, Oxford University Press, 2015), at 444, 448.

[35] Judgment Pursuant to Article 74 of the Statute, *The Prosecutor v. Thomas Lubanga Dyilo* (hereafter *Lubanga*), Case No. ICC-01/04-01/06, Trial Chamber, 14 March 2012, § 608.

[36] *The Prosecutor v. Germain Katanga* (Reasons for the Oral Decision on the Motion Challenging the Admissibility of the Case) (Article 19 of the Statute), ICC-01/04-01/07-1213-tENG, Trial Chamber II, 18 June 2009, (hereafter Katanga), §§ 30–32.

to pin the ordinary meaning of the text. In this instance though, the text itself was unhelpful. Citing this, the Court placed reliance on the context and supplementary interpretive tools instead.

Comparatively, at the Special Court for Sierra Leone (SCSL), the literal approach did not find much traction. It seems that the primary reason for the disuse of the textual rule is that the Court was largely faced with cases arising out of the conscription of child soldiers and the practice of having bush wives. These were both areas that were completely new to IHL and the SCSL was at the helm of the effort to add meaning to them.[37] It is only exceptionally that the Court invoked the plain and ordinary meaning. Most often this was done when decoding statements made by the AFRC leaders where they referred to themselves as "government" or to their "bush wives".[38] On the IHL regime governing child soldiers, the Court typically resorted to the plain meaning when ascertaining whether or not conscription necessarily required the recruited children to *participate* in hostilities.[39] In his separate opinion in the *Gbao et al.* decision, referring to the text of Article 4 of the SCSL Statute which defined conscription as the act of "enlisting of children into armed forces or using them to actively participate in hostilities", Justice Thompson found that the disjunctive "or" did not need both elements to be present.[40]

Contextual Interpretation

While the text was definitively considered to be a starting point by most tribunals, it was also equally accepted that the law did not exist in a vacuum. The events and discussions preceding the adoption of legal texts are particularly determinative as to the meaning that should be anointed to

[37] N. B. Novogrodsky, After the Horror: Child Soldiers and the Special Court for Sierra Leone, in C. Jalloh (ed.), "The Sierra Leone Special Court and its Legacy: The Impact for Africa and International Criminal Law" (New York, Cambridge University Press, 2013), at 361–372; Judgment, *The Prosecutor v. Alex Tamba Brima, Brima Bazzy Kamara, Santigie Borbor Kanu*, Case No. SCSL-04-16-T, Trial Chamber, 20 June 2007 (hereafter AFRC), § 703.

[38] Ibid, §§ 1155, 1089.

[39] Judgment, *Prosecutor v. Issa Hassan Sesay, Moris Kallon and Augustine* Gbao, SCSL-04-15-T, Trial Chamber I, 2 March 2009.

[40] *Ibid*, Separate Concurring Opinion of Justice Bankole Thompson Filed Pursuant to Article 18 of the Statute, § 30.

the law.[41] In domestic law, in cases where the text is ambiguous, it is replaced by a reading of the 'context', that is the circumstances in which the text was adopted. Here, text and context are mutually exclusive. Compared to domestic law however, international legal interpretation is inclined to consider the context in conjunction with and not separate from the text, as evidenced by Article 31(3) of the Vienna Convention on the Law of Treaties.[42]

Sandorski explains that drafters' intent is particularly significant for IHL given that the entire regime consists of self-executing norms.[43]

In other words, this means that IHL, by design, does not have the bandwidth to rely on in situ or post facto interpretations. It is tied to before the fact guidance. Importantly, the *Delalić* Chamber of the ICTY treated contextual interpretation as a variant of the literal rule.[44] The ICC Appeals Chamber, too, has found that interpreting the text itself requires the interpreter to "read the provision in entirety and in conjunction with its context".[45] Context finds equal force in the identification of custom as well.[46]

The versatility of literal readings has motivated international criminal tribunals to even borrow specific interpretive formulae from national jurisdictions. In *Blaskić*, the ICTY referenced the rule of *ejusdem generis*, which commentators describe as a linguistic device that preserves the specificity of legal language. The point of contention in this case was whether crimes against property could be prosecuted as crimes against humanity

[41] J. D'Aspremont, "The Systemic Integration of International Law by Domestic Courts: Domestic Judges as Architects of the Consistency of the International Legal Order" in Fouchald and Noellkaemper (eds), *The Practice of International and National Courts and the (De-)Fragmentation of International Law* (Oxford, Hart Publishing, 2012), at 151 ff.

[42] Vienna Convention on the Law of Treaties, *supra* note 14, at Art. 31 (3).

[43] J Sandorski, "Opieka konsularna a opieka nad jeńcami wojennymi w świetle sprawy kombatantów afgańskich" in J. Biaáocerkiewicz, M. Balcerzak and A. Czeczko-Durlak (eds), Księga Jubileuszowa Profesora Tadeusza Jasudowicza (Toruń: TNOiK, 2004), at 363–398.

[44] Judgment, *Prosecutor v. Zejnil Delalić, Zdravko Mucic also known as "Pavo", Hazim Delic, Esad Landzo also known as "Zenga"*, ICTY-96-21-T, Trial Chamber, 16 November 1998 (hereafter Delalić), § 166.

[45] Judgment on the Prosecutor's Application for Extraordinary Review of Pre-Trial Chamber I's 31 March 2006, *Situation in the Democratic Republic of the Congo* (Decision Denying Leave to Appeal), ICC-01/04-168, 13 July 2006, § 33.

[46] *Final Report: Statement of Principles Applicable to the Formation of General Customary International Law* International Law Association Committee on Formation of Customary (General) International Law, (2000) 17, available at www.ila-hq.org/index.php/committees?committeeID=22.

and/or war crimes. The Appeals Chamber disagreed with the Defence's argument invoking the *ejusdem generis* rule—the application of which would only allow crimes against *persons* to qualify.[47] Differently, Judges Van den Wyngaert and Morrison of the ICC applied *ejusdem generis* to the residual clause of "other inhumane acts" in Article 7(1)(k) to disqualify the crime of pillage from being prosecuted as a crime against humanity.[48]

Limitations of the Text

While there are certainly benefits of a literal approach in so far as it increases the durability of laws and limits interpretive discretion of judges, textual allegiance can often injure victims too. This is an important line of inquiry given that international criminal tribunals have applied textual readings to endorse completely opposite meanings of the impugned words which have had the effect of legitimizing State sponsored crimes.[49] As Schabas notes, loyalty to the text bodes often conflates into the strict construction of core crimes.[50] For a field of law such as IHL that is only now beginning to find its feet, exclusive reliance on the text can become a gatekeeper for victim experiences and the full emancipatory potential of IHL.

Moreover, literal readings cement the dominance of the written text, showing the door to visual and other non-textual features of the law.[51] This is noteworthy because international criminal law and IHL both rely heavily on their expressive and reparative features, most of which are visual and experiential rather than textual.[52]

Such non-textual features typically find genesis in non-Western epistemologies. Therefore, the preference for text not only ends up eliminating the more reparative features of the law, it also writes out the injustices

[47] Judgment, *Prosecutor v. Tihomir Blaškić* (IT-95-14-A), Appeals Chamber, 29 July 2004, § 148.

[48] Separate Opinion of Judge Christine Van den Wyngaert and Judge Howard Morrison, *The Prosecutor v. Jean-Pierre Bemba Gombo* (ICC-01/05–01/08), Appeals Chamber, 14 June 2018, § 63.

[49] Judgment, *Prosecutor v. Tadić* (ICTY-94-1-T), Trial Chamber, 7 May 1997, § 639; Judgment, *Prosecutor v. Milan Martić* (ICTY-95-11-T), Trial Chamber, 12 June 2007, § 50.

[50] W. A. Schabas, *An Introduction to the International Criminal Court* (New York, 5th edn., Cambridge University Press, 2017), at 201.

[51] N. M. Rajkovic, "The Visual Conquest of International Law: Brute Boundaries, the Map, and the Legacy of Cartogenesis", 31 *Leiden Journal of International Law* (2018), at 267.

[52] I. Tallgren, "Come and See? The Power of Images and International Criminal Justice", 17(2) *International Criminal Law Review* (2017), at 259–280.

meted out to peoples of color. Affixing ordinary meaning and subjecting all parties in the trial to the same ordinary meaning runs the risk of invisibilizing the linguistic and cultural pluralism that is inherent to international forums.[53] This challenge has plagued both IHL and international criminal law right from their genesis. Illustratively, a major talking point at the time of the drafting of the Geneva Conventions was their drafting language. Until 1929, the Geneva Conventions were exclusively drafted in French.[54] In 1949, plenipotentiaries to the drafting conference agreed that both French and English should be regarded as equally authentic texts of the Conventions, each informing and complementing the other.[55] This, however, is no guarantee of convergence. In fact, anticipating divergence, the drafters decided that the French and English versions would be presumed to have the same meaning and made all efforts to ensure that the two versions coincided in meaning and form.[56] Despite these efforts, the truth remains that only French and English—colonial languages—were chosen for the authentic text, diminishing the claims of other languages to international humanitarian law. Following the proposals by Latin American delegations attending the Diplomatic Conference of the Geneva Conventions, translations were made available in Russian and Spanish.[57] But these translations were considered secondary in status to the authentic versions, readily displaced by the English/French version in case of divergence. In so doing, a colonial hierarchy was enforced amongst the languages chosen.[58] Notwithstanding the attempts to enforce linguistic consistency, divergent readings were still generated and necessitated resort to other rules of interpretation. Linguistic disputes have continued to

[53] Philip Allott famously described treaties as disagreements reduced to writing. His critique was based on the simplification of cultural differences when drawing up a text. P Allott, "The Concept of International Law", 10 *European Journal of International Law* (1999), at 43.

[54] Commentary to the Protocol Additional to the Geneva Conventions of 12 August 1949, and relating to the Protection of Victims of International Armed Conflicts (Protocol I), 8 June 1977, at Art. 102.

[55] *Rule 38 of the Rules of Procedure, Final Record of the Diplomatic Conference of Geneva of 1949*, Vol. I, at 187–188.

[56] M. Villiger, *Commentary on the 1969 Vienna Convention on the Law of Treaties* (Martinus Nijhoff Publishers, 2009), at 450–462.

[57] Final Record of the Diplomatic Conference of Geneva of 1949, Vol. II-B, at 371.

[58] O. Ammann, "Language Bias in International Legal Scholarship: Symptoms, Explanations, Implications and Remedies", 33(3) *European Journal of International Law* (2022), 821–850.

manifest at the ICC too. The Court has six official languages, including Arabic and Chinese.[59] Any reading that pedestalizes only certain languages from this list and ignores others will not do justice to the Statute or its stakeholders.[60] In recognition of this, Judge Kaul consulted the meaning of 'State or organizational policy' under Article 7(2)(a) of the Statute in all official languages.[61] Sadly, such efforts remain few and exceptional.

The choice of official languages opens the door to more limitations of textual readings. At the ICTR, much of the litigation arose out of innuendo-filled speeches and posters, both of which would have otherwise easily circumvented the plain meaning test.[62] The trials of Charles Taylor at the SCSL and Dominic Ongwen at the ICC are also particularly instructive as to these limitations. In *Ongwen*, the crux of the case was to understand the meaning of "childhood" in the Acholi context—both on the point of whether Ongwen was indeed a minor as per the Rome Statute and whether he was aware that he was conscripting "child" soldiers.[63] A literal reading of the Acholi terms *kadoge/kadogi* both of which translate to children would have been plainly insufficient to protect the rights of the accused. As the Defence showed, the term "*kadoge*" was typically used for anyone younger than oneself.[64]

Relatedly, in Taylor's trial, one of the Prosecution's key witnesses was Joseph ZigZag Marzah who was a former member of Taylor's National Patriotic Front of Liberia.[65] Given that Marzah was only fluent in the Creole language, the Court had to rely on simultaneous translations into

[59] Rome Statute, *supra* note 33, at Article 50(1).

[60] L. Swigart, "Now you see it, now you don't: culture at the International Criminal Court" in J. Fraser and B. McGonigle Leyh (eds), *Intersections of Law and Culture at the ICC* (Edward Elgar, 2020), at 14, 16.

[61] Dissenting Opinion of Judge Hans-Peter Kaul to Situation in the Republic of Kenya, Decision Pursuant to Article 15 of the Rome Statute on the Authorization of an Investigation into the Situation in the Republic of Kenya, ICC-01/09-1, Pre-Trial Chamber II, 31 March 2010, §§ 37–38.

[62] Judgment and Sentence, *Prosecutor v. Ferdinand Nahimana*, ICTR-99-52-T, Trial Chamber, 3 December 2003, §§ 160, 161, 310.

[63] Judgment, *The Prosecutor v Dominic Ongwen*, ICC-02/04-01/15, Trial Chamber, 4 February 2021, § 2328; A. L. Nistor, "Culture as evidence and the construction of (un) certainty in the Dominic Ongwen trial", Armed Groups and International Law blog, 15 April 2021, available online at https://armedgroups-internationallaw.org/2021/04/15/ongwen-blog-symposium-culture-as-evidence-and-the-construction-of-uncertainty-in-the-dominc-ongwen-trial/ (last visited 5 September 2021).

[64] *Ibid.*

[65] Transcript, *The Prosecutor v. Charles Ghankay Taylor*, SCSL-2003-OI-PT, § 6018.

English. As a result, much of Marzah's phrases—"passport sized diamond", "dressed up in human being form"—were not comprehendible to the Court.[66] Sadly, despite the wealth of substantive evidence in it, Marzah's testimony—owing to the difficulty faced in deciphering it—was reduced to merely sensational significance.[67]

4.3 Purposive Approach

Pedigree of the Rule

Tribunals interpreting IHL soon realized that strict construction would make IHL more arcane and difficult to apply. This realization triggered the turn to the purposive approach. Per Savigny's account, the purposive approach is a search for the effect that the "law intended to achieve".[68] Other descriptions of the approach differ slightly. The VCLT, for instance, prescribes a search for the object and purpose of the law.[69] In both *Delalić* and *Tadić*, the ICTY found that strict construction pits the State/legislature as an adversary of the victim.[70] The purposive approach, in comparison, was less antagonizing.

In the case of the *ad hoc* tribunals, the mandate to apply norms which "were beyond doubt a part of customary law" encouraged and facilitated attempts to read beyond the text.[71] Since the text of the constitutive Statutes of the tribunals left much to conjecture, deciphering purpose offered a useful anchor for the tribunals' interpretive efforts. Notwithstanding its evidentiary challenges,[72] the purposive approach allowed the *ad hoc* tribunals to steer a "necessary development in broadening individual criminal responsibility to respond to modern international inter-ethnic conflict".[73] In the famed paragraphs 166 and 168 of the *Tadić*

[66] Ibid, §§ 5878–5879.

[67] G. Anders, "Testifying about Uncivilized Events: Problematic Representations of Africa in the Trial against Charles Taylor", 24 *Leiden Journal of International Law* (2011), at 937.

[68] F. Karl von Savigny, *System des heutigen römischen Rechts* (Bei Veit und Comp, 1840), at 217.

[69] Vienna Convention on the Law of Treaties, *supra* note 14, at Art. 31(1).

[70] *Delalić*, *supra* note 44, § 410; *Tadić* (Decision on Appellant's Motion for the Extension of the Time-Limit and Admission of Additional Evidence) IT-94-1-A, Appeals Chamber, 15 October 1998, § 73.

[71] ICTY Report, *supra* note 8, §§ 33–34.

[72] Ammann, *supra* note 12, at 140.

[73] *Delalić*, *supra* note 44, § 163.

decision, the ICTY observed that "Article 4 of Geneva Convention IV, if interpreted in light of its object and purpose, is directed to the protection of civilians to the maximum extent possible".[74] This purpose—lofty as it sounds—meant that Article 4 could not be limited by narrow formal bonds such as nationality. *Tadić* was just the beginning of a series of functional readings. The teleological approach, first applied in *Tadić*, was later defended in *Delalić* and the *Hadžihasanović* decisions.[75] Similarly, when the SCSL was tasked with prosecuting defendants charged with the crime of conscription of child soldiers, a crime about which little was known at the time, the purposive approach proved far more useful. Being a hybrid court that shares more features with domestic criminal courts than international courts, the SCSL was not comfortable with determining strict liability for international crimes. This led to a natural proclivity for purposive readings. When determining liability for conscription of child soldiers, the Court extended liability to non-State actors by observing that IHL was "intended to apply to all parties in an internal armed conflict".[76] In the *AFRC* decision, the Trial Chamber went so far as to openly acknowledge that "IHL is not grounded in formalistic postulations".[77]

Challenges to Application

It is no revelation that the purposive tool is more difficult to apply than it is to describe. Many attempts have been to unpack the method and nature of the approach. The primary attack levelled against the application of the purposive approach has been that of judicial activism, that the law-making predilections of the tribunal militates against international law's grounding in State consent.[78] The bold statements furnished by tribunals in support of broad, purposive interpretations hardly ever justify the application

[74] *Tadić*, *supra* note 18, §§ 166, 168.

[75] Judgment, *Prosecutor v. Zejnil Delalic, Zdravko Mucic also known as Pavo, Hazim Delic and Esad Landžo also known as Zenga*, IT-96-21, Appeals Chamber, 20 February 2001, § 86; Judgment, *The Prosecutor v. Enver Hadžihasanović and Amir Kubura* (IT-01-47-T), Trial Chamber, 15 March 2006, § 171.

[76] AFRC, § 734.

[77] *Ibid.*

[78] A. M. Danner, "When Courts Make Law: How the International Criminal Tribunals Recast the Laws of War", 59 *Vanderbilt Law Review* (2006), at 1, 18.

of the interpretive approach and its suitability for the facts at case.[79] This lack of reasoning only clouds the case for clarity. Perhaps understandably then, purposive readings are accused of introducing excessive flexibility/indeterminacy into otherwise strictly circumscribed legal regimes.[80]

The second line of attack has been directed at the deontological basis of the tool.[81] In other words, what value is the approach trying to advance?[82] Is it righteousness or justice? Is it the intent of the drafters? Some scholars suggest that the object and purpose approach is an ode to "common sense and good faith".[83] The case law, instead, suggests that purposive readings uncover the *fundamental* values and philosophical orientations of the legal regime.[84] The *Furundžija* decision of the ICTY[85] and the *Ntaganda* decision of the ICC both illustrate that rule interpreters are mainly interested in advancing what is desirable for the law.[86]

The third continuing challenge has been to identify whose object and purpose are being interpreted. Is it the object and purpose of the field of IHL more generally? Or of the specific provision under study? Or of international criminal law? As the ICJ has noted, treaties typically have multiple objectives, not all of which sit well with the vision underlying specific provisions.[87] International criminal law is vowed to legality and fair labelling,[88] whereas IHL is committed to governing warfare and reducing damage to victims. This makes it all the more important for courts to clarify which purpose they are singling out.[89]

[79] Grover, *supra* note 6, at 550.

[80] See fn 1273 of Ammann, *supra* note 12.

[81] J. Klabbers, "Some Problems Regarding the Object and Purpose of Treaties", 8 *Finnish Yearbook of International Law* (1997), at 138.

[82] A. Ross, *On Law and Justice* (Lawbook Exchange, 2004), at 121ff.

[83] *Draft Articles on the Law of Treaties with Commentaries*, International Law Commission, (ILC Draft Articles), UN Doc. A/6309/Rev. 1 (1966), at Art. 27, at 221.

[84] A. Barak, *Purposive Interpretation* (Princeton, Princeton University Press, 2005) (hereafter Barak), at 5.

[85] V. Oosterveld, "Gender and the Charles Taylor Case at the Special Court for Sierra Leone", 19 *William and Mary Journal of Women and the Law* (2012), at 7, 25.

[86] C. Kenny and Y. McDermott, "The Expanding Protection of Members of a Party's Own Armed Forces under International Criminal Law", 68 *International Comparative Law Quarterly* (2019), at 943–976.

[87] Judgment and merits, *Case concerning Kasikili/Sedudu Island (Botswana v. Namibia)*, ICJ Reports 1999, 13 December 1999, at 1045, 1074, § 45.

[88] D. Robinson, "The Identity Crisis of International Criminal Law", 21 *Leiden Journal of International Law* (2008), at 925, 931.

[89] Ammann, *supra* note 12, at 550.

In *Tadić*, the Chamber's reasoning was anchored in the object and purpose of Article 4 of Geneva Convention IV, which was to extend "safeguards afforded by the Geneva Convention to those civilians who are not subject to the allegiance and control of the State in whose hands they may find themselves".[90] Citing this, the Appeals Chamber abandoned a nationality-based reading of protected persons. Differently though, in *Hadžihasanović*, when expanding the limits of command responsibility of military superiors, the Trial Chamber admitted that the object and purpose of Additional Protocol I—which was to affirm protections available to victims of armed conflict—were the same as that of IHL more broadly.[91] Here, the ICTY moved to identifying the object and purpose of IHL more generally. In *Ntaganda too* the ICC was required to determine whether members of DPH were victims of intra-party sexual crimes.[92] When extending IHL protections to such victims, the ICC was guided by the purpose of the regime to not let sexual crimes during conflict go unpunished.[93] It interpreted the purpose of the regime, rather than the purpose of specific provisions. The SCSL took a different route. In the *Norman* case, it noted that the purpose of customary law was to "represent the common standard of behaviour within the international community".[94] That is why non-state actors could not be exempted from customary IHL prohibitions on the conscription of child soldiers.

As Barak explains, the purpose of the law could be either subjective or objective.[95] A subjective purpose refers to the intention of the interpreters and authors—the judges, lawyers, academics.[96] Objective intent is a reference to the purpose of the system, the Statute. This tends to veer into a philosophical assessment of the objectives of IHL and criminal sanction more generally. The ICTY has confirmed its reading of intent as objective intent in *Delalić* when it noted that "the international community can

[90] *Tadić*, *supra* note 18, § 162.

[91] *Hadžihasanović* (Separate and Partially Dissenting Opinion of Judge Hunt Command Responsibility Appeal), Case No. IT-01-47-AR72, Appeals Chamber, § 22.

[92] Judgment, *Prosecutor v. Bosco Ntaganda* (ICC-01/04-02/06), Trial Chamber VI, 8 July 2019.

[93] *Ntaganda*, Second decision on the Defence's challenge to the jurisdiction of the Court in respect of Counts 6 and 9, ICC-01/04-02/06-1707, § 46.

[94] Decision on Preliminary Motion based on lack of Jurisdiction, *Prosecutor v. Sam Hingo Norman*, SCSL-2004-14-AR72, 31 May 2005.

[95] Barak, *supra* note 84, at 15.

[96] *Ibid.*

only come to grips with the hydra-headed elusiveness of human conduct through a reasonable as well as a purposive interpretation of existing provisions of international customary law".[97] The *Tadić* case, however, is an telling example of how the judges' own aspirations for the Court's legacy inevitably colour the application of the teleological approach. Compared to the avowed goals of the ICTY, Dusko Tadić was a small fish—as a prison guard. That his trial has now become the touchstone of IHL norms is mainly the doing of the Tribunal itself. As Alvarez has expertly reasoned, cases with lower stakes and lesser "political temperatures" allowed the bar and bench to test out the substantive purposive principles of IHL with more ease.[98] That different ICTY Chambers have arrived at different conclusions when attempting teleological readings of the same provision only augurs this accusation. As aforementioned, while the *Delalić* Chamber found that the purpose of IHL is to ensure that victims are protected to the maximum extent possible,[99] the Chamber in *Furundžija* found that IHL was designed for "protecting human dignity".[100] This only lends more weight to the concern that judges might be forwarding interpretations that are suited to their own predilections and their expectations of the international criminal justice project.

4.4 Effectiveness

Another interpretive approach that is prominently applied in tandem with purposive interpretation is the effectiveness approach. Linderfalk deconstructs the approach as one which zeroes in on readings that avoid situations where a part of the treaty is rendered normatively useless.[101] The rationale is to preserve the original consent/agreement of the treaty parties.[102] Effectiveness can be invoked to serve two purposes. The first is to

[97] *Delalić*, *supra* note 44, § 170.

[98] J. Alvarez, "Rush to Closure: Lessons of the Tadić Judgment", 96 *Michigan Law Review.* (1998), at 2031, 2093.

[99] *Delalić*, *supra* note 44, § 168.

[100] Judgment, *Prosecutor v. Anto Furundžija*, IT-95-17/1, Trial Chamber, 10 December 1998, § 184.

[101] U. Linderfalk, *On the Interpretation of Treaties. The Modern International Law as Expressed in the 1969 Vienna Convention on the Law of Treaties* (1st edn., Springer, 2007), at 579.

[102] H. Lauterpacht, "Restrictive Interpretation and the Principle of Effectiveness in the Interpretation of Treaties", 26 *British Yearbook of International Law* (1949), at 284.

prevent treaties from becoming futile. The second is to maximize the effect of the treaty.[103] Like the teleological approach, effectiveness has been critiqued for its constructivism and the overwhelming discretion that it vests in interpreting bodies.[104]

The *ad hoc* tribunals have often applied the effectiveness approach in questions relating to IHL. One area in which effective interpretation has been in vogue is the delimitation of jurisdiction over IHL violations. In the *Tadić* case, a key point of contention was whether violations of Common Article 3 of the Geneva Conventions fell within the jurisdiction of the tribunal.[105] The Appeals Chamber, in what is often touted to be an overly broad reading,[106] ruled that Article 3 of the Tribunal's Statute allowed the ICTY to exercise jurisdiction over all residual crimes, so as to "ensure that no serious violation of international humanitarian law is taken away from the jurisdiction of the International Tribunal".[107] The "overall control test" devised in *Tadić* is another classic instance of the ICTY simplifying triggers to its jurisdiction in order to avoid a circumstance where certain conflicts remain unregulated.[108] Jurisdiction was also hotly contested during the establishment of the SCSL. In a move to "right-size" the Tribunal, the Secretary-General proposed a narrow personal jurisdiction for the Court, limited to individuals who bore the "greatest responsibility".[109] Despite initial disagreement, the Court ultimately read its personal jurisdiction broadly to encompass both "killer-perpetrators and political military leaders".[110] Although this was not accompanied by a

[103] Ch. Schreuer, "Comments", in R. Hoffman and C. Tams (eds), *International Investment Law and General International Law: From Clinical Isolation to Systemic Integration* (1st edn., Baden Baden, Nomos, 2011), at 2.

[104] J. D. Fearon and A. Wendt, "Rationalism vs. Constructivism: A Skeptical View", in W. Carlsnaes, T. Risse and B. A. Simmons (eds). *Handbook of International Relations* (Sage, 2002), at 52–72.

[105] *Tadić*, *supra* note 18, §§ 73, 83.

[106] Alvarez, *supra* note 98, at 2093.

[107] *Tadić*, *supra* note 18, § 91.

[108] *Ibid*, § 131.

[109] *Report of the Secretary General on the establishment of a Special Court for Sierra Leone* (hereafter SCSL Agreement), UN Doc. S/2000/915, 4 Oct. 2000, § 29.

[110] Ch. Jalloh, "SCSL Symposium: The Continued Relevance of the Contributions of the Sierra Leone Tribunal to International Criminal Law", Opinio Juris, 15 March 2021, available online at http://opiniojuris.org/2021/03/15/scsl-symposium-the-continued-relevance-of-the-contributions-of-the-sierra-leone-tribunal-to-international-criminal-law/ (last visited on 5 September 2021).

declaratory invocation of effectiveness, the Court seems to have been motivated by the need to secure the relevance of IHL and the effectiveness of its constitutive statute.

Another area in which effectiveness has been influential is the classification of armed conflicts. Once the ICTY had made a name for itself, as higher-ranked leaders came to be tried, the Tribunal was more inclined to classify conflicts as international.[111] Scholars surmise that perhaps this was because international armed conflicts allowed the grave breaches regime to be applied.[112] Soon after, the Tribunal realized that the conflict in Yugoslavia was, in fact, only *vicariously* waged between States. The ground reality revealed a more amorphous, fragmented set of conflicts at play. This explains the growing recognition of parallel conflicts and the recurring classification of internal conflicts.[113] However, in the *Hadžihasanović* case, the ICTY strikingly found that NIACs to be a residual type of armed conflict.[114] Given that the Prosecutor had not recorded the international nature of the armed conflict as a material fact, it was considered, "by default", to be an internal conflict.[115] Such an interpretation has recurred in the ICC. The Trial Chamber of the ICC, in the *Lubanga* case, found that the threshold for international armed conflicts had not been met.[116] However, the Chamber did not apply the same rigour in testing whether the threshold for non-international armed conflicts had been met. In the Katanga confirmation decision, the Prosecution sought to characterize the conflict as an "internal conflict".[117] Even though the Prosecution had little to no evidence to offer to prove the level of organization of the forces warring with the forces allegedly controlled by the accused,[118] the Chamber sided with the Prosecution's labelling of the conflict.[119] Bartels rightly

[111] Judgment, *Prosecutor* v. *Ljube Boškoski and Johan Tarčulovski*, Case No. IT-04-82-T, Trial Chamber, 10 July 2008, para. 293; *Tadić*, *supra* note 18, § 81.

[112] R. Bartels, "The Classification of Armed Conflicts by International Criminal Courts and Tribunals", 20 (4) *International Criminal Law Review* (2020), at 595–668.

[113] *Tadić*, § 84; *Lubanga* (Decision on the confirmation of charges), Pre-Trial Chamber, § 209.

[114] Hadžihasanović, *Trial* Judgment, *supra* note 70, § 27.

[115] *Ibid.*

[116] *Lubanga*, Confirmation Decision, *supra* note 108, §§ 210–211.

[117] Defence Observations Pursuant to Regulation 55(3)(b) of the Regulations of the Court, *Prosecutor v. Germain Katanga and Mathieu Ngudjolo Chui*, Case No. ICC-01/04-01/07, 1 May 2012, § 2.

[118] Ibid, § 24.

[119] *Katanga*, Case No. ICC-01/04-01/07, Trial Chamber, 7 March 2014, §§ 1212–1215 and 1229.

observes that this was another occasion where the Court's conclusions were based not on the strength of the Prosecution case but on the lack thereof.[120] In her dissenting opinion, Judge Wyngaert.[121] found that the Chamber's position was motivated by the need to preserve the effectiveness of ICL in the proximate future than the culpability of the accused in the case.

Although the SCSL has been relatively freed of the burden of classifying armed conflicts, effectiveness has permeated its reasoning through different routes. The SCSL was repeatedly faced with defendants accused of the crime of conscription of child soldiers. At the time of the setting up of the Court, the conventional understanding of conscription was circumscribed to State policies "requiring citizens to serve in their armed forces".[122] However, in the Liberian/Sierra Leonese context, conscription was exclusively alleged against members of non-state armed groups. Judge Robertson, in the *Norman* decision, emphasized that the key element of conscription was compulsion.[123] So long as this objective criterion was met, the status of the perpetrator was no bar to charging the crime of conscription. With this in mind, the Trial Chamber in *AFRC* recognized that an orthodox interpretation of conscription would render its penalization futile. Instead, it found that the crime could be committed by members of non-state armed groups, a reading which was understood to preserve the effectiveness of the law of armed conflict.[124]

4.5 Subsequent Practice and Evolutionary Interpretation

From the early 1990s, there has been growing recognition that treaties are not static documents and should assume a more "living" function.[125,126] Courts then began to devise interpretive aids that would do service to the

[120] Bartels, *supra* note112, fn 57.

[121] Katanga, Minority Opinion of Judge Christine Van den Wyngaert, Katanga confirmation, fn 382.

[122] AFRC, § 734.

[123] Dissenting Opinion of Justice Robertson, *supra* note 94, §§ 1 and 5.

[124] AFRC, § 734.

[125] Quoting the *Tyrer v. United Kingdom*, ECtHR, App No 5856/72, A/26, [1978] 2.

[126] R. Higgins, "Some Observations on the Inter-Temporal Rule in International Law", in J. Makarczyk (ed.), *Theory of International Law at the Threshold of the 21st Century—Essays in Honour of Krysztof Skubilewski* (1997), at 181.

evolving nature of treaties. One way was to refer to the subsequent practice of treaty signatories to inform the interpretation of the treaty.[127] This method is recognized in Article 31(3) of the VCLT. The VCLT, however, prescribes strict conditions for the successful invocation of Article 31(3)(b), requiring such practice to be directed at the application of the treaty and that such practice be accepted by other signatories.[128] The alternative is to accord changing meanings to reflect the changing times.[129] This is otherwise known as the evolutionary approach. Compared to treaties where evolutionary readings demand interpretive exertion and justification, customary law is the home ground for evolutionary approach.[130] Here, it is important to clarify that evolutionary readings do not always lead to progressive results. Evolutionary interpretation has a more neutral quality to it.[131]

The evolutionary approach has found immense currency in the IHL jurisprudence of international criminal tribunals.[132] In fact, the International Military Tribunal was the first to encourage dynamic, evolving readings of IHL, given that is centrally dependent on contemporary military practice/abstentions.[133] The ICTY/ICRR jurisprudence on sexual crimes also leans towards the application of evolutionary interpretation. Although rape was expressly prohibited in the statutes of the ICTY

[127] G. Fitzmaurice, "The Law and Procedure of the International Court of Justice, 1951–4: Treaty Interpretation and Other Treaty Points", 33 *British Yearbook of International Law* (1957), at 203, 210.

[128] G. Nolte, *Second report on subsequent agreements and subsequent practice in relation to treaty interpretation*, UN doc A/CN.4/671, 26 March 2014, § 60.

[129] J. Arato, "Subsequent Practice and Evolutive Interpretation: Techniques of Treaty Interpretation over Time and Their Diverse Consequences", 9 *Law and Practice of International Courts and Tribunals* (2010), at 443.

[130] N. Arajärvi, *The Changing Nature of Customary International Law: Methods of Interpreting the Concept of Custom in International Criminal Tribunals* (London & New York: Routledge, 2014), at 25.

[131] *Hatton and Others v United Kingdom*, App no 36022/97 (ECtHR [GC], 8 July 2003), *Joint Dissenting Opinion of Judges Costa, Ress, Türmen, Zupancic and Steiner*, § 2.

[132] *Tadić*, *supra* note 18, § 18; Joint Separate Opinion of Judges McDonald and Vohrah, *The Prosecutor v. Dražen Erdemović*, ICTY-96-22-A, Appeals Chamber, 7 Oct. 1997, § 3.

[133] Judgment and Sentence, *Trial of German Major War Criminals (Goering et al.)*, International Military Tribunal (Nuremberg) Sept. 30 and Oct. 1, 1946 (Cmd. 6964, HMSO, London).

and ICTR,[134] there was no internationally available definition for the crime until the ICTR's *Akayesu* decision. Confronted by mounting evidence of rape against the Tutsi women, the ICTR examined various domestic and international definitions of the crime as well as the ways in which modes of committing sexual crimes had transformed over the years.[135] The Tribunal chose to reject an anatomical approach requiring penetration and endorsed a more gender-neutral, consent-based understanding that relies on the effect of the act on the victim.[136] In the *Musema* judgement that followed, the ICTR observed that such a definition was better equipped to "accommodate evolving norms of criminal justice" and was aligned with the contemporary trends in national practice.[137] This seems to clearly evoke the value and weight of the changing times. Similarly, in *Kunarac*, the ICTY referred to the evolving definition of slavery—mapping the gradual erosion of the notion of chattel slavery following the adoption of the 1926 Slavery Convention.[138]

The *ad hoc tribunals* also engineered a sea change in the status requirement of war crimes, from not recognizing the victimhood of combatants to finding that civilian status is not a condition for proof of victimhood.[139] This evolution was grounded largely in contemporaneous practice.[140] This trend has trickled down to the SCSL and ICC too, with the latter recently finding that sexual crimes committed by members of armed forces against

[134] Statute of the International Tribunal for the Prosecution of Persons Responsible for Serious Violations of International Humanitarian Law Committed in the Territory of the Former Yugoslavia since 1991 (adopted 25 May 1993 UN SC Resolution 827), at Art. 5(g) (hereafter ICTY Statute); Statute of the International Criminal Tribunal for the Prosecution of Persons Responsible for Genocide and Other Serious Violations of International Humanitarian Law Committed in the Territory of Rwanda and Rwandan Citizens Responsible for Genocide and Other Such Violations Committed in the Territory of Neighbouring States, between 1 February 1994 and 31 December (adopted 9 November 1994 by UN SC Resolution 955) (hereafter ICTR Statute), at Art. 3(g).

[135] Judgment, *The Prosecutor v. Jean-Paul Akayesu*, ICTR-96-4, Trial Chamber, 2 September 1998, §§ 416–417.

[136] *Ibid*, § 688.

[137] Judgment and Sentence, *Prosecutor v. Alfred Musema*, Case No. ICTR-96–13-T, Trial Chamber, 27 January 2000, § 228.

[138] Judgment, *Prosecutor v. Dragoljub Kunarac, Radomir Kovac, Zoran Vukovic*, IT-96-23 & 23/1, Trial Chamber, 22 February 2001, § 117.

[139] Judgment, *Prosecutor v Zdravko Tolimir*, IT-05-88/2-A, Appeals Chamber, 8 April 2015, § 142.

[140] Judgment, *Prosecutor v Vidoje Blagojević, Dragan Jokić*, IT-02-60-T, Trial Chamber, 17 January 2005, § 544; *Tadić*, *supra* note 18, § 638.

their own also qualify as war crimes.[141] The Court's reading was hailed by some scholars for its evolutionary victim-oriented approach.[142] At the SCSL, national practice (legislative and judicial) was key to Justice Doherty's finding in Taylor that forced marriages were recognized as prohibited under customary law.[143]

4.6 Normativity and Politics of Interpretation

As much as interpretation is an exercise to add more meaning to the law, it is deeply embedded in concerns about reception and legitimacy. Perhaps anticipating this, Fish aptly refers to interpretation as a "game".[144]

Unlike domestic criminal courts, which enjoy a high degree of latitude, international criminal tribunals are heavily dependent on political and financial support of States. The tribunals that this chapter studies neatly cover the full extent of the spectrum of such dependence. The *ad hoc* tribunals, for instance, were fairly independent. Having been set up by a one-stop resolution of the UN Security Council, the *ad hoc* tribunals enjoyed a fair share of delegated responsibilities without having to regularly consult the Security Council members.[145] This allowed the tribunals the liberty to innovate and renovate IHL, without fear of reprisal. Sadly, future tribunals did not enjoy identical liberties. One could argue that the higher fetters on such tribunals were informed by the lessons learnt from the design of the *ad hoc* tribunals. The SCSL, for instance, was created by an agreement between the UN and the government of Sierra Leone.[146] The Court thrives on the cooperation and goodwill between Member States of the UN and the government of Sierra Leone.[147] The Court's administrative and prosecutorial functions heavily rely on voluntary contributions by UN Member States. The Court has also been required to

[141] *Ntaganda*, *supra* note 93, § 62.

[142] S. Deuitch, "Putting the Spotlight on the Terminator: How the ICC Prosecution of Bosco Ntaganda Could Reduce Sexual Violence during Conflict", 22 *William & Mary Journal of Women & Law* (2016), at 655.

[143] AFRC, Justice Doherty dissenting, §§ 16-57.

[144] Fish, *supra* note 16, at 15.

[145] G. P. Lombardi "Legitimacy and the Expanding Power of the ICTY", 37 *New England Law Review* (2003), at 4, 889.

[146] SCSL Agreement, *supra* note 109, at 104.

[147] *Fifth Report of the Secretary-General on the United Nations Mission in Sierra Leone*, S/2000/751, 31 July 2000, § 9ff.

seek assistance from sister courts to find premises and detention facilities for its trials.[148] The ICC, as a treaty creature, is completely reliant on the support and compliance of State parties.[149] These modes of working play a crucial role in their choice of interpretive approaches and their proclivity towards interpretive conservatism.

Upon comparing the practices of the *ad hoc* tribunals, the ICC, and the SCSL, certain (inter-connected) patterns become visible. Firstly, it would not be incorrect to say that with greater external monetary dependence, the tendency to invoke the literal approach becomes higher. Perhaps this is because the personal and substantive jurisdictional scope is strictly circumscribed. More likely it is because such tribunals have much to lose if they overstay or overstep their mandate. This also explains why more dependent courts prefer abbreviated indictments[150] and invest more time in justifying why the literal approach is not appropriate.[151]

Secondly, and perhaps slightly contradictorily, the growing moral force of the prosecution of IHL violations has generated a higher willingness on the part of tribunals to move beyond the text. The ICC was rooted and operationalized in a climate seeped in the abhorrence surrounding IHL violations and the moral high ground of prosecution.[152] The normative weight of the Prosecution case itself seems to have justified the recourse to the effectiveness of teleological approaches. As discussed above, in *Katanga* and *Lubanga*, the Prosecution failed to convincingly establish that the threshold for an NIAC had been met. The Court, in both cases, made an NIAC classification possible presumably only because the

[148] S. Sanusi, "SCSL Practice on Cooperation with the Host State and Third States: A Contribution to Africa and International Criminal Justice", in C. Jalloh (ed.), *The Sierra Leone Special Court and its Legacy: The Impact for Africa and International Criminal Law* (New York, Cambridge University Press, 2013), 469–480.

[149] N. Roht-Arriaza, "Institutions of International Justice", 52 (2) *Journal of International Affairs* (1999), at 473, 474.

[150] C. Rose, "Troubled Indictments at the Special Court for Sierra Leone: The Pleading of Joint Criminal Enterprise and Sex-Based Crimes", 7 *Journal of International Criminal Justice* (2009), at 353–72.

[151] Concurring Opinion of Judge Van den Wyngaert, *The Prosecutor v. Mathieu Ngudjolo Chui*, Case No. ICC-01/04-02/12, 18 December 2012, § 20.

[152] B. A.Simmons and J. Hyeran, "Measuring Norms and Normative Contestation: The Case of International Criminal Law", *Faculty Scholarship at Penn Law* (2019), at 2055, available online at https://scholarship.law.upenn.edu/faculty_scholarship/2055 (last visited 5 September 2021).

Prosecution case was seen as morally stronger.[153] The sheer strength of the normative case against child soldiering or perpetrating brutal sexual crimes on bush wives compelled the SCSL to find interpretive tools to make adjustments to the IHL framework.

Thirdly, the interpretive practices are deeply tied to the degree of fragmentation in the state of the art. The *ad hoc* tribunals came into being at a time when IHL and IHRL were considered to be separate silos. Theodor Meron's famed 2000 article "The Humanization of Humanitarian Law" was among the first to invite attention to IHL's gradual transition from interstate obligation to individual rights, a change orchestrated by the growing presence of IHRL.[154] Echoing McCormack and Mathews,[155] Meron observed that humanitarian concerns have been traditionally downplayed in IHL.[156] The "fear of proliferation, the need or lack of need for specific weapons, and the difficulty of effective defense" have occupied more primary roles.[157] The resounding support for self-contained regimes for tribunals made it difficult for the *ad hoc* tribunals to resist fragmentation of IHL/IHRL.[158] But soon enough, the *ad hoc* tribunals occupied a central role in the move to re-interpret IHL treaties using the lens of humanization, batting to centre it around the value of human dignity.[159] The convergence engineered by the *ad hoc* tribunals did not escape backlash, with States and military troops fearing that excessive humanization would trigger more resistance to compliance with IHL norms.[160] By the time the SCSL came into operation, there was a growing consensus that the gulf between IHL, IHRL, and individual criminal responsibility had to be diminished. The IHL regime governing child soldiering began to move

[153] T. McCormack, "Challenges in Applying Article 8 of the Rome Statute", in S. Linton, G. Simpson and W. A. Schabas (eds), *For the Sake of Present and Future Generations: Essays on International Law, Crime and Justice in Honour of Roger S. Clark* (Leiden, Brill, 2015), at 353.

[154] T. Meron, "The Humanization of Humanitarian Law", 94 *American Journal of International Law*, (2000), at 239.

[155] R. J. Mathews, T. L. H. McCormack, "The Influence of Humanitarian Principles in the Negotiation of Arms Control Treaties", 834 *International Review of the Red Cross* (1999), at 331.

[156] Meron, *supra* note 154, at 240–241.

[157] *Ibid.*

[158] Interestingly, in *Tadić*, the Court observed that "every tribunal is a self-contained system (unless otherwise provided)", *Tadić*, *supra* note 18, § 458.

[159] *Furundžija*, *supra* note 100, § 183.

[160] Meron, *supra* note 154, at 241.

away from "reciprocal restraints on warfare" to norms hoisted on IHRL instruments.[161] This vested great liberty on newer tribunals to apply evolutionary and purposive readings.

Fourthly, the choice of interpretive approaches is motivated by the likelihood of compliance by other IHL stakeholders. Closing on the heels of the Nuremberg Tribunal, the *ad hoc* tribunals were imbued with a piercing sense of retribution and deterrence.[162] The rationale of starting with "small fish" like Dusko Tadić itself was to create a formidable precedent of individual criminal responsibility.[163] However, the *ad hoc* tribunals had little luck with ensuring compliance with their judgements. On a more interpretive level, this could be because the tribunals struggled to reconcile their roles as rule interpreters and the limitations (legal and pragmatic) of *ex post facto* judgements on conduct during armed conflicts. This struggle had lasting ramifications since the tribunals were in operation at a time when the conflict was in progress. In the *Gotovina* judgement, for instance, the Trial Chamber found that all the "impact sites located more than 200 metres from a target deemed legitimate served as evidence of an unlawful artillery attack". This finding—albeit constructed using expert evidence—was blind to the spontaneity of wartime decisions. Military commanders were quick to reject the Tribunal's mechanical 200-metre standard. *Gotovina* was written off as a blind spot in the Tribunal's jurisprudence.[164] After *Gotovina*, the tribunal came to appreciate the value of finding intersection points that are compatible with both IHL and ICL. Later jurisprudence emerging out of the Tribunals was more mindful of reception amongst and compliance by military leaders. The SCSL existed in a different climate—where the civil war had ended. Funded by external donors, the SCSL represented a moment of institution-building and signalling, in so far as it allowed the international community to stage an intervention to condemn child soldiering.[165] The SCSL was hesitant to make value

[161] N. B. Novogrodsky, "Litigating Child Recruitment before the Special Court for Sierra Leone", 7 *San Diego International Law Journal* (2006), at 421, 425.

[162] ICTY Report, *supra* note 8; ICTR Report, *supra* note 8; In *Delalić*, the Chamber considered deterrence to be the most important aim of punishment. *Delalić*, *supra* note 44, § 1234. Subsequently recalled by Trial Judgment, *The Prosecutor v. Tihomir Blaskić*,. IT-95-14-T, Trial Chamber, 3 March 2000, § 761.

[163] Swart, *supra* note 27, at 1001.

[164] J. N. Clark, "Courting Controversy: The ICTY's Acquittal of Croatian Generals Gotovina and Markač", 11(2) *Journal of International Criminal Justice* (2013), at 399–423.

[165] Novogrodsky, *supra* note 161, at 362–364.

judgements about wartime decisions. The Court's consistent jurisprudence excluding child defendants from prosecutions[166] and its recognition of child soldiering and forced marriages as punishable crimes has brought much-needed clarity to members of the armed forces.[167] The Court's decision to confine itself to a limited set of defendants has provided a useful "template" for other criminal tribunals to follow.[168]

4.7 Conclusion

This chapter is a brief attempt to reflect on and deconstruct the interpretive practices of international criminal tribunals in relation to IHL norms. Typically, inquiries into interpretive practices reveal much about the future behaviours of judicial bodies and help stakeholders make informed decisions about the efficacy of such institutions more generally.[169] In an IHL setting though, interpretative exercises are a direct understudy into norm reception by the soldiers and victims embroiled in wartime situations. As one of the chief interpreters of IHL norms in a regime that is marked by the lack thereof, international criminal tribunals have gradually begun to factor in the more expressive aspects of their jurisdiction into their application of interpretive tools. Albeit not exhaustive, this chapter shows how the ad hoc tribunals, the SCSL, and the ICC applied conventional interpretive tools to add meaning to norms governing newer crimes. More importantly, the chapter shows how increasing financial dependence, the moral force of Prosecution narratives, the state of the art of IHL/IHRL, and the likelihood of compliance impact which interpretive tool is invoked and how it is applied. It is hoped that this study offers useful lessons for the tribunals that are being conceived now and that it eventually encourages more public conversations about norm robustness in IHL among actors on the ground.

[166] *Special Court Prosecutor Says He Will Not Prosecute Children*, Press Release, Special Court for Sierra Leone (2 November 2002), available online at http://www.sc-sl.org/LinkClick.aspx?fileticket=XRwCUe%2baVhw%3d&tabid=196 (last visited 5 September 2021).

[167] Novogrodsky, *supra* note 161, at 368.

[168] *Ibid*, at 368.

[169] G. Schwarzenberger, *International Law as Applied By International Courts and Tribunals*, vol. 1 (3rd edn., Steven and Sons, 1957).

CHAPTER 5

Human Rights Rules and Principles in the Legal Regime of the International Criminal Court: Refining the Super-Legality Approach

Sergii Masol

5.1 Introduction

Article 21 of the Rome Statute of the International Criminal Court (ICC Statute) is titled 'Applicable law'. It has a threefold structure. Paragraph 1 establishes the strict hierarchy of the sources of law to be used by the International Criminal Court (ICC). Paragraph 2 stipulates that the ICC is not bound by its jurisprudence. Lastly, paragraph 3 obliges the ICC to comply with the human rights consistency test.

To be precise, Article 21(3) of the ICC Statute stipulates: 'The application and interpretation of law [...] must be consistent with internationally recognized human rights, and be without any adverse distinction founded

S. Masol (✉)
University of Cologne, Cologne, Germany
e-mail: sergii.masol@alumni.eui.eu

M. Faix, O. Svaček (eds.), *ICC Jurisprudence and the Development of International Humanitarian Law*, Global Issues,
https://doi.org/10.1007/978-3-031-45994-8_5

on grounds such as gender as defined in article 7, paragraph 3, age, race, colour, language, religion or belief, political or other opinion, national, ethnic or social origin, wealth, birth or other status'.[1] In addition, references to external human rights norms are possible via Article 21(1)(b) ('where appropriate, applicable treaties and the principles and rules of international law')[2] or Article 21(1)(c) ('general principles of law derived [...] from national laws of legal systems of the world including, as appropriate, the national laws of States that would normally exercise jurisdiction over the crime, provided that those principles are not inconsistent with [...] [the ICC] Statute and with international law and internationally recognized norms and standards'). These sources of law stand hierarchically lower than the ICC statutory framework ('[i]n the second place' and '[f]ailing that' respectively), but international human rights law as a part of international law is broader and more adjustable to the ICC context than the concept of internationally recognised human rights.[3] Article 21(1)(b) and Article 21(1)(c) are not scrutinised in the present chapter because internationally recognised human rights in treaty law, customary international law or general principles of law are already used in examining

[1] Rome Statute of the International Criminal Court (adopted 17 July 1998, entered into force 1 July 2002), 2187 UNTS 90 (hereafter ICC Statute), at Art. 21(3). See also ibid, at Art. 7(3) ('[T]he term "gender" refers to the two sexes, male and female, within the context of society. The term "gender" does not indicate any meaning different from the above').

[2] It is widely acknowledged that this provision indirectly refers to customary international law. See, for example, Judgment pursuant to Article 74 of the Statute, *Prosecutor v Jean-Pierre Bemba Gombo* (ICC-01/05-01/08-3343), Trial Chamber III, 21 March 2016, § 71; N. Clarenc Bicudo, 'Article 21. Droit applicable', in J. Fernandez, X. Pacreau and M. Ubeda-Saillard (eds), *Statut de Rome de la Cour pénale internationale: Commentaire article par article*, Vol. I (2nd edn., Paris: Pedone, 2019) 957–976, at 964–965; M. deGuzman, 'Article 21. Applicable Law', in K. Ambos (ed.), *Rome Statute of the International Criminal Court: Article-by-Article Commentary* (4th edn., Munich/Oxford/Baden-Baden: C.H. Beck/Hart/Nomos, 2022) 1129–1148, at 1138–1141; A. Pellet, 'Applicable Law', in A. Cassese, P. Gaeta and J. Jones (eds), *The Rome Statute of the International Criminal Court: A Commentary*, Vol. II (Oxford: Oxford University Press, 2002) 1051–1084, at 1072; W. Schabas, *The International Criminal Court: A Commentary on the Rome Statute* (2nd edn., Oxford: Oxford University Press, 2016), at 521–523. See *contra* G. Fletcher and J. Ohlin, 'Reclaiming Fundamental Principles of Criminal Law in the Darfur Case', 3 *Journal of International Criminal Justice* (2005) 539–561, at 559.

[3] G. Edwards, 'International Human Rights Law Challenges to the New International Criminal Court: The Search and Seizure Right to Privacy', 26 *Yale Journal of International Law* (2001) 323–412, at 387; C. Paulussen, Male captus bene detentus? *Surrending Suspects to the International Criminal Court* (Antwerp/Oxford/Portland: Intersentia, 2010), at 796, 801, 826.

the statutory framework under Article 21(1)(a) as a part of the human rights consistency test under Article 21(3).[4] Although human rights norms are undoubtedly applicable before the ICC, the place of this test in the edifice of applicable law remains unclear.

On the one hand, it has been contended that Article 21(3) of the ICC Statute contains a super-legality norm.[5] What does it mean? Internationally recognised human rights are superior to any other legal norms outlined in Article 21(1), including those of the ICC Statute itself.[6] This structure, accurately called 'a multiplicity of hierarchies',[7] is derived from the duty of the ICC not only to interpret but also to apply the law consistently with internationally recognised human rights.[8] On the other hand, some legal

[4] Paulussen, *supra* note 3, at 825. Cf. J. Gebhard, *Necessity or Nuisance? Recourse to Human Rights in Substantive International Criminal Law* (Baden-Baden: Nomos, 2018), at 81 (arguing that Article 21(1)(b) 'is the more appropriate source of law', because Article 21(3) guarantees only procedural human rights).

[5] Pellet, *supra* note 2, at 1077–1082.

[6] Ibid; P. Currat, 'L'interprétation du Statut de Rome', 20 *Revue québécoise de droit international* (2007) 137–163, at 155; Gebhard, *supra* note 4, at 40; G. Werle and F. Jeßberger, *Principles of International Criminal Law* (4th edn., Oxford: Oxford University Press, 2020), at 92; Paulussen, *supra* note 3, at 824; K. Zeegers, *International Criminal Tribunals and Human Rights Law: Adherence and Contextualization* (The Hague: T.M.C. Asser Press, 2016), at 73; A. Zahar and G. Sluiter, *International Criminal Law: A Critical Introduction* (Oxford: Oxford University Press, 2008), at 280; Corrigendum to the Brief in support of the "Notice of appeal by Witnesses DRC-D02-P-0236, DRC-D02- P-0228 and DRC-D02-P0350 against the *Décision relative à la demande de mise en liberté des témoins détenus* DRC-D02-P-0236, DRC-D02-P-0228 *et* DRC-D02-P-0350 issued by Trial Chamber II on 1 October 2013 (ICC-01/04-01/07-3405)" (ICC-01/04-01/07-3408), *Prosecutor v Germain Katanga* (ICC-01/04-01/07-3411-Corr-tENG), Duty Counsel, 9 October 2013, § 15. See also M. Arsanjani, 'The Rome Statute of the International Criminal Court', 93 *American Journal of International Law* (1999) 22–43, at 28–29.

[7] G. Bitti, 'Article 21 of the Statute of the International Criminal Court and the treatment of sources of law in the jurisprudence of the ICC', in C. Stahn and G. Sluiter (eds), *The Emerging Practice of the International Criminal Court* (Leiden/Boston: Martinus Nijhoff, 2009) 285–304, at 287.

[8] Ibid, at 303; Pellet, *supra* note 2, at 1080; L. Grover, *Interpreting Crimes in the Rome Statute of the International Criminal Court* (Cambridge: Cambridge University Press, 2014), at 263; V. Nerlich, 'Article 21(3) of the ICC Statute: Identifying and Applying "Internationally Recognized Human Rights"', in P. Lobba and T. Mariniello (eds), *Judicial Dialogue on Human Rights: The Practice of International Criminal Tribunals* (Leiden/ Boston: Brill Nijhoff, 2017) 73–89, at 75.

academics have firmly opposed such a far-reaching construction of Article 21(3) of the ICC Statute.[9]

Therefore, the main question is whether the human rights consistency test under Article 21(3) of the ICC Statute can be treated as a trump card to neutralise all other legal arguments. If so, what are the contours of this super-legality norm? Robert Alexy's *Theorie der Grundrechte* is a useful theoretical framework that can help to fine-tune the place of human rights rules and principles in the ICC legal regime by softening the sharp angles of opposing scholarly opinions and seemingly inconsistent judicial decisions.

At the outset, the present chapter provides a background distinction between rules and principles in the light of Robert Alexy's *Theorie der Grundrechte*, in addition to examining the applicability of this theory to international law. After that, the discussion proceeds with an analysis of the relevant case law of the ICC, contributing to the scholarly debate on the super-legality approach to Article 21(3) of the ICC Statute. In this respect, the present chapter uses the methods of treaty interpretation and the above-mentioned *Theorie der Grundrechte*.

5.2 Robert Alexy's *Theorie der Grundrechte*

Rules and Principles

For Robert Alexy, who built his *Theorie der Grundrechte* on Ronald Dworkin's model, '[e]very norm is either a rule or a principle'.[10] The former shall be applied in an all-or-nothing fashion after the determination of the scope of its application, whereas the latter shall be applied in a more-or-less fashion.[11] Principles are optimisation requirements and the weight of reasons behind them differs from case to case depending on what is to the greatest extent factually and legally possible in the light of any opposing principles and rules.[12] This explains the gist of their interpretation. To interpret principles means to assess their weight in regard to others, while

[9] See e.g. G. Hafner and C. Binder, 'The Interpretation of Article 21(3) ICC Statute: Opinion Reviewed', 9 *Austrian Review of International and European Law* (2004) 163–190.

[10] R. Alexy, *Theorie der Grundrechte* (Baden-Baden: Nomos, 1994), at 77.

[11] Ibid, at 75–77.

[12] Ibid.

to interpret rules means to determine the ambit of their application.[13] Thus, any collision between competing principles is resolved by the act of balancing; any seeming collision between rules and principles is non-existent (and a more careful examination of their content is needed); and any collision between rules is resolved by either regarding one of them as an exception to another or declaring one of them invalid, in particular, by means of the maxims *lex posterior derogat legi priori* or *lex specialis derogat legi generali*.[14] Clashes between rules cannot occur in theory, but they may surface in legal practice.[15] In the ICC legal regime, a conflict may transpire in the exercise of discretionary powers by the ICC, but less likely as a direct discrepancy between statutory norms and human rights norms.[16]

The sharpest criticism at Robert Alexy's *Theorie der Grundrechte* has been levelled by Jürgen Habermas, who thinks that the irrational weighing of human rights principles is necessarily goal-oriented and may result in their sacrifice to collective ends.[17] In response, Robert Alexy has given evidence of a weight formula proving that rational balancing is possible.[18]

Applicability to International Law

In his work, *Theorie der Grundrechte*, Robert Alexy rationally reconstructed constitutional rights reasoning in Germany. However, his theory is not confined to the norms of German constitutional law. On the contrary, it is applicable 'to all jurisdictions where judges wrestle with rights adjudication', as emphasised in the description of the book's English-language edition.[19] Such generality is enabled by the substantive openness

[13] M. Scheinin, 'Core Rights and Obligations', in D. Shelton (ed.), *The Oxford Handbook of International Human Rights Law* (Oxford: Oxford University Press, 2013) 527–540, at 535.

[14] Alexy, *supra* note 10, at 77–79.

[15] M. Scheinin, 'Terrorism and the Pull of "Balancing" in the Name of Security', in M. Scheinin et al., *Law and Security—Facing the Dilemmas* (San Domenico di Fiesole: EUI Working Paper, Law, 2009) 55–63, at 55.

[16] Zahar and Sluiter, *supra* note 6, at 280.

[17] J. Habermas, *Faktizität und Geltung: Beitrage zur Diskurstheorie des Rechts und des demokratischen Rechtsstaats* (Frankfurt am Main: Suhrkamp Verlag, 1998), at 309 et seq.

[18] R. Alexy, *A Theory of Constitutional Rights* (Oxford: Oxford University Press, 2002), at 388 et seq. Nevertheless, this formula does not exclude irrationality altogether. Scheinin, *supra* note 15, at 57.

[19] See Description (R. Alexy, J. Rivers, A Theory of Constitutional Rights), available online at https://global.oup.com/academic/product/a-theory-of-constitutional-rights-9780199584239?cc=de&lang=en&# (visited 27 January 2023).

and formal abstraction of the theoretical underpinnings.[20] Moreover, the original title of Robert Alexy's *magnum opus* suggests something broader than *Verfassungsrecht*, even though Julian Rivers translated this book into English as *A Theory of Constitutional Rights*. Thus, the theory in question can be applicable to the norms of international law.[21]

International criminal law usually contains rules, as these norms need to be precise and predictable. For example, international crimes are expressed as prohibition of certain kinds of behaviour. At the same time, there are instances where the definitions of international crimes refer to human rights law. For instance, the ICC Statute proscribes the war crime of '[w]ilfully depriving a prisoner of war or other protected person of the rights of fair and regular trial'.[22] Such references are also possible via Article 21(3) of the ICC Statute. In *Lubanga*, Judge Elizabeth Odio Benito thus clarified the statutory prohibition of war crimes of conscription, enlistment and use of child soldiers in the light of human rights law, particularly the Convention on the Rights of the Child.[23]

[20] J. Rivers, 'A Theory of Constitutional Rights and the British Constitution', in Alexy, *supra* note 18, xvii-li, at xviii.

[21] T. Kleinlein, *Konstitutionalisierung im Völkerrecht: Konstruktion und Elemente einer idealistischen Völkerrechtslehre* (Heidelberg: Springer, 2012), at 663–669.

[22] ICC Statute, *supra* note 1, at Art. 8(2)(a)(vi).

[23] Judgment pursuant to Article 74 of the Statute, *Prosecutor v Thomas Lubanga Dyilo* (ICC-01/04-01/06-2842), Trial Chamber I, 14 March 2012, Separate and Dissenting Opinion of Judge Odio Benito, § 6.

In turn, the majority of human rights—often being broadly defined[24] and innately linked to morality[25]—express primarily principles.[26] For example, the limitation clause of the right to freedom to manifest one's religion or beliefs provides for the balancing test under the International Covenant on Civil and Political Rights: this freedom 'may be subject only to such limitations as are prescribed by law and are necessary to protect public safety, order, health, or morals or the fundamental rights and freedoms of others'.[27] However, there are certain rights which are non-derogable in a state of emergency, absolute and without limitation clauses. They express rules that leave no room for balancing. One of the notable examples is the prohibition of torture and inhuman or degrading treatment or punishment.[28]

[24] S. Egan, 'The Doctrinal Approach in International Human Rights Law Scholarship', in L. McConnell and R. Smith (eds), *Research Methods in Human Rights* (London/New York: Routledge, 2018) 24–41, at 35 ('usually very general'); J. Smits, *The Mind and the Method of the Legal Academic* (Cheltenham/Northampton: Edward Elgar, 2012), at 72 (claiming that 'undisputed [fundamental] rights do not exist and, in so far as they are generally recognized, they are so indeterminate that they offer only little guidance in deciding a dispute'). See also A. Danner and J. Martinez, 'Guilty Associations: Joint Criminal Enterprise, Command Responsibility and the Development of International Criminal Law', 93 *California Law Review* (2005) 75–169, at 89–90 (noting that some, albeit not all, norms of international human right law are contingent and aspirational).

[25] E. Klein, 'Zum (völker-)rechtlichen Unter- und Hintergrund von Menschenrechtsverträgen: Gibt es ein menschenrechtliches corpus iuris?', 55 *Archiv des Völkerrechts* (2017) 303–323, at 303–307; M.D.A. Freeman, *Lloyd's Introduction to Jurisprudence* (9th edn., London: Sweet & Maxwell, 2014), at 1287. Cf. C. Tomuschat, *Human Rights: Between Idealism and Realism* (3rd edn., Oxford: Oxford University Press, 2014), at 9 (differentiating moral values from human rights based on such values).

[26] Scheinin, *supra* note 15, at 56. For a similar view, see L. Gradoni, 'The Human Rights Dimension of International Criminal Procedure', in G. Sluiter et al. (eds), *International Criminal Procedure: Principles and Rules* (Oxford: Oxford University Press, 2013) 74–95, at 86.

[27] International Covenant on Civil and Political Rights (adopted 16 December 1966, entered into force 23 March 1976), 999 UNTS 171, at Art. 18(3).

[28] M. Scheinin, 'Characteristics of Human Rights Norms', in C. Krause and M. Scheinin (eds), *International Protection of Human Rights: A Textbook* (2nd edn., Turku/Åbo: Åbo Akademi University, 2012) 19–37, at 32. See *contra* S. Greer, 'Is the Prohibition against Torture, Cruel, Inhuman and Degrading Treatment Really 'Absolute' in International Human Rights Law?', 15 *Human Rights Law Review* (2015) 101–137, at 134–137.

5.3 The Priority of Human Rights Norms in the Case Law

The distinction between processes of interpretation and application is embedded in the ICC legal framework. As already mentioned, the ICC has a duty not only to interpret but also to apply the law consistently with internationally recognised human rights. The latter obligation presupposes that human rights law can set aside any applicable law listed under Article 21(1) of the ICC Statute.[29] Thus, internationally recognised human rights become an additional source of law in the ICC legal regime.[30] Has the ICC harnessed Article 21(3) for the purposes of both interpretation and application?

Interpretation

In one set of decisions, the ICC used 'the general principle of interpretation set out in article 21 (3)'—together with the customary rules of interpretation set forth in the Vienna Convention on the Law of Treaties—in order to confirm that the statutory framework of the disclosure process

[29] Pellet, *supra* note 2, at 1080; Gradoni, *supra* note 26, at 83; Zeegers, *supra* note 6, at 83–84. Cf. Nerlich, *supra* note 8, at 88–89 (reserving this function only for internationally recognised human rights which are *jus cogens*). See *contra* J. Powderly, 'The Rome Statute and the Attempted Corseting of the Interpretative Judicial Function: Reflections on Sources of Law and Interpretative Technique', in C. Stahn (ed.), *The Law and Practice of the International Criminal Court* (Oxford: Oxford University Press, 2015) 444–498, at 486 (arguing that 'Article 21(3) does not override the [ICC] Statute as such, but rather comes into effect when more than one interpretation [...] is possible, dictating that the interpretation that best conforms with human rights must be adopted').

[30] Bitti, *supra* note 7, at 303; S. Bailey, 'Article 21(3) of the Rome Statute: A Plea for Clarity', 14 *International Criminal Law Review* (2014) 513–550, at 535–536; Paulussen, *supra* note 3, at 821–822. See *contra* Schabas, *supra* note 2, at 515; R. Young, '"Internationally Recognized Human Rights" before the International Criminal Court', 60 *International and Comparative Law Quarterly* (2011) 189–208, at 193; P. Saland, 'International Criminal Law Principles', in R. Lee (ed.), *The International Criminal Court: The Making of the Rome Statute: Issues, Negotiations, Results* (The Hague/London/Boston: Kluwer Law International, 2002) 189–216, at 214.

did not deviate from internationally recognised human rights.[31] This way of reasoning does not militate against the super-legality approach (which includes interpretation) and the ICC could—and perhaps should—have stopped there. What has caused trouble however, is its further emphasis on 'the need to safeguard the uniqueness of the [ICC] criminal procedure [as] [...] one of the primary considerations in contextual interpretation of the [ICC Statute]'.[32] The second argument is not only *de trop* but also neglects the explicit requirements of Article 21(3). Indeed, their 'mandatory and specific content [...] appears to prevent Judges from adjusting the content of human rights law to the unique ICC-context'.[33]

In *Lubanga*, Pre-Trial Chamber I preferred the practice of witness familiarisation to the one of witness proofing due to the latter's non-existence under any source of applicable law listed in Article 21(1), which in itself barred any resort to internationally recognised human rights.[34] Rebecca Young has rightly criticised this approach for overlooking that a determination of the (non-)existence of applicable law 'is itself a process of interpretation of the law, which [...] must be informed by article 21(3)'.[35]

[31] Annex I to the Decision on the Final System of Disclosure and the Establishment of a Timetable, *Prosecutor v Thomas Lubanga Dyilo* (ICC-01/04-01/06-102), Pre-Trial Chamber I, 15 May 2006, § 2; Decision Establishing General Principles Governing Applications to Restrict Disclosure pursuant to Rule 81(2) and (4) of the Rules of Procedure and Evidence, *Prosecutor v Thomas Lubanga Dyilo* (ICC-01/04-01/06-108-Corr), Pre-Trial Chamber I, 19 May 2006, § 7. See also, among many others, Decision on the Joinder of the Cases against Germain Katanga and Mathieu Ngudjolo Chui, *Prosecutor v Germain Katanga* (ICC-01/04-01/07-257), Pre-Trial Chamber I, 10 March 2008, at 7; Decision on the powers of the Pre-Trial Chamber to review *proprio motu* the pretrial detention of Germain Katanga, *Prosecutor v Germain Katanga and Mathieu Ngudjolo Chui* (ICC-01/04-01/07-330), Pre-Trial Chamber I, 18 March 2008, at 10–12; Decision on the Set of Procedural Rights Attached to Procedural Status of Victims at the Pre-Trial Stage of the Case, *Prosecutor v Germain Katanga and Mathieu Ngudjolo Chui* (ICC-01/04-01/07-474), Pre-Trial Chamber I, 13 May 2008, §§ 57, 78; Decision on the Prosecution's Application for a Warrant of Arrest against Omar Hassan Ahmad Al Bashir, *Prosecutor v Omar Hassan Ahmad Al Bashir* (ICC-02/05-01/09-3), Pre-Trial Chamber I, 4 March 2009, §§ 44, 126.

[32] Annex I to the Decision, *supra* note 31, § 4.

[33] G. Sluiter, 'Human Rights Protection in the ICC Pre-Trial Phase', in Stahn and Sluiter, *supra* note 7, 459–475, at 463 (admitting, however, that an overly 'rigid stance on this matter should be rejected').

[34] Decision on the Practices of Witness Familiarisation and Witness Proofing, *Prosecutor v Thomas Lubanga Dyilo* (ICC-01/04-01/06-679), Pre-Trial Chamber I, 8 November 2006, §§ 10–42.

[35] Young, *supra* note 30, at 201.

Application

In *Lubanga*, the ICC famously held: 'Human rights underpin the [ICC] Statute; every aspect of it [...]. Its provisions must be interpreted and more importantly applied in accordance with internationally recognized human rights'.[36] As a result, it grounded the power to grant a stay of proceedings on neither a source under Article 21(1), nor the doctrine of inherent/implied powers,[37] but rather on Article 21(3). In *Gbagbo*, this was expressed in pellucid terms: '[T]he correct legal basis for dealing with [...] requests [for a stay of proceedings] was article 21(3)'.[38] Crucially, Article 21(3) does not distinguish between human rights in substantive and procedural law; nor should it.[39] Although the provision in question does not preclude the ICC from incorporating new substantive doctrines or norms into its legal framework,[40] the norm-generating function has

[36] Judgment on the Appeal of Mr. Thomas Lubanga Dyilo against the Decision on the Defence Challenge to the Jurisdiction of the Court pursuant to Article 19(2)(a) of the Statute of 3 October 2006, *Prosecutor v Thomas Lubanga Dyilo* (ICC-01/04-01/06-772), Appeals Chamber, 14 December 2006, § 37. See also, among many others, Judgment in the Appeal by Mathieu Ngudjolo Chui of 27 March 2008 against the Decision of Pre-Trial Chamber I on the Application of the Appellant for Interim Release, *Prosecutor v Germain Katanga and Mathieu Ngudjolo Chui* (ICC-01/04-01/07-572), Appeals Chamber, 9 June 2008, § 15; Decision on the fitness of Laurent Gbagbo to take part in the proceedings before this Court, *Prosecutor v Laurent Gbagbo* (ICC-02/11-01/11-286-Red), Pre-Trial Chamber I, 2 November 2012, § 45.

[37] O. Svaček, 'Applicable Law, Interpretation, Inherent and Implied Powers—A Brief Rendezvous with the ICC', 7 *Czech Yearbook of Public and Private International Law* (2016) 342–354, at 351–352 (noting that the ICC could have reached the same conclusion with the help of this doctrine, but preferred Article 21(3) as a much stronger legal ground).

[38] Judgment on the appeal of Mr. Laurent Koudou Gbagbo against the decision of Pre-Trial Chamber I on jurisdiction and stay of the proceedings, *Prosecutor v Laurent Gbagbo* (ICC-02/11-01/11-321), Appeals Chamber, 12 December 2012, § 100. See also Decision on the Applications for Participation in the Proceedings of VPRS 1, VPRS 2, VPRS 3, VPRS 4, VPRS 5 and VPRS 6, *Situation in the Democratic Republic of the Congo* (ICC-01/04-101-tENG-Corr), Pre-Trial Chamber I, 17 January 2006, § 81; Decision on the Prosecution's Application, *supra* note 31, § 44 (considering Article 21(3) as a gap-filling tool for a *lacuna* in the ICC Statute, the Rules of Procedure and Evidence and Elements of Crimes).

[39] K. Gallant, 'International Human Rights Standards in International Organizations: The Case of International Criminal Courts', 19 *Nouvelles études pénales* (2004) 397–404, at 402.

[40] Bedont, B. 'Gender-Specific Provisions in the Statute of the International Criminal Court', in F. Lattanzi and W. Schabas (eds), *Essays on the Rome Statute of the International Criminal Court*, Vol. I (Ripa Fagnano Alto: il Sirente, 1999) 183–210, at 185. See *contra* N. Wagner, 'A Critical Assessment of Using Children to Participate Actively in Hostilities in *Lubanga*: Child Soldiers and Direct Participation', 24 *Criminal Law Forum* (2013) 145–203, at 191–193.

usually been limited to procedural matters.[41] This fact can be explained not only by the relative precision of the statutory definitions of international crimes but also by the types of challenges faced by the ICC at the early stages of its existence.[42] Yet some of the vexed problems relating to substantive law, such as the prohibition of war crimes of conscription, enlistment and use of child soldiers, are emerging.[43] What comes into play here is the *nullum crimen sine lege* principle, which itself is an internationally recognised human right.[44] Hence, the super-legality approach remains intact.

The *Lubanga* Appeals Chamber recalled 'the hierarchy of applicable law [...] provided for in article 21',[45] thereby tacitly demonstrating that

[41] O. Svaček, 'The International Criminal Court and Human Rights: Achievements and Challenges', in D. Moura Vicente (ed.), *Towards a Universal Justice? Putting International Courts and Jurisdictions into Perspective* (Leiden/Boston: Brill Nijhoff, 2016) 206–221, at 207, 214; A. Jones, 'Insights into an Emerging Relationship: Use of Human Rights Jurisprudence at the International Criminal Court', 16 *Human Rights Law Review* (2016) 701–729, at 721; B. Krzan, 'Human Rights and International Criminal Law', in B. Krzan (ed.), *Prosecuting International Crimes: A Multidisciplinary Approach* (Leiden/Boston: Brill Nijhoff, 2016) 153–175, at 172–173; Gebhard, *supra* note 4, at 63–64, 81, 246.

[42] D. Scalia, 'Human Rights in the Context of International Criminal Law: Respecting them and Ensuring Respect for Them', in R. Kolb and G. Gaggioli (eds), *Research Handbook on Human Rights and Humanitarian Law* (Cheltenham/Northampton: Edward Elgar Publishing, 2013) 575–589, at 582, 585.

[43] For a discussion, see S. Masol, 'War Crimes of Conscription, Enlistment and Use of Child Soldiers: Expendable Human Rights Rhetoric of the International Criminal Court', 3 *Journal of International Law of Peace and Armed Conflict—Humanitäres Völkerrecht* (2020) 193–208.

[44] M. Boot, *Genocide, Crimes against Humanity, War Crimes: Nullum Crimen Sine Lege and the Subject Matter Jurisdiction of the International Criminal Court* (Antwerp/Oxford/New York: Intersentia, 2002), at 366–368; K. Gallant, *The Principle of Legality in International and Comparative Law* (Cambridge: Cambridge University Press, 2009), at 3, 331 et seq.; S. Garibian, *Le crime contre l'humanité au regard des principes fondateurs de l'Etat moderne: naissance et consécration d'un concept* (Brussels: Bruylant; Geneva/Zurich/Basel: Schulthess, 2009), at 400. See also Universal Declaration of Human Rights, GA Res. 217A (III), UN Doc. A/810, 10 December 1948, at Art. 11 (2); International Covenant on Civil and Political Rights, *supra* note 27, at Art. 15.

[45] Judgment on the appeals against the "Decision establishing the principles and procedures to be applied to reparations" of 7 August 2012, *Prosecutor v Thomas Lubanga Dyilo* (ICC-01/04-01/06-3129), Appeals Chamber, 3 March 2015, § 154. See also Judgment pursuant to article 74 of the Statute, *Prosecutor v Germain Katanga* (ICC-01/04-01/07-3436-tENG), Trial Chamber II, 7 March 2014, § 39. See *contra* Garibian, *supra* note 44, at 393 (claiming that Article 21 establishes an express order of consideration rather than a hierarchy of sources).

the hierarchy concerns the whole of Article 21, that is, including paragraph 3. The only possible consequence is that the applicable law having its own hierarchy under Article 21(1) is also subordinated to internationally recognised human rights. Yet in another decision, Trial Chamber I noted that 'Article 21 [...] requires the Chamber to apply first the [ICC] Statute, Elements of Crimes and Rules of the ICC'.[46] Here, no human rights issues were at stake, which can explain the ICC's non-use of Article 21(3).

Does the reasoning of the Appeals Chamber trump that of Trial Chamber I? The answer is no. Article 21(2) denies the *stare decisis* doctrine even when it comes to the rulings of the Appeals Chamber.[47] In any event, inconsistencies in jurisprudence should be avoided lest they cause confusion and uncertainty, which in turn have repercussions on the effectiveness, fairness and legitimacy of the law.[48]

Perhaps the best example of this bewilderment is the asylum saga in *Katanga and Ngudjolo.* In 2011, Trial Chamber II delayed the return of three detained witnesses to the Democratic Republic of the Congo, enabling them to exercise their right to apply for asylum and their right to an effective remedy in the Netherlands: '[T]he Chamber is unable to apply article 93(7) of the [ICC] Statute in conditions which are consistent with internationally recognised human rights, as required by article 21(3)'.[49] In

[46] Decision Regarding the Practices Used to Prepare and Familiarise Witnesses for Giving Testimony at Trial, *Prosecutor v Thomas Lubanga Dyilo* (ICC-01/04-01/06-1049), Trial Chamber I, 30 November 2007, § 44.

[47] See e.g. Judgment pursuant to Article 74 of the Statute, *supra* note 2, § 74; Werle and Jeßberger, *supra* note 6, at 91–92. See *contra* А. Кузнецов, 'Международное уголовное право: понятие, признаки, система', 7(2) *Журнал прикладных исследований* (2022) 196–203, at 201.

[48] Jones, *supra* note 41, at 729; Y. McDermott, *Fairness in International Criminal Trials* (Oxford: Oxford University Press, 2016), at 31. Cf. M. Shahabuddeen, 'Consistency in the Case Law of the ICTY', in G. Venturini and S. Bariatti (eds), *Individual Rights and International Justice: Liber Fausto Pocar* (Milan: Giuffrè, 2009) 899–911, at 900–902 (claiming that inconsistencies should be avoided, but sometimes certain variety may be useful to making an informed choice).

[49] Decision on an Amicus Curiae application and on the *"Requête tendant à obtenir presentations des témoins DRC-D02-P-0350, DRC-D02-P-0236, DRC-D02-P-0228 aux autorités néerlandaises aux fins dásile"* (articles 68 and 93(7) of the Statute), *Prosecutor v Germain Katanga and Mathieu Ngudjolo Chui* (ICC-01/04-01/07-3003-tENG), Trial Chamber II, 9 June 2011, § 73. See also Redacted Decision on the request by DRC-DOI-WWWW-0019 for special protective measures relating to his asylum application, *Prosecutor v Thomas Lubanga Dyilo* (ICC-01/04-01/06-2766-Red), Trial Chamber I, 5 August 2011, §§ 72–88.

other words, it adopted the super-legality approach, according to which any applicable law may be declared inapplicable in a certain case.[50] Importantly, the human rights consistency test does not make the applicable law—*in casu* Article 93(7)—void; such a consequence stems only from a violation of *jus cogens*.[51] This notwithstanding, in 2013, when the witnesses were still incarcerated in the ICC Detention Unit and their asylum applications remained pending, Trial Chamber II not only turned its previous understanding of Article 21(3) upside down but also complicated the problem even further:

> [A]rticle 21 […] enshrines […] the primacy of the […] [ICC] Statute […] over the other sources of law […]. [But the 2011 decision implied that if] the witnesses' asylum application […] [succeeded], the Chamber would exceptionally afford precedence to internationally recognised human rights [due to two factors]: the risk of the immediate violation of a fundamental norm of international customary law whose peremptoriness finds increasing recognition among States and from which no derogation is permitted (*jus cogens*) and the impossibility of applying the [ICC] Statute in compliance with this norm […]. [T]he only means to adhere to the peremptory norm of *non-refoulement* was to suspend article 93(7) […] temporarily and not apply it should the asylum claims succeed.[52]

Firstly, and contrary to the 2013 decision, the 2011 decision considered the *non-refoulement* principle as a norm of customary international law[53] and did not mention *jus cogens* at all. If this customary norm, which must, pursuant to Article 21(1)(b), be applied in the second place, prevailed over the ICC Statute, then—due to the absence of any other legal rationale for an exception to the 'primacy-of-the-Statute' postulate—the ICC must have adopted the super-legality approach. Secondly, and contrary to what the 2013 decision implies, Article 21(3) enunciates only one category of rights—internationally recognised human rights—without any

[50] Pellet, *supra* note 2, at 1081.

[51] Ibid.

[52] Decision on the application for the interim release of detained Witnesses DRC-D02-P-0236, DRC-D02-P-0228 and DRC-D02-P-0350, *Prosecutor v Germain Katanga* (ICC-01/04-01/07-3405-tENG), Trial Chamber II, 1 October 2013, §§ 29–30.

[53] Decision on an Amicus Curiae application, *supra* note 49, §§ 64, 68.

explicit differentiation between peremptory and non-peremptory norms.[54] Even if we assume that the *non-refoulement* norm is peremptory, the requirements of Article 21(3) become futile, because such a norm shall, by its very nature, override any others. Thus, the primacy of internationally recognised human rights remains intact. In conclusion, although the 2011 and 2013 decisions are appallingly inconsistent, neither rebuts the super-legality approach.

In 2014, the witnesses were at long last ordered to return to the Democratic Republic of the Congo, because, inter alia, Article 21(3) 'does not require the Court to violate its obligations pursuant to article 93 (7) [...], [...] [while the opposite view] would seriously damage the Court's ability to enter into future cooperation agreements with States'.[55] This reasoning seems to be more policy-oriented than legal. The judicial *denouement* of the asylum saga is an apologetic recourse to sovereignty and state cooperation, on which the ICC legal regime rests.[56]

[54] Decision on the application for the interim release of detained Witnesses, *supra* note 52, Dissenting Opinion of Judge Van den Wyngaert (ICC-01/04-01/07-3405-Anx), § 6; A. Davidson, 'Human Rights Protection before the International Criminal Court: Assessing the Scope and Application of Article 21(3) of the Rome Statute', 18 *International Community Law Review* (2016) 72–101, at 95–96; G. Bitti, 'Article 21 and the Hierarchy of Sources of Law before the ICC', in Stahn, *supra* note 29, 411–443, at 439; Pellet, *supra* note 2, at 1081. Cf. V.-D. Degan, 'On the Sources of International Criminal Law', 4 *Chinese Journal of International Law* (2005) 45–83, at 82–83 (claiming that the sole function of Article 21(3) is the acknowledgement of *jus cogens* norms in international human right law); Nerlich, *supra* note 8, at 88–89 (drawing parallels between the functions of Article 21(3) and *jus cogens*).

[55] Order on the implementation of the cooperation agreement between the Court and the Democratic Republic of the Congo concluded pursuant article 93(7) of the Statute, *Prosecutor v Mathieu Ngudjolo Chui* (ICC-01/04-02/12-158), Appeals Chamber, 20 January 2014, § 26 (emphasis omitted).

[56] Cf. Decision on the Defence Motion for Interlocutory Appeal on Jurisdiction, *Prosecutor v Duško Tadić* (IT-94-1), Appeals Chamber, 2 October 1995, § 58 ('It would be a travesty of law and a betrayal of the universal need for justice, should the concept of State sovereignty be allowed to be raised successfully against human rights'); Werle and Jeßberger, *supra* note 6, at 70 (claiming that in clashes between sovereignty and human rights international criminal law favours the latter).

5.4 A Dethronement of Internationally Recognised Human Rights?

The scholarly community is divided on the question of where to place human rights in the ICC legal regime. Notably, Gerhard Hafner and Christina Binder have advanced essentially five arguments against the super-legality approach to Article 21(3) of the ICC Statute.[57] Nevertheless, all of them can be refuted with the help of Robert Alexy's *Theorie der Grundrechte*, as described above, and the methods of treaty interpretation.

Literal Interpretation

The first argument based on the literal interpretation of Article 21(3) of the ICC Statute is that internationally recognised human rights are not placed at the top of the applicable law.[58] However, this is easily rebutted by an *argumentum a contrario*. If we assume that the application of a statutory norm violates human rights, can the ICC apply it? Article 21(3) plainly says that its application 'must be consistent' with them. This phrase denotes an obligation.[59] In Robert Alexy's terminology, it is a rule. There are no exceptions thereto.[60]

Structure and Wording

The second argument is based on the structure and wording of Article 21 of the ICC Statute. The drafters did not include the concept of internationally recognised human rights in paragraph 1, placing it at the end of

[57] Hafner and Binder, *supra* note 9, at 174–176.

[58] Ibid, at 174. See also K. Gallant, 'Individual Human Rights in a New International Organization: The Rome Statute of the International Criminal Court', in M.C. Bassiouni (ed.), *International Criminal Law. Volume III—Enforcement* (2nd edn., Ardsley, New York: Transnational Publishers, Inc., 1999) 693–722, at 702–703; Clarenc Bicudo, *supra* note 2, at 972. See *contra* Davidson, *supra* note 54, at 83–84; Paulussen, *supra* note 3, at 827.

[59] D. Akande, 'Sources of International Criminal Law', in A. Cassese (ed.), *The Oxford Companion to International Criminal Justice* (Oxford: Oxford University Press, 2009) 41–53, at 47; Davidson, *supra* note 54, at 95. Cf. Gebhard, *supra* note 4, at 64 ('the explicit right').

[60] G. Pikis, *The Rome Statute for the International Criminal Court: Analysis of the Statute, the Rules of Procedure and Evidence, the Regulations of the Court and Supplementary Instruments* (Leiden/Boston: Martinus Nijhoff, 2010), at 89.

the article, although they could, for example, have formulated it as 'subject to its consistency with human rights, the Court shall apply'.[61]

However, Ida Caracciolo has praised that Article 21—and, by implication, its third paragraph—harmoniously gives the finishing touch to Part II (dealing with the definitions of crimes, amongst others) and immediately precedes Part III (on the general principles of criminal law) of the ICC Statute.[62] It is submitted that the mere location of a provision is simply irrelevant. For instance, Article 52 of the Charter of Fundamental Rights of the European Union is at the end of the treaty despite its paramount importance for the European Union system of human rights protection. Similarly, the location of paragraph 3 at the end of Article 21 of the ICC Statute does not militate against it acting as a *chapeau*.[63]

As regards the formulation, the proposed version would have been less problematic, but it is by no means the only one that can support the super-legality approach. Indeed, Robert Alexy has maintained that 'the same norm can be expressed by [...] [various] formulations'.[64]

Contextual Interpretation

The third argument is based on the contextual interpretation of Article 21(3) of the ICC Statute. A reference is made to Article 69(7) of the ICC Statute concerning '[e]vidence obtained by means of a violation of *this Statute or internationally recognized human rights*'.[65] Such evidence 'shall not be admissible if: (a) The violation casts substantial doubt on the reliability of the evidence; or (b) The admission of the evidence would be antithetical to and would seriously damage the integrity of the proceedings'.[66]

[61] Hafner and Binder, *supra* note 9, at 174. See also Clarenc Bicudo, *supra* note 2, at 972. See *contra* Paulussen, *supra* note 3, at 827–828; Zeegers, *supra* note 6, at 76. Cf. G. Hochmayr, 'Applicable Law in Practice and Theory: Interpreting Article 21 of the ICC Statute', 12 *Journal of International Criminal Justice* (2014) 655–679, at 676 (saying that the analysis of its wording does not give a clear answer).

[62] I. Caracciolo, 'Applicable Law', in Lattanzi and Schabas, *supra* note 40, 211–232, at 225.

[63] C. Chamberlain, *Children and the International Criminal Court: Analysis of the Rome Statute through a Children's Rights Perspective* (Cambridge/Antwerp/Portland: Intersentia, 2015), at 48; Akande, *supra* note 59, at 47.

[64] Alexy, *supra* note 10, at 43.

[65] ICC Statute, *supra* note 1, at Art. 69(7) (emphasis added).

[66] Ibid.

For Gerhard Hafner and Christina Binder, the disjunctive 'or' between the ICC Statute and internationally recognised human rights signals that the former is placed on the same footing as the latter.[67] Yet the word 'or' can mean 'and' and 'or', the caveat being that 'or' negates any mandatory cumulative effect of the options. If 'or' meant exclusive disjunction, it would lead to manifestly absurd results. For instance, one cannot gainsay that the right to liberty exists both under Article 55(1)(d) of the ICC Statute and as an internationally recognised human right. Moreover, nothing in the drafting history indicates that 'or' has been used for exclusive disjunction. Hence, it is inclusive and may point to either (i) the ICC Statute or (ii) internationally recognised human rights, or (iii) both. Option (i) is possible when the ICC Statute affords a higher level of protection than external human rights. For example, a violation of Article 67(1)(a) does not necessarily entail a violation of any human rights treaties or customary international law, but at the same time, Article 67(1)(a) is consistent with them because they prescribe minimum guarantees. Option (ii) is possible when the ICC Statute is simply silent regarding certain rights, such as the right to freedom of expression. Option (iii) can be exemplified by the above-mentioned right to liberty.

This does not, however, relieve us of the fact that Article 69(7) permits the admission of illegally obtained evidence.[68] How can the ICC apply the law inconsistently with internationally recognised human rights, contrary to Article 21(3)? Robert Alexy's *Theorie der Grundrechte* helps us to explain this problem. It is submitted that the rule on admissibility under Article 69(7) must be read within the delineated scope of its application: it constitutes an exception to the rule on consistency under Article 21(3) in all cases involving the admission of evidence.

In any event, the ICC is not totally anti-human-rightist as far as the 'fruit of the poisonous tree' dilemma is concerned. Not every human rights violation will be tolerated even when it comes to the admission of evidence. The prohibition of torture is one of the representative

[67] Hafner and Binder, *supra* note 9, at 174. See *contra* Paulussen, *supra* note 3, at 828 (conjecturing that internal consistency should not be exaggerated, because different parts of the ICC Statute were drafted separately).

[68] To be fair, such a provision is not unique. An absolute and automatic exclusionary rule exists in neither the criminal law of most national legal systems, nor the law of the ad hoc international criminal tribunals. A.M. Thake, 'The (In)Admissibility of Unlawfully Obtained Evidence at the International Criminal Court', 28 *Hague Yearbook of International Law* (2015) 161–187, at 163, 169–174.

examples.[69] Judicial discretion will, however, be exercised on the basis of the two safeguards under Article 69(7) concerning the non-reliability of evidence and the detriment of evidence to the integrity of proceedings. At a minimum, one of these conditions must be met for evidence to be declared inadmissible.[70] Nevertheless, this does not lessen the indignation of critics. Alexander Zahar and Göran Sluiter have highlighted 'a mockery of human rights law as an indivisible set of minimum legal standards'.[71] For Andrew Walker, references to ethics and integrity rather than the rights of the accused result in the preponderance of political expediency over the ideal of the rule of law.[72] Salvatore Zappalà has also expressed concern over the excessive breadth of the norm on the admission of evidence, but he believes that it is fairly satisfactory owing to the professionalism of judges, the requirement to provide detailed reasoning and the availability of the right to appeal.[73]

Thomas Lubanga invoked Article 69(7) in the proceedings on the confirmation of charges, claiming that evidence obtained in the Democratic Republic of the Congo by means of the search and seizure of a witness's house by the national authorities, and with the presence of an investigator from the Office of the Prosecutor of the ICC, had to be declared inadmissible due to the breach of the right to privacy. Pre-Trial Chamber I found a breach of this right.[74] Yet it rejected the notion that the evidence obtained

[69] See, for example, D. Piragoff and P. Clarke, 'Article 69. Evidence', in Ambos, *supra* note 2, 2037–2088, at 2087; W. Jasiński, 'Admissibility of Illegally Obtained Evidence in Proceedings before International Criminal Courts', in Krzan, *supra* note 41, 201–223, at 221; *Report of the Special Rapporteur on torture and other cruel, inhuman or degrading treatment or punishment*, Juan E. Méndez, UN Doc. A/HRC/25/60, 10 April 2014, §§ 17 et seq.

[70] Judgment on the appeals of Mr. Jean-Pierre Bemba Gombo, Mr. Aimé Kilolo Musamba, Mr. Jean-Jacques Mangenda Kabongo, Mr. Fidèle Babala Wandu and Mr. Narcisse Arido against the decision of Trial Chamber VII entitled "Judgment pursuant to Article 74 of the Statute", *Prosecutor v Jean-Pierre Bemba Gombo, Aimé Kilolo Musamba, Jean-Jacques Mangenda Kabongo, Fidèle Babala Wandu and Narcisse Arido* (ICC-01/05-01/13-2275-Red), Appeals Chamber, 8 March 2018, § 280.

[71] Zahar and Sluiter, *supra* note 6, at 382. See *contra* Jasiński, *supra* note 69, at 222–223.

[72] A. Walker, 'When a Good Idea Is Poorly Implemented: How the International Criminal Court Fails to Be Insulated from International Politics and to Protect Basic Due Process Guarantees', 106 *West Virginia Law Review* (2004) 245–304, at 281–282.

[73] S. Zappalà, *Human Rights in International Criminal Proceedings* (Oxford: Oxford University Press, 2003), at 253.

[74] Decision on the confirmation of charges, *Prosecutor v Thomas Lubanga Dyilo* (ICC-01/04-01/06-803-tEN), Pre-Trial Chamber I, 29 January 2007, § 81.

in such an unlawful way 'should be automatically excluded' and it ruled that 'the judges have the discretion to seek an appropriate balance between the [ICC] Statute's fundamental values in each concrete case'.[75] The ICC proceeded to consider paragraphs (a) and (b) of Article 69(7). As regards the former, it noted that the violation in question did not cast any substantial doubt on the reliability of evidence because the content of the items seized would have been the same even if the principle of proportionality had been fully respected.[76] As regards the latter, the ICC recalled: '[I]n the fight against impunity, it must ensure an appropriate balance between the rights of the accused and the need to respond to victims' and the international community's expectations [...]. Although no consensus has emerged on this issue in international human rights jurisprudence, the majority view is that only a serious human rights violation can lead to the exclusion of evidence'.[77]

The ICC concluded that the integrity of proceedings had not been infringed, and hence the evidence was declared admissible. Still, how can the ICC measure the seriousness of a human rights violation? Does the end justify the means? Georges Abi-Saab has taken a stand against any reliance on this Machiavellian maxim when it comes to the methods of obtaining evidence in international criminal law, but even so, he has urged liberal consideration of the admissibility of evidence.[78]

Teleological Interpretation

The fourth argument is that the vague concept of internationally recognised human rights cannot impede the realisation of the object and purpose of the ICC.[79] More specifically, international crimes under its jurisdiction 'must not go unpunished and [...] their effective prosecution

[75] Ibid, § 84. See also Decision on the confirmation of charges, *Prosecutor v Callixte Mbarushimana* (ICC-01/04-01/10-465-Red), Pre-Trial Chamber I, 16 December 2011, § 61.

[76] Decision on the confirmation of charges, *supra* note 74, § 85.

[77] Ibid, § 86.

[78] G. Abi-Saab, 'International Criminal Tribunals and the Development of International Humanitarian and Human Rights Law', in E. Yakpo and T. Boumedra (eds), *Liber Amicorum—Judge Mohammed Bedjaoui* (The Hague/London/Boston: Kluwer Law International, 1999) 649–658, at 658.

[79] Hafner and Binder, *supra* note 9, at 175.

must be ensured'.[80] Justice appears to be measured by the outcome that is favourable to victims.[81]

This way of thinking resembles the cogitation of judges in Nuremberg and Tokyo, although we should not retrospectively excoriate the International Military Tribunals for their human rights faults, which were, probably, not deemed egregious at a time of crude retributivism.[82] Hans Kelsen had little doubt that 'it is more important to bring the war criminals to justice than to respect [...] the rule against *ex post facto* law, which [...] was never unrestrictedly recognized'.[83] But international human rights law substantially developed and gained legitimacy during the Cold War, and after that was relied on to legitimate the establishment of modern international criminal tribunals.[84]

[80] ICC Statute, *supra* note 1, Preamble.

[81] For criticism, see D. Jacobs 'A Tale of Four Illusions: The Rights of the Defense before International Criminal Tribunals', in C. Rohan and G. Zyberi (eds), *Defense Perspectives on International Criminal Justice* (Cambridge: Cambridge University Press, 2017) 561–586, at 579–580.

[82] L. Sunga, 'Full Respect for the Rights of Suspect, Accused and Convict: from Nuremberg and Tokyo to the ICC', in M. Henzelin and R. Roth (eds), *Le droit pénal à l'épreuve de l'internationalisation* (Paris/Brussels/Geneva: L.G.D.J./Bruylant/Georg, 2002) 217–239, at 222; M.C. Bassiouni, 'Enforcing Human Rights through International Criminal Law and through an International Criminal Tribunal', in L. Henkin and J.L. Hargrove (eds), *Human Rights: An Agenda for the Next Century* (Washington, D.C.: The American Society of International Law, 1994) 347–382, at 359; С. Егоров, 'Приговор Нюрнбергского Трибунала и ответственность физических лиц за международные преступления', 4 *Московский журнал международного права* (2015) 90–102, at 93.

[83] H. Kelsen, 'The Rule against Ex Post Facto Laws and the Prosecution of the Axis War Criminals', *Judge Advocate Journal* (1945), No. 3, 8–12 and 46, at 11.

[84] O. Martelly, 'La légitimation des juridictions pénales internationales par la consécration dans leurs Statuts d'un droit commun du procès équitable autour de l'article 14 du PIDCP', *Annuaire de Justice pénale internationale et transitionnelle* (2014) 49–81; T. Rauter, *Judicial Practice, Customary International Criminal Law and* Nullum Crimen Sine Lege (Cham: Springer, 2017), at 52. At the same time, the human rights *telos* of the modern international criminal tribunals may empower victims, thereby bringing in the Nuremberg rhetoric through the back door. ICC Press Release, 'ICC Prosecutor visits Egypt and Saudi Arabia' (ICC-CPI-20080509-MA13), 9 May 2008, available online at www.icc-cpi.int/Pages/item.aspx?name=press+release+media+advisory_+icc+prosecutor+visits+egypt+and+saudi+arabia (visited 27 January 2023); Prosecutor of the ICC, Statement to the Press, Abidjan, Côte d'Ivoire, 20 July 2013, available online at www.icc-cpi.int/iccdocs/PIDS/wu/ED181_ENG.pdf (visited 27 January 2023), at 2; A. Cassese, 'The International Criminal Tribunal for the Former Yugoslavia and Human Rights', 4 *European Human Rights Law Review* (1997) 329–352, at 332; R. De Gouttes, 'Droit pénal et droits de l'homme', *Revue de science criminelle et de droit pénal comparé* (2000), No. 1, 133–144, at 139; E. van Sliedregt, 'International Criminal Law', in M. Dubber and T. Hörnle (eds), *The Oxford Handbook of Criminal Law* (Oxford: Oxford University Press, 2015) 1139–1162, at 1142.

One of the foundations and aims of present-day international criminal law is to foster abidance by human rights.[85] The culminating inclusion of Article 21(3) in the ICC Statute is the verbalised proof of this tectonic shift. Even if the above-mentioned quotation from the statutory Preamble sets out the only *raison d'être* of the ICC (which is debatable), it cannot reduce the requirements of Article 21(3) to zero.[86] Nowadays respect for human rights—particularly, the right to a fair trial—is regarded as a precondition for, or a means to mete out, justice in the ICC legal regime and criminal law generally.[87] It also underlies the legitimacy of international criminal tribunals.[88] In this connection, the *Lubanga* Appeals Chamber has noted: 'Where fair trial becomes impossible because of breaches of the fundamental rights of the suspect or the accused by his/her accusers, it would be a contradiction in terms to put the person on trial [...]. A fair trial is the only means to do justice. If no fair trial can be held,

[85] В. Буткевич, 'Міжнародне кримінальне право', in В. Буткевич (ed.), *Міжнародне право. Основні галузі* (Київ: Либідь, 2004) 676–719, at 700, 702; C.C. Jalloh and A. DiBella, 'Equality of Arms in International Criminal Law: Continuing Challenges', in W. Schabas, Y. McDermott and N. Hayes (eds), *The Ashgate Research Companion to International Criminal Law: Critical Perspectives* (Farnham/Burlington: Ashgate, 2013) 251–287, at 287; J. Ohlin, 'Goals of International Criminal Justice and International Criminal Procedure', in G. Sluiter et al. (eds), *International Criminal Procedure: Principles and Rules* (Oxford: Oxford University Press, 2013) 55–68, at 58, 63.

[86] Cf. P. Robinson, 'Ensuring Fair and Expeditious Trials at the International Criminal Tribunal for the Former Yugoslavia', 11 *European Journal of International Law* (2000) 569–589, at 572, 580, 583 (arguing that the object and purpose of the Statute of the International Criminal Tribunal for the former Yugoslavia is the achievement of a fair trial, but the broader purpose is the prosecution of individuals for international crimes).

[87] T. Margueritte, 'International Criminal Law and Human Rights', in W. Schabas and N. Bernaz (eds), *Routledge Handbook of International Criminal Law* (Abingdon: Routledge, 2010) 435–452, at 446; А. Мезяев, *Защита прав обвиняемых в современном международном уголовном процессе: актуальные вопросы теории и практики* (Казань: Университет управления «ТИСБИ», 2014), at 25; Danner and Martinez, *supra* note 24, at 167; De Gouttes, *supra* note 84, at 137–138.

[88] Decision on Prosecution's Motion for Order Appointing Counsel to Assist Vojislav Šešelj with his Defence, *Prosecutor v Vojislav Šešelj* (IT-03-67-PT), Trial Chamber II, 9 May 2003, § 21; D. Luban, 'Fairness to Rightness: Jurisdiction, Legality, and the Legitimacy of International Criminal Law', in S. Besson and J. Tasioulas (eds), *The Philosophy of International Law* (Oxford: Oxford University Press, 2010) 569–588, at 579–580; E. Maculan, 'Judicial Definition of Torture as a Paradigm of Cross-fertilisation: Combining Harmonisation and Expansion', 84 *Nordic Journal of International Law* (2015) 456–481, at 457; McDermott, *supra* note 48, at 22–25, 140–141, 147, 178.

the object of the judicial process is frustrated and the process must be stopped'.[89]

It appears that this reasoning does not accord with that of the *Lubanga* Pre-Trial Chamber in the decision on the confirmation of charges. One of the ways of dealing with the juxtaposition of a fair trial and justice is to delimit their scope of application, that is, to consider that the right to a fair trial exists independently from the duty to prosecute international crimes.[90] In other words, both are and remain rules. This approach seems to have been adopted by the *Lubanga* Appeals Chamber. Another way of thinking is that the right to a fair trial constitutes a principle that can be balanced. This approach seems to have been adopted by the *Lubanga* Pre-Trial Chamber. However, the same norm cannot be a rule and a principle in the light of Robert Alexy's *Theorie der Grundrechte*.[91] This seeming logjam has a way out with the aid of the core-and-mantle model of human rights norms. Martin Scheinin has argued that 'most, if not all, human rights include an inviolable core with the character of a rule, surrounded by a much broader principle that is valid at the level of the legal order as a whole'.[92] Hence, there is a core—to be precise, a number of cores—of the right to a fair trial and a broader principle surrounding them. Balancing in the non-core dimension occurred in the decision on the confirmation of charges, but the cores of the right to a fair trial were not violated on any of the occasions.

Preparatory Work

Finally, Gerhard Hafner and Christina Binder refer to Mahnoush Arsanjani's frequently quoted opinion: 'While the original intention behind [Article 21(3)] may have been to limit the court's powers [...], it

[89] Judgment on the Appeal of Mr. Thomas Lubanga Dyilo, *supra* note 36, § 37. See also Judgment on the Appeal of the Prosecutor against the decision of Trial Chamber I entitled "Decision on the consequences of non-disclosure of exculpatory materials covered by Article 54(3)(e) agreements and the application to stay the prosecution of the accused, together with certain other issues raised at the Status Conference on 10 June 2008", *Prosecutor v Thomas Lubanga Dyilo* (ICC-01/04-01/06-1486), Appeals Chamber, 21 October 2008, § 77.

[90] See, mutatis mutandis, *Jurisdictional Immunities of the State (Germany v. Italy: Greece intervening)*, International Court of Justice, Judgment of 3 February 2012, ICJ Reports (2012) 99, at 140–141, § 94.

[91] Alexy, *supra* note 10, at 71 et seq.

[92] Scheinin, *supra* note 15, at 56. See also Scheinin, *supra* note 13, at 532–535.

could have the opposite effect and broaden [its] competence'.[93] Their argument does not, however, benefit from resorting to the preparatory work of the ICC Statute. The fact that the drafters initially wanted to constrain the ICC finds no support in what they eventually agreed on and signed.[94] Indeed, the *travaux préparatoires* can bolster virtually any construction,[95] which is one of the reasons the Vienna Convention on the Law of Treaties vests them with merely an auxiliary role in interpretation.[96] Moreover, most negotiations at the Rome Conference were informal and there are no complete written records.[97] A related pragmatic argument that the norm-generating function of Article 21(3) may arouse profound mistrust of the ICC as a foremost criminal tribunal[98] is not compelling due to the aforesaid importance of human rights in international criminal law, including the *nullum crimen sine lege* principle under Article 22 of the ICC Statute.

5.5 Conclusions

Article 21(3) of the ICC Statute can be harnessed for two purposes. Firstly, it can be used to interpret international criminal law and other norms. Secondly, it can enable judges to set aside statutory norms and rely on external human rights norms, thus underscoring the supremacy of human rights in the ICC legal regime. Despite the importance of state cooperation for the effectiveness of the ICC, it is submitted that the super-legality approach to Article 21(3) is, legally speaking, largely correct. Yet this

[93] Arsanjani, *supra* note 6, at 29. See also Clarenc Bicudo, *supra* note 2, at 972. Cf. Corrigendum to the Brief, *supra* note 6, para. 8 ('the drafters of the [ICC] Statute left it to the judges to undertake an evolutive interpretation of the statutory provisions'); Davidson, *supra* note 54, at 86 (arguing that the conceptualisation of Article 21(3) as incorporating a 'living instrument' doctrine precludes it from turning into a dead letter).

[94] Akande, *supra* note 59, at 47.

[95] W. Schabas, 'Interpreting the Statutes of the ad hoc Tribunals', in L.C. Vohrah et al. (eds), *Man's Inhumanity to Man—Essays on International Law in Honour of Antonio Cassese* (The Hague/London/New York: Kluwer Law International, 2003) 847–888, at 868.

[96] O. Dörr, 'Article 32. Supplementary Means of Interpretation', in O. Dörr and K. Schmalenbach (eds), *Vienna Convention on the Law of Treaties: A Commentary* (2nd edn., Berlin: Springer, 2018) 617–633, at 618–620.

[97] R. Cryer, H. Friman, D. Robinson and E. Wilmshurst, *An Introduction to International Criminal Law and Procedure* (3rd edn., Cambridge: Cambridge University Press, 2014), at 149–150.

[98] Krzan, *supra* note 41, at 170.

approach is not omnipotent if it is examined in the light of Robert Alexy's *Theorie der Grundrechte*, particularly his distinction between rules and principles. Serving as a conflict-avoidance technique, Article 21(3) places internationally recognised human rights rules above any other rules (including those in the ICC Statute), except for those that are *jus cogens* and the rule on the admission of evidence under Article 69(7), which, however, has its own human rights safeguards. At the same time, Article 21(3) is less helpful to the exercise of balancing. Human rights principles can yield to other principles so long as the inviolable core(s) of the former is/are not breached.

PART II

Developments in Respect of the Substantive Elements of International Criminal Law

CHAPTER 6

The Contribution of the International Criminal Court Towards Conflict Classification from *Lubanga* to *Ongwen*: Demystifying or Muddying the Notion of 'protracted armed conflict' Under Article 8(2)(f) of the Rome Statute?

Martha M. Bradley

6.1 Introduction

This chapter presents an examination of the intensity threshold of Article 8(2)(f) of the Rome Statute and the consequences of the introduction of the notion of 'protracted armed conflict' in the second part of this

M. M. Bradley (✉)
Department of Public Law, Faculty of Law, and South African Research Chair for International Law, University of Johannesburg, Johannesburg, South Africa
e-mail: mbradley@uj.ac.za

M. Faix, O. Svaček (eds.), *ICC Jurisprudence and the Development of International Humanitarian Law*, Global Issues,
https://doi.org/10.1007/978-3-031-45994-8_6

provision.[1] Article 8(2)(f) of the Rome Statute determines the scope of application, that is, the arena in which the types of war crimes listed in Article 8(2)(e) of the Rome Statute must be committed in order for the International Criminal Court (ICC) to exercise jurisdiction over such violations. With regard to the broader theme of this volume, which relates to child soldiers, it should be noted that the type of war crimes listed in Article 8(2)(e) of the Rome Statute includes the conscription of of children under the age of 15 years into an armed force or group or using them to actively participate in hostilities.[2] The inclusion of the phrase 'protracted armed conflict' in the second sentence of Article 8(2)(f) possibly creates a requirement for a threshold of violence higher than the minimum intensity of violence associated with protracted armed violence and could, in fact, creates a new category of non-international armed conflicts in the context of the Rome Statute.[3]

Several scholars, including the author of this chapter, have contributed to the body of literature that is concerned with the interpretative conundrum posed by the inclusion of 'protracted armed conflict' in the final sentence of Article 8(2)(f) of the Rome Statute through employing the

[1] Rome Statute of the International Criminal Court (adopted 17 July 1998, entered into force 1 July 2002), 2187 UNTS 90 (hereafter Statute).

[2] Rome Statute, *supra* note 1, at Art. 8(2)(e)(vii).

[3] *Cf.* Rome Statute, *supra* note 1, Art. 8(2)(d) which reads: 'Paragraph 2(c) applies to *armed conflicts not of an international character* and thus does not apply to situations of internal disturbances and tensions, such as riots, isolated and sporadic acts of violence or other acts of a similar nature.' Rome Statute Art. 8(2)(f) provides as follows: 'Paragraph 2(e) applies to *armed conflicts not of an international character* and thus does not apply to situations of internal disturbances and tensions, such as riots, isolated and sporadic acts of violence or other acts of a similar nature. It applies to armed conflicts that take place in the territory of a state when there is *protracted armed conflict* between governmental authorities and organized armed groups or between such groups' (emphasis added). See also C. Gray, 'The Meaning of Armed Conflict: Non-International Armed Conflict', in M.E. O'Connell (ed.), *What is War: An Investigation in the Wake of 9/11* (Leiden/Boston: Martinus Nijhoff, 2012) at 72.

rules of treaty interpretation.[4] For this reason, that type of examination will not be repeated in this chapter.[5] The results of treaty interpretation, however, have proved inconclusive; scholarly opinion offers strong arguments, both for[6] and against the creation of a diverse notion of 'intensity'[7] and, consequently, of a new category of non-international armed conflict as a result of the inclusion of the wording 'armed conflict not of a pro-

[4] These scholars include C. Kress, 'War Crimes Committed in Non-International Armed Conflict and the Emerging System of International Criminal Justice', 30 *Israel Yearbook on Human Rights* (2001) 104, at 118; N Quenivet, 'Applicability Test of Additional Protocol II and Common Article 3 for Crimes in Internal Armed Conflict', in D. Jinks et al. (eds), *Applying International Humanitarian Law in Judicial and Quasi-Judicial Bodies* (The Hague: T.M.C. Asser Press, 2014); A. Cullen, 'The Concept of Non-International Armed Conflict in the Rome Statute of the International Criminal Court: Interpreting the Threshold Contained in Article 8(2)(f): Rome Statute of the International Criminal Court', in A. Cullen, *The Concept of Non-International Armed Conflict in International Humanitarian Law* (United Kingdom: Cambridge University Press, 2010) at 69, 82, 174–185, 206; see J. Pejic, 'The Protective Scope of Common Article 3: More Than Meets the Eye', 93 *IRRC* (2011) at 202; S. Sivakumaran, *The Law of Non-International Armed Conflict* (New York: Oxford University Press, 2012) 192–194; see Y. Dinstein, *Non-International Armed Conflicts in International Law* (United Kingdom: Cambridge University Press, 2014) 190; K. Ambos, *Treatise on International Criminal Law: Volume II: The Crimes and Sentencing* (Oxford: Oxford University Press, 2014) 543; M. Cortier, 'War Crimes', in R. O'Keefe, *International Criminal Law* (1st edn., New York: Oxford University Press, 2015) 312–314; O Triffterer and K Ambos *Rome Statute of the International Criminal Court: A Commentary* (3rd edn, Oxford: C.H. Beck, 2016) 441; K. Dörmann et al. (eds), *International Committee of the Red Cross: Commentary on the First Geneva Convention: Convention (I) for the Amelioration of the Conditions of the Wounded and Sick in Armed Forces in the Field* (Cambridge: Cambridge University Press, 2016) paras 424–437 of the Commentaries on Common Article 3, at 160–161, paras 443–444; M.M. Bradley, 'The "Intensity" Threshold in Article 8(2)(f) of the Rome Statute: The Conundrum Created by the Term "Protracted Armed Conflict" and the Possibility of a New Category of Non-International Armed Conflict' 42 *South African Yearbook of International Law* (2017) 79.

[5] For an in-depth examination of Art. 8(2)(f) of the Rome Statute through the law of treaty interpretation, see A. Cullen, 'The Definition of Non-International Armed Conflict in the Rome Statute of the International Criminal Court: An Analysis of the Threshold of Application Contained in Article 8(2)(f)' 212 *Journal of Conflict and Security Law* (2008) 419–445; Bradley, *supra* note 4, at 49–68; and S. Sivakumaran, 'Identifying an Armed Conflict Not of an International Character', in S. Stahn and G. Sluiter (eds), *The Emerging Practice of the International Criminal Court* (The Hague: Martinus Nijhoff, 2009) at 373–377.

[6] S. Vité, 'Typology of Armed Conflicts in International Humanitarian Law: Legal Concepts and Actual Situations', 91 *Review of the Red Cross* (2009) 82; Bradley, *supra* note 4, at 42; Dinstein, *supra* note 4, at para. 610.

[7] Sivakumaran, *supra* note 4, at 192–195; Cullen, *supra* note 5, at 419–445.

tracted nature'.[8] The content of the notion of 'intensity' in respect of Article 8(2)(f) of the Rome Statute, therefore, is a matter of dispute and this interpretive conundrum requires clarification in the form of the decisions of the ICC.[9] This is the primary research purpose of this contribution to examine the intensity threshold represented in Article 8(2)(f) of the Rome Statute in terms of the wording 'protracted armed conflict' by means of an in-depth analysis of the relevant case law of the ICC. Such an analysis in this chapter is a means of finding an answer to the conundrum of whether the contribution of the ICC in defining the construct of 'protracted armed conflict' demystifies this notion, or whether it simply creates further confusion in terms of understanding the elements necessary to constitute a non-international armed conflict under Article 8(2)(f) of the Rome Statute.

Questions may be raised as to why conflict classification matters in relation to the prosecution of alleged war criminals under the Rome Statute.[10] The fact is that the identification of the existence of an armed conflict informs the two contextual elements inherent in war crimes.[11] Sassoli explains that international criminal law and the international criminal jus-

[8] See Dinstein, *supra* note 4, at para. 610 explaining the consequence of a higher threshold test unique to art 8(2)(f) of the Rome Statute.

[9] The case law of the International Criminal Court, as judicial decisions, classifies as sources of persuasive value as per Art. 38(1)(d) of the Statute of the International Court of Justice (adopted 26 June 1945, entered into force 24 October 1945) TS No 993 (hereafter ICJ Statute). For an overview of the rules of interpretation applicable to the Rome Statute itself, see A. de Beer and M. Bradley, 'Appellate Deference *De Novo* Analysis of Evidence: The Decision of the Appeals Chamber in *Prosecutor Jean-Pierre Bemba Gombo* '22 *Yearbook of International Humanitarian Law* (2019) 153, at 156–161.

[10] For an overview of the importance of conflict classification in respect of war crime adjudication, see M. Bradley, '"Protracted Armed Conflict": A Conundrum. Does Article 8(2)(f) of the Rome Statute Require an Organized Armed Group to Meet the Organisational Criteria of Additional Protocol II?' 3 *South African Journal of Criminal Justice* (2019), 291 at 299–300.

[11] In *Situation in the Democratic Republic of the Congo in the Case of the Prosecutor v Bosco Ntaganda*, decided on 8 July 2019, Trial Chamber VI confirmed that the existence of an armed conflict was vital in the context of war crime prosecution as two requirements must be met in determining each war crime confirmed in a particular case: first, that the conduct in question (the alleged commission of a war crime) took place 'in the context of and was associated with' the relevant category of armed conflict; second, that the alleged perpetrator of a war crime indeed was aware of factual circumstances that established the existence of an armed conflict. Judgment, *Situation in the Democratic Republic of the Congo in the Case of The Prosecutor v Bosco Ntaganda* (01/04-02/06), Trial Chamber VI, 8 July 2019, § 698.

tice system support the international humanitarian law regime by the provision of enforcement mechanisms.[12] The war crime provisions in the Rome Statute create an enforcement platform in the form of the ICC to adjudicate the most serious violations of international humanitarian law (criminalized and codified in the Rome Statute as war crimes) that fall within the jurisdiction of this court.[13] Conflict classification is a preliminary to the application of all international humanitarian law and, equally, is a preliminary issue in war crime adjudication by international criminal courts and tribunals in the sense that war crimes are committed only during armed conflict.[14] It is owing to the link between international criminal law and international humanitarian law in the context of conflict classification that this contribution slots into the general theme of this volume.

This chapter is structured in two sections. In the first substantive section (Sect. 6.2) the author gives content to the interpretative conundrum introduced by the inclusion of the second part of Article 8(2)(f).[15] The consequences of this interpretative conundrum for conflict classification that are specific to the ICC are illustrated through an examination of the relationship between the minimum threshold of the notion of intensity demanded to trigger the existence of a non-international armed conflict that equates to 'protracted armed conflict' and the element of duration that may or may not be considered an additional element introduced in Article 8(2)(f) of the Rome Statute through the inclusion of the phrase 'protracted armed conflict'. In the second substantive section of this chapter (Sect. 6.3), the relevant cases where the ICC had to determine the existence of an article 8(2)(f)-type conflict are surveyed. The purpose of this analysis is to establish whether the ICC interpreted Article 8(2)(f) as simply requiring the *Tadic* formulation[16] as demanded by Article 8(2)(d)

[12] M. Sassoli, *International Humanitarian Law: Rules, Controversies, and Solutions to Problems Arising in Warfare* (Cheltenham, UK/Northampton, MA: Edward Elgar Publishing, 2019) at para. 9.5.4.

[13] *Ibid.*

[14] Sassoli, *supra* note 12, at para. 9.5.5.

[15] Rome Statute, *supra* note 1, at Art. 8(2)(f).

[16] See Decision on the Defence Motion for Interlocutory Appeal on Jurisdiction, *Prosecutor v Dusko Tadic aka 'Dule'* (IT-94-1-A), Appeals Chamber, 19 July 1998, § 70 and Opinion and Judgment, *Prosecutor v Dusko Tadic a/k/a 'Dule'* (IT-94-1-T 7), Trial Chamber I, 7 May 1997, § 561. As per the *Tadic* formulation for a situation to transform into the realm of non-international armed conflict, the non-state party or parties to such situation have to be sufficiently organized and the fighting between the parties has to equate protracted armed violence.

of the Rome Statute, or whether the ICC interpreted Article (8)(2)(f) of the Rome Statute as demanding an additional temporal element. The author of this contribution refers to the latter as a '*Tadic*-plus' approach to the notion of 'protracted armed conflict'. The relevant cases are surveyed in chronological order, from the first case, which is *Lubanga*,[17] to the most recent case at the time of publication, the *Ongwen*[18] decision of 2021. In Sect. 6.4, a conclusion is drawn, and the author answers the question of whether the contribution of the ICC towards conflict classification from *Lubanga* to *Ongwen* confuses or clarifies the notion of 'protracted armed conflict' under Article 8(2)(f) of the Rome Statute.

6.2 An Interpretative Conundrum: Protracted Armed Conflict, Protracted Armed Violence and Duration

Non-international armed conflicts are defined in Article 8(2)(d) of the Rome Statute as armed conflicts not of an international character, which means that the term does not apply to 'situations of internal disturbances and tensions such as riots, isolated and sporadic acts of violence or other acts of a similar nature'. This definition mimics the understanding of a non-international armed conflict or 'armed conflict not of an international character' in terms of Common Article 3 and customary international humanitarian law.[19] The term 'armed conflict' is not defined in the relevant treaty law under either the law of armed conflict or the Rome Statute

[17] Judgment Pursuant to Art. 74 of the Judgment, *The Prosecutor v Thomas Lubanga Dyilo* (ICC-01/04-01/00), Trial Chamber, 14 March 2012.

[18] Trial Judgment, *Situation in Uganda in the Case of The Prosecutor v Dominic Ongwen* (ICC-02/04-01/15), Trial Chamber IX, 4 February 2021.

[19] Common Article 3 is common to all four Geneva Conventions. Geneva Convention I for the Amelioration of the Condition of the Wounded and Sick in Armed Forces in the Field (adopted 12 August 1949, entered into force 21 October 1950) 75 UNTS 31 (First Geneva Convention); Geneva Convention II for the Amelioration of the Condition of Wounded, Sick and Shipwrecked Members of Armed Forces at Sea (adopted 12 August 1949, entered into force 21 October 1950) 75 UNTS 85 (Second Geneva Convention); Geneva Convention III Relative to the Treatment of Prisoners of War (adopted 12 August 1949, entered into force 21 October 1950) 75 UNTS 135 (Third Geneva Convention); Geneva Convention IV Relative to the Protection of Civilian Persons in Time of War (adopted 12 August 1949, entered into force 21 October 1950) 75 UNTS 287 (Fourth Geneva Convention). The customary international law status of Common Article 3 was confirmed by the International Court of Justice in the *Nicaragua* case. *Military and Paramilitary Activities in and Against Nicaragua (NicaraguaUnited States)*, Merits, (Judgment) of 27 June 1986 [1986] ICJ Rep 14, 103, at para. 218.

of the ICC itself. The Appeals Chamber of the International Criminal Tribunal for the former Yugoslavia (ICTY), however, contributed a clarification in delineating what it considered to be the characteristics of armed conflict in *Prosecutor v. Dusko Tadic a/k/a 'Dule': Decision on the Defence Motion for the Interlocutory Appeal on Jurisdiction*.[20] The Appeals Chamber phrased its understanding as follows: 'An armed conflict exists whenever there is a resort to armed force between States or *protracted armed violence* between governmental authorities and *organized armed groups* or between such groups within a State.'[21] This construct is often referred to as the *Tadic* formula.

The first part of Article 8(2)(f) of the Rome Statute mimics the scope of application and definition of an Article 8(2)(d)-type armed conflict.[22] This means that the *Tadic* formula must be met for an Article 8(2)(f)-type armed conflict to exist. Up to this point, defining a non-international armed conflict in the context of Article 8 of the war crimes provision of the Rome Statute is not problematic. Article 8(2)(f) of the Rome Statute, however, consists of two parts, and at this point the situation becomes confusing. The drafters added a second sentence to Article 8(2)(f) of the Rome Statute which does not appear in Article 8(2)(d) of the Rome Statute. This sentence reads: 'It applies to armed conflicts that take place in the territory of a State when there is protracted armed conflict between governmental authorities and organized armed groups or between such groups.'[23] This second part of Article 8(2)(f) of the Rome Statute determines that an armed conflict must be 'protracted'. The phrase 'protracted armed conflict' may or may not imply that an additional (higher) threshold of violence requirement co-exists with the intensity of violence

[20] See *Tadic (Decision on the Defence Motion for Interlocutory Appeal on Jurisdiction)*, *supra* note 16, para. 70.

[21] *Ibid* (emphasis added).

[22] The instructive part of Art. 8(2)(d) of the Rome Statute, *supra* note 1, reads: 'applies to *armed conflicts not of an international character* and thus does not apply to situations of internal disturbances and tensions, such as riots, isolated and sporadic acts of violence or other acts of a similar nature'. Similarly, the first sentence of Art. 8(2)(f) determines: 'applies to *armed conflicts not of an international character* and thus does not apply to situations of internal disturbances and tensions, such as riots, isolated and sporadic acts of violence or other acts of a similar nature'.

[23] Rome Statute, *supra* note 1, Art. 8(2)(f).

requirement inherent in the first part of this provision.[24] This possibly fuels the debate that the notion of intensity inherent in Article 8(2)(f) differs from that in Article 8(2)(d) of the Rome Statute.[25] If such an additional threshold of violence requirement exists under Article 8(2)(f) of the Rome Statute, it could be argued that this provision creates a new category of non-international armed conflict.[26] It is specifically the threshold of violence requirement that is contentious and needs to be explored in order to fully comprehend the meaning of the notion of 'intensity' as a constitutive element of a non-international armed conflict in accordance with the Rome Statute.[27] This requirement relates to the intensity of violence requirement which makes it necessary for the degree of violence to be 'protracted' for a situation to be transformed into a non-international armed conflict.[28]

At this juncture, a brief overview of the threshold of violence under the *Tadic* formulation is offered as a way of illustrating the confusion that arises pertaining to 'protracted armed violence' as the minimum threshold of the notion of intensity in contradistinction to duration as an additional element to protracted armed violence under the construct, 'protracted armed conflict'.[29] The notion of 'intensity' is defined in any treaty. The notion was introduced by the ICTY in *Tadic*.[30] The 2016 Commentary on the First Geneva Convention of the International Committee of the Red Cross (ICRC) considers the understanding of the notion of intensity as

[24] See Cullen, *supra* note 4, 128, where he cites Sonja Boelaert-Suominen's comments on the meaning of the term 'protracted'.

[25] See note 4.

[26] *Ibid.*

[27] *Ibid.*

[28] *Tadic* (Decision on the Defence Motion for Interlocutory Appeal on Jurisdiction), *supra* note 16.

[29] For an overview of the notion of intensity under *Tadic*, see M.M. Bradley 'Additional Protocol II: Elevating the minimum threshold of intensity?' *International Review of the Red Cross* (2021) 1, at 9–14.

[30] *Tadic* (Decision on the Defence Motion for Interlocutory Appeal on Jurisdiction), *supra* note 16, para. 70. For a discussion of the role of the jurisprudence of the International Criminal Tribunal for the former Yugoslavia in the development of the notion of 'protracted armed violence', see M. Hrnjaz and J. Simentić Popović, 'Protracted Armed Violence as a Criterion for the Existence of Non-International Armed Conflict: International Humanitarian Law, International Criminal Law and Beyond', *Journal of Conflict and Security Law* (2020) 7–11.

formulated in the *Tadic* case to be widely accepted.[31] The purpose of the notion of intensity is to provide for a minimum threshold to the fighting that must be met in order to satisfy the second constitutive element—the existence of protracted armed violence—of a non-international armed conflict.[32]

The 2016 ICRC Commentary acknowledges that there is a point at which the intensity requirement that defines a non-international armed conflict applies to situations formerly regarded as instances of 'sporadic violence', resulting in their reclassification as armed conflicts not of an international character in that, at a later point, the fighting comes to resemble 'protracted armed violence'.[33] A contemporary understanding of the notion of 'intensity' thus depends on the meaning of the term 'protracted armed violence'.[34] Case law of international courts and tribunals promotes a better understanding of what is meant by the term 'protracted' as the decisions suggest several indicative factors that may be employed to determine whether or not violence is protracted.[35] In the *Haradinaj*

[31] Dörmann et al., *supra* note 4, para. 435. The 2016 Commentary on the First Geneva Convention has been consulted to aid in the interpretation of the construct 'protracted armed violence'. Commentaries are important analytical tools, constituting '[a] teaching that explores the meaning of the provision—looking at its object and purpose, situating it in context, considering its drafting history, analysing subsequent practice, and canvassing relevant literature—can prove influential'. The ICRC Commentaries constitute an especially invaluable subsidiary source. Sandesh Sivakumaran, 'The Influence of Teachings of Publicists on the Development of International Law', 66 *International and Comparative Law Quarterly* (2017) 1–32, at 15. These commentaries fill the role of publicist within the ambit of Art. 38(1)(d) of the Statute of the International Court of Justice (adopted 26 June 1945, entered into force 24 October 1945), TS No. 993 (hereafter ICJ Statute).

[32] *Tadic* (Decision on the Defence Motion for Interlocutory Appeal on Jurisdiction), *supra* note 16, para. 70. For a general overview of the notion of intensity, see Sivakumaran, *supra* note 4, 167–170; International Law Association, 'The Hague Conference (2010): Use of Force: Final Report on the Meaning of Armed Conflict in International Law', in O'Connell, *supra* note 3, at 15 and 20; Dörmann et al., *supra* note 4, paras 423–428; Bradley, *supra* note 28, at 10–11.

[33] Dörmann et al., *supra* note 4, para. 427.

[34] A. Cullen, 'Article 3 Common to the Four Geneva Conventions of 1949 and the Threshold of Non-International Armed Conflict in International Humanitarian Law', in Cullen, *supra* note 4, at 27–29.

[35] Judgment, *Prosecutor v. Boškoski and Tarculovski* (IT-04-82-T), Trial Chamber, 10 July 2008, §§ 199–203; *Lubanga* (Judgment Pursuant to Article 74 of the Statute), *supra* note 17, para. 538; Judgment, *Prosecutor v. Ramush Haradinaj Idriz Balaj Lahi Brahimaj* (IT-04-84-T), Trial Chamber, 3 April 2008, § 52, § 49; Dörmann et al., *supra* note 4, para. 432.

case,[36] the Trial Chamber considered how the criterion of 'protracted violence' had been established in practice[37] and, consequently, it determined that the following indicative factors (which is a non-exhaustive list) are present in order to decide whether the duration of the violence indeed was protracted:

> [T]he number, duration and intensity of individual confrontations; the type of weapons and other military equipment used; the number and caliber of munitions fired; the number of persons and type of forces partaking in the fighting; the number of casualties; the extent of material destruction; and the number of civilians fleeing combat zones. The involvement of the UN Security Council may also be a reflection of the intensity of a conflict.[38]

The purpose of these indicative factors is for them to be used to assess whether a specific armed clash or conflict situation is sufficiently intense to satisfy the minimum threshold of protracted armed violence and, thus, transform the incident into an armed conflict not of an international character.[39] The indicative factors developed by the ICTY in relation to 'protracted violence' are considered an important contribution as subsequently

[36] *Haradinaj, supra* note 35, para. 49.

[37] Trial Chamber I did so by examining the cases of *Tadic* (Decision on the Defence Motion for Interlocutory Appeal on Jurisdiction), *supra* note 16; Judgment, *Prosecutor v. Zejnil Delalic Zdravko Mucic, also known as 'Pavo', Hazim Delic Esad Landzo also known as 'Zenga'* (IT-96-21-T), Trial Chamber, 16 November 1998, §§ 183–192; *Milosevic, supra* note 23; Judgment, *Prosecutor Kordic and Cerkez* (IT-95-14/2-A), Appeals Chamber, 17 December 2004, § 341; Judgment, *Prosecutor v Sefer Halilovic* (IT 01-48-T), Trial Chamber, 16 November 2005; Judgment, *Prosecutor v Fatmir Limaj, Haradin Bala, Isak Musliu* (IT-03-66-T), 30 November 2005, Trial Chamber II, 171–173; *The ProsecutorEnver Hadzihasanovic Amir Kubara* Case No. IT-01-47-T Trial Chamber 15 March 2006; Judgment, *Prosecutor v. Martic* (IT-95-1+R61), Trial Chamber, 8 March 1996, at 41; and Trial Judgment, *Prosecutor v. Mile Mrksic, Miroslav Radic, Veselin Sljivancanin* (IT-95-13/1-T), Trial Chamber, 27 September 2007.

[38] *Haradinaj, supra* note 35, para. 49.

[39] *Ibid.*

they have been adopted by various other international courts and tribunals, including the ICC.[40]

It is important to emphasize that these indicative factors are not conditions that need to exist concurrently, nor is any one of these factors in itself constitutive in nature.[41] For example, 'duration' is not a decisive indicator but should be considered when making an assessment of whether or not a situation is intense enough to equate to 'protracted armed violence' in terms of Common Article 3.[42] A clear understanding of the relationship between duration and protracted armed violence is vital as it clarifies the tension caused by the introduction of the construct 'protracted armed conflict' in the final sentence of Article 8(2)(f) of the Rome Statute. In terms of the notion of intensity associated with a non-international armed conflict (under Common Article 3 and Article 8(2)(d) of the Rome Statute), duration is included in the assessment of protracted armed violence. Duration is not a constitutive factor on its own account.[43] Scholars

[40] *Haradinaj, supra* note 35, para 49. See Bradley who provides examples of international courts and tribunals employing this threshold test: 'Other international tribunals and courts, such as the International Criminal Court (ICC), have confirmed the indicative factors developed by the International Criminal Tribunal for the Former Yugoslavia in relation to "protracted violence". For instance, in the *Lubanga* case, the ICC contributed to the jurisprudence by explaining its understanding of "protracted violence" in relation to Common Article 3. The ICC utilized the indicative factors used by Trial Chamber II of the International Criminal Tribunal for the Former Yugoslavia in the *Mrksic* case to determine whether the violence was sufficiently protracted. The International Criminal Tribunal for Rwanda referred to these indicative factors as forming part of an "evaluation test" which it employed to determine whether situations were mere internal disturbances and tensions or whether they constituted armed conflicts in the legal sense. In the *Akayesu* case, Chamber I of the International Criminal Tribunal for Rwanda concluded in its assessment of the intensity requirement that the evaluation of this threshold requirement was not dependent on a subjective judgment by the parties to the conflict but that it was an objective test.' M. Bradley, 'Revisiting the Notion of "Intensity" Inherent in Common Article 3: An Examination of the Minimum Threshold Which Satisfies the Notion of "Intensity" and a Discussion of the Possibility of Applying a Method of Cumulative Assessment', 17 *International Comparative Law Review* (2017) 7–38, at 21–22, referring to *Lubanga, supra* note 17, para. 538; Judgment, *Prosecutor v. Akayesu* (ICTR-96-4-T), Chamber I, 2 September 1998, § 627; Judgment and Sentence, *Prosecutor v. Georges Anderson Nderubumwe Rutanganda* (ICTR-96-3-T, 26), Trial Chamber I, 6 December 1999, § 93; Judgment and Sentence, *Prosecutor v. Alfred Musema* (ICTR-96-13-A), Trial Chamber, 27 January 2000, §§ 248–251.

[41] *Ibid.* See also Bradley, *supra* note 40, at 19.

[42] For a discussion of the relationship between 'duration' and 'intensity', see Dörmann et al., *supra* note 4, paras 438–444; Sivakumaran, *supra* note 4, at 167–168, paras 88–97; Bradley, *supra* note 28, at 9–14.

[43] *Ibid.*

agree with this position that duration is not a separate requirement in addition to protracted armed violence.[44] Lewis explains that jurisprudence illustrates that the duration dimension often is factored into the 'broader analysis of the intensity of hostilities' as but a single criterion that is taken into account in the assessment of the existence of a non-international armed conflict.[45] The inclusion of the phrase 'protracted armed conflict' in Article 8(2)(f) arguably imposes an additional temporal element to the *Tadic* criterion. Simply put, the constitutive elements inherent in a 'protracted armed conflict' may equate to the *Tadic* formulation plus duration.

6.3 Case Law of the International Criminal Court

Lubanga 2012 (Tadic Plus)

Thomas Lubanga Dyilo was the commander-in-chief of the *Forces Patriotiques pour la Liberation du Congo* (FPLC).[46] The FPLC was the armed military wing of a Congolese political party, the *Union des Patriots Congolais* (UPC).[47] In the situation that existed in the Democratic Republic of the Congo (DRC), the UPC participated as an apolitical grouping that had the FPLC as its fighting arm between 2 June 2003 and December 2003.[48] Among other charges, the Prosecutor of the ICC under Articles 8(2)(e)(vii) and 25(3)(a) of its Statute charged Thomas Lubango Dyilo with the war crime of conscripting and enlisting children under the age of 15 years into an organized armed group, a charge of particular importance in this context.[49] The armed group in this case is the

[44] Bradley, *supra* note 28, at 9–14; Moir interprets the case law of the ICTY to suggest that, in an assessment of protracted armed violence, indicative factors concerned with the method of fighting should bear more weight than duration, and confirms that he also considers duration to be only one factor. L. Moir, 'The Concept of Non-International Armed Conflict', in A. Clapham, P. Gaeta and M. Sassòli (eds), *The 1949 Geneva Conventions: A Commentary* (Oxford: Oxford University Press, 2015) 410, para. 53; Sivakumaran, *supra* note 4, at 167–169.

[45] D. A. Lewis, 'The Notion of "Protracted Armed Conflict" in the Rome Statute and the Termination of Armed Conflicts Under International Law: An Analysis of Select Issues', 101 *International Review of the Red Cross* (2019) 1091, at 1099.

[46] Decision on the Confirmation of Charges, *Situation in the Democratic Republic of the Congo in the Case of The Prosecutor v. Thomas Lubanga Dyilo* (ICC-01/04-01/06), Pre-Trial Chamber I, 29 January 2007, §§ 7 and 8.

[47] *Lubanga* (Decision on the Confirmation of Charges) *supra* note 46, para. 7.

[48] *Ibid*, paras 9 and 227–237.

[49] *Ibid*, para. 9; Rome Statute, *supra* note 1.

FPLC.[50] The accused was also charged with the legal violation of employing these children to actively participate in the hostilities in the context of an armed conflict not of an international character.[51] These types of war crimes fall under Article 8(2)(e) category war crimes, as included in the Rome Statute. For this reason, it was necessary for Pre-Trial Chamber I to review the events that had occurred between 2 June 2003 and late December 2003 in order for the ICC to be able to exercise jurisdiction over these types of war crimes.[52] Such crimes must be committed in the type of conflict described in Article 8(2)(f) of its Statute.[53]

In its preliminary assessment of the existence and nature of the conflict in Ituri during the period applicable to the war crime charges, Pre-Trial Chamber I defined the requirements constituting an Article 8(2)(f)-type NIAC as follows: 'The Chamber notes that article 8(2)(f) of the Statute makes reference to "protracted armed conflict" between ... [organized armed group]. In the opinion of the Chamber, this focuses on the need for the armed groups in question to have the ability to plan and carry out military operations *for a prolonged period of time*.'[54]

In its factual assessment of the indicators of the notion of intensity, Pre-trial Chamber I treated protracted armed violence as the threshold of intensity and duration separately as a temporal element.[55] This represents a departure from the ICTY's approach that duration is but an element of 'protracted armed violence'.[56] The instructive part of paragraph 253 reads: 'In the instant case, the Chamber finds that an armed conflict of a certain degree of intensity *and extending from at least June 2003 to December 2003* existed in the territory of Ituri.'[57]

The use of the conjunction 'and' is significant as it demands the presence not only of protracted armed violence but also a temporal element which is that of duration. The word 'and' may be replaced by 'also', 'plus', 'together with', or 'in addition to'.[58] The Court's assessment in paragraph 235 of the notion of intensity in the view of this author supports the

[50] *Lubanga* (Decision on the Confirmation of Charges) *supra* note 46, paras 9 and 227–237.

[51] *Ibid.*

[52] *Lubanga* (*Decision on the Confirmation of Charges*) *supra* note 46, paras 227–229, read together with Rome Statute Arts 8(2)(e) and 8(2)(f).

[53] *Ibid.*

[54] *Lubanga* (*Decision on the Confirmation of Charges*) *supra* note 46, para. 234.

[55] *Ibid.*

[56] See note 40.

[57] *Lubanga* (*Decision on the Confirmation of Charges*) *supra* note 46, para. 235.

[58] M. O'Neill and E. Summers, *Collins English Thesaurus* (7th edn., Glasgow: HarperCollins, 2015) at 36.

interpretation that paragraph 234 demands *Tadic*-plus duration as the elements that must be satisfied to constitute a 'protracted armed conflict' under Article 8(2)(f) of the Rome Statute.

Sivakumaran has commented on paragraph 234 of *Lubanga* (Decision on Confirmation of Charges).[59] Sivakumaran cautions that even though a superficial reading of the *Lubanga* understanding of Article 8(2)(f) as articulated in paragraph 234 might suggest a threshold unique to an Article 8(2)(f)-type non-international armed conflict where duration is emphasized, this is not necessarily the case.[60] Sivakumaran suggests that the inclusion of the term 'prolonged' merely is a language error as the original French text of *Lubanga* (Decision on Confirmation of Charges), like the original French text of *Tadic*, refers to 'protracted' as *prolongée* and that *prolongée* in French often is interchangeable with duration.[61] Sivakumaran further argues that the *Tadic* formulation contains the temporal element of duration as part of the broader notion of protracted armed violence and that, therefore, there is no greater focus on duration by Pre-Trial Chamber I in *Lubanga*.[62] Sivakumaran considers the confusion caused by paragraph 234 to be the result of a poor translation.[63]

Hrnjaz and Popovic, on the other hand, maintain that it simply is not possible to conclude with certainty that Pre-Trial Chamber I in paragraph 234 of *Lubanga* (Decision on Confirmation of Charges) meant 'duration' to be interpreted as part of the intensity criterion or if duration in fact constitutes an independent criterion required to qualify a situation as an Article 8(2)(f)-type non-international armed conflict.[64] Vite, for example, interprets paragraph 234 as conferring a distinct meaning on Article 8(2)(f) by defining a specific threshold of applicability.[65] According to Vite, this threshold necessitates an additional temporal requirement:

> The ICC Pre-Trial Chamber … thus apparently wanted to confer a distinct meaning on this provision, defining a specific threshold of applicability. The Chamber made it clear that this threshold is characterized by two conditions: (a) the violence must achieve a certain intensity and be protracted; (b)

[59] Sivakumaran, *supra* note 4, at 195.
[60] *Ibid.*
[61] *Ibid.*
[62] *Ibid.*
[63] *Ibid.*
[64] Hrnjaz and Popović, *supra* note 30, at 15–17.
[65] Vite, *supra* note 6 at, 82.

an armed group with a 'degree of organisation', particularly the ability to 'plan and carry out military operations for a prolonged period of time' must be involved.[66]

Vite considers paragraph 234 to demand a stricter scope of application than the *Tadic* formula from situations if they are to equate to protracted armed conflict under Article 8(2)(f) of the Rome Statute.[67] As argued elsewhere, the author of this contribution aligns her view with Vite's interpretation that *Lubanga* (Decision on Confirmation of Charges) demands a *Tadic*-plus duration test to be met to satisfy Article 8(2)(f).[68]

In paragraph 506 of *Lubanga* (Judgment Pursuant to Article 74 of the Statute), Trial Chamber II confirmed that determining the nature of an armed conflict is a fundamental requirement of the charges under Articles 8(2)(b)(xxvi) and 8(2)(e)(vii) of the Rome Statute.[69] In paragraph 506, Trial Chamber II went further than demanding the *Tadic* formulation alone as being the correct assessment for the existence of an Article 8(2)(f)-type non-international armed conflict, as the final sentence of paragraph 506 reads: '*Additionally*, Article 8(2)(f) of the Statute stipulated that the conflict must be "protracted" for these purposes.'[70] The use and placement of the term 'additionally', in the view of this author, are significant; the adverb 'additionally' can be substituted by 'further', 'besides' or 'as well as'.[71] The placement of 'additionally' following the reference to the *Tadic* criteria suggests that an armed conflict under Article 8(2)(f) demands an extra criterion of protraction.[72] Therefore, an Article 8(2)(f)-type non-international armed conflict differs from a traditional non-international armed conflict as provided for in Article 8(2)(d) of the Rome Statute.

Vite draws a similar conclusion.[73] Vite interprets paragraph 506 as demanding that an Article 8(2)(f)-type conflict not only meets the threshold of intensity equivalent to protracted armed violence but that the

[66] *Ibid.*

[67] *Ibid.*

[68] Bradley, *supra* note 4, at 69–73.

[69] *Lubanga* (Judgment Pursuant to Article 74 of the Statute) *supra* note 17, paras 503 and 504.

[70] *Ibid*, para. 506.

[71] O'Neill and Summers, *supra* note 58, at 15.

[72] This author makes a similar argument in her article; Bradley, *supra* note 4, at 70–71.

[73] Vite, *supra* note 6, at 83.

violence furthermore should be protracted.[74] In its factual assessment of the existence of an Article 8(2)(f) protracted conflict, Trial Chamber II fails to explain or give content to its understanding of the meaning of 'protracted'.[75] Trial Chamber II, however, clarifies that a protracted armed conflict does not necessitate the threshold test associated with Additional Protocol II.[76]

Scholarly opinion was activated in response to the uncertainty created by Trial Chamber III by the wording of paragraph 506 of *Lubanga*.[77] Scholars such as Vite and the author of this contribution view paragraph 506 as necessitating a *Tadic*-plus duration construct.[78] On the other hand, Sivakumaran and Dinstein disagree with this view.[79] Hrnjaz and Popovic propose that there is merit in both views.[80] Hrnjaz and Popović comment on Trial Chamber I's interpretation of the elements necessary to equate a situation to an Article 8(2)(f)-type non-international armed conflict.[81] They interpret the reliance by Trial Chamber I on the *Mrškić* case as being aligned with the ICTY's approach in that duration forms part of the notion of intensity of which the minimum threshold test equals 'protracted armed violence'.[82] The author of this contribution holds a different opinion and finds that the language of paragraph 506 of *Lubanga* (Judgment) is in line with paragraph 234 (Confirmation), as well as the factual assessment of intensity as indicated by Trial Chamber I and Pre-Trial Chamber II, and that they clearly necessitate a *Tadic*-plus approach.

Katanga 2014 (Inconclusive)

The accused, Germain Katanga, served as a military leader in a predominantly Ngiti combatant group at the time that the alleged war crimes were

[74] *Ibid.*

[75] *Lubanga* (Judgment Pursuant to Article 74 of the Statute) *supra* note 17, para. 536.

[76] *Ibid.*

[77] Vite, *supra* note 6, at 82; Bradley, *supra* note 4, at 73; Dinstein, *supra* note 4, at 191; Sivakumaran, *supra* note 4, at 195; Sivakaumaran, *supra* note 5, at 378–379; Hrnjaz and Popović, *supra* note 30, at 16–17.

[78] Vite, *supra* note 6, at 82; Bradley, *supra* note 4, at 73.

[79] Dinstein, *supra* note 4, at 191; Sivakumaran, *supra* note 4, at 195; Sivakaumaran, *supra* note 5, at 378–379.

[80] Hrnjaz and Popović, *supra* note 30, at 16–17.

[81] *Ibid*, 17.

[82] *Ibid.*

committed.[83] This armed group is known as the *Force de Resistance Patriotique en Ituri* (FRPI).[84] Germain Katanga was the FRPI's most senior military commander at the time the alleged war crimes were committed during the attack on the Bogoro village.[85] Brigadier-General Katanga and other commanders of the FRPI and Front for National Integration (FNI) allegedly incurred individual criminal responsibility in the context of Article 25(3)(a) of the Rome Statute for the commission of war crimes owing to the fact that they agreed to a common plan to 'wipe out' Bogoro.[86] The accused was charged with various war crimes, including war crimes listed in Article 8(2)(e) of the Rome Statute.[87]

In pursuit of defining the term 'armed conflict not of an international character', Trial Chamber II, additionally, relied on the definition cited in Article 8(2)(f) of its Statute.[88] First, the Trial Chamber reflected that two categories of participants are considered parties to such a conflict.[89] The first category is if one of the fighting forces belongs to the state and the opposition forces represent one or more organized armed groups.[90] The second category is if organized armed groups fight one another without

[83] Trial Judgment, *Situation in the Democratic Republic of the Congo in the Case of The Prosecutor v. Germain Katanga* (ICC-01/04-01/07), Trial Chamber II, 7 March 2014, § 6.

[84] *Ibid.*

[85] *Ibid*, para. 12.

[86] *Ibid*, para. 33.

[87] *Ibid*, paras. 10, 24, 28, 30, 31 and 32. Germain Katanga was accused of various war crimes which included his facilitation of the use of children to actively participate in hostilities. This is a war crime under the Rome Statute in the context of international armed conflict (Art. 8(2)(b)(xxvi)) and armed conflict not of an international nature (Art. (8)(2)(e)(vii)). Germain Katanga was also charged with the commission of sexual slavery through others (Art. 25(3)(a)), which constitutes a war crime if committed during armed conflict, whether international (Art. 8(2)(b)(xxii)) or non-international in nature (Art. 8(2)(e)(vi). Further, the charges against him included the commission of rape through others (Art. 25(3)(a)) which is criminalized by the Rome Statute, whether this crime is committed during an armed conflict characterized as international (Art. 8(2)(b)(xxii)) or non-international (Art. 8(2)(e)(vi)). He also allegedly directed attacks against civilians, which constitutes a war crime when committed either during an international armed conflict (as codified in Art. 8(2)(b)(i) of the Rome Statute) or during a non-international armed conflict as stipulated in Art. 8(2)(e)(i) of the Rome Statute. Additionally, Germain Katanga was charged with pillage as well as the destruction of property, which are war crimes in the context of both international armed conflict (Arts 8(2)(b)(xvi) and 8(2)(b)(xiii)) and non-international armed conflict (Arts 8(2)(e)(v) and 8(2)(e)(xii)).

[88] *Katanga* (Trial Chamber) *supra* note 83, para. 1184.

[89] *Ibid.*

[90] *Ibid.*

the involvement of the governmental fighting forces.[91] The Trial Chamber then referred to the jurisprudence of Trial Chamber I and cited the *Lubanga* judgement.[92] In the *Lubanga* case, the Trial Chamber stated: 'Article 8(2)(f) of the Statute requires only the existence of a "protracted" conflict between "organized armed groups"'.[93] In so doing, Trial Chamber II emphasized that two essential threshold requirements determine whether or not a situation can be classed as 'an armed conflict not of an international character' in the ambit of Article 8(2)(f) of the Rome Statute.[94] The first criterion requires an armed group to be 'organized'; the second relates to the threshold of violence criterion which it terms a 'protracted conflict'.[95] The Trial Chamber listed a number of non-exhaustive factors that serve to aid in the assessment of whether or not a 'body' or non-state actor fighting force constitutes an organized armed group.[96] It pointed out that on its own none of the factors listed was singularly determinative.[97]

The second criterion emphasized by Trial Chamber II that must be satisfied in order to establish whether or not an Article 8(2)(f)-type armed conflict exists is the issue of whether or not the armed conflict is protracted.[98] In determining whether an armed conflict not of an international character existed or, rather, if the armed conflict it had to assess was protracted, Trial Chamber II found it imperative to consider its intensity since, in its view, Article 8(2)(f) prescribes that the violence must be more than sporadic or isolated:

In appraising the intensity of a potential conflict, the ICTY has held that the bench must have regard to, inter alia, the seriousness of attacks and potential increase in armed clashes; their spread over territory and over a period of time; the increase in the number of armed forces; the mobilization and the distribution of weapons among both parties to the conflict; as well as whether the conflict has attracted the attention of the UN Security Council and, if so, whether any resolutions on the matter

[91] *Ibid.*

[92] See *Lubanga* (Judgment Pursuant to Article 74 of the Statute) *supra* note 17, para. 536, as cited in *Katanga* (Trial Chamber) *supra* note 83, para. 1185.

[93] *Ibid.*

[94] *Katanga* (Trial Chamber) *supra* note 83, para. 203.

[95] *Ibid.*

[96] *Ibid.*

[97] *Ibid.*

[98] *Ibid.*

have been passed. This approach, in the view of the Chamber, is expedient, and so it will proceed.[99]

There is no explicit reference to the term 'protracted armed conflict' in paragraph 1187 of *Katanga*.[100] At first glance, this assessment seems to reflect the protracted armed violence threshold as the threshold employed in order to determine whether or not the threshold of violence in the situation before the Court had been satisfied in order to establish the existence of an organized armed conflict not of an international character under Article 8(2)(d) of the Rome Statute, in Common Article 3 and in customary international law.[101]

The Trial Chamber's analysis above suggests that there is no third threshold requirement that necessitates an Article 8(2)(f) conflict to be a 'protracted armed conflict'.[102] Should there be no additional criterion, the absence of such a requirement makes the second sentence included in Article 8(2)(f) of the Rome Statute redundant. Consequently, it is unclear whether all armed conflicts not of an international character essentially are a 'protracted armed conflict'.

An alternative argument is that the Trial Chamber included the indication that an armed conflict has to take place 'over a period of time' precisely to allude to the fact that the armed conflict must be 'protracted' in nature. This line of thinking may be supported by the tribunal's assessment of whether the facts before it are sufficient to meet the threshold requirements inherent in Article 8(2)(f) of its Statute.[103] However, when Trial Chamber II assessed whether the specific situation that took place at Bogoro on 24 February 2003 met the threshold requirement which determines if a situation is a 'protracted armed conflict' as included in Article 8(2)(f) of the Rome Statute, its response was positive.[104] In its assessment, the Trial Chamber specifically gave weight to the fact that the military operations were conducted over a protracted period.[105] Hence, Trial Chamber II reflected the interpretation of the term 'protracted armed conflict' previously given by Trial Chamber I in the *Lubanga* case.[106]

[99] *Katanga* (Trial Chamber) *supra* note 83, para. 1187.
[100] *Ibid.*
[101] *Ibid.*
[102] Rome Statute, *supra* note 1.
[103] See *Katanga* (Trial Chamber) *supra* note 83, paras 1209, 1217 and 1218.
[104] *Ibid.*
[105] *Ibid.*
[106] *Ibid.*

Whether *Katanga* demands a *Tadic*-plus formulation or merely necessitates the *Tadic* formulation is unclear.[107]

Bemba 2016 (Tadic-Plus)

In the *Bemba* case, the Prosecutor of the ICC under the terms of Article 28(a) of its Statute charged Mr Bemba with war crimes effectively in respect of his role as a military commander.[108] Mr Bemba is a national of the DRC.[109] He allegedly committed the crimes listed in the charges brought against him in the context of the hostilities that took place in the territory of the Central African Republic between 26 October 2002 and 15 March 2013.[110] The war crimes of rape and pillage, with which the accused was charged, require the existence of an armed conflict that meets the threshold requirements included in Article 8(2)(f) of the Rome Statute.[111]

In the evaluation by Pre-Trial Chamber III in *Bemba* Decision Pursuant to Article 61(7)(a) of whether the facts of this case satisfied these threshold requirements, the Chamber paid specific attention to the intensity of

[107] See Hrnjaz and Popović, *supra* note 30, who agree that *Katanga* is confusing. Hrnjaz and Popvic observe: 'The Trial Chamber in the *Katanga* case followed the approach of *Lubanga* Trial Chamber. It quoted Article 8(2)(F) and paragraph 70 of the *Tadic* judgment, and then the *Mrskic* and *Lubanga* cases, making the duration of the conflict part of the intensity criterion. It is interesting to note, however, that in the part of the Decision that dealt with the intensity of the conflict the Trial Chamber stated: "With specific reference to its foregoing review of the attacks that followed assault on Bogor, the Chamber finds that the armed conflict was both protracted and intense owing, inter alia, to its duration and the volume of attacks perpetrated throughout the territory of Ituri from January 2002 to May 2003." The statement that the conflict was both protracted and intense could prima facie suggest that the Trial Chamber considered the term "protracted" not as the part of the intensity criterion, but as an independent criterion for the existence of NIAC. Yet, the very next sentence of the Decision declares that in the Chamber's view, the evidence before it suffices to fulfil the intensity of the conflict requirement in the scope of intensity criterion.'

[108] Decision Pursuant to Article 61(7)(a) and (b) of the Rome Statute on the Charges of the Prosecutor Against Jean-Pierre Bemba Gombo, *Situation in the Central African Republic In the Case of the Prosecutor v. Jean-Pierre Bemba Gombo* (ICC-01/05-01/08), Pre-Trial Chamber II, 15 June 2009, § 2. These charges were brought in respect of the facilitation of the crimes against humanity of murder (Art. 7(1)(a)) and rape (Art. 7(1)(g)), and the war crimes of murder (Art. 8(2)(c)(i)), rape (Art. 8(2)(e)(vi)) and pillaging (Art.i (8)(2)(e)(v)) under the Rome Statute.

[109] *Ibid.*

[110] *Ibid.*

[111] *Ibid*, para. 127.

violence threshold and the protracted character of the conflict.[112] In its assessment, Pre-Trial Chamber II attended to the differentiating threshold requirements under Article 8(2)(d) and Article 8(2)(f), respectively.[113] Specifically, in paragraph 226, Pre-Trail Chamber II remarked:

> With respect to the contextual element of crimes enumerated in Article 8(2)(e) of the Statute, Article 8(2)(f), second sentence of the Statute *further adds* that [i]t applies to armed conflicts that take place in the territory of a State when there is protracted armed conflict between governmental authorities and organized armed groups or between such groups.

The emphasis in the above observation created by the adverbial phrase 'further adds' contributes a meaning of 'in addition', 'on top of', 'as well as'.[114] The use of the phrase 'further adds' may be construed as referencing an additional requirement of a 'protracted armed conflict' on top of *Tadic*.

In its factual assessment of the existence of a non-international armed conflict meeting the contextual requirements set out under Articles 8(2)(c) and (e) of the Rome Statute, Pre-Trial Chamber II explicitly acknowledges in paragraph 235 the possibility of Article 8(2)(f) establishing a different threshold from that in Article 8(2)(f). This author now enlarges upon the significance of paragraph 235 of *Bemba* Decision Pursuant to Article 61(7)(a):

> The Chamber is also mindful that the wording of Article 8(2)(f) of the Statute differs from that of Article 8(2) (d) of the Statute, which requires the existence of a 'protracted armed conflict' and thus *may* be seen to require a higher or additional threshold to be met—a necessity which is not set out in Article 8(2)(d) of the Statute. The argument can be raised as to whether this requirement may nevertheless be applied also in the context of Article 8(2)(d) of the Statute. However, irrespective of such a possible interpretative approach, the Chamber does not deem it necessary to address this argument, as the period in question covers approximately five months and is therefore to be regarded as 'protracted' in any event.[115]

[112] *Ibid*, paras. 137–140.

[113] *Ibid*, paras. 225 and 226.

[114] *Collins English Thesaurus*, *supra* note 58.

[115] *Bemba* (Decision Pursuant to Article 61(7)(a) and (b) of the Rome Statute) *supra* note 108, para. 235.

The selection of a modality 'may' by Pre-Trial Chamber II is noted in that its use is to indicate the possibility that Article 8(2)(f) demands a different or additional threshold from that in Article 8(2)(e).[116] This choice of verb may indicate that the Court has adopted a cautious approach in an effort to evade directly indicating in its understanding that 'protracted armed conflict' demands *Tadic*-plus duration as the minimum threshold in the requirements under Article 8(2)(f).[117] Pre-Trial Chamber II adds in paragraph 235 a defence of its choice not to pursue an examination of the possibility of a higher threshold being created in Article 8(2)(f).[118] Pre-Trial Chamber II merely asserts that owing to the duration of the conflict, approximately five months, clearly an Article 8(2)(f) protracted armed conflict exists.[119] If protraction is met in terms of Article 8(2)(f), the Article 8(2)(c) conflict exists and no further analysis into the interpretive conundrum is demanded. Pre-Trial Chamber II has attempted to avoid giving content to the construct 'protracted armed conflict', as included in Article 8(2)(f) by declaring that approximately five months satisfies the minimum temporal requirement needed to equate to protraction.[120] The wording 'as the period in question covers approximately five months and is therefore to be regarded as "protracted" in any event' nevertheless is suggestive of an interpretation that Pre-Trial Chamber II took 'duration' into account separately from 'protracted armed violence' in its assessment of determining whether the situation in Ituri constituted an Article 8(2)(f)-type non-international armed conflict.[121]

At the trial stage in *Bemba* (Judgment pursuant to Article 74 of the Statute), Trial Chamber III attempted to supply content to the phrase 'protracted armed conflict',[122] resulting in the distinctive phrasing noted in the second and third sentences of paragraph 139: 'When assessing whether an armed conflict not of an international armed character was protracted, however, 'different' chambers of this court emphasizes the

[116] *Ibid*; O'Neill and Summers, *supra* note 71, at 482.

[117] *Bemba* (Decision Pursuant to Article 61(7)(a) and (b) of the Rome Statute) *supra* note 108, para. 235.

[118] *Ibid.*

[119] *Ibid.*

[120] *Ibid.*

[121] *Ibid.*

[122] Judgment pursuant to Article 74 of the Statute, *Situation in the Central African Republic in the Case of The Prosecutor v Jean-Pierre Bemba Gombo* (ICC-01/05-01/08), Trial Chamber III, 21 March 2016, § 139.

duration of the violence as a relevant factor. This corresponds to the approach taken by the Chambers of the ICTY.'[123]

Trial Chamber III reiterated Pre-Trial Chamber II's conclusion that Article 8(2)(f) through the formulation in the second sentence[124] demands, in addition to the threshold established under Article 8(2)(c), the existence of a 'protracted armed conflict'. Trial Chamber III reports that Pre-Trial Chamber II did not find it necessary to examine further a possible distinction of threshold owing to the temporal scope of the situation before it; it determined that the period of almost five months was 'protracted'.[125] In response, Trial Chamber III reflects that raising the possibility of a distinction in the terms of Articles 8(2)(d) and 8(2)(f) would be significant in the current case only if the conflict before it had not been protracted, which has not been disputed.[126] Trial Chamber III on this occasion missed an opportunity, perhaps intentionally, in 2016 to clarify this interpretive conundrum.

An alternative reading of paragraph 139 of *Bemba* (Judgment pursuant to Article 74 of the Statute) in the view of this author in the light of the wording '***different chambers of this court emphasizes the duration of the violence as a relevant factor***, specifically the term 'emphasizes', suggests that 'duration' is a separate requirement additional to the *Tadic* threshold.[127] Trial Chamber III declares that different chambers of this court have ***emphasized*** duration of violence as a relevant factor in assessing whether an armed conflict not of an international character is protracted.[128] This reading places the declaration to be in line with the understanding that Article 8(2)(f) demands *Tadic*-plus duration and indicates that 'duration' is a separate requirement.[129] If it is accepted that the Court stated that duration was assessed in determining whether a non-international armed conflict existed, then it entails that duration formed part of the assessment of the notion of intensity, in which case the sentence would read 'when assessing if the notion of intensity of an armed conflict has been met, different chambers of this Court emphasized the duration of violence as a

[123] *Ibid.*
[124] *Ibid.*
[125] *Ibid.*
[126] *Ibid.*
[127] *Ibid.*
[128] *Ibid.*
[129] *Ibid.*

relevant factor'.[130] This corresponds with the approach taken by the ICTY.[131]

The deliberation by Trial Chamber II that in its approach, as explained in paragraph 139 of *Bemba* (Judgment pursuant to Article 74 of the Statute), it followed that of the ICTY adds to the confusion in that an emphasis on 'duration' as not in line with ICTY practice.[132] ICTY case law reports 'duration' as but one factor indicative of the existence of protracted armed violence.[133] The ICTY intended to avoid a situation where an overemphasis on 'duration' would be counterproductive and preclude conflicts that in a short time become protracted from the protective scope of the law of non-international armed conflict.[134]

In support of the view that *Bemba* (Judgment Pursuant to Article 74 of the Statute) interprets Article 8(2)(f) to demand *Tadic*-plus duration, this author examines paragraphs 662 and 663 of the decision where Trial Chamber III specifically assesses the 'intensity threshold and protracted character of the conflict'.[135] It is of interest to note that this is the phrase which is the heading of the conflict classification part of the judgement rather than a simple reference to the notion of intensity or protracted armed violence.[136] The conclusion is that the heading pre-empts a *Tadic*-plus duration approach as essentially that means protracted armed violence plus duration.

In paragraph 662, Trial Chamber III assesses the facts of the situation in Ituri between 26 October 2002 and late February 2003.[137] The *Haradinaj* factors are employed to assess the facts holistically.[138] On this basis, the Court stated that the intensity threshold exceeding 'situations of internal disturbances and tensions, such as riots, isolated and sporadic acts of violence and other acts of a similar nature' had been met.[139] The assessment of the classification of the conflict does not end there;[140] after con-

[130] *Ibid.*
[131] *Haradinaj*, *supra* note 35, para. 49.
[132] *Bemba* (Judgment pursuant to Article 74 of the Statute) *supra* note 122, para. 139.
[133] *Bemba*, *supra* note 122, para. 139; *Haradinaj*, *supra* note 35, para. 49.
[134] *Haradinaj*, *supra* note 35, para. 49.
[135] *Bemba* (Judgment pursuant to Article 74 of the Statute) *supra* note 122.
[136] *Ibid*, para. 329.
[137] *Ibid*, para. 662.
[138] *Ibid.*
[139] *Ibid*, para. 663.
[140] *Ibid.*

firming that the notion of intensity has been met under Articles 8(2)(d) and (f), Trial Chamber III comments that the duration requirement that constitutes a protracted armed conflict under Article 8(2)(f) also has been fulfilled.

In the view of this author, paragraph 663 can only be construed in a manner similar to Pre-Trial Chamber II in *Bemba* [Decision Pursuant to Article 61(7)(a) and (b)].[141] Trial Chamber III confirmed the definition of protracted armed conflict as requiring *Tadic*-plus duration:

> In light of the above, the Chamber finds beyond reasonable doubt that the armed conflict reached a sufficient level of intensity for purposes of Articles 8(2)(d) and 8(2)(f), namely, one exceeding 'situations of internal disturbances and tensions, such as riots, isolated and sporadic acts of violence or other acts of a similar nature'. On the basis of the length of the armed conflict, namely more than four and a half months, and the regular hostilities, the Chamber also finds beyond reasonable doubt that the armed conflict was 'protracted' within the meaning of Article 8(2)(f).[142]

The final sentence in paragraph 663 confirms that this Trial Chamber as well as the Pre-Trial Chamber in *Bemba* differentiated an Article 8(2)(d)-type non-international armed conflict necessitating the *Tadic* formula and an Article 8(2)(f)-type non-international armed conflict which demands *Tadic*-plus duration. Paragraph 663 of *Bemba* (Judgment Pursuant to Article 74), as does *Bemba* (Decision Pursuant to Article 61(7)(a) and (b)), confirms four and a half months as a sufficient length of time to fulfil the temporal threshold requirement demanded by a definition of 'protracted' in 'protracted armed violence'. Lewis interprets *Bemba* as confirming that 'protracted armed conflict', as included in Article 8(2)(f) of the Rome Statute, constitutes a unique category of non-international armed conflict[143] and agrees that according to *Bemba*, under Article 8(2)(f), a protracted non-international armed conflict apparently, at a minimum, lasts five months.[144]

141 *Ibid*, para. 235.
142 *Ibid*, para. 663.
143 Lewis, *supra* note 45.
144 *Ibid*.

Al Mahdi 2016 (Tadic-Plus)

Mr Ahmad Al Faqi Al Mahdi, the accused, is a Mali national.[145] The Prosecutor of the ICC charged him with the commission of the war crime of attacking objects protected under Article 8(2)(e)(iv) of the Rome Statute.[146] A plea agreement was reached and the accused tendered an admission of guilt.[147] This war crime was committed in the context of the non-international armed conflict that took place during the period in question between the Malian government and organized armed groups.[148]

In the *Al Mahdi* case (Judgment and Sentencing) the only confirmed charge referred to the war crime of attacking cultural property which is codified under Article 8(2)(e)(iv) of the Rome Statute.[149] This case is unique in that Trial Chamber VIII exclusively had to determine the existence of a protracted armed conflict under Article 8(2)(f).[150] This article determines the scope of application, that is, the type of non-international armed conflict in which the kind of war crimes listed in Article 8(2)(e) of the Rome Statute must be committed to fulfil the contextual requirement of the existence of this specific category of non-international armed conflict. Indeed, in *Lubanga*,[151] *Katanga*,[152] *Bemba*,[153] *Ntaganda*[154] and *Ongwen*[155] charges were confirmed under Articles 8(2)(c) and (e). Trial Chamber VIII, therefore, had a unique opportunity to specifically assess

[145] Judgment and Sentence, *Situation in the Republic of Mali in the Case of the Prosecutor v. Ahmad Al Faqi Al Mahdi* (ICC-01/12-01/15), Trial Chamber VIII, 27 September 2016, § 9.

[146] *Ibid*, para. 2.

[147] *Ibid*, paras. 3 and 7.

[148] *Ibid*, para. 45.

[149] *Ibid*.

[150] *Ibid*, para. 11.

[151] *Lubanga* (Judgment Pursuant to Article 74 of the Judgment) *supra* note 17; *Lubanga* (Decision on the Confirmation of Charges, Pre-Trial Chamber I) *supra* note 46.

[152] *Katanga* (Trial Chamber) *supra* note 83.

[153] *Bemba* (Decision Pursuant to Article 61(7)(a) and (b) of the Rome Statute) *supra* note 108; *Bemba* (Judgment pursuant to Article 74 of the Statute) *supra* note 122.

[154] Warrant of Arrest, *Situation in the Democratic Republic of the Congo in the Case of the Prosecutor v. Bosco Ntaganda* (ICC-01/04-02/06-2), Pre-Trial Chamber I, 24 August 2006; Decision Pursuant to Article 61(7)(a) and (b) of the Rome Statute on the Charges of the Prosecutor Against Bosco Ntaganda, *Situation in the Democratic Republic of the Congo in the Case of the Prosecutor v. Bosco Ntaganda* (ICC-01/04-02/06), Pre-Trial Chamber II, 9 June 2014; *Ntaganda* (Judgment) *supra* note 11.

[155] *Ongwen* (Trial Judgment) *supra* note 18.

the content and definition of an Article 8(2)(f)-type protracted non-international armed conflict.[156]

In *Al Mahdi* (Judgment and Sentence), Trial Chamber VIII assessed whether or not the situation before it constituted a non-international armed conflict.[157] Interestingly, the opening lines of paragraph 49 refer to the existence of a non-international armed conflict without reference to protracted armed conflict or to Article 8(2)(f).[158] This omission could be construed as suggesting that the Court considered a non-international armed conflict to be the same as a protracted armed conflict, in other words, Article 8(2)(f) necessitates merely the *Tadic* formula.[159] The assessment of the organizational degree and intensity threshold by Trial Chamber VIII, however, is superficial when compared to other decisions concerned with conflict classification before the ICC.[160] It could be that the situation in Mali was clear-cut or that because of the guilty plea, Trial Chamber VIII did not deem it necessary to interrogate the elements of Article 8(2)(f). The instructive part of paragraph 49, where Trial Chamber VII assesses intensity, reads as follows:

> With respect to the requirement that the armed violence must meet a certain minimum level of intensity to be distinguished from mere internal disturbances and tensions, the Chamber notes that the facts that these groups exercised control over such a large part of Mali *for such a protracted period*—with the resulting effect on the civilian population concerned—clearly demonstrates a sufficient degree of intensity of the conflict.[161]

Trial Chamber VIII considered territorial control over a large part of territory for a lengthy period as sufficient evidence that the intensity threshold equated with the minimum threshold of protracted armed violence.[162] The phrasing 'must meet a certain minimum level of intensity to be distinguished from mere internal disturbances and tensions' equates to the minimum threshold of protracted armed violence which is demanded from a

[156] *Al Mahdi* (Judgment and Sentence) *supra* note 145.
[157] *Ibid*, para. 49.
[158] *Ibid*.
[159] *Ibid*.
[160] *Ibid*.
[161] Para. 49 (emphasis added).
[162] *Ibid*.

traditional non-international armed conflict.[163] The wording used in paragraph 49, in the view of this author, does not distinguish between a traditional non-international armed conflict and a protracted armed conflict, even though, for purposes of this specific case, the situation under assessment indeed meets the threshold test inherent in Article 8(2)(f) of the Rome Statue.[164]

The assessment of the situation in Mali by Trial Chamber VIII uses the phrasing associated with the description of the scope of application of Additional Protocol II.[165] Duration and territorial control are constitutive requirements under Article 1(1) of Additional Protocol II.[166] The drafting history of Article 8(2)(f) reveals that the threshold of Additional Protocol II was removed from the final formulation of Article 8(2)(f) by the Sierra Leone compromise of 'protracted armed conflict', which may or may not demand an additional temporal requirement.[167] The use of Additional Protocol II-style language in paragraph 49 with its emphasis on territorial control and duration suggests that Trial Chamber VIII considered a non-international armed conflict in the context of Article 8(2)(f) to demand a temporal requirement and thought it correct to explicitly emphasize duration.[168]

The absence of reference to Article 8(2)(f) in paragraph 49 may be justified in that logically Article 8(2)(f) determines the scope of application (existence of a non-international armed conflict) for charges under Article 8(2)(e) of the Rome Statute and that Trial Chamber VII, therefore, merely refers to 'an armed conflict not of an international character'.[169] It is the opinion of the author that paragraph 49 of the *Al Mahdi* case does not provide clarity with respect to whether or not Article 8(2)(f) demands a different threshold criterion or additional elements than does Article 8(2)(d). The explicit mention of duration seemingly elevates duration as a

[163] *Ibid.*

[164] *Ibid.*

[165] Geneva Protocol II Additional to the Geneva Conventions of 12 August 1949, and Relating to the Protection of Victims of Non-International Armed Conflict (adopted 8 June 1977, entered into force 7 December 1978) 1125 UNTS 609 (Additional Protocol II), Art. 1(1).

[166] *Ibid.* For an examination of the duration requirement inherent in Art. 1(1) of Additional Protocol II, see Bradley, *supra* note 28, at 14–26.

[167] *Al Mahdi* (Judgment and Sentence) *supra* note 145, para. 49.

[168] *Ibid.*

[169] *Ibid.*

factor, but the manner in which the instructive part of paragraph 49 is phrased refers to prolonged territorial control rather than the intensity of the fighting.[170] This author views *Al Mahdi* as adding to the confusion surrounding the 'protracted armed conflict' interpretive conundrum. Trial Chamber VIII missed an opportunity to address the elements demonstrated by a 'protracted armed conflict' perspective.

Ntaganda 2019 (Tadic)

An arrest warrant for Bosco Ntaganda was issued by Pre-Trial Chamber I on 22 August 2006.[171] Mr Ntaganda was believed to have occupied the position of Deputy Chief of General Staff for Military Operations of the FPLC at the time that the alleged crimes were committed in the region of Ituri, Uganda.[172] Owing to his position as a high-ranking official, the accused was charged with criminal liability under Article 25(3)(a) of the Rome Statute for the commission of war crimes related to the enlistment,[173] conscription[174] and use[175] of children under the age of 15 years to actively participate in hostilities.[176]

Pre-Trial Chamber I, in its opinion, asserted that the ICC had jurisdiction to prosecute Mr Ntaganda for the commission of the crimes listed above.[177] These crimes are categorized as crimes against humanity and war crimes, which allegedly were committed between June 2002 and December 2003.[178] Some of the war crimes that Mr Ntaganda allegedly committed are listed under Article 8(2)(e) of the Rome Statute and, thus, the Pre-Trial Chamber had to determine whether at the time an Article 8(2)(f)-type armed conflict existed in Ituri.[179] It found that reasonable grounds existed to believe that a protracted armed conflict had taken place in Ituri from July 2002 to December 2003.[180]

[170] *Ibid.*
[171] *Ntaganda* (Warrant of Arrest) *supra* note 154, at 2.
[172] *Ibid*, at 5.
[173] Rome Statute, *supra* note, Arts 8(2)(b)(xxvi) and 8(2)(e)(vii).
[174] *Ibid*, Arts 8(2)(b)(xxvi) and 8(2)(e)(vi).
[175] *Ibid.*
[176] *Ntaganda* (Warrant of Arrest) *supra* note 154, at 5.
[177] *Ibid*, at 2.
[178] *Ibid.*
[179] *Ibid.*
[180] *Ibid.*

Pre-Trial Chamber I specifically uses the term 'protracted armed conflict', which is specific to Article 8(2)(f) of the Rome Statute.[181] The arrest warrant does not reveal much information concerning the factors that Pre-Trial Chamber I considered in arriving at its conclusion, but does reveal a time frame.[182] It explicitly mentions that the situation, which the Pre-Trial Chamber believed to be an assessment based on 'reasonable grounds', occurred between June 2002 and December 2003.[183] This situation lasted for a period of approximately 18 months. The duration of this situation, which was considered to be a 'protracted armed conflict', is in line with previous decisions of the courts as well as with the literal interpretation of the provision that considers the general understanding of the term 'protracted' to imply that an armed conflict is not short-lived.[184] It should be noted that 'duration' is not emphasized so as not to support a conclusion that it is a separate element in addition to protracted armed violence.[185]

In *Ntaganda* (Decision Pursuant to Articles 61(7)(a) and (b) of the Rome Statute), the Pre-Trial Chamber confirmed that the situation described in the arrest warrant was an Article 8(2)(f)-type armed conflict.[186] In order to reach this conclusion, the Pre-Trial Chamber assessed the organisational and intensity thresholds related to the situation that had taken place in Ituri between June 2002 and December 2003.[187] In its assessment, the Pre-Trial Chamber specifically highlights the ability of the UPC and FPLC to carry out military operations over a prolonged period.[188] It also indicated that the fighters owned heavy weaponry, which included rocket launchers, mortars and grenade launchers.[189] The nature of these weapons contributes to a high degree of violence, and they were used during multiple and frequent attacks that occurred for the duration of the conflict.[190] This assessment did not place too great an emphasis on the fact that the situation had been prolonged in nature in order to con-

[181] *Ibid.*

[182] *Ibid.*

[183] *Ibid.*

[184] *Lubanga* (Judgment Pursuant to Article 74 of the Statute) *supra* note 17, paras 563 and 567; *Katanga* (Trial Judgment) *supra* note 83, paras 1209, 1217 and 1218.

[185] *Ntaganda* (Warrant of Arrest) *supra* note 154, at 5.

[186] *Ntaganda* (Pre-Trial) *supra* note154, para. 17.

[187] *Ibid.*

[188] *Ibid.*

[189] *Ibid.*

[190] *Ibid*, at 24–30.

clude that a protracted armed conflict had existed in Ituri at the time when the crimes with which Mr Ntaganda was charged had been committed, but 'duration' was treated to be a factor as per the approach followed by the ICTY in general.[191] The above may be interpreted as revealing that Pre-Trial Chamber I and Pre-Trial Chamber II considered protracted armed violence the correct threshold constituting an Article 8(2)(f)-type armed conflict.[192]

The Trial Chamber's assessment of 'protracted armed violence' and the relationship between duration and protracted armed violence in *Ntaganda* (Judgment) is now the focus.[193] A close reading of paragraphs 701 to 703 of *Ntaganda* (Judgment) suggests that Trial Chamber VI considered there to be a single type of non-international armed conflict for war crimes committed under Articles 8(2)(c) and (e);[194] an interpretation that is supported by the wording of paragraph 701 and the specific reference to the construct 'armed conflict not of an international character' rather than referencing the distinction between an 'armed conflict not of an international character' and 'protracted armed conflict' as found in the text of Articles 8(2)(c) and (f):

> Although paragraphs (2)(d) and (f) of Article 8 provide some guidance, the Court's legal framework does not define the term 'armed conflict not of an international character' as referred to in paragraphs (2)(c) and (e). However, noting that paragraph 2(e) and the elements of crimes explicitly refer to 'the established framework of the international law of armed conflict', the Chamber adopts the definition of 'armed conflict not of an international character' introduced by the ICTY Appeals Chamber in 1995, which has since been accepted by states as authoritative and has become part of state practice. Therefore, it will consider that such a conflict exists in case of 'protracted armed violence between governmental authorities and organized armed groups or between such groups within a state.[195]

Paragraph 701 specifically employs 'armed conflict not of an international character' as the singular type of conflict of application to war crimes committed under Articles 8(2)(c) and (e), and then cites the *Tadic* formula as

[191] *Ibid.*
[192] *Ibid*; Rome Statute, *supra* note 1, Art. 8(2)(f).
[193] *Ntaganda* (Judgment) *supra* note 11, paras 701–703.
[194] *Ibid.*
[195] *Ibid*, para. 701.

the correct test for Article 8(2)(d) and 8(2)(f)-type non-international armed conflicts.[196] At this juncture, no additional temporal requirement is mentioned.[197] Paragraph 703 confirms that this two-prong test determines the existence of a non-international armed conflict under Articles 8(2)(c) to (f):

> In order to distinguish situations of internal disturbances and tensions, such as riots, isolated and sporadic acts of violence, or other acts of a similar nature from a non-international armed conflict, (i) at least two organized armed groups need to have been involved in (ii) armed violence of a certain intensity.[198]

The Trial Chamber's assessment of the intensity confirms this preliminary assessment that Trial Chamber VI in *Ntaganda* interprets Article 8(2)(f) to refer to a traditional non-international armed conflict and not to a protracted armed conflict demanding *Tadic*-plus as an additional temporal requirement.[199] In the assessment of the intensity threshold of the situation in Ituri between July 2002 and January 2003, Trial Chamber VI clearly followed the same approach as Pre-Trial Chambers I and II in not emphasizing duration or treating it as a separate element.[200] The Chamber considered the frequency of attacks, the involvement of the UN and the European Union, the conclusion of cease-fire agreements, as well as the type of weapons used during the attacks.[201] It is clear that in *Ntaganda*, an Article 8(2)(f)-type conflict was interpreted as being similar to that of a traditional non-international armed conflict and that the *Tadic* test is the correct assessment method.

Ongwen 2021 (Tadic-Plus)

At the time of writing, the most recent case relating to an adjudication of the enlistment of child soldiers and, consequently, the classification of a non-international armed conflict under Article 8(2)(f) of the Rome Statute is *The Situation in Uganda In the Case of the Prosecutor v. Dominic*

[196] *Ibid.*
[197] *Ibid.*
[198] *Ibid*, para. 703.
[199] *Ibid*, paras 720–722.
[200] *Ibid.*
[201] *Ibid*, paras 720–724.

Ongwen, decided on 4 February 2021.[202] The accused, Dominic Ongwen, was charged with over 90 counts of war crimes as well as crimes against humanity committed as a member of the Lord's Resistance Army (LRA)[203] allegedly committed in Northern Uganda between 1 July 2002 and 31 December 2005.[204] These charges include using children under the age of 15 years to actively participate in hostilities as a war crime (Article 8(2)(e)(vii)) and conscription of children under the age of 15 into an armed group as a war crime.[205] Dominic Ongwen entered the ranks of the LRA unwillingly at first as an abducted child soldier.[206] During the period covered by the charges, Ongwen was 24 to 27 years old.[207]

As the crimes are listed in Article 8(2)(e) of the Rome Statute, Article 8(2)(f) determines the threshold test of the type of conflict that must exist at the time of the charges which requires that there is a 'protracted armed conflict'. In order to assess whether the contextual elements of war crimes have been met, Trial Chamber IX set out to consider the classification of the situation as a non-international armed conflict.[208] First, it assessed the organizational criteria of the LRA and found that its fighting force constituted an organized armed group.[209] In the context of this contribution, Trial Chamber IX's assessment of intensity throughout the period of the charges is significant as is notable by the formulation in paragraph 2810: 'Accordingly, the military conflict was of such intensity that surpassed the threshold required by the contextual elements of war crimes. It was also protracted in nature, noting that it spanned the entire period relevant to the charges, i.e., 1 July 2002 to 31 December 2005.'[210]

In the view of this author, the final sentence introduces a dual requirement that goes further than 'protracted armed violence' as represented by the wording 'it was *also* protracted in nature'.[211] The adverb 'also' is synonymous with 'and', 'too', 'further', 'plus', 'in addition', 'additionally',

[202] *Ongwen* (Judgment) *supra* note 18.
[203] *Ibid*, para. 32; Confirmation Decision at 71–104.
[204] *Ibid*, para. 1.
[205] *Ibid*, para. 36.
[206] *Ibid*, para. 27.
[207] *Ibid*, para. 31.
[208] *Ibid*, paras 2807–2809.
[209] *Ibid*.
[210] *Ibid*, para. 2810.
[211] *Ibid*.

and 'as well as'.[212] The *Collins English Thesaurus* defines the term 'also' as 'in addition'.[213] Paragraph 2810 of *Ongwen* thus can be read in a manner so as to interpret the threshold of an Article 8(2)(f)-type armed conflict as demanding intensity plus duration, in which duration is seen as a separate requirement. The latter part of the final sentence of paragraph 2810 clarifies what Trial Chamber IX means with protraction as it refers to a specific lengthy period, namely, 31 months (from 1 July 2002 to 31 December 2005). Trial Chamber IX may be construed as supporting confirmation of a three-element test of *Tadic*-plus duration.[214]

There is a need for caution in that in paragraph 2811, the Court's classification of the conflict is a reduction to 'not of an international character'.[215] It may be argued that this suggests a singular category of non-international armed conflict under the Rome Statute. In the view of this author, reading paragraph 2811 in the context of paragraph 2810 is misleading.[216] Paragraph 2811, if read in the context of the sequence of the argument, serves as a prelude to paragraph 2812 that relates to the discussion that there had been no internationalization of the conflict.[217] The reference to non-international armed conflict as a single concept in paragraph 2811 is not concerned with the classification of the conflict under Article 8(2)(e) and Article 8(2)(f) but, rather, with the question of the internationalization of the conflict.[218] This author interprets *Ongwen* to consider an Article 8(2)(f)-type conflict to be different from a traditional armed conflict and to demand *Tadic*-plus duration as its assessment test.

6.4 Conclusion

This chapter offers a comprehensive overview of the contribution of the International Criminal Court either in demystifying or in creating greater confusion surrounding the definition under Article 8(2)f of the Rome Statute of the notion of 'protracted armed conflict'. It provides an in-depth analysis of the *Lubanga*, *Katanga*, *Bemba*, *Al Mahdi*, *Ntaganda*

[212] *Collins English Thesaurus*, *supra* note 58, at 31.
[213] *Ibid.*
[214] *Ongwen*, *supra* note18, para. 2810.
[215] *Ongwen*, *supra* note 18.
[216] *Ibid.*
[217] *Ibid.*
[218] *Ibid.*

and *Ongwen* cases. This examination of case law is needed owing to the interpretative conundrum that arises from the inclusion of the second sentence of Article 8(2)(f) of the Rome Statute which introduced as an addition the notion of 'protracted armed violence' to the wording in Article 8(2)(d) of the Rome Statute. The consequence is the possibility that a different category of non-international armed conflict is presented in Article 8(2)(f).

The rules of treaty interpretation proved inconclusive as a technique in clarifying the elements required to constitute an Article 8(2)(f)-type non-international armed conflict. The relevant cases of the ICC are interpreted in order to determine, as is the case for Article 8(2)d, whether fulfilling the determinations of the *Tadic* formula alone satisfies the demands for the existence of an Article 8(2)(f)-type non-international armed conflict or whether an additional temporal requirement was introduced owing to the inclusion of the wording 'protracted armed violence'. These cases are considered in chronological order from the first case of *Lubanga* in 2012 to the most recent case of *Ongwen* decided in 2021.

An examination of *Lubanga* (Decision on the Confirmation of Charges) and *Lubanga* (Judgment Pursuant to Article 74 of the Statute) reveals that Pre-Trial Chamber I and Trial Chamber II understand the criteria for the existence of an Article 8(2)(f)-type non-international armed conflict to incorporate a demand that the situation assessed fulfils the *Tadic* formula plus a temporal element. Further evidence in support is provided by an assessment of the facts. It is noted that scholars offer various interpretations of these decisions, but the author of this contribution is of the opinion that *Lubanga* supports a *Tadic*-plus duration approach. An examination of the *Katanga* case did not prove helpful since it is unclear from the interpretation of the notion of intensity by Trial Chamber II as well as its assessment of the facts whether or not 'duration' was considered an element additional to the *Tadic* formula.

In the *Al Mahdi* case (Judgment and Sentencing), the only confirmed charge was brought under Article 8(2)(e)(iv) of the Rome Statute which makes this case unique. Trial Chamber VIII had to determine exclusively the existence of a protracted armed conflict under Article 8(2)(f) of the Rome Statute. The emphasis on duration in the factual assessment of the situation in Mali for the period of the charges may be considered indicative of the fact that Trial Chamber VIII followed a *Tadic*-plus duration approach. However, the Chamber did not explicitly engage in examining the definition of 'protracted armed violence'. In the view of this author, the *Al Mahdi* case is a missed opportunity to provide clarification of the notion of 'intensity' as demanded under Article 8(2)(f) of the Rome Statute.

In *Ntaganda* (Decision Pursuant to Articles 61(7)(a) and (b) of the Rome Statute) and *Ntaganda* (Judgment), Pre-Trial Chamber II and Trial Chamber VI interpret Article 8(2)(f) as demanding a situation to satisfy the *Tadic* formula in order to be classified as a non-international armed conflict under this provision. An analysis of the language used (the reference to non-international armed conflict, in general, and no explicit reference to protracted armed conflict) clearly indicated that in *Ntaganda*, non-international armed conflicts under Articles 8(2)(d) and (f) were regarded as belonging to the same category of non-international armed conflict in that the *Tadic* formula was found applicable under both provisions. Furthermore, in the assessment of the intensity threshold of the situation in Ituri between July 2002 and January 2003, Pre-Trial Chamber II and Trial Chamber VI clearly followed the same approach in treating 'duration' as no more than one indicator of 'protracted armed violence'. *Ntaganda* clearly supports an interpretation that an Article 8(2)(f)-type conflict is similar in type to a traditional non-international armed conflict and that the *Tadic* test is the correct method of assessment.

A close reading of paragraph 2810 of *The Situation in Uganda In the Case of the Prosecutor v. Dominic Ongwen* reveals that Trial Chamber IX in this case understands a protracted armed conflict under Article 8(2) of the Rome Statute to exist if the *Tadic* formula plus an additional temporal element is fulfilled. This interpretation is further supported in the analysis of the assessment by Trial Chamber IX of the situation in Northern Uganda between 1 July 2002 and 31 December 2005. This most recent case can thus be aligned with the conclusions in *Lubanga* and *Bemba*.

Regrettably, the analysis of the case law of the ICC has not resulted in 'demystifying' the notion of 'protracted armed conflict'. Rather, the differing interpretations produced have occluded the understanding of the relationship between 'protracted armed violence' and 'duration' in respect of an Article 8(2)(f)-type non-international armed conflict. In the context of the broader theme in this publication relating to the recruitment and enlistment of child soldiers as a war crime, a question arises as to whether the interpretative conundrum posed by the ambiguity inherent in Article 8(2)(f) of the Rome Statute creates an obstacle to prosecution. In the view of this author, the recruitment and enlistment of children into organized armed groups is not a spontaneous event and is a phenomenon associated with armed conflicts of some longevity. On the other hand, other types of war crimes may fail prosecution under the higher threshold (*Tadic*-plus duration) if committed at the outset of a conflict.

Acknowledgement Author would like to thank the anonymous reviewers for their valuable input on this chapter. She would also like to thank Ondřej Svaček, Martin Faix and Jessie Phyffer for comments on earlier drafts.

CHAPTER 7

The International Criminal Court and the Protection of Child Soldiers against Intra-Party Violence

Gus Waschefort

7.1 Introduction

Equal to the horrors suffered by children conditioned and exploited to perpetrate horrific violence on their battlefield adversaries is the violence they themselves endure often at the hands of their commanders and comrades.[1] The *Ntaganda* case of the International Criminal Court (ICC)

[1] This reality is illustrative of the hypocrisy in the fact that Art. 38 of the Convention on the Rights of the Child (CRC), which prohibits the recruitment and use of children younger than fifteen for direct participation in hostilities, is the only prevision of the CRC that provides for a lower-age threshold for protection than younger than eighteen. Indeed, Art. 6(2) compels states "to the maximum extent possible the survival and development of the child [younger than eighteen]". Yet, these states can lawfully use fifteen-year-olds for direct participation in hostilities.

G. Waschefort (✉)
Essex Law School and Armed Conflict Hub, University of Essex, Colchester, UK

Member, Guernica 37 Chamber, London, UK
e-mail: g.waschefort@essex.ac.uk

M. Faix, O. Svaček (eds.), *ICC Jurisprudence and the Development of International Humanitarian Law*, Global Issues,
https://doi.org/10.1007/978-3-031-45994-8_7

exposed a fault line in the core of international humanitarian law (IHL), which had the potential to cause a chink in the armour the law affords children affected by armed conflict.[2] Ntaganda relied on an obscure, yet orthodox interpretation of IHL, challenging the jurisdiction ratione materiae of the court to prosecute him at once for the use of children for active participation in hostilities, and the rape and sexual slavery of the same children as war crimes.[3] The basis for the argument is that 'the laws of armed conflict do not protect members of armed groups from acts of violence directed against them by their own forces'.[4] In particular, the defence argued that 'the established framework of international law' imports a status requirement in regard to the victim of the crime, the status requirement being that protection is reserved for '(i) persons taking no active part in the hostilities; (ii) members of armed forces who have laid down their arms; and (iii) those placed "hors de combat" by sickness, wounds, detention, or any other cause'.[5] Trial Chamber VI dismissed Ntaganda's challenge and the Appeals Chamber confirmed this finding,[6] however, these decisions sharply divided high-profile members of the IHL and

[2] Judgment, *Ntaganda*, (ICC-01/04-02/06-2359), Trial Chamber VI, 8 July 2019 (hereafter *Ntaganda*, Trial Chamber Judgment); Judgment, *Ntaganda*, (ICC-01/04-02/06-2782), Appeals Chamber VI, 12 September 2022 (hereafter *Ntaganda*, Appeals Chamber Judgment).

[3] Application on behalf of Mr. Ntaganda challenging the jurisdiction of the Court in respect of Counts 6 and 9 of the Document containing the charges, *Ntaganda*, (ICC-01/04-02/06-804), Trial Chamber VI, 1 September 2015 (hereafter *Ntaganda* challenge to Counts 6 and 9).

[4] Ibid, § 28.

[5] Ibid, § 21.

[6] Second decision on the Defence's challenge to the jurisdiction of the Court in respect of Counts 6 and 9, *Ntaganda* (ICC-01/04-02/06-1707), Trial Chamber VI, 4 January 2017 (hereafter Ntaganda Trial Chamber Decision on challenge to Counts 6 and 9), § 54; and Judgment on the Appeal of Mr Ntaganda against the "Second decision on the Defence's challenge to the jurisdiction of the Court in respect of Counts 6 and 9", *Ntaganda*, (ICC-01/04-02/06-1962), Appeals Chamber, 15 June 2017 (hereafter Ntaganda Appeals Chamber Decision on challenge to Counts 6 and 9), § 71.

international criminal law (ICL) communities.[7] The *Ntaganda* case has indeed given rise to considerable commentary, the thrust of which supports the Court's conclusion.[8] The aim of this chapter is to make a more discrete, yet vital contribution to the understanding of this issue by analysing whether children continue to enjoy special protection in terms of IHL once they are enlisted, conscripted or used for active participation in hostilities, and whether such children enjoy protection against sexual violence on an intra-party basis, as a matter of law.

The first substantive section of the chapter situates the debate by expressing the orthodox understanding of the passive personal scope of applicability ratione personae of IHL, it then canvasses the ICC's jurisprudence in the *Lubanga* and *Ntaganda* cases.[9] This analysis sheds light on how the Office of the Prosecutor's (OTP) trial strategy evolved not only from *Lubanga* to *Ntaganda*, but across the course of the *Ntaganda* case.

[7] Examples of critique of the position adopted by the ICC includes, Y. McDermott, 'ICC extends War Crimes of Rape and Sexual Slavery to Victims from Same Armed Forces as Perpetrator', IntLawGrrls, 5 January 2017, available at https://ilg2.org/2017/01/05/icc-extends-war-crimes-of-rape-and-sexual-slavery-to-victims-from-same-armed-forces-as-perpetrator/ (last visited 9 February 2023); and K.J. Heller, 'ICC Appeals Chamber Says A War Crime Does Not Have to Violate IHL', OpinioJuris, 15 June 2017, available at http://opiniojuris.org/2017/06/15/icc-appeals-chamber-holds-a-war-crime-does-not-have-to-violate-ihl/ (last visited 9 February 2023). In contrast, the following commentators support the conclusion reached by the ICC, but have added additional legal argumentation: P.V. Sellers, 'Ntaganda: Re-Alignment of a Paradigm', in F. Pocar (ed.), *The Additional Protocols 40 Years Later: New Conflicts, New Actors, New Perspectives* (Milan: Franco Angeli, 2018) 116–136; and M. Longobardo, 'The Criminalisation of Intra-party Offences in Light of Some Recent ICC Decisions on Children in Armed Conflict', 19 *International Criminal Law Review* (2019) 600–634. Svaček suggests that both the *Ntaganda*, Trial Chamber and Appeals Chamber Judgments fall foul of the principle of legality, yet he supports an interpretation of the applicable IHL which renders protection to child on an intra-party basis, O. Svaček, 'Brothers and Sisters in Arms as Victims of War Crimes: Ntaganda Case Before the ICC', 8 *Czech Yearbook of Public and Private International Law* 8(1) (2017) 346–357.

[8] See, for example, Longobardo, *supra* note 7, whose detailed analysis brings into question the provenance of the orthodox interpretation of IHL as not applying on an intra-party basis. Sellers, *supra* note 7, at 127–131, suggests that the continuing application of the child protective norms in IHL provides an adequate basis to prosecute a perpetrator both for the enlistment, conscription and use of children, as well as sexual violence perpetrated against them.

[9] Judgment, *Lubanga* (ICC-01/04-01/06-2842), Trial Chamber I, 14 March 2012 (hereafter *Lubanga*, Trial Chamber Judgment); Judgment, *Lubanga*, (ICC-01/04-01/06-3121), Appeals Chamber VI, 1 December 2014 (hereafter *Lubanga*, Appeals Chamber Judgment).

This evolution lies at the heart of Ntaganda's ultimate challenge to the Court's jurisdiction. The enquiry then progresses to consider intra-party violations in the context of the continued special protection of children during armed conflict. While Sellers has advocated for this position in response to the *Ntaganda* affair,[10] this section of the chapter addresses several issues that remains outstanding, including: whether such special protection includes the cumulative elements of the war crime of rape and sexual slavery; the question whether the norms that afford children special protection during armed conflict can be invoked on an intra-party basis; and the unintended pitfalls of reliance on the law of international armed conflict (IAC) as an expression of customary international law, as it relates to the special protection of children during non-international armed conflict (NIAC). In the context of the *Ntaganda* case, the Court was correct to address the issue in both the context of IAC as well as NIAC, as it is only at judgment when the conflict is finally classified, a lesson the OTP learned the hard way in the *Lubanga* case.[11] However, none of the relevant submissions or decisions in the *Ntaganda* case, nor any of the resulting academic commentary have adequately and lucidly disentangled the arguments relevant to IAC and those relevant to NIAC. Additionally, the implications of the ICC's embrace of 'active participation in hostilities' as a broader concept than 'direct participation in hostilities' for the question of intra-party violations as a potential bar to prosecution is for the first time analysed.[12] Finally, in the conclusion the micro-level analysis presented informs some macro reflexion on the theme of this volume: development of IHL in the jurisprudence and practice of the ICC.

[10] Sellers, *supra* note 7, at 127–131.

[11] The *Lubanga* Arrest Warrant charged Lubanga under Art. 8(2)(e) of the Rome Statute of the International Criminal Court (adopted 17 July 1998, entered into force 1 July 2002), 2187 UNTS 90 (hereafter Rome Statute) which requires a nexus to a NIAC. However, the Pre-Trial Chamber found the conflict at the relevant time to have been an IAC, requiring charges to argued under Art. 8(2)(b), *Lubanga* (Confirmation of Charges Decision), §§ 200–237. At judgment, the Trial Chamber determined that the conflict was at the relevant time a NIAC, as originally argued by the OTP, *Lubanga*, Trial Chamber Judgment, §§ 523–567. For the procedural history, see, M.E. Kurth, 'The *Lubanga* Case of the International Criminal Court: A Critical Analysis of the Trial Chamber's Findings on Issues of Active Use, Age, and Gravity', 5 *Goettingen Journal of International Law* (2013) 431–453, at 435–436.

[12] *Lubanga*, Trial Chamber Judgment, § 261.

7.2 Situating the Debate

The orthodox interpretation of IHL as not applying on an intra-party basis is premised on the traditional understanding of the passive personal scope of applicability ratione personae of IHL:

> In international armed conflicts, international humanitarian law formally recognizes and defines distinct categories of persons who do not or no longer directly participate in hostilities as 'protected persons'. These are the wounded, sick and shipwrecked, prisoners of war, and civilians. While no formal categories of 'protected persons' exist in non-international armed conflict, the applicable international humanitarian law nevertheless grants material protection to those who do not or no longer actively participate in hostilities.[13]

This expression is indeed misleading, as the law on the conduct of hostilities by and large serve to protect combatants and fighters, for example, restrictions on means and methods of armed conflict.[14] Additionally, IHL provides special protection to several identified sub-categories of persons, including children. However, to benefit from such special protection, the individual must first fall within the scope of applicability ratione personae of IHL.[15] The orthodox and restrictive understanding of the passive personal scope of applicability ratione personae can be premised on three bases: that there is a general rule of IHL that so limits the scope of application of the body of law as a whole[16]; that the scope of application of each IHL convention is so limited[17]; or that each individual protective

[13] J. Kleffner, 'Scope of Application of International Humanitarian Law', in D. Fleck, (ed.), Handbook of International Humanitarian Law (4th edn., Oxford: Oxford University Press, 2021) 50–80, at 63.

[14] Ibid, at 64.

[15] Ibid, at 63.

[16] Clapham, for example, posits that IHL as whole 'does not cover how an armed group treats its own forces'. See, A. Clapham, 'Human Rights Obligations for Non-State-Actors: Where are We Now?', in F. Lafontaine and F. Larocque (eds), *Doing Peace the Rights Way: Essays in International Law and Relations in Honour of Louise Arbour* (Antwerp: Intersentia, 2018) 11–26, at 16.

[17] For example, Heller, *supra* note 7, states that, 'IHL protection does not "generally" apply only to civilians and combatants hors de combat. On the contrary, *each and every IHL convention applies only* to those two categories of individuals' (own emphasis).

norm of IHL has inherent in it such a status limitation.[18] In the *RUF* case, the Special Court for Sierra Leone held that,

> The law of international armed conflict regulates the conduct of combatants *vis-à-vis* their adversaries and persons *hors de combat* who do not belong to any of the armed groups participating in the hostilities. [...] It is trite law that an armed group cannot hold its own members as prisoners of war. The law of international armed conflict was never intended to criminalise acts of violence committed by one member of an armed group against another, such conduct remaining first and foremost the province of the criminal law of the State of the armed group concerned and human rights law. In our view, a different approach would constitute an inappropriate re-conceptualisation of a fundamental principle of international humanitarian law.[19]

However, very little detailed discussion had taken place of this issue prior to it arising in the *Ntaganda* case. Perhaps the most widely cited view is that of Cassese, who resolutely advocated that 'an offence [...] committed by a combatant against another combatant belonging to the same belligerent [...], is not a war crime, although the armed conflict may have been the occasion for the offence'.[20] Kleffner and Sivakumaran prophetically engaged in considerably more detailed discussion of the issue. Kleffner concludes that both Common Article 3 of the Geneva Conventions (CA3) and Article 75 of Additional Protocol I to the Geneva Conventions (API) has some effect on an intra-party basis.[21]

[18] Judgment, *The Prosecutor* vs. *Isa Hassan Sesay, Moris Kallon and Augustine Gbao* (hereafter RUF case) (SCSL-04-15-T), Trial Chamber I, 2 March 2009, §§ 1452–1453. This was in part the argument made by Ntaganda's defence team, although as it relates to the charges against him, the argument was confined to those rules of IHL that proscribe rape and sexual slavery. See, *Ntaganda* (Challenge to Counts 6 and 9), *supra* note 3.

[19] *RUF* case, ibid, §§ 1452–1453.

[20] A. Cassese, *International Criminal Law* (3rd edn., Oxford: Oxford University Press, 2013), at 78.

[21] J. Kleffner, 'Friend or Foe? On the Protective Reach of the Law of Armed Conflict: A Note on the SCSL Trial Chamber's Judgment in the Case of *Prosecutor v. Sesay, Kallon and Gbao*', in M. Matthee, B. Toebes and M. Brus, *Armed Conflict and International Law: In Search of the Human Face: Liber Amicorum in Memory of Avril McDonald* (The Hague: T.M.C. Asser Press, 2013) 285–302; and J. Kleffner, 'The Beneficiaries of the Rights Stemming from Common Article 3', in A. Clapham, P. Gaeta and M Sassoli (eds), *The 1949 Geneva Conventions: A Commentary* (Oxford: Oxford University Press, 2015) 433–447.

Sivakumaran submits that 'things are not quite as self-evident as the traditional position suggests'.[22] He proceeds to identify a catalogue of norms that have intra-party effect.[23]

The focus of this contribution is to consider whether at the individual normative level the special protection afforded children during armed conflict continues to operate to provide protection to children against sexual violence even when they no longer belong to the categories of persons traditionally included in the passive personal scope of applicability ratione personae of IHL. If this is indeed the case, it disproves restrictive interpretations of such scope of application of IHL at the regime and convention level.

From Lubanga to Ntaganda

While the issue of intra-party violations arose for the first time before the ICC during 2017 in the *Ntaganda* case, the antecedent history of the ICC's first prosecution in the *Lubanga* case feeds into this issue in manners that were not fully appreciated at the time of the conclusion of that case. The tie between these cases exists both in relation to the overlapping substantive issues, which were ultimately addressed through curiously diverging trial strategies, as well as the relationship of the accused. Both men were prosecuted for overlapping offences committed in their capacity as senior leaders within the *Union des Patriotes Congolais* (UPC), including its military wing the *Forces Patriotiques pour la Libération du Congo* (FPLC). The offences for which both were prosecuted were committed during a narrow time window between August 2002 and December 2003

[22] S. Sivakumaran, *The Law of Non-International Armed Conflict*, (Oxford: Oxford University Press, 2012), at 246–249.
[23] Ibid.

during the particularly gruesome Ituri Conflict in north-eastern Democratic Republic of the Congo (DRC).[24]

Notwithstanding extensive critique of international criminal mechanisms' historic failure to properly include sexual violence in their proceedings,[25] the ICC infamously charged Lubanga only with the war crime of conscripting or enlisting children under the age of fifteen years into an armed group and using them to participate actively in hostilities.[26] However, on 22 May 2009, the legal representatives of twenty-seven victims who participated in the trial successfully requested the Trial Chamber to consider a legal re-characterisation of the facts in order to expand the charges against Lubanga to include sexual slavery both as a crime against humanity and a war crime applicable to IAC and NIAC, and the war

[24] The Decision on the Confirmation of Charges determined that there was sufficient evidence to establish substantial grounds to believe that Lubanga committed the war crime of enlisting and conscripting children under the age of fifteen years into the FPLC and using them to participate actively in hostilities during both the periods covering early September 2002 to 2 June 2003 and 2 June to 13 August 2003. Decision on the Confirmation of Charges, *Lubanga*, (ICC-01/04-01/06-803), Pre-Trial Chamber I, 29 January 2007, §§ 406–408 (hereafter *Lubanga*, Confirmation of Charges Decision). In the Decision on the Confirmation of Charges in the Ntaganda case it was determined that there were substantial grounds to believe that UPC/FPLC soldiers and Ntaganda himself committed the war crime of enlistment and conscription of children under the age of fifteen years between 6 August 2002 and 31 December 2003; the war crime of using children under the age of fifteen years to participate actively in hostilities between 6 August 2002 and 30 May 2003; and that UPC/FPLC soldiers committed the war crimes of rape and sexual slavery against child soldiers between 6 August 2002 and 31 December 2003. Decision Pursuant to Article 61(7)(a) and (b) of the Rome Statute on the Charges of the Prosecutor Against Bosco Ntaganda, *Ntaganda*, (ICC-01/04-02/06-309), Trial Chamber II, 9 June 2014, § 74 (hereafter *Ntaganda*, Confirmation of Charges Decision).

[25] For a compelling critique see, R. Copelon, 'Gender Crimes as War Crimes: Integrating Crimes against Women into International Criminal Law', 46 *McGill Law Journal* (2000) 217–240. At 224–229 Copelon chronicles to troubled trial history in the first successful international prosecution for sexual violence as a crime against humanity in: Judgement, *The Prosecutor v. Jean-Paul Akayesu*, (ICTR-96-4-T), Trial Chamber, 2 September 1998.

[26] Charges were only brought under Art. 8(2)(b)(xxvi) and 8(2)(e)(vii) of the Rome Statute, see *Lubanga*, (Confirmation of Charges Decision), *supra* note 24. For critique of the narrow scope of charges see, International Federation for Human Rights, *Democratic Republic of the Congo: Breaking the Cycle of Impunity* (2008), available online at https://www.fidh.org/IMG/pdf/DRCsexualcrimeseng2008.pdf (last visited 9 February 2023); and K.O. Smith, '*Prosecutor v. Lubanga*: How the International Criminal Court Failed the Women and Girls of the Congo', 54(2) *Howard Law Journal* (2011) 467–500.

crimes of inhuman and cruel treatment, applicable to IAC.[27] However, on appeal, the Trial Chamber's decision was correctly reversed on the basis that the proposed legal re-characterisation of the facts would exceed the facts and circumstances described in the charges, which is inconsistent with the applicable regulation.[28]

The Trial Chamber rendered its verdict on 14 March 2012, convicting Lubanga as joint perpetrator for the enlistment, conscription and use for active participation in hostilities of children younger than fifteen (as separate offences).[29] Lubanga was sentenced to fourteen years imprisonment.[30] The judgment and sentence were unsuccessfully appealed.[31] In a separate and dissenting opinion to the Trial Chamber judgment, Judge Odio Benito argued that sexual violence to which the children enlisted, conscripted and used by Lubanga's forces were subjected, should be included in the *actus reus* of the offence of using children to participate actively in hostilities.[32] In particular, she argued:

> By failing to deliberately include within the legal concept of "use to participate actively in the hostilities" the sexual violence and other ill-treatment suffered by girls and boys, the Majority of the Chamber is making this critical aspect of the crime invisible [...] I thus consider it necessary and a duty of the Chamber to include sexual violence within the legal concept of "use to participate actively in the hostilities", regardless of the impediment of the Chamber to base its decision pursuant to Article 74(2) of the Statute.[33]

[27] *Lubanga* (Decision Giving Notice to the Parties and Participants that the Legal Characterization of the Facts may be Subject to Change in Accordance with Regulation 55(2) of the Regulations of the Court), (ICC-01/04-01/06-2049), Trial Chamber I, 14 July 2009. The charges that were contemplated were, sexual slavery pursuant to Art. 7(l)(g) or 8(2)(b)(xxii) or 8(2)(e)(vi) of the Rome Statute, and inhuman and / or cruel treatment pursuant to Art. 8(2)(a)(ii) or 8(2)(c)(i) of the Rome Statute.

[28] Judgment on the appeals of Mr Lubanga Dyilo and the Prosecutor against the Decision of Trial Chamber I of 14 July 2009, *Lubanga*, (ICC-01/04-01/06-2205), Appeals Chamber, 8 December 2009, § 112. For a detailed overview of the procedural history see, A.C. Diala, 'Victims' Justice and Re-Characterizing Facts in the *Lubanga* Trial at the ICC', 7 *Eyes on the ICC* (2010) 59–84. For more critical commentary see, S. Merope, 'Recharacterizing the Lubanga Case: Regulation 55 and the Consequences for Gender Justice at the ICC', 22(3) *Criminal Law Forum* (2011), 311–346.

[29] *Lubanga*, Trial Chamber Judgment, §§ 1351–1357.

[30] *Lubanga* (Decision on Sentence pursuant to Article 76 of the Statute), (ICC-01/04-01/06-2901), Trial Chamber I, 10 July 2012, §§ 98–99 (hereafter *Lubanga*, Sentencing Decision).

[31] *Lubanga*, Appeals Chamber Judgment, § 529.

[32] Separate and Dissenting Opinion of Judge Odio Benito, *Lubanga*, Trial Chamber Judgment, §§ 15–21.

[33] Ibid, § 16.

Judge Odio Benito's analysis is unconvincing and ill conceived.[34] It flies in the face of any reasonable interpretation of the underlying offence, and thus offends the principle of legality.[35] Indeed, Article 74(2), to which she referred, expressly provides 'the decision shall not exceed the facts and circumstances described in the charges and any amendments to the charges'. Moreover, considering the Appeal Chamber's earlier finding which barred legal re-characterisation of the facts, and consequently expansion of the charges to include sexual offences, her approach is somewhat disingenuous, as it amounts to a second bite at the cherry. Nevertheless, as we shall see, her opinion provides an interesting antecedent to the charges brought against Lubanga's compatriot, Bosco Ntaganda.

There is no doubt that the OTP was aware of the sexual violence perpetrated by members of Lubanga's forces against the children they enlisted and conscripted.[36] The narrow scope of charges brought against Lubanga is thus premised on trial strategy, the strength of which remains questionable. Arguments to the effect that the OTP not only failed the victims of Lubanga and his co-perpetrators but failed in its obligations in terms of the Rome Statute are well known and will not be re-canvased.[37] However, the issue of intra-party violations, which arose later in the *Ntaganda* case illustrates that the matter is more complicated than the critique against the OTP in regards to Lubanga suggests. Lubanga's victims were themselves children enlisted and conscripted by his forces. Victims' concern with the narrowness of charges brought against Lubanga, as reflected in the pro-

[34] Kurth, *supra* note 11, at 439–442; N. Jørgensen,' Child Soldiers and the Parameters of International Criminal Law', 11(4) *Chinese Journal of International Law* (2012) 657–688, at 679–684; J. Tan, 'Sexual Violence Against Children on the Battlefield as a Crime of Using Child Soldiers: Square Pegs in Round Holes and Missed Opportunities in Lubanga', 15 *Yearbook of International Humanitarian Law* (2012) 117–151, at 138–139. *Contra*: K. Gallagher, 'Towards a Gender-Inclusive Definition of Child Soldiers: *The Prosecutorial v. Thomas Lubanga*', 7 *Eyes on the ICC* (2010–2011) 115–136, at 125–129.

[35] K. Ambos, 'The First Judgment of the International Criminal Court (*Prosecutor v. Lubanga*): A Comprehensive Analysis of the Legal Issues', 12(2) *International Criminal Law Review* (2012) 115–153, at 137; and Tan, *supra* note 34, at 142–145.

[36] Smith, *supra* note 26, at 468–469.

[37] See, inter alia, Smith, *supra* note 26, at 477; and Merope, *supra* note 28, at 312–313. Art. 54 (1)(b) of the Rome Statute puts forward the duties of the prosecutor: 'Take appropriate measures to ensure the effective investigation and prosecution of crimes within the jurisdiction of the Court, and in doing so, respect the interests and personal circumstances of victims and witnesses, including age, gender as defined in article 7, paragraph 3, and health, and take into account the nature of the crime, in particular where it involves sexual violence, gender violence or violence against children'.

ceedings to expand the scope of charges, centred on the failure to address other conduct to which they fell victim.[38] Which, a fortiori, were committed on an intra-party basis. This suggests that for those who subscribe to the orthodox understanding that IHL does not provide for intra-party violations, the OTP in the *Lubanga* case had limited options.

While there are no such indications, there is the possibility that the OTP anticipated additional charges related to violations against child members of the UPC would complicate the prosecution based on the orthodox understanding that IHL does not provide for intra-party violations. Should this indeed be the case, the lack of official record of such reasoning is not surprising, as it would be contra the long-term interests of the OTP to make such concerns public. Nevertheless, as the *Ntaganda* case illustrates the challenges posed by the vexed issue of intra-party violations were not insurmountable and does not vindicate the OTP for its failure to institute additional charges against Lubanga. Moreover, the historical record leaves little doubt that the victims of the catalogue of abuses perpetrated by Lubanga's forces go well beyond members of the UPC. Indeed, the lessons learned by the OTP in the *Lubanga* case are evident when considering its procedural history in parallel to that of the *Ntaganda* case. The warrant of arrest for Lubanga was issued under seal on 10 February 2006 and the first warrant of arrest for Ntaganda was issued under seal a mere six months later on 22 August 2006.[39] Both warrants confined the charges against the accused to the enlistment, conscription and use for active participation in hostilities of children younger than fifteen.[40] The *Lubanga* Trial Chamber Judgment, including Judge Odio Benito's dissent, was delivered on 14 March 2012. At this stage, any concerns by the OTP regarding the potential impact of the issue of intra-party violations on prosecution for child enlistment, conscription and use on the one hand, and their ill-treatment on the other, had been jettisoned. A second warrant of arrest for Ntaganda was issued four months after the *Lubanga* judgement on 13 July 2012, expanding the charges against

[38] See generally, Joint Application of the Legal Representatives of the Victims for the Implementation of the Procedure under Regulation 55 of the Regulations of the Court, *Lubanga*, (ICC-01/04-01/06-1891), Trial Chamber I, 24 May 2009.

[39] Warrant of Arrest, *Lubanga*, (ICC-01/04-01/06-8), Pre-Trial Chamber I, 22 August 2006 (hereafter *Lubanga* Arrest Warrant); and Warrant of Arrest, *Ntaganda*, (ICC-01/04-02/06-2), Pre-Trial Chamber I, 22 August 2006 (hereafter *Ntaganda* first Arrest Warrant).

[40] Ibid.

Ntaganda to include an additional three counts of crimes against humanity, consisting in murder, rape and sexual slavery, and persecution, and four counts of war crimes consisting of murder, attacks against the civilian population, rape and sexual slavery, and pillaging.[41]

On 1 September 2015, Ntaganda first challenged the subject-matter jurisdiction of the Court as it related to the coexistence of the charge of enlisting, conscripting, and using children in hostilities, and the rape and sexual slavery of such children. The essence of the challenge was that 'the laws of armed conflict do not protect members of armed groups from acts of violence directed against them by their own forces'.[42] As such, Ntaganda cannot be prosecuted for the rape and sexual slavery of children whom he enlisted, conscripted and used for active participation in hostilities. It was only on 4 January 2017 that the Trial Chamber made a finding on the substance, by dismissing the challenge.[43] In essence, the Trial Chamber dismissed the challenge based on five points of reasoning: (1) the structure and chapeau of Article 8 of the Rome Statute is broader than simply that determined by the grave breaches provisions and CA3[44]; (2) the fact that most prohibitions of rape and sexual slavery in IHL relate to those hors de combat and civilians does not limit the scope of protection from such conduct[45]; (3) such a restrictive approach to rape and sexual slavery is incompatible with the aims IHL[46]; (4) the Trial Chamber determined that the jus cogens status of sexual slavery as well as rape in the context of armed conflict, provides additional support for its rejection of the challenge, as no derogation from these provisions are allowed[47]; and, finally, (5) Article 75 of API applies as a matter of law on an intra-party basis.[48]

On 15 June 2017 the Appeals Chamber confirmed the Trial Chamber's decision and added minimally to the already scant legal reasoning of the Trial Chamber.[49] The Appeals Chamber determined that neither the chapeau to Articles 8(2)(b) and (e) of the Rome Statute, nor the underlying offences of rape and sexual slavery stipulate a requirement that the victims

[41] Warrant of Arrest, *Ntaganda*, (ICC-01/04-02/06-36), Pre-Trial Chamber II, 13 July 2012 (hereafter *Ntaganda*, second Arrest Warrant).

[42] *Ntaganda* (Challenge to Counts 6 and 9), *supra* note 3, at § 28.

[43] *Ntaganda* (Trial Chamber Decision on challenge to Counts 6 and 9), *supra* note 6.

[44] Ibid, at § 44.

[45] Ibid, at § 47.

[46] Ibid, at § 48.

[47] Ibid, at §§ 51–52.

[48] Ibid, at § 46.

[49] *Ntaganda* (Appeals Chamber Decision on challenge to Counts 6 and 9), *supra* note 6.

be 'protected persons' under the Geneva Conventions or 'persons taking no active part in the hostilities' in terms of CA3.[50] Further, IHL, as a component of the 'established framework of international law', does not contain a general norm limiting protection to 'protected persons' under the Geneva Conventions or 'persons not taking active part in hostilities' under CA3.[51] Moreover, the Trial Chamber's finding that the status requirement generally observed in IHL prohibitions of rape and sexual slavery does not serve to limit the scope of victims of these offences under the Rome Statute, was affirmed.[52]

7.3 Intra-Party Violations of the Special Protection Afforded Child Participants in Hostilities

Sellers argues that the special protection afforded to children during armed conflict continues to operate even after the relevant children become participants in hostilities.[53] As this special protection includes protection against sexual violence, children recruited or used by a given armed group or force are protected, as a matter of law, from sexual violence perpetrated by fellow member of the group or force.[54] The issue of the continued special protection of children once they become participants in hostilities has largely gone unnoticed, and worst still, it is often assumed that together with loss of protection against direct targeting, children also lose all residual special protection. This is indeed the crux of the interpretation that IHL excludes intra-party violations, however, the language of the applicable conventional law is clear that at least some protection persists, for example, it is not controversial that children continue to benefit from protection against use in hostilities even after they become members of armed forces.[55] While I agree with Sellers' position, meticulous legal

[50] Ibid, § 46.

[51] Ibid, §§ 57–63.

[52] Ibid, § 64.

[53] Sellers, *supra* note 7, at 127–131.

[54] Ibid.

[55] As conceded by Ntaganda's defence team and discussed in further detail below. See, *Ntaganda* (Challenge to Counts 6 and 9), *supra* note 3, § 30. Technically, however, this would only be the case in IAC, as in order for 'membership' on an organized armed group to operate such that it can be deemed to exclude intra-party violations, the given child, a fortiori, need to be a direct participant in hostilities.

analysis is needed to address gaps in her approach. Additionally, the implications of the ICC adopting an expansive definition of active participation in hostilities, rather than the IHL standard of direct participation, has not yet been considered in adequate detail, and certainly not in relation to the possibilities it poses in respect of intra-party violations.

The Persistence of Special Protection of Children Once they Participate in Hostilities

Sellers' approach rests on the following suggested features of Article 77 of API and Article 4 of Additional Protocol II to the Geneva Conventions (APII): (1) they specifically provide children with special protection including against rape and sexual slavery; and (2) this special protection persists after a child becomes a participant in hostilities.[56] The interpretation of the relevant provisions of the Additional Protocols calls for a rather technical analysis that engages these provisions holistically. While both provisions provide for the special protection of children, Article 77 of API is titled 'protection of children', whereas Article 4 of APII is titled 'fundamental guarantees', and provides protection to different categories of persons, including children—a feature that complicates interpretation of the provision. Article 77 of API provides that in the context of IAC:

> 1. Children shall be the object of special respect and shall be protected against any form of indecent assault. The Parties to the conflict shall provide them with the care and aid they require, whether because of their age or for any other reason.
>
> 2. The Parties to the conflict shall take all feasible measures in order that children who have not attained the age of fifteen years do not take a direct part in hostilities and, in particular, they shall refrain from recruiting them into their armed forces. In recruiting among those persons who have attained the age of fifteen years but who have not attained the age of eighteen years, the Parties to the conflict shall endeavour to give priority to those who are oldest.
>
> 3. If, in exceptional cases, despite the provisions of paragraph 2, children who have not attained the age of fifteen years take a direct part in hostilities and fall into the power of an adverse Party, they shall continue to benefit from the special protection accorded by this Article, whether or not they are prisoners of war.
>
> [...]

[56] Sellers, *supra* note 7, at 127–131.

The parallel provision applicable to NIAC is reflected in Article 4 of APII:

> 1. All persons who do not take a direct part or who have ceased to take part in hostilities, whether or not their liberty has been restricted, are entitled to respect for their person, honour and convictions and religious practices. They shall in all circumstances be treated humanely, without any adverse distinction. It is prohibited to order that there shall be no survivors.
>
> 2. Without prejudice to the generality of the foregoing, the following acts against the persons referred to in paragraph 1 are and shall remain prohibited at any time and in any place whatsoever:
>
> [...]
>
> (e) outrages upon personal dignity, in particular humiliating and degrading treatment, rape, enforced prostitution and any form of indecent assault;
>
> (f) slavery and the slave trade in all their forms;
>
> [...]
>
> 3. Children shall be provided with the care and aid they require, and in particular:
>
> (a) they shall receive an education, including religious and moral education, in keeping with the wishes of their parents, or in the absence of parents, of those responsible for their care;
>
> (b) all appropriate steps shall be taken to facilitate the reunion of families temporarily separated;
>
> (c) children who have not attained the age of fifteen years shall neither be recruited in the armed forces or groups nor allowed to take part in hostilities;
>
> (d) the special protection provided by this Article to children who have not attained the age of fifteen years shall remain applicable to them if they take a direct part in hostilities despite the provisions of sub-paragraph (c) and are captured;
>
> [...]

Special Protection against Rape and Sexual Slavery

The protection against any form of indecent assault offered by API is certainly sufficiently broad to include all the elements of rape and sexual slavery as defined in Article 8(2)(b)(xxii) of the Rome Statute.[57] While the ongoing nature of special protection is addressed below, it is important

[57] However, the charges in *Ntaganda* related to the equivalent NIAC provision, contained in Art. 8(2)(e)(vi) of the Rome Statute.

that Article 77(3) clarifies that its reference to continued special protection includes the totality of such protection offered 'by this Article', that is, Article 77 as a whole. The matter is more complicated in relation to APII. This is because Article 4 of APII provides protection for two distinct classes of persons: paragraphs 1 and 2 provide protection to 'all persons who do not take a direct part or who have ceased to take part in hostilities, whether or not their liberty has been restricted', and paragraph 3 provides protection to 'children'. The provision provides that 'the special protection *provided by this Article* to children who have not attained the age of fifteen years' shall remain applicable to them even if they are used for DPH in contravention of Article 4(3)(c) of APII (own emphasis). However, it does not clarify whether the scope of such special protection is limited to paragraph 3, or instead whether it incorporates the protection offered by paragraphs 1 and 2. While the language 'this Article' is suggestive that the totality of protection offered by Article 4 is included, children who participate in hostilities are expressly excluded from the scope of application ratione personae of paragraphs 1 and 2.

An interpretation that excludes paragraphs 1 and 2 from the ongoing special protection of children per paragraph 3(d) would imply that such ongoing special protection is limited to receiving an education (including religious and moral education) and the obligation that appropriate steps be taken to facilitate the reunion of separated families. As such, a good faith interpretation of Article 4(3)(d) of APII done in accordance with the ordinary meaning of the terms in their context and in light of the object and purpose of APII compels a conclusion that the ongoing special protection of children includes the mutatis mutandis application of paragraphs 1 and 2 of Article 4 to children. Article 4(1) provides broad protection for the respect of the person and their honour, and it calls for humane treatment in all circumstances. The travaux préparatoires of APII fully supports this conclusion. In both the 1975 and 1976 drafts of APII, the special protection of children was dealt with in draft Article 6bis, while the fundamental guarantees were provided for in Article 6.[58] Article 6bis provided: 'in addition to the protection conferred by Article 6, women and children

[58] See the Draft Protocol Additional to the Geneva Conventions of August 12, 1949, and Relating to the Protection of Victims of International Armed Conflicts, Following the Second Session of the Diplomatic Conference, (1975), at Art. 6 and 6bis; and Draft Protocol Additional to the Geneva Conventions of August 12, 1949, and Relating to the Protection of Victims of International Armed Conflicts, Following the Third Session of the Diplomatic Conference, (1976), at Art. 6 and 6bis.

shall be the object of special respect and shall be protected against rape, enforced prostitution, and any form of indecent assault'.[59] The amalgamation of Articles 6bis and 6, made redundant the need for explicit protection for children against rape, enforced prostitution and indecent assault, as this protection was afforded through paragraphs 1 and 2 of the fundamental guarantees. This was confirmed as the agreed understanding among the plenipotentiaries during an exchange between the representative of Pakistan and Canada on 3 June 1977.[60]

Article 4(2) of APII more specifically prohibits 'outrages upon personal dignity, in particular humiliating and degrading treatment, rape, enforced prostitution and any form of indecent assault'. Accordingly, the special protection provided by Article 4 of APII also includes all the elements of rape and sexual slavery as defined in Article 8(2)(e)(vi) of the Rome Statute.

The Continuing Nature of Special Protection Once a Child Participates in Hostilities

There are significant distinctions between the norms proscribing child recruitment and use in the two protocols, which have direct bearing on the issue of intra-party violations. Uniquely, APII provides a more stringent obligation to refrain from using children in hostilities, when compared to API.[61] The prohibition is not confined to what is feasible in the circumstances, and children are not protected only against use for direct participation in hostilities, as is the case in API. However, there is a need to define more precisely what threshold of participation is included in Article 4(3)(c) of APII, which speaks of being 'allowed to take part in hostilities'. The threshold should not be interpreted too liberally. The nature of organised armed groups is often such that family units form an integral part of the dynamic of the group. Thus, regarding any form of contribution to the group as amounting to taking part in hostilities may well conflict with the right to family life of group members, including

[59] Ibid.

[60] *Official Record of the Diplomatic Conference on the Reaffirmation and Development of International Humanitarian Law Applicable in Armed Conflicts*, Geneva (1974–1977) Volume VII 90–92 CDDH/SR 50 during the fiftieth plenary meeting on 3 June 1977.

[61] S. Fatima, *Protecting Children in Armed Conflict* (Oxford: Hart Publishing, 2018), at 184; M. Happold, *Child Soldiers in International Law* (Manchester: Manchester University Press, 2005), at 66–67; M.A. Drumbl, 'Reimagining Child Soldiers in International Law and Policy' (Oxford: Oxford University Press, 2012), 139.

children. Nevertheless, Article 4(3)(c) of APII certainly protects children against a lower threshold of participation than Article 77(2) of API. The threshold established by the ICC in regard to active participation in hostilities presents a good starting point to consider an appropriate threshold for purposes of Article 4(3)(c) of APII.

In the context of the *Ntaganda* case, Sellers offers reliance on Article 77 of API as an expression of customary international law which then applies also to NIAC as a solution to 'jurisdictional pre-requisites' that may stand in the way of the generality of 'the principle that each party bears responsibility for any form of indecent assault against children.[62] There is a major pitfall in such reliance being placed on Article 77 of API in the context of NIAC, as one effectively throws the baby out with the bathwater by losing the enhanced protection offered by APII. Indeed, one of the concerning features of the development of IHL through international criminal tribunals is the conflation of the law of international and non-international armed conflict. This may seem justified on the basis of the increased convergence of these bodies of law as a consequence of customary international law.[63] However, this approach loses sight of the differing nature of the law of NIAC and has the unintended consequence that in areas such as child soldiering the threshold of protection offered by the conventional law of NIAC is in effect lowered.[64] The ICRC's

[62] Sellers, *supra* note 7, at 128–129.

[63] For example, Greenwood discusses in detail the *obiter dictum* discussion in the *Tadic* case regarding the extent to which the law on the conduct of hostilities in IAC were deemed to apply as customary international law to NIAC. He comments, 'It is open to question whether the Appeals Chamber was wise to raise such an important matter in this way, rather than waiting for a case which actually required a decision on the content of this part of humanitarian law. It is also doubtful whether the practice discussed in this part of the decision really sustains some of the inferences drawn from it'. C. Greenwood, 'The Development of International Humanitarian Law by the International Criminal Tribunal for the Former Yugoslavia', *Max Planck Yearbook of United Nations Law* (1998) 97–140, at 128–131. Droege and Giorgou provides an overview of these developments in their analysis of the development of IHL, see, C. Droege and E. Giorgou, 'How International Humanitarian Law Develops', 920–921 *International Review of the Red Cross* (2022) 1798–1839, at 1812–1815.

[64] For example, Kretzmer, Ben-Yehuda and Furth present a compelling argument that the scope for lawful use of lethal force during NIAC is much narrower than during IAC. In contrast, the ICRC Customary Law Study suggests that, because of development through customary international law, the scope for the use of such force is identical across both regimes. See, D. Kretzmer, A. Ben-Yehuda and M. Furth, 'Thou shall not kill": the use of lethal force in non-international armed conflicts', 47(2) *Israel Law Review* (2014) 191–224.

Customary International Humanitarian Law study is guilty of similar logic. Indeed, the very first sentence of the commentary to rule 137 misstates the lex lata: 'Additional Protocols I and II prohibit the participation of children in hostilities'.[65] Both protocols prohibit the use of children in hostilities, not the participation in hostilities by children. That aside, the Customary Law Study articulates a single norm for application in both IAC and NIAC, effectively watering down the more protective features of Article 4(3)(c) of APII.

Moreover, it is vital to guard against treaty norms, including codifications of customary international law having a chilling effect on the actual development of customary international law. This risk becomes evident when considering the extent to which the ICRC Customary Law Study is accepted without much consideration.[66] Indeed, the use of children for direct participation in hostilities serves as an excellent example. Almost all sources suggest that the customary standard is that children younger than fifteen may not be used for direct participation.[67] The ICRC Customary Law Study, for example, provides, 'although there is not, as yet, a uniform practice regarding the minimum age for participation in hostilities, there is agreement that it should not be below 15 years of age'.[68] Such a claim is not at all supported by the evidence. There is in fact not a single state internationally who's legal and policy framework provides for direct participation in hostilities of children younger than eighteen, outside of extraordinary circumstances, as provided for in the "all feasible measures" standard. Indeed, very few customary norms that enjoy wide or even universal support is premised on such strong state practice and opinio juris.

[65] Rule 137 provides, 'children must not be allowed to take part in hostilities'. J.-M. Henckaerts, L. Doswald-Beck, Customary International Humanitarian Law, Volume I: Rules (New York, International Committee of the Red Cross, Cambridge, 2005), at 485.

[66] M. Milanovic and S. Sivakumaran, 'Assessing the authority of the ICRC Customary IHL Study: How does IHL develop?', 920–921 *International Review of the Red Cross* (2022) 1856–1897.

[67] The ICRC Customary Law Study, for example, provides in the commentary to Rule 137, that, 'although there is not, as yet, a uniform practice regarding the minimum age for participation in hostilities, there is agreement that it should not be below 15 years of age'. Such a claim is not at all supported by the evidence. There is in fact not a single state internationally who's legal and policy framework provides for direct participation in hostilities of children younger than eighteen, outside of extraordinary circumstances, as provided for in the "all feasible measures" standard. Indeed, very few customary norms that enjoy wide or even universal support is premised on such strong state practice and opinio juris.

[68] Commentary to Rule 137, *supra* note 65.

Instead of conflating the law of IAC and NIAC as a singular expression of customary international law, the correct protective result is achieved by a proper parallel application of Article 4 of APII and Article 77 of API. As previously mentioned, due to the practicalities of war crimes trials, the Court in the *Ntaganda* case was correct in addressing the issue in both the context of IAC and NIAC. However, this approach should be seen as arguments made in the alternative, since the conflict is yet to be classified, rather than a process through which the line between the law of IAC and that of NIAC becomes obscured.

The question of ongoing special protection of children rests on the language expressed in each of the Additional Protocols. Article 77(3) of API provides, 'If, in exceptional cases, despite the provisions of paragraph 2, children who have not attained the age of fifteen years take a direct part in hostilities and fall into the power of an adverse Party, *they shall continue to benefit from the special protection* accorded by this Article, whether or not they are prisoners of war' (own emphasis). Article 4(3)(d) of APII provides, 'the special protection provided by this Article to children who have not attained the age of fifteen years *shall remain applicable to them* if they take a direct part in hostilities despite the provisions of sub-paragraph (c) and are captured' (own emphasis).

In Article 77(3) of API there is a tension between the context of children who 'fall into the power of an adverse Party' and the language that 'they shall continue to benefit from the special protection'. Article 4(3)(d) of APII presents similar tension in addressing the context of children who directly participate in hostilities 'and are captured', while suggesting 'special protection [...] shall remain applicable to them'. Both formulations allow three possibilities: (1) the emphasis is to be placed on the ongoing nature of special protection, after all something cannot be deemed to be continuing or to remain applicable, if at one point it ceases and is only reactivated upon a change in circumstances, that is, falling into the hands of an adverse party or being captured, (2) the listed contexts of falling into the hands of an adverse party or being captured are prerequisites or triggers for continued special protection, meaning such protection cease to apply once the child participates in hostilities, (3) the drafters included the reference to context, as they deemed the special protection not to be operational on an intra-party basis. Thus, while children continue to be the beneficiaries of such special protection throughout, it is only once they fall into the hands of an adverse party or are captured that such special protection can be invoked to any material consequence.

The commentary to Article 77 of API offer little by way of clarification. The discussion focuses on children who are detained, and it is unclear whether more general statements are to be read in this narrower context. For example, potentially the most useful part of the commentary states, 'Finally, all children who are in the situation just referred to can rely on the provisions of Article 77, even if they are prisoners of war or protected persons under the fourth Convention'.[69] However, the 'situation just referred to' was children under fifteen years who participates in hostilities under conditions that exclude prisoner-of-war status, but amount to protected person under the fourth Geneva Convention.[70] Rather oddly, on this issue the most illuminating part appears in the commentary to Article 4(3)(d) of APII, but in reference to Article 77(3) of API.[71] The commentary offers reasons for the weaker protection against child use for participation in hostilities in API when compared to APII, and specifically provides that such weaker protection 'leaves the door open to exceptions which justify the provision that if children under fifteen nevertheless participate in hostilities, they still continue to enjoy the special protection laid down for children'.[72] This is unambiguous. The commentary to APII further provides:

> It should be recalled that the aim of this provision is to guarantee children special protection in the turmoil caused by situations of conflict. For this reason it seemed useful to specify in this sub-paragraph that children will continue to enjoy privileged rights in case the age limit of fifteen years laid down in subparagraph (c) is not respected. In this case making provision for the consequences of any possible violation tends to strengthen the protection.[73]

The commentary to rule 136 of the ICRC Customary Law study supports this position:

[69] B. Zimmermann et al., *Commentary on the Additional Protocols of 8 June 1977 to the Geneva Conventions of 12 August 1949*, (Geneva: International Committee of the Red Cross, 1987), at Art. 77.

[70] Ibid.

[71] Ibid, at Art. 4(3)(d).

[72] Ibid.

[73] Ibid.

> Lastly, it should be noted that Additional Protocol I provides that children who do take a direct part in hostilities and fall into the power of an adverse party shall continue to benefit from the special protection to which they are entitled, whether they are prisoners of war or not.[16] None of the rules which identify such special protection, such as the prohibition of sexual violence (see Rule 93) and the obligation to separate children from adults in detention (see Rule 120) provide for an exception in the event that children have taken part in hostilities. In addition, none of the practice supporting the prohibition of the participation of children in hostilities provides that they should be deprived of their special protection if they do participate in hostilities.[74]

While these commentaries support rather strongly the conclusion that special protection continues to apply throughout and need not be re-triggered by any specific context, neither addresses the question as to against whom such special protection can be invoked. Children are clearly the beneficiaries of the special protection; however, which parties incur obligations in IHL owed to these children? IHL is often conceived of as a regime of international law in terms of which obligations are owed between warring parties, precluding obligations being owed by an armed group or armed force to its constituent members.[75] However, this framing is premised on the fallacy that absent an express rule on intra-party violations, the nature of IHL obligations is somehow defined independently of individual protective norms. The more plausible position is reflected in the Commentaries of the International Law Commission (ILC) to the Draft Articles on Responsibility of States for Internationally Wrongful Acts of 2001 (Draft Articles), which recognises that 'an internationally wrongful act may involve legal consequences in the relations between the State responsible for that act and persons or entities other than States'.[76] The ILC Commentary further confirmed that whether persons or non-state entities

[74] Commentary to Rule 136, *supra* note 65.

[75] See, for example, Clapham, *supra* note 16, at 16; M. Cottier and J. Grignon, 'Paragraph 2(b)(xxvi): Conscription or Enlistment of Children and their Participation in Hostilities', in O. Triffterer and K. Ambos (eds), *The Rome Statute of the International Criminal Court: A Commentary* (3rd edn, Munich: CH Beck-Hart-Nomos, 2015) 519–528, at 523.

[76] Draft Articles on Responsibility of States for Internationally Wrongful Acts, with Commentaries (2001), 2(2) *Yearbook of the International Law Commission, 2001*, (New York and Geneva: United Nations, 2007), (adopted by International Law Commission, GA Res A/56/10), at Art. 28, 87–88, § 3.

are entitled to invoke responsibility on their own account will be determined by the particular primary rule.[77]

The very formulation of the prohibition of the recruitment and use of children presents an exception to a rigid understanding of intra-party violations: it is trite that the use for direct participation in hostilities of children previously unlawfully recruited amounts to a further violation of IHL.[78] Indeed, as much was conceded by Ntaganda's defence team: 'The fact that the crime of using child soldiers to participate actively in hostilities can be committed by a perpetrator against members of his own party to the conflict, is an express exception to the principle that war crimes can only be committed against members of the adversaries or those in the hands of a party to the conflict by virtue of being detained or interned'.[79] This peculiarity of the obligation created in terms of the prohibition against the recruitment and use of children emphatically illustrates that the relevant provisions do indeed provide for special protection that can be invoked on an intra-party basis. There is a grotesque irony in the suggestion that commission of an offence as abhorrent as the use for active participation in hostilities of children younger than fifteen can shield the perpetrator from prosecution for the rape and sexual slavery of the same child victims. The Trial Chamber in *Ntaganda* recalled the general principle of law that 'there is a duty not to recognise situations created by certain serious breaches of international law', moreover 'one cannot benefit from one's own unlawful conduct'.[80] There is indeed much to say

[77] Ibid, at 95. For further discussion see, M. Sassòli, 'State responsibility for violations of international humanitarian law', 848 *International Review of the Red Cross* (2002) 401–434, at 418–419; L. Hill-Cawthorne, 'Rights under international humanitarian law' 28 *European Journal of International Law* (2017) 1187–1215, at 1206–1207; R. Hoffman (co-rapporteur), *Art 6. Declaration of International Law Principles on Reparation for Victims of Armed Conflict*, International Law Association (2010), available at https://www.ila-hq.org/en_GB/documents/conference-report-the-hague-2010-10 (last visited 13 February 2023), at 13–21.

[78] The Appeals Chamber of the Special Court for Sierra Leone put it thus, 'these modes of recruiting children [enlistment; conscription and use] are distinct from each other and liability for one form does not necessarily preclude liability for the other'. See Judgment, *The Prosecutor v. Moinina Fofana and Allieu Kondewa* (hereafter CDF) (SCSL-04-14-A), Appeals Chamber, 28 May 2008, § 139.

[79] *Ntaganda* (Challenge to Counts 6 and 9), § 30.

[80] *Ntaganda*, Trial Chamber Judgment, § 53.

about the importance of preventing manifestly unjust conclusions based on legal-technical interpretation, as would be required in terms of a "thick" conception of the rule of law.

Intra-Party Violations and the Dialectics of Active Versus Direct Participation in Hostilities

The question as to whom are regarded as members of an armed force or group for purposes of intra-party violations is not readily clear. In IAC the determination is status-based and thus more straightforward, 'members of the armed forces' is a term of art, with several legal consequences.[81] The notion of membership in an organized armed group is more complex.[82] The structure of non-state armed groups in NIACs is such that an affiliation to such a group, such as being a cook or collecting firewood and water, can surely not be regarded as amounting to a form of membership of the group with the consequences of losing IHL protection.[83] Membership in such groups may often also be more transient. The defence in *Ntaganda* made their submissions in the context of a NIAC, and their substantive argument focused heavily on the scope of protection ratione personae offered by CA3.[84] In this context, there are two possible bases for Ntaganda's argument: (1) the child soldiers in question fall outside of the protective scope of IHL on the basis of their membership of the UPC; or (2) they fall outside of the protective scope of IHL on the basis that they are direct participants in hostilities. The language of CA3 is clear: 'Persons taking no active part in the hostilities, *including* members of armed forces who have laid down their arms and those placed hors de combat by sickness, wounds, detention, or any other cause, shall in all circumstances be treated humanely, without any adverse distinction

[81] For example, see, Commentary to Rule 3, *supra* note 65.

[82] For discussion in the context of Common Article 3 to the Geneva Conventions, see, Kleffner, 'The Beneficiaries of the Rights Stemming from Common Article 3', *supra* note 21, at 435–436.

[83] There is a concern the broad protection offered by Art. 4(3)© of the Protocol Additional to the Geneva Conventions of 12 August 1949, and relating to the Protection of Victims of Non-International Armed Conflicts (hereafter APII) against the use of children younger than fifteen for indirect participation in hostilities may equate these children to members of the group whose lose IHL protection. This is, however, not a justified conclusion.

[84] See generally, *Ntaganda* (Challenge to Counts 6 and 9), *supra* note 3.

founded on race, colour, religion or faith, sex, birth or wealth, or any other similar criteria' (own emphasis).[85]

The question whether a person falls within the protective scope of CA3 is determined based on conduct, not status. The included examples of members of armed forces who have laid down their arms and those placed hors de combat are just that, examples. This is evident from the language '*including* members of armed forces'.[86] It is well established in ICL that the offences of enlistment, conscription and use of children for active participation in hostilities are separate offences. For instance, the Trial Chamber held in *Lubanga*, 'it follows that the status of a child under fifteen who has been enlisted or conscripted is independent of any later period when he or she may have been "used" to participate actively in hostilities'.[87] Those children who have been enlisted or conscripted by Ntaganda, but who does not actively participate in hostilities fall within the scope of protection of CA3. They can thus not be excluded from a charge under Article 8(2)(e)(vi) for rape and sexual slavery. The position of children who are in fact used for participation in hostilities is somewhat more complex.

As previously discussed, the law of NIAC absolutely prohibits the use of children younger than fifteen for participation in hostilities, whereas the law of IAC only requires parties to a conflict to take all feasible measures not to use such children for direct participation in hostilities (DPH).[88] The notion of DPH is a term of art in IHL that is of fundamental importance as this is the standard that allows the principle of distinction to be operationalised in respect of fighters who do not have the status of combatants as well as civilians.[89] Yet, at the same time, it is the standard that

[85] Geneva Conventions, Common Art. 3(1), (own emphasis).

[86] Kleffner, 'The Beneficiaries of the Rights Stemming from Common Article 3', *supra* note 21, at 435–437.

[87] *Lubanga*, Trial Chamber Judgment, § 609.

[88] APII, Art. 4(3)(c) and Protocol Additional to the Geneva Conventions of 12 August 1949 and relating to the Protection of Victims of International Armed Conflicts, Art. 77(2).

[89] For example, Rule 6 of the ICRC Customary Law Study provides, 'Civilians are protected against attack, unless and for such time as they take a direct part in hostilities', *supra* note 65. This is a distillation of Art. 51(3) API and Art. 13(3) APII.

determines whether a child is unlawfully used in international armed conflict.[90] DPH as a protective threshold thus acts as a check on DPH as a targeting threshold and vice versa.[91] The Rome Statute departs from this standard, by proscribing the use of children 'to participate actively in hostilities'.[92] The debate as to whether these standards are synonymous predates the Rome Statute, as CA3 to the Geneva Conventions refer to "active part in the hostilities"; in contrast, the Additional Protocols refers to "direct participation in hostilities". The thrust of pre-ICC jurisprudence confirms the synonymity of the terms, a particular compelling factor is that the authoritative French texts of the conventions and protocols uses consistent terminology—*participent directemen*.[93] Thus, the conclusion that 'direct' and 'active' should be deemed the same is justified, and indeed, until such time that the ICC diverged, the dominant view was that these were the same standards. However, in the *Lubanga Confirmation of Charges* decision, the ICC held that while active participation encompasses DPH, it is considerably broader: ' "Active participation" in hostilities means not only direct participation in hostilities, combat in other words, but also covers active participation in combat-related activities such as scouting, spying, sabotage and the use of children as decoys, couriers or at military check-points'.[94]

[90] API, at Art. 77(2). There is debate as to whether the notion of DPH should be singularly construed across the various contexts it is used in the Geneva Convention Framework. The ICRCs *Interpretive Guidance on the Notion of Direct Participation in Hostilities* provides that the Guidance 'examines the concept of direct participation in hostilities only for the purposes of the conduct of hostilities'. However, this does not necessarily imply that the standard should be differently construed, but rather that the Guidance excludes contexts other than the conduct of hostilities from consideration, and thus in effect leaves this question open. See, for example, Fatima, *supra* note 61, at 182–183; and N. Melzer, *Interpretive Guidance on the Notion of Direct Participation in Hostilities under International Humanitarian Law*, International Committee of the Red Cross (ICRC), May 2009, available online at https://shop.icrc.org/interpretive-guidance-on-the-notion-of-direct-participation-in-hostilities-under-international-humanitarian-law-pdf-en.html (last visited 13 February 2023), at 11.

[91] For my previous more detailed analysis of this, see G. Waschefort, *International Law and Child Soldiers* (Oxford: Hart Publishing, 2015), at 62–68.

[92] Rome Statute, *supra* note 11, at Art. 8(2)(b)(xxvi) and Art. 8(2)(e)(vii).

[93] Kleffner, 'The Beneficiaries of the Rights Stemming from Common Article 3', *supra* note 21, at 436–439. Compare: Geneva Conventions, at Common Art. 3(1), API, at Arts. 43(2), 47(2)(b), 51(3), 67(1)(e), 77(2) and 77(3), as well as APII, at Arts. 4(1), 4(3)(d) and 13(3).

[94] *Lubanga* (Confirmation of Charges Decision), *supra* note 24, § 261.

It is vital to emphasise that the ICC has not reinterpreted DPH to be a broader concept than otherwise determined, rather it held that active participation in hostilities, as used in the Rome Statute is a different and broader standard than DPH. Indeed, unlike the case with the Geneva Conventions and Additional Protocols where the French text uses consistently the equivalent langue to 'direct participation' (*participent directemen*), the French text of the Rome Statute uses the equivalent to 'active participation' (*participer avtivement*). As such, this ICC authority has no bearing on, for example, determining the targetability of an individual on the basis of the degree of their participation in hostilities. Within the Geneva Convention treaty regime direct and active participation is generally and must be interpreted as synonymous. The ICC's interpretation of active participation as used in the Rome Statute as broader than DPH is a peculiarity of the drafting history of the Rome Statute and does not impact upon the meaning afforded to that term in CA3.[95]

The level of participation of children who in fact participate in hostilities may fall into a range of categories, including participation falling short of both active and direct participation; participation amounting to active participation in terms of the Rome Statute, but falling short of DPH in terms of IHL; participation amounting to both active participation in terms of the Rome Statute as well as DPH in terms of IHL. Where the active participation threshold is met, but not DPH, the use of such child will amount to a war crime under the Rome Statute, but the child will not lose protection against direct attack. Where the threshold of both active and direct participation is met, such use will amount to a war crime and the child will lose protection against direct attack as a matter of IHL. The ICRC Interpretive Guidance on the Notion of DPH provides that a fighter will be regarded as being a direct participant in hostilities, and thus lose protection against attack, for such time that they maintain a continuous

[95] The ICC premised its reasoning as to the meaning of 'active participation' on a Report of the Preparatory Committee on the Establishment of an International Criminal Court. In this sense, the conclusion is not one premised on the legal meaning of 'active participation in hostilities' in international law, but rather as a concept defined specifically for the purposes of the ICC. Indeed, there is a circularity to the argument of the Court in this regard. See, *Lubanga* (Confirmation of Charges Decision) *supra* note 24, § 261; and *Report of the Preparatory Committee on the Establishment of an International Criminal Court*, (A/CONF.183/2/Add.1) (14 April 1998), available online at https://digitallibrary.un.org/record/253772?ln=en (visited 13 February 2023), at 21 (fn. 12).

combat function (CCF).[96] This is relevant to the *Ntaganda* matter, as child soldiers forming part of Ntaganda's forces, may be regarded as having such a CCF. However, the actions of the fighter still must reach the threshold of direct participation to trigger the loss of protection, which is then maintained for the duration of the CCF.[97]

Thus, the charges brought against Ntaganda in relation to the use of children for active participation in hostilities, and the rape and sexual slavery of these children, can be successfully prosecuted without the prosecution establishing beyond reasonable doubt that these children ever directly participated in hostilities in a manner that precludes them from protection under CA3. It may be that in fact the level of participation did meet that of DPH. However, should they choose to go down this path, the onus will be on the defence to establish this as a matter of fact, which necessarily requires conceding the actus reus elements of the war crime of using children for active participation in hostilities.

7.4 Conclusion

Given the meteoric rise of child soldiering as a social and legal issue in the ICC era,[98] this norm perhaps better than any other provides a vantage point from which to take stock of the impact of the jurisprudence and practice of the ICC on the development of IHL—an issue ripe for consid-

[96] Interpretive Guidance, *supra* note 90, at 27–36.

[97] Ibid, Principle II provides, 'In non-international armed conflict, organized armed groups constitute the armed forces of a non-State party to the conflict and consist *only of individuals whose continuous function it is to take a direct part in hostilities*' (own emphasis).

[98] It is hard to imagine today that prior to the adoption of the Rome Statute on 17 July 1998, child soldiering was a peripheral issue in international law. Machel's ground-breaking report that shone the spotlight of international attention on the plight of children associated with fighting forces was released less than two years prior and there had never been an international or domestic prosecution for the military use or recruitment of children. Bassiouni, the Chairman of the Drafting Committee for the Diplomatic Conference, commented during 2000 that the child soldier offence in the Rome Statue in the context of non-international armed conflict (NIAC), is "progressive". See, M.C. Bassiouni, 'The Normative Framework of International Humanitarian Law: Overlaps, Gaps and Ambiguities', 75(3) *International Law Studies* (2000) 1–55, at 20. Scharf, the US Representative at the Rome Conference, went further, 'the use of children under the age of 15 years in hostilities was not currently a crime under customary international law and was another area of legislative action outside the purview of the Conference'. See, *United Nations Diplomatic Conference of Plenipotentiaries on the Establishment of an International Criminal Court, Committee of the Whole*, Summary Record of the 4th Meeting, A/CONF.183/C.1/SR.4, 20 November 1998, § 54.

eration, astutely identified by the editors of this volume. Yet, this meteoric rise against the backdrop of a dearth of jurisprudence and analysis on the issue at the time of the establishment of the ICC meant the war crime of enlistment, conscription, and use of children in hostilities was always going to pose challenges. Absent a general rule or design feature in IHL precluding intra-party violations, the strength of the claim that such violations are not supported in IHL rests on the idea that each protective norm individually excludes intra-party application ratione personae. The firm conclusion of this contribution is that both Article 77 of API and Article 4 of APII affords special protection to children such that they are protected against sexual violence, including rape and sexual slavery; this protection continues to apply after a child is enlisted, conscripted or used in hostilities, and is not subject to any additional status requirement.

The war crimes regime remained in its infancy throughout the period between the trial of Breaker Morant and his co-accused during the Second Boer War and the Nuremburg and Tokyo tribunals following World War II. The ad hoc tribunals for the former Yugoslavia and Rwanda forced the regime to progress rapidly through its school-age development. Yet, it was still heavily reliant on its single parent: IHL—this is evident through jurisprudence such as the influential *Tadic* case which has clarified as much about IHL as it has about ICL.[99] While it has not completely flown the nest, during the ICC era, the war crimes regime has entered adolescence—with development comes greater independence. ICL is indeed reaching a stage of development where greater divergence from IHL and international human rights law should be welcomed. The relationship with these regimes will become toxic if development within ICL, which happens at lightning pace when compared to IHL, monopolizes the understanding and development of IHL. In time, the interpretive principle of systemic integration as provided for in the Vienna Convention on the Law of Treaties will increasingly become the appropriate vehicle through which to consider the impact of IHL in the application of norms of ICL, rather than a relationship of direct dependence as exists to date.[100] Indeed, the differing objectives of IHL and ICL causes strain in the alignment of these

[99] The Trial Chamber as well as Appeals Chamber of the ICTY rendered several decisions of immense importance in the understanding of both IHL and ICL during the course of the prosecution of Duško Tadić. The most significant of which is Decision on the Defence Motion for Interlocutory Appeal on Jurisdiction, *Tadić* (IT-94-1-AR72), Appeals Chamber, 2 October 1995.

[100] Vienna Convention on the Law of Treaties, at Art. 31(3)(c).

regimes.[101] Such a shift is already happening, as is evidenced by the Trial Chamber and Appeals Chamber in *Ntaganda* placing significant reliance on the text of Article 8 of the Rome Statute in reaching the conclusion that there is no status requirement for prosecuting intra-party sexual violence committed against child members of the UPC/FPLC. It should also be said that in relation to the ICC, the sentiment that 'the law of war crimes is, in essence, the criminal phase of humanitarian law', overstates the relationship.[102] Indeed, the war crime of child use, conscription and enlistment serves well as an example. As extensively discussed, this war crime utilizes a standard of active participation in hostilities, which is dramatically more expansive than the IHL notion of DPH, which applies to child use in IAC. Additionally, the Rome Statute includes child enlistment as opposed to recruitment. There is considerable debate as to whether recruitment is broad enough to include voluntary enlistment.[103] The only stumbling block to such divergence is the principle of legality, which does not hamper the ICC in this context, as the Rome Statute does not provide for retrospective jurisdiction.[104] It is nonsensical to suggest that the constituent elements of an underlying offence can diverge from established IHL, but the chapeau to the provision cannot.

[101] See, for example, R. Bartels, 'Discrepancies between international humanitarian law on the battlefield and in the courtroom: the challenges of applying international humanitarian law during international criminal trials', in M. Matthee, B. Toebes and M. Brus, *Armed Conflict and International Law: In Search of the Human Face: Liber Amicorum in Memory of Avril McDonald* (The Hague: T.M.C. Asser Press, 2013) 339–378; and R. Bartels, 'Dealing with the Principle of Proportionality in Armed Conflict in Retrospect: The Application of the Principle in International Criminal Trials', 46(2) *Israel Law Review* (2013) 271–315.

[102] R. Cryer, 'International Criminal Law', in M. D. Evans (ed), *International Law* (5th edn., Oxford: Oxford University Press, 2018) 743–773, at 752.

[103] The following authorities suggest, as put by Schabas, 'enlisting, suggests something more passive [than recruitment], such as putting the name of a person on a list', W. Schabas, *An Introduction to the International Criminal Court* (Cambridge: Cambridge University of Press, 2001), at 50; G. van Bueren, *The International Law on the Rights of the Child* (Amsterdam: Kluwer, 1998), at 337; 61 Dissenting Opinion of Justice Robertson, Decision on Preliminary Motion Based on Lack of Jurisdiction, *Prosecutor v. Sam Hinga Norman*, (SCSL-2004-14-AR72(E)), Appeals Chamber, 31 May 2004, § 27. In contrast, the following authorities suggest that recruitment includes enlistment and conscription, S. Sivakumaran, 'War Crimes before the Special Court for Sierra Leone', 8 *Journal of International Criminal Justice* (2010) 1009–1034, at 1012; Fatima, *supra* note 61, at 185; Longobardo, *supra* note 7, at 605; *Lubanga*, Trial Chamber Judgment, § 607.

[104] The ad hoc and hybrid tribunals of the past was confined to customary international law, as their respective statutes were drafted ex post facto the temporal jurisdiction of the tribunal. While the drafting committee of the Rome Statute was tasked with drafting a statute that reflects customary international law, there were no legal bars to exceeding custom at the time, as in fact the drafters did in several instances. See, Bassiouni, *supra* note 98, at 20; and Scharf, *supra* note 98, § 54.

CHAPTER 8

'Regularly Constituted' Courts of Non-State Armed Groups Between Rome and Geneva

René Provost

8.1 Introduction

Zones of armed conflict are spaces of disorder. While this may seem a truism, the disorder of war is not limited to the violence that is one of the defining features of armed conflict. While armed hostilities are the conceptual core around which the concept of warfare has been constructed, they are echoed and amplified in the dislocation of social structures in a more pervasive fashion. Even during war, much of life goes on for many people in a manner that is not directly affected by the use of armed force, and yet all social relations are transformed by the onslaught of war. The disorder of war spills also into the legal realm, bringing insecurity to aspects of life

R. Provost (✉)
McGill University, Montreal, QC, Canada
e-mail: rene.provost@mcgill.ca

M. Faix, O. Svaček (eds.), *ICC Jurisprudence and the Development of International Humanitarian Law*, Global Issues,
https://doi.org/10.1007/978-3-031-45994-8_8

covered by both civil and criminal law.[1] Belligerents have an interest in managing that insecurity, mirroring the civilian population's right to legal security, resulting in a practice of the administration of justice in zones of conflict that is distinct from justice in peacetime.[2] The distinctiveness of the administration of justice in times of war is amplified when the belligerent in question is not a state but a non-state armed group wielding authority over a territory and a population, whether in an international or non-international armed conflict. Further to abuses committed in the name of law and order before and during World War II, states agreed in Common Article 3 of the 1949 Geneva Conventions to establish a set of minimum conditions to the exercise of public authority in the name of justice as part of even the barebones regime regulating non-international armed conflicts.

Common Article 3 prohibits "the passing of sentences and the carrying out of executions without previous judgment pronounced by a regularly constituted court, affording all the judicial guarantees which are recognised as indispensable by civilised peoples". This legal standard is echoed in a diffracted fashion in Article 6 of the 1977 Additional Protocol II, which prohibits the passing of sentences and execution of penalties "except pursuant to a conviction pronounced by a court offering the essential guarantees of independence and impartiality". While Common Article 3 was not listed among the grave breaches that triggered a duty to prosecute of extradite, violations of this provision came to be considered as war crimes, first as a matter of customary law and then as a specific crime under the 1998 Rome Statute of the International Criminal Court. The Rome Statute, in Article 8(2)(c)(iv), criminalizes the violation of this standard as a war crime, using language that is nearly identical to that of Common Article 3.

In many armed conflicts around the world, non-state armed groups establish their own courts to administer justice, including the passing of sentences and, sometimes, the ordering of executions.[3] Is it possible to

[1] See L. Gayer, 'La «normalité de l'anormal»: recomposer le quotidien en situation de guerre civile', (2018) *Critique internationale*, at 181; S. C. Lubkemann, *Culture in Chaos: An Anthropology of the Social Condition in War* (University of Chicago Press, 2010).

[2] See R. Provost, 'Accountability for International Crimes Within Insurgent Groups', in: M. Bergsmo and T. Song (eds), *Military Self-Interest in Accountability for Core International Crimes* (2nd edn., Torkel Opsahl, 2018).

[3] The analysis presented here is derived from a segment of a broader study of the administration of justice by non-state armed groups in conflict zones, published as R. Provost, *Rebel Courts: The Administration of Justice by Armed Insurgents* (New York, Oxford University Press, 2021).

imagine that rebel courts can meet the requirements set out in Common Article 3 and Article 6 of Protocol II to lawfully administer justice, even in capital cases, as a defence to an indictment under Article 8(2)(c)(iv) of the Rome Statute? The one element of consensus about these requirements is that the notion of a 'regularly constituted' court and the content of the minimum judicial guarantees are left undefined in the Geneva Conventions and the Rome Statute. In order to identify the fundamental attributes of a regularly constituted court, it is necessary to weave together elements of international criminal law, international humanitarian law, and international human rights law.

Although many abuses have been committed in the name of the administration of justice in situations of armed conflicts, prosecutions for the corresponding war crime have been relatively rare, and what little there is has attracted limited attention.[4] In state practice, the prosecution of Omar Sakhanh before Swedish courts for executing a sanction authorized by a court of the Free Syrian Army that was not regularly constituted seem to be the only recent example that deals with the administration of justice by a non-state armed group.[5] For the very first time, the issue has come before an international tribunal, further to the indictment of Al Hassan ag Abdoul Aziz under Article 8(2)(c)(iv) of the Rome Statute in relation to his role as de facto chief of police in Timbuktu when that city was under the control of Ansar Dine/Al-Qaida in the Islamic Maghreb (AD/AQIM).[6] Shortly upon taking control of Timbuktu in April 2012, AD/AQIM established its own Islamic court composed of eight judges connected to the group, seated in the *La Maison* hotel located in the centre of

[4] See J. DePiazza, 'Denial of Fair Trial as an International Crime: Precedent for Pleading and Proving It under the Rome Statute', 15 *Journal of International Criminal Justice* (2017), at 257; D. Marchesi, 'The War Crimes of Denying Judicial Guarantees and the Uncertainties Surrounding Their Material Elements', 54 *Israel Law Review* (2021), at 174.

[5] *Prosecutor v. Omar Haisam Sakhanh,* Stockholms tingsrätt (Stockholm District Court), B 3787–16, Judgment of 16 February 2017, available online (in Swedish) at http://www.ejiltalk.org/wp-content/uploads/2017/03/Stockholms-TR-B-3787-16-Dom-2017-02-16.pdf, with a partial English translation in (2018) 16 *Journal of International Criminal Justice*, at 403–424; confirmed by *Prosecutor v. Omar Haisam Sakhanh*, Svea hovrätt (Svea Court of Appeal), B 2259–17, Judgment of 31 May 2017; leave to appeal was denied by the Supreme Court of Sweden, B 3157–17, 20 July 2017. See Provost, *supra* note 3, at 1–2.

[6] *The Prosecutor v. Al Hassan Ag Abdoul Aziz Ag Mohamed Ag Mahmoud*, Version amendée et corrigée du Document contenant les charges, ICC-01/12-01/18, 2 July 2019, hereafter Al Hassan (Document contenant les charges), §§ 11, 24 (available only in French).

town. From May 2012, the Islamic court issued decisions relating to criminal matters but also private actions to recover debts, settle property disputes, decide family matters, etc.[7] In its decision confirming the charges, the ICC Preliminary Chamber concluded that Al Hassan did not have authority over the AD/AQIM Islamic court but that he directly supervised and sometimes participated in the public execution of sentences imposed by that court.[8] The punishments were claimed by the Islamic court to be derived from Shari'a, and included the execution of murderers, the amputation of the hands of thieves, and the lashing of adulterers, alcohol drinkers, tobacco smokers, and people failing to abide by the dress code imposed by AD/AQIM.[9] The defence vigorously contested the prosecution's suggestion that the Islamic court was 'inherently illegal' because it was not established pursuant to Malian law, maintaining that whether a court is regularly constituted must be determined under international humanitarian law.[10]

The ICC Preliminary Chamber in *Al Hassan* concluded that the AD/AQIM Islamic court was not a regularly constituted court, and thus that the accused could not lawfully execute its judgments. The Chamber came to this conclusion by following an approach adopted in the ICC Elements of Crimes whereby the requirement of regular constitution is replaced by that of the independence and impartiality of the tribunal.[11] In this chapter, I challenge the validity of this confusion between the concept of the regular constitution of a court and its independence and impartiality as inconsistent with the Rome Statute, contrary to Article 9(3). I first map out the concept of a 'regularly constituted' court (2) before tackling the relationship of that concept to that of 'independence and impartiality' that appears as a substitute in Additional Protocol II (3).

[7] Ibid, § 139.

[8] *The Prosecutor v. Al Hassan Ag Abdoul Aziz Ag Mohamed Ag Mahmoud*, Décision de la Chambre préliminaire relative à la confirmation des charges, ICC-01/12-01/18, 13 November 2019, hereafter Al Hassan (Décision de la Chambre préliminaire), §§ 711–723, 888–892 & 968–975 (available only in French).

[9] Ibid, §§ 133–136.

[10] *The Prosecutor v. Al Hassan Ag Abdoul Aziz Ag Mohamed Ag Mahmoud*, Defence Submissions for the Confirmation of Charges, ICC-01/12-01/18, 9 July 2019, hereafter Al Hassan (Defence Submissions for the Confirmation of Charges), §§ 254–255.

[11] *Al Hassan* (Décision de la Chambre préliminaire), *supra* note 8, § 376; K. Dörmann, *Elements of War Crimes under the Rome Statute of the International Criminal Court: Sources and Commentary* (New York, Cambridge University Press, 2003), at 408.

8.2 'Regularly Constituted' Courts

In Article 8(2)(c)(iv), the Rome Statute defines as a war crime "the passing of sentences and the carrying out of executions without previous judgment pronounced by a regularly constituted court". This is language that is taken without any change from Common Article 3, indicating that the meaning to be given to the concept of a 'regularly constituted court' must be derived first and foremost from international humanitarian law. In this section, I first explore the most plausible interpretation of the expression 'regularly constituted' courts under international humanitarian law before considering its relation to the human rights standard that a tribunal be 'established by law'.

Regularly Constituted Courts in Humanitarian Law

In a report on the situation in Ireland in the 1880s, the Earl of Carnarvon bemoaned that "the greatest mischief lay in the informal courts" established by the Irish National League to handle land disputes in its effort to undermine British rule and resist the injustice of English courts: "And when I say 'informal' courts, perhaps I should say 'formal', for they were formal in every respect except that they were secret. ... They were regularly constituted, went into evidence on each side in a regular manner, and under a system of carefully drawn rules, proceeded by written records, and were in complete communication with the Central Body in Dublin".[12] This example, taken from a very different setting, makes the point that we can think of a court as regularly constituted despite the fact that it operates in violation of the national law of a state. In the context of the interpretation of the expression 'regularly constituted' in Common Article 3 of the Geneva Conventions, the first question would be to assess whether this is a concept defined in international humanitarian law. The only other use of the expression 'regularly constituted court' can be found in Article 75(4) of Additional Protocol I, which refers to an 'impartial and regularly constituted Court', but without providing any further specificity to the expression. Article 66 of the Fourth Geneva Convention for its part uses the expression 'properly constituted court' to describe a non-military

[12] Sir A. Hardinge, *The Life of Henry Howard Molyneux Herbert, Fourth Earl of Carnarvon, 1831–1890*, vol. 3 (Humphrey, 1925), at 252; cited in D. Jordan, 'The Irish National League and the "Unwritten Law": Rural Protest and Nation-Building in Ireland 1882–1890', 158 *Past & Present* 146 (1998), at 161.

courts in occupied territory, although the equally authentic French version uses '*régulièrement constitués*' in both Common Article 3 and Article 66. The 1958 ICRC commentary explains that a properly or regularly constituted court "definitely excludes all special tribunals" in favour of ordinary military tribunals established "in accordance with the recognized principles governing the administration of justice".[13] This actually does little to dim the uncertainty surrounding the notion of a regularly constituted court, as it is not specified whether these 'recognized principles' are those derived from public international law or from the domestic legal order of the occupying state.

The United States, because of both its history and its constitutional framework, has had a very significant although not unique engagement with this issue. Since the mid-nineteenth century occupation of Mexico by US troops, it has been the accepted practice that a commander may establish military commissions that have a broad jurisdiction over ordinary criminal offences normally dealt with by civilian courts as well as over violations of the laws and customs of war, inasmuch as they are all geographically and temporally connected to the theatre of war or zone of occupation.[14] There are two aspects of this practice that have some significance for the construction of the concept of a regularly constituted court under international humanitarian law: the fact that military commissions are an emanation of the executive rather than the legislative branch, and the invocation of the laws of war as the foundation of the authority to establish such courts. Unlike courts-martial with jurisdiction over members of the US military, there was for more than a century and a half of their existence no statutory basis for the establishment of military commissions. The executive power to create these court was felt to fall under the power to conduct hostilities in times of war, not a matter for the legislature.[15] A similar pattern was followed in the United Kingdom, where courts operating in Germany after World War II to try enemy soldiers for war crimes were established not by a statute of Parliament but by royal warrant pursuant to the royal prerogative, in other words a purely

[13] International Committee of the Red Cross, *Commentary on the Fourth Geneva Convention* (International Committee of the Red Cross, 1958), at 340.

[14] W. Winthrop, *Military Law and Precedents* (2nd edn., US Government Printing Office, 1920), at 834–835; D. F. Vagts, 'Military Commissions: A Concise History', 101 *American Journal of International Law* (2007), at 35.

[15] Winthrop, *supra* note 14, at 831, 835.

executive decision.[16] In the United States, this power is seen to emanate not only from constitutional law but also from what is referred to as the 'common law of war'.[17] The legality of military commissions under domestic and international law has been challenged in a series of cases before the US Supreme Court, most significantly the *Quirin*, *Yamashita*, and *Hamdan* cases, leading to judgments that illuminate the concept of a regularly constituted court.[18]

In *Quirin*, dealing with a group of German saboteurs arrested on US soil during World War II, President Roosevelt had issued a proclamation establishing a military commission to try the men and to block access to regular courts. The US Supreme Court, in denying habeas corpus, rejected an argument that the commission ought to have been established by statute, seeming to find that the constitution incorporated into US law not only the substantive war crimes under international law but also the wherewithal to sanction them.[19] In *Yamashita*, related to the prosecution of the commander of Japanese forces in the Philippines, the Court rejected a claim that *Quirin* implied that the military commission created for him was subject to the Articles of War, a statute offering various guarantees he was denied. Instead, the majority held that the commission "was not convened by virtue of the Articles of War, but pursuant to the common law of war".[20] Unusually for such a case at the time, this triggered a vigorous dissent from Justice Rutledge, protesting that "the tribunal, specially constituted for the particular trial" was not in accord with basic concepts of American law.[21]

After a half-century of abeyance, military commissions were revived to deal with the presumed authors of the 9/11 attacks, leading to a challenge by one Guantanamo Bay detainee, Salim Hamdan. In its 2006 decision,

[16] United Nations War Crimes Commission, *Law Reports of Trials of War Criminals*, vol. XV, published for the United Nations War Crimes Commission by His Majesty's Stationary Office (1949), at 28–29 (also on the legal basis of Australian and Canadian war crimes courts); A. P. V. Rogers, 'War Crimes Trials under the Royal Warrant: British Practice 1945–1949', 39 *International & Comparative Law Quarterly* 780 (1990), at 788–89 (offering a detailed analysis of the British decision to proceed without a statute).

[17] See e.g. L. Lauer, 'The International War Criminal Trials and the Common Law of War', 1 *St. John's Law Review 18.* (1945).

[18] *Ex Parte Quirin*, 317 US 1 (1942); *In Re Yamashita*, 327 US 1 (1946); *Salim Ahmed Hamdan v. Donald H. Rumsfeld*, 548 US 557 (2006) (hereafter Hamdan v. Rumsfeld).

[19] *Quirin*, *supra* note 18, at 28–29.

[20] *Yamashita*, *supra* note 18, n. 402, at 20.

[21] Ibid, at 44–45. See also *Duncan v. Kahanamoku*, 327 U.S. 304 (1946).

the US Supreme Court found that, in some respects, matters broadly stood as they did for *Yamashita*, with commissions still expressly regulated neither by the Constitution nor by statute.[22] One important change since the previous decisions in 1946, however, was the adoption of the 1949 Geneva Conventions and, with it, the explicit requirement of a 'regularly constituted court'. Justice Stevens for the Court recalled the excoriation of specially constituted tribunals in the *Yamashita* dissent and linked it to the ICRC commentary of Common Article 3 whereby the notion of a regularly constituted court "definitely excludes all special tribunals", to conclude that a tribunal not established by law could not be regularly constituted.[23] This idea is framed more broadly by Justice Kennedy in his concurring opinion:

> Whatever the substance and content of the term "regularly constituted" as interpreted in this and any later cases, there seems little doubt that it relies upon the importance of standards deliberated upon and chosen in advance of crisis, under a system where the single power of the Executive is checked by other constitutional mechanisms. All of which returns us to the point of beginning—that domestic statutes control this case.[24]

In dissent, Justice Alito basically agrees with this approach, arguing that the domestic law of the state in question is the only possible body of law that could regulate the regular constitution of court, but interpreting US law as offering that support.[25] On the opposite, Justice Thomas, arguing that "the common law of war is flexible, responsive to the exigencies of the present conflict, and deferential to the judgment of military commanders", held that the mere longevity of this practice, more than 150 years, shows that military commissions are regularly constituted.[26] In reaction to

[22] *Hamdan v. Rumsfeld*, *supra* note 18, at 590.

[23] Ibid, at 632.

[24] Ibid, at 637.

[25] Ibid, 727 ("In order to determine whether a court has been properly appointed, set up, or established, it is necessary to refer to a body of law that governs such matters. I interpret Common Article 3 as looking to the domestic law of the appointing country because I am not aware of any international law standard regarding the way in which such a court must be appointed, set up, or established, and because different countries with different government structures handle this matter differently. Accordingly, "a regularly constituted court" is a court that has been appointed, set up, or established in accordance with the domestic law of the appointing country").

[26] Ibid, at 691, 720–721.

the striking down of military commissions by the Supreme Court, Congress enacted the *Military Commissions Act* of 2006 to provide the statutory foundation that most judges considered necessary for a court to be regularly constituted.[27] Strikingly, the Act sought to pre-empt any further discussion of the issue under consideration by explicitly stating that the military commissions thus validated were 'regularly constituted court' under Common Article 3.[28] The *Military Commissions Act* of 2009 stepped back from this jurisdictional overreach by eliminating this language, leaving it to courts to determine whether the revamped military commissions correspond to regularly constituted courts pursuant to international humanitarian law.[29]

The conclusion that most members of the US Supreme Court arrived at, that a regularly constituted court must be established pursuant to the domestic law of the relevant state, mirrors the ICRC statement of the corresponding customary international law norm.[30] Some have taken this to imply that non-state armed groups cannot regularly constitute a court pursuant to Common Article 3, as it would be extremely unlikely that national law would authorize a rebel court.[31] The evolution of the

[27] Military Commissions Act of 2006, 10 U.S.C., §§ 948a-950w. This was further amended by the Military Commissions Act of 2009.

[28] Ibid, § 948b(f) ("Status of Commissions Under Common Article 3. A military commission established under this chapter is a regularly constituted court, affording all the necessary 'judicial guarantees which are recognized as indispensable by civilized peoples' for purposes of common Article 3 of the Geneva Conventions"). See C. M. Vázquez, 'The Military Commissions Act, the Geneva Conventions, and the Courts: A Critical Guide', 101 *American Journal of International Law* 73 (2007).

[29] D. Weissbrodt, 'International Fair Trial Guarantees' in A. Clapham and P. Gaeta (eds), *The Oxford Handbook of International Law in Armed Conflict* (New York: Oxford University Press, 2014), at 436.

[30] International Committee of the Red Cross, Customary International Humanitarian Law Database, Rule 100, available online at https://ihl-databases.icrc.org/customary-ihl/eng/docs/v1_rul_rule100 ("A court is regularly constituted if it has been established and organized in accordance with the laws and procedures already in force in a country").

[31] A.-M. La Rosa and C. Wuerzner, 'Armed Groups, Sanctions and the Implementation of International Humanitarian Law', 90 *International Review of the Red Cross* (2008) 327, at 340; J. Somer, 'Jungle Justice: Passing Sentence on the Equality of Belligerents in Non-International Armed Conflict', 89 *International Review of the Red Cross* (2007) 655, at 671–672; S. Sivakumaran, 'Courts of Armed Opposition Groups—Fair Trials or Summary Justice?', 7 *Journal of International Criminal Justice* (2009) 489, at 498; International Committee of the Red Cross, *Commentary on the Additional Protocols of 8 June 1977 to the Geneva Conventions of 12 August 1949* (International Committee of the Red Cross and Martinus Nijhoff, 1987), § 4600.

jurisprudence of the US Supreme Court examined earlier can be taken to challenge a rigid equation between the regular constitution of courts and statutory authorization under the domestic law of the state. To do so would, for instance, present a challenge to the legality of international courts like the ICTY or ICTR that were not established pursuant to the domestic legal order of any given state.[32] The central concern animating the requirement that criminal law be administered by a regularly constituted court is not the defence of state sovereignty but rather the humanitarian protection of those tried in conflict zones. Returning to the statement by Justice Rutledge in *Yamashita* against ad hoc courts created specifically to try one person, and to Justice Kennedy's reflection in *Hamdan* that a requirement of regular constitution speaks to the need for advanced and deliberate consideration of the means to administer justice in a manner that prevents abuses, we can agree that states normally carry out such deliberation by way of legislation, although in unusual circumstances perhaps they could do so otherwise. Non-state armed groups, for their part, are less systematically reliant on legislation, although some may indeed have fixed rules that capture such deliberate consideration. If a court was established pursuant to rebel law, then it could meet the requirement of a regularly constituted court.[33] Otherwise, rather than a focus on formal outcomes of deliberative processes, the analysis should investigate whether the court was established with a broad mandate to administer justice by way of a norm of general application, as opposed to being a tool devised to arrive at a specific result in a given case. Thus, states and non-state armed groups can both be taken to be able to regularly constitute courts, even if through somewhat different means. As such, this exemplifies the type of substantive rather than formal equality of belligerents.[34]

[32] D. Fleck, 'Comment—Perspectives on Courts Established by Armed Opposition Groups', in H. Krieger (ed.), *Inducing Compliance with International Humanitarian Law* (Cambridge University Press, 2015), 181 note 1.

[33] International Committee of the Red Cross, *Commentary on the Second Geneva Convention* (Cambridge University Press, 2017), § 714.

[34] R. Provost, 'The Move to Substantive Equality in International Humanitarian Law: A Rejoinder to Marco Sassòli and Yuval Shany', 93 *International Review of the Red Cross* (2011), 437.

Courts Established by Law in Human Rights Law

The question of whether a court is regularly constituted pursuant to Common Article 3 and, in turn, Article 8(2)(c)(iv) of the Rome Statute is related to the human rights standard that a court be 'established by law'. International human rights law remains applicable during armed conflicts, even if the obligations it imposes must be adapted to the specificity of these unusual circumstances. Both treaty and customary human rights norms related to due process require that a judicial decision be taken by a court established by law. Thus, Article 14(1) of the International Covenant on Civil and Political Rights provides in part that "In the determination of any criminal charge against him, or of his rights and obligations in a suit at law, everyone shall be entitled to a fair and public hearing by a competent, independent and impartial tribunal established by law". One crucial difference between the humanitarian law norm of a regularly constituted court and the human rights standard of a court established by law is that whereas the former is applicable only with respect to criminal matters, the former cover both civil and penal matters. The ambiguous reference in Article 14(1) of the Covenant to 'a suit at law' is clarified by the French version which employs the expression "*des contestations sur ses droits et obligations de caractère civil*".[35] The human rights requirement of a court established by law thus equally applies to the rebel administration of justice in non-criminal matters, which is a very significant dimension of insurgent governance in many armed conflicts.

Turning to the substance of the human rights norm that a civil or criminal court must be 'established by law', it has been interpreted to normally require that states provide for the constitution of their courts by way of statutes adopted by the relevant legislative body, as opposed to a fiat of the executive branch.[36] One limited exception accepted by the Human Rights Committee under the Covenant on Civil and Political Rights relates to

[35] *Human Rights Committee, General Comment 32 (Article 14),* U.N. Doc. CCPR/C/GC/32, 23 August 2007, §§ 16–17. See S. Joseph and M. Castan, *The International Covenant on Civil and Political Rights: Cases, Materials, and Commentary* (Oxford University Press: Oxford, 2013), at 434. The American Convention on Human Rights specifies in its equivalent provision that it applies to "the determination of his rights and obligations of a civil, labor, fiscal, or any other nature".

[36] *Human Rights Committee,* ibid, § 3; *Caso Barreto Leiva* vs. *Venezuela,* IACtHR, Judgment, 17 November 2009, § 76; *Coëme and Others v. Belgium,* ECtHR, Appl. Nos 32492/96, 32547/96, 32548/96, 33209/96, and 33210/96, Judgment, 22 June 2000, § 98.

religious or customary courts, although their jurisdiction is to be limited and under supervision of state courts.[37] In an amicus curiae brief submitted to the ICC in the *Bemba* trial, Amnesty International argued that a 'competent authority' in Article 28 of the Rome Statute must be interpreted to conform to the human rights requirement of a court established by law, and that a court of a non-state armed group would not normally meet this condition.[38] The ICC Trial Chamber in its decision did not directly address the impact of this human rights norm, but it did hold against the accused that "he was the competent authority to investigate and prosecute the crimes", and that his failure to empower members of his group to do so attracted responsibility pursuant to Article 28 of the Rome Statute.[39] On appeal, the Appeals Chamber found that the Trial Chamber had erred in appreciating factual limits to a remote commander's material ability to establish a courts-martial to sanction violations by his troops, thus implicitly proclaiming the legal right, indeed duty, to do so.[40] In a different context, the ICTY Appeals Chamber in the *Tadic* case considered a defence argument that the ICTY itself was not 'established by law' because its creation resulted from a resolution of the UN Security Council rather than from a statutory instrument enacted by a legislative body. The ICTY found that a court could be 'established by law' by a range of decision-making bodies that was not limited to legislative assemblies, inasmuch as it was set up in a manner consistent with the rule of law

[37] *Human Rights Committee*, ibid, § 32. For example, the *Dina* customary court system in Madagascar, which imposed capital punishment further to summary trials failing to meet fair trial guarantees, was not seen as established by law: *Human Rights Committee, Concluding Observations on Madagascar*, UN doc CCPR/C/MDG/CO/3, 11 May 2007, § 16.

[38] Amicus Curiae Observations on Superior Responsibility submitted pursuant to Rule 103 of the Rules of Procedure and Evidence, *Situation in the Central African Republic in the Case of the Prosecutor v. Jean-Pierre Bemba Gombo*, (ICC-01/05-01/08-406), Pre-Trial Chamber II, 20 April 2009, at 15–16, available at http://www.legal-tools.org/doc/9efb78/. The one exception conceded there are the courts of the Confederate States during the US Civil War.

[39] Trial Judgment, *Situation in the Central African Republic in the case of the Prosecutor v. Jean-Pierre Bemba Gombo*, (ICC-01/05-01/08) 21 March 2016 (hereafter Prosecutor v. Bemba), § 733.

[40] Appeals Judgment, *Situation in the Central African Republic in the case of the Prosecutor v. Jean-Pierre Bemba Gombo*, (ICC-01/05-01/08 A), 8 June 2018, §§ 167–169. The deduction is warranted on the basis of the deference due on appeal to the Trial Chamber as trier of facts, whereas no such deference obtains in relation to questions of law: *Situation in the Democratic Republic of the Congo in the Prosecutor v. Thomas Lubanga Dyilo*, Appeals judgment, 1 December 2014, (ICC-01/04-01/06 A 5), §§ 16–28.

requirements respecting fair trial guarantees.[41] The ICTY decision does stand as a rebuttal of the principle that a court established by law can only be established by way of national legislation, in the domestic legal orders of states; rather, the international context of the creation of the ICTY means that this norm corresponds to a different establishment process. If the international community is not structured around a tryptic of executive, legislative and judicial branches that mirrors the constitutional orders of states, then necessarily a 'court established by law' must correspond to a different process.

This finding can be transposed to the establishment of courts by non-state armed groups, in the sense that these groups typically do not have a constitutional structure that replicates that of states. It follows that, for armed groups, the process to constitute a 'court established by law' will not necessarily entail the enactment of a statute. The European Court of Human Rights considered a situation that bears many similarities to the rebel administration of justice in *Ilascu v Moldova and Russia*, in which the applicant challenged the legality of their detention and treatment pursuant to decisions of the courts of the 'Moldavian Republic of Transdniestria', an autonomous entity not recognized under international law. With respect to the legality of such courts under the European Convention on Human Rights, the Court noted:

> In certain circumstances, a court belonging to the judicial system of an entity not recognised under international law may be regarded as a tribunal "established by law" provided that it forms part of a judicial system operating on a "constitutional and legal basis" reflecting a judicial tradition compatible with the Convention, in order to enable individuals to enjoy the Convention guarantees.[42]

[41] *The Prosecutor v. Duško Tadic*, Decision on the Defence Motion for interlocutory Appeal on Jurisdiction (IT-94-AR72), 2 October 1995, §§ 41–47.

[42] *Ilascu v Moldova and Russia*, ECtHR, Appl. No 48787/99, (2004) ECHR 318, § 460; *Güzelyurtlu v. Cyprus and Turkey*, ECtHR, Grand Chamber, Judgment, Appl. No 36965/07, 29 January 2019, §§ 248–249. See J. Willms, 'Courts of Armed Groups—a Tool for Inducing Higher Compliance with International Humanitarian Law?' in H. Krieger (ed.), *Inducing Compliance with International Humanitarian Law* (Cambridge, Cambridge University Press, 2015), at 156. On the issue of the exhaustion of local remedies, the European Court has seemed to show itself open to the possibility that an applicant may be required to seek remedies before the courts of a non-state entity before turning to the Strasbourg court: Provost, *supra* note 3, at 412–413.

The Court found that legal requirements for what constitutes a court must take into account the existence of an armed conflict, such that what may be needed for a court to be established by law by an armed opposition group in a conflict zone would not necessarily correspond to the full array of requirements normally demanded of states in peace time.[43] All of these elements seem to align with those associated with the concept of a 'regularly constituted court' pursuant to Common Article 3 and international humanitarian law more generally, centrally the need for deliberate consideration by an established authority to constitute a court of general jurisdiction that will apply 'law' broadly defined. Returning to the *Al Hassan* case, the question is thus whether AD/AQIM, having established its authority over Timbuktu, constituted the Islamic court pursuant to a deliberate decision to create a court of general jurisdiction applying an identified body of law. On the basis of this criteria, it certainly is not evident that the Islamic court fails to meet the requirement of regular constitution under Article 8(2)(c)(iv) of the Rome Statute.

8.3 Judicial Guarantees of Independence and Impartiality

The requirement that a court be regularly constituted is not the only one imposed by Article 8(2)(c)(iv) of the Rome Statute as a condition of the lawfulness of the imposition of a sentence and the carrying out of execution in an armed conflict. In addition, the provision requires that the court afford "all judicial guarantees which are generally recognized as indispensable". Once again, the wording is nearly identical to that of Common Article 3, with the omission of the outdated and offensive reference to 'civilized nations'. This element is also found in Article 6(2) of Additional Protocol II, which demands "a court offering the essential guarantees of independence and impartiality". The prosecution in *Al Hassan* argued that the AD/AQIM Islamic court in Timbuktu was neither independent nor impartial, a claim that the Pre-Trial Chamber provisionally found reasonable.[44] This requirement raises two distinct questions, which will be discussed in turn: first, what is the relationship between the condition that

[43] *Hassan v UK*, ECtHR, Grand Chamber, Judgment, Application No 29750/09, 16 September 2014, §§ 104–106.

[44] *Al Hassan* (Document contenant les charges), *supra* note 6, §§ 425–433; *Al Hassan* (Décision de la Chambre préliminaire), *supra* note 8, §§ 416–427.

a court be 'regularly constituted' and its ability to afford judicial guarantees? And second, how are the concepts of judicial independence and impartiality to be understood under international humanitarian law when applied to the courts of non-state armed groups?

Fairness as Rightness

In the formulation codified in Common Article 3, to repeat the full statement of the rule, a lawful conviction and sentence must be issued by "a regularly constituted court, affording all the judicial guarantees which are recognized as indispensable by civilized peoples". The formulation adopted in 1977 in Article 6(2) of Protocol II differs in significant ways from Common Article 3, referring to "a court offering the essential guarantees of independence and impartiality", but omitting any mention of the regular constitution of the tribunal. A third variant is used in Article 75(4) of Additional Protocol I, applicable to an international armed conflict, requiring that a conviction be "pronounced by an impartial and regularly constituted court respecting the generally recognized principles of regular judicial procedure". The least that can be said is that the use of different formulations in these three treaty provisions casts a degree of uncertainty as to the institutional features required of a court under humanitarian law.

One approach to resolve this uncertainty, adopted by the ICRC in its commentaries to Protocol II and Common Article 3, holds that the requirement that the court be regularly constituted simply has been abandoned in Protocol II. For the ICRC, the need for regular constitution "is replaced by" the need for independence and impartiality.[45] The rationale for this interpretation rests on the assumption that a court can only be 'regularly constituted' if it is established pursuant to the laws of the state, which is surely unlikely for a rebel court. As a result, if insurgents are ever to be able to administer justice in territory under their control, then the regularly constituted requirement must be jettisoned in favour of independence and impartiality. This seems an awkward approach in at least two

[45] International Committee of the Red Cross, *supra* note 31, § 4600; International Committee of the Red Cross, *Commentary on the Third Geneva Convention* (Cambridge University Press, 2020), § 729; P. Akhavan, 'Judicial Guarantees' in A. Clapham, P. Gaeta and M. Sassòli (eds), *The 1949 Geneva Conventions: A Commentary* (New York, Oxford University Press, 2015), at 1223; Marchesi, *supra* note 4, at 197.

ways: first, it goes beyond a teleological interpretation of the Conventions and Protocol II, to instead posit a conclusion that is neither stated in nor derivable from the instruments (armed groups must be able to establish courts) in order to justify a particular reading of Common Article 3 and Article 6(2) of Protocol II. The second problem is that Additional Protocol II was not adopted to amend or change the Geneva Conventions but rather to supplement them. There is nothing in the text or in the travaux préparatoires of Protocol II that suggests an intent to delete the regularly constituted requirement found in Common Article 3. It is important to remember that the scope of application of the Protocol is narrower than that of Common Article 3, such that any armed conflict governed by the newer Protocol will *also* be governed by Common Article 3. There would be a certain paradox, if not contradiction, in loosening the institutional requirement for the regular constitution of courts in an armed conflict that is defined more narrowly in part on the basis of a demand that armed groups be more structured and responsible.[46] In its study of customary humanitarian law, the ICRC in Rule 100 maintains both requirements of a regular constitution and independence and impartiality for international as well as non-international armed conflicts, a position that appears to mirror more accurately the interplay of Common Article 3 and Article 6(2) of Protocol II.[47]

A slightly different approach is taken in the Elements of Crimes adopted pursuant to the Rome Statute of the ICC. The Statute itself, in Article 8(2)(c)(iv), provides for jurisdiction over serious violations of Common Article 3, formulating the requirement for a 'regularly constituted court' with the same wording as the Geneva Conventions. One can note that the drafters of the Rome Statute did not slavishly transpose the wording of the Geneva Conventions in this provision, as they eliminated in the latter part of that sentence the reference to "civilized peoples" that is found in the older treaty. Pursuant to Article 9 of the Rome Statute, the Assembly of States Parties may adopt Elements of Crimes to "assist the Court in the interpretation and application of articles 6, 7 and 8". The Elements of Crimes must be consistent with the Rome Statute (Art. 9(3)) and, as such, are not binding on the Court. It is fair to say, however, that they are

[46] Protocol Additional to the Geneva Conventions of 12 August 1949, and relating to the Protection of Victims of Non-International Armed Conflicts (Protocol II), 9 June 1977, at Art. 1(1).

[47] International Committee of the Red Cross, *supra* note 20, Rule 100.

considered highly persuasive.[48] The Elements of Crimes related to Article 8(2)(c)(iv) subsume the requirement that the court be "regularly constituted" into the requirement touching on due process:

> War Crime of Sentencing or Execution Without Due Process [...]
>
> There was no previous judgement pronounced by a court, or the court that rendered judgement was not "regularly constituted", that is, it did not afford the essential guarantees of independence and impartiality, or the court that rendered judgement did not afford all other judicial guarantees generally recognized as indispensable under international law.[49]

The argument here is no longer that the rule has changed so that requirement for a court to be 'regularly constituted' has been replaced by one that it be independent and impartial, as suggested by the ICRC in its commentary, but rather that the requirement of regular constitution be interpreted as met if a court is independent and impartial.

The challenge in Rome was that the crimes in non-international armed conflicts were primarily defined in relation to the more universally agreed-upon Common Article 3, but that Additional Protocol II had come to supplement international humanitarian law in significant ways that should be reflected in international criminal law. An initial Belgian proposal for this Element of Crime had clearly differentiated three situations that would correspond to a violation of Article 8(2)(c)(iv): there was no previous judgment; the court was not regularly constituted; the court did not afford essential guarantees of independence and impartiality.[50] Somehow, during the negotiation process, this accurate rendering of the rule was mushed into the paragraph reproduced above which introduces significant confusion in the elements of this particular crime. Under the Elements of Crimes, there is no longer any independent substance associated with the requirement of regular constitution, which is wholly subsumed into that of independence and impartiality. As noted by Jonathan Somer, there is here clearly a tension between the binding wording of the Rome Statute and the interpretation suggested by Elements of Crimes.[51] More than an

[48] Dörmann, *supra* note 11, at 8.

[49] Ibid, at 408.

[50] *Proposal by Belgium concerning article 8, paragraph 2 (c) (iv) of the Statute of the International Criminal Court*, UN Doc. PCNICC/1999/WGEC/DP.13 (28 July 1999), available online at https://www.legal-tools.org/doc/e51c85/pdf/

[51] Somer, *supra* note 31, at 675.

inconsistency, it seems difficult not to conclude that the position adopted in the Elements of Crimes is incoherent, something that did not seem to trouble the ICC Pre-Trial Chamber in *Al-Hassan* when it endorsed this approach.[52] Indeed, the Pre-Trial Chamber accurately notes that the drafters of the Elements of Crimes 'discarded Common Article 3' and its requirement of regularly constitution in favour of a test of independence and impartiality said to be an 'objective criterion'.[53] The problem with this reasoning is that the drafters of the Elements of Crimes did not discard only the requirement of Common Article 3 but also, more problematically, the requirement of Article 8(2)(c)(iv) of the Rome Statute, something the Elements of Crimes manifestly cannot lawfully do pursuant to the explicit limit set by Article 9 of the Statute.[54]

The basic and obvious central point is that the substance of the requirement of regular constitution of a court is quite different from that of independence and impartiality: one relates to the process whereby a decision to create a court is taken, and the other to the institutional features of this court. It is not hard to find examples of courts established in the most regular way that fail to afford basic guarantees of independence and impartiality, as in the previous example of the official courts of Syria under Bashar Al-Assad. Conversely, it is not unimaginable that a court might well be independent and impartial and yet fail to have been regularly constituted. Vigilante justice could perhaps be done with independence and impartiality, but it would not be the product of a regularly constituted body. The point is, as explored in the previous subsection, that the regular constitution of courts and their independence and impartiality are mutually reinforcing features that contribute to the fair administration of justice. This also ties back to the relevance of the human rights norm that

[52] *Al Hassan,* (Décision de la Chambre préliminaire), *supra* note 8, § 376.

[53] Ibid, § 377 ("À cet égard, les travaux préparatoires des Eléments des crimes illustrent la volonté des rédacteurs d'établir un critère objectif en établissant un lien entre la notion de tribunal régulièrement constitué et les garanties statutaires. Les rédacteurs se sont dégagés de l'article 3 commun aux quatre Conventions de Genève et n'ont pas retenu la proposition de la Belgique pour la rédaction des Éléments des crimes concernant l'article 8-2-c-iv du Statut, proposition qui érigeait l'absence d'un tribunal régulièrement constitué comme troisième possibilité pour caractériser le crime, indépendamment du respect des principes d'indépendance ou d'impartialité par le tribunal, ou du respect des garanties judiciaires généralement reconnues en droit international").

[54] *The Prosecutor v. Omar Hassan Ahmad Al Bashir*, Decision on the Prosecution's Application for a Warrant of Arrest against Omar Hassan Ahmad Al Bashir (ICC-02/05-01/09), Pre-Trial Chamber I, 4 March 2009, § 128.

tribunals be not only independent and impartial but also 'established by law'. No one seems to have suggested that, under human rights law, if a court is shown to be independent and impartial, then ipso facto it becomes established by law.

As noted by Miriam Gur-Arye and Alon Harel, criminal law is an 'agent-dependent enterprise', in that it matters not only how well justice is done, but also who is doing it.[55] What the requirement of regular constitution in Common Article 3 and Article 8(2)(c)(iv) of the Rome Statute conveys is a sense that rightness is not wholly reducible to fairness.[56] This echoes the need for justice to be administered by institutions and practices established through deliberate consideration by an established authority, forming part of the broader governance by non-state armed groups. As a result, the creation of a court able to afford guarantees of independence and impartiality is a requirement distinct from its regular constitution. The implication in *Al Hassan* is that, if the accused is shown to have executed sentences issued by the AD/AQIM Islamic court, he must establish *both* that this court was regularly constituted *and* that it was independent and impartial.

Institutional Requirements of Independence and Impartiality

Turning to substance, what are the institutional features of a rebel court that will be demanded to show that it can afford judicial guarantees of independence and impartiality? The wording used to describe the required guarantees varies from one provision to the next. It can be noted that the reference to "judicial guarantees which are recognized as indispensable by civilized nations" in Common Article 3 sought to capture an international minimum standard that would avoid the variations found among national legal systems at the time. In 1949, there was no binding international human rights instrument that could provide a common statement of judicial guarantees, and 'civilized nations' was the accepted short-hand to ensure that basic norms such as the presumption of innocence would

[55] M. Gur-Arye and A. Harel, 'Taking Internationalism Seriously: Why International Criminal Law Matters' in J. D. Ohlin and F. Mégret (eds), *Oxford Handbook of International Criminal Law* (New York, Oxford University Press, 2018).

[56] See the argument by David Luban that courts can give themselves legitimacy by the fairness of the justice they provide: D. Luban, 'Fairness to Rightness: Jurisdiction, Legality, and the Legitimacy of International Criminal Law' in S. Besson and J. Tasioulas (eds), *The philosophy of international law* (New York, Oxford University Press 2010), at 579.

obtain everywhere.[57] The fact that Article 8(2)(c)(iv) of the Rome Statute eliminates the last three words ('by civilized nations') and the Elements of Crimes' outright replacement of these words by a reference to international law do not correspond to a change in the law, but are merely a reflection of the evolution of the international legal context in which Common Article 3 must be interpreted. As was made explicit during the drafting of Article 6(2) of Additional Protocol II, all these varied statements can be taken today as reflecting the essential guarantees of independence and impartiality as entrenched in international human rights law, most particularly in Article 14 of the ICCPR, as adjusted to reflect the particular context of an armed conflict.[58]

The twin requirements of independence and impartiality are interdependent and overlap to some extent. Thus, the fact that the corresponding provision in Additional Protocol I, Article 75(4), omits the mention of independence to refer only to "an impartial and regularly constituted court", is not taken to signal a different standard. That said, particular attributes have been associated with guarantees of judicial independence, on the one hand, and of judicial impartiality, on the other.

Independence speaks to the autonomy of a court in its consideration of cases. In particular, in international human rights law, various bodies have underscored the need for an arm's length relationship between courts and the executive and legislative branches of government. This translates into rules dealing with the appointment, tenure, and removal of judges such that the position is not so fragile as to make its holders susceptible to pressures from the coequal branches of government.[59] If a judicial body is structured in a manner that allows the leadership of a non-state armed groups to simply direct what decisions are issued, then there is no sense of

[57] See *Diplomatic Conference for the Establishment of International Conventions for the Protection of Victims of War*, Vol. II-B (Geneva, 1949) 83; International Committee of the Red Cross *Commentary on the Second Geneva Convention*, *supra* note 33, § 705; on civilization as a common standard in international law, see M. Koskenniemi, *The Gentle Civilizer of Nations: The Rise and Fall of International Law, 1870–1960* (Cambridge, Cambridge University Press, 2002), at 132–136.

[58] M. Bothe, *New Rules for Victims of Armed Conflicts: Commentary on the Two 1977 Protocols Additional to the Geneva Conventions of 1949* (2nd edn., Nijhoff, 2013), at 748.

[59] *Human Rights Committee*, *supra* note 35, at 5–6. See also *UN Basic Principles on the Independence of the Judiciary, adopted by the Seventh United Nations Congress on the Prevention of Crime and the Treatment of Offenders held at Milan from 26 August to 6 September 1985 and endorsed by General Assembly resolutions 40/32 of 29 November 1985 and 40/146 of 13 December 1985.*

independence, and indeed the body in question can hardly merit the label of a court.[60] For instance, witnesses in the *Bemba* trial before the ICC testified that the courts-martial created within the *Mouvement de libération du Congo* were largely a charade meant to hide the fact that judges were merely executing orders issued by their superiors.[61] The prosecutor in *Al Hassan* claimed that the AD/AQIM Islamic court was instrumentalized by the group to carry out its plan, that there was systematic interference by the leadership in the judicial process, and that 'important decisions' were really taken by the leader of the armed group.[62]

Of course, this vision of independence reflects the administration of justice by states through a formal court system operating in peace time. Non-state armed groups, even when they are institutionally sophisticated and exercise broad governance authority, rarely will be constituted in separate and coequal branches of government. As we can see in the operation of the non-state courts of the Islamic State and the Taliban, for example, the rebel administration of justice remains marked by the context of armed hostilities in its design, objectives, and operation.[63] Even in groups like the LTTE that have distinct military and political wings, the division does not carry with it any notion of a judicial branch that stands apart from the rest of the movement.[64]

Is it possible, in that context, to have a rebel court that would be considered independent? Transposing the substance of judicial independence to armed groups, we can already note that rebel courts need not be entirely disconnected from such groups in order to be independent, no more than state courts need to be disconnected from the government apparatus. Insurgent courts can be an arm of the rebellion just as state courts can be an arm of the sovereign authority of the state. In both cases, there is no legitimate expectation that the court will be neutral vis-à-vis the policies of the government or armed group.[65] Courts are, after all, a tool of

[60] Ibid, at 6 ("A situation where the functions and competencies of the judiciary and the executive are not clearly distinguishable or where the latter is able to control or direct the former is incompatible with the notion of an independent tribunal").

[61] *Prosecutor v. Bemba*, Trial Judgment, *supra* note 39, at 299, 300, note 1861.

[62] *Al Hassan* (Document contenant les charges), *supra* note 6, §§ 428–429.

[63] See Provost, *supra* note 3, at 103–140.

[64] Ibid, at 220–248.

[65] M. Sassòli, 'L'administration d'un territoire par un groupe armé peut-elle être régie par le droit?' in M. Hottelier, M. H. Randall and A. Flückiger (eds), *Etudes en l'honneur du Professeur Thierry Tanquerel. Entre droit constitutionnel et droit administratif: questions autour du droit de l'action publique* (Genève, Schulthess, 2019), at 271.

governance. It takes political capital to make people obey summons and respect decisions of a court, and that political capital will surely be found at least in part in the more general authority of the armed group as a whole rather than only in the rebel courts themselves.[66] The model offered by the House of Justice in Houran, a court jointly established by nearly one hundred armed groups in Southern Syria which was said to demand that judges have no affiliation with any armed group, thus would be rather unique, possibly as a reflection that it handled not only individual cases but also disputes among the different armed groups.[67] More commonly, rebel judges will be linked to the armed group but exercise their judicial authority with a degree of autonomy from its hierarchy.

One type of state courts that could reasonably be thought to provide a better comparator to insurgent courts are military courts, both because they are attached to the armed forces and because they are designed to operate, at least some of the times, in situations of armed hostilities. The question of the independence of courts-martial has attracted significant attention and criticism, especially in their consistency with human rights requirements that courts be independent and impartial. Considerable work has been done in this respect by the United Nations, first under the aegis of the Sub-Commission on the Promotion and Protection of Human Rights and its Special Rapporteur Emmanuel Decaux, and later by successive Special Rapporteurs on the Independence of Judges and Lawyers appointed by the Human Rights Council.[68] In the context of the administration of justice by state armed forces, independence has been understood

[66] N. Coburn, 'Informal Justice and the International Community in Afghanistan' (United States Institute of Peace, 2013) 26, available online at: https://www.usip.org/publications/2013/04/informal-justice-and-international-community-afghanistan (accessed 28 July 2020).

[67] Geneva Call, Administration of Justice by Armed Non-State Actors (Report from the 2017 Garance Talks), Geneva, 2018, at 10 (statement by Esmat Alabasi). External observers noted that armed groups divided the number of judges each could appoint to the Houran House of Justice, casting some doubt as to their independence: M. Sosnowski, 'The Syrian Southern Front: Why It Offers Better Justice and Hope than Northern Front' (*Syria Comment*, 9 July 2015), available at: https://www.joshualandis.com/blog/the-syrian-southern-front-why-it-offers-better-justice-and-hope-than-northern-front-by-marika-sosnowski/(accessed 15 August 2018).

[68] See especially: *Report submitted by Mr. Emmanuel Decaux to the Sub-Commission on the Promotion and Protection of Human Rights on the administration of justice through military tribunals*, UN Doc. E/CN.4/Sub.2/2004/7; *Report of the Special Rapporteur Gabriela Knaul on the independence of judges and lawyers*, UN Doc. A/68/285 (2013).

to relate to the status of judges and the autonomy of the military judiciary. As regards status, in some countries, military justice is administered by civilian judges (e.g. Belgium, France), while in others the court is composed of service members but they are accorded protections similar to civilian judges (e.g. Russia, Turkey, Spain); in the majority of countries, however, judges do not have special status and remain subject to the chain of command and military discipline (e.g. Argentina, Brazil, Cameroun, United States, Israel).[69] In many cases, national law envisages the possibility that operational officers and enlisted men, rather than officers with legal training attached to the armed forces legal services or judge advocate general, can serve as decision-makers on judicial panels or juries.[70] As regards the autonomy of military justice, external interference can take place at the level of the laying of charges, confirmation of the judgment, and possibility of appeal. Here again, state practice remains widely variable, from outright interference (e.g. China, Cameroon) to a process of confirmation of decisions by political authorities (e.g. Egypt, Ireland, Chile).[71]

No particular distrust of the independence of military courts can be discerned in international humanitarian law. Article 84 of the Third Geneva Convention provides in a very strict manner that "a prisoner of war shall be tried only by a military court", unless the detaining state's own troops may be tried by a civilian court. The ICRC Commentary makes clear that the latter is the exception rather than the rule, and the fact that the court will be trying an enemy is not incompatible with its independence.[72] The same provision specifies that in all cases the court must "offer the essential guarantees of independence and impartiality as generally recognised". A similarly positive disposition towards military courts is evident in Article 66 of the Fourth Geneva Convention, under which civilians in occupied territory may be tried by the "properly constituted, non-political military courts" of the occupying power for offences

[69] Knaul Report, ibid, §§ 26–28; G. Giudicelli-Delage, 'Les garanties procédurales et le droit au recours—rapport de synthèse' in E. Lambert-Abdelgawad (ed), *Juridictions militaires et tribunaux d'exception en mutation: perspectives comparées et internationales* (Archives contemporaines, 2008) 466; G. Nolte and H. Krieger, 'Comparison of European Military Law Systems', in G. Nolte (ed), *European Military Law Systems* (Walter de Gruyter, 2003), at 156–171.

[70] See, e.g. United States Uniform Code of Military Justice, 10 U.S.C, at Art. 25, § 825.

[71] Giudicelli-Delage, *supra* note 69, at 466–467.

[72] International Committee of the Red Cross, *Commentary on the Third Geneva Convention*, *supra* note 45, §§ 3600–3604, 3614.

against its security. The rationale for favouring military courts in situations of occupation is the fact that an occupying force will necessarily bring along its own courts, in order to deal with the inevitable offences and crimes committed by its own forces; as such, these courts will be available in situ, an option preferable to moving civilians charged with an offence to the national territory of the occupant or, one presumes, to the creation of civilian courts of the occupying forces.[73] The role of military courts was left untouched in Additional Protocol I, despite a provision that significantly augmented the due process guarantees owed to anyone prosecuted for an offence related to the conflict, a notion broad enough to include both prisoners of war and civilians in occupied territory (Art. 75(4), Additional Protocol I). All these provisions apply only to situations of international armed conflicts, with no explicit reference to military courts in Common Article 3 or Additional Protocol II.

The picture of the independence of military tribunals that emerges from the jurisprudence of international human rights bodies is radically different. The caselaw of the European Court of Human Rights, the Inter-American Court and Commission of Human Rights, and the African Commission of Human and Peoples' Rights is replete with findings that military courts fail to meet the requirement of independence under international human rights law. Key flashpoints have focused on the lack of insulation of military investigators, prosecutors, and judges from the line of hierarchical authority within the army, on whether violations of human rights should properly fall within the jurisdiction of military courts, on a practice of transferring the prosecution of civilians to military tribunals in situations of emergency or under antiterrorism measures, and on the observance of due process guarantees in military justice.[74] It is interesting

[73] International Committee of the Red Cross, *Commentary on the Fourth Geneva Convention*, *supra* note 13, at 340.

[74] See Knaul Report, *supra* note 53, at 8–19. For a survey of various decisions touching on all these points. See also Ch. M. Cerna, 'The Inter-American System and Military Justice', in A. Duxbury and M. Groves (eds), *Military Justice in the Modern Age* (Cambridge University Press, 2016); F. Andreu-Guzman, 'Les tribunaux militaires et juridictions d'exception dans le système onusien des droits de l'homme', in É. L. Adbelgawad (ed), *Juridictions militaires et tribunaux d'exception en mutation: perspectives comparées et internationales* (Archives contemporaines, 2008); J. Daniel, 'Les tribunaux militaires et juridictions d'exception à l'épreuve de la jurisprudence de la Cour européenne des droits de l'homme', in Adbelgawad, *supra* note 74; É. L. Adbelgawad, 'Les tribunaux militaires et juridictions pénales spéciales sous le contrôle de la Commission africaine des droits de l'homme et des peuples', in Adbelgawad, *supra* note 74.; J. Bucherer, *Die Vereinbarkeit von Militärgerichten mit dem Recht auf ein faires Verfahren gemäß Art. 6 Abs. 1 EMRK, Art. 8 Abs. 1 AMRK und Art. 14 Abs. 1 des UN-Paktes über bürgerliche und politische Rechte* (Heidelberg, Springer, 2010), 37–101.

to note, in that respect, that a number of states have entered reservations aiming to exclude their military justice system from the full application of human rights conventions.[75] Despite repeatedly concluding to the inadequacy of military courts under human rights law, regional human rights courts have not gone so far as to conclude that military courts are inherently unable to meet the requirements of independence and impartiality.[76]

As always, the delineation of the institutional requirements for state courts under international law must be adapted to the reality and limitations of the administration of justice by non-state armed groups. The fact that armed groups are never as large and complex a governance apparatus as a state has been underscored already. Where the state operates on the basis of many internal divisions, among branches of government and within each branch among various services, insurgents tend to have organizational structures that are both more fluid and more integrated. Thus, as noted by Daragh Murray in his lucid exploration of the human rights obligations of non-state armed groups, the entire discussion of military justice in human rights law is coloured by the assumption that there is an available civilian justice system operating in parallel.[77] Nowhere is this more evident than in the Inter-American doctrine of the 'right to the natural judge' (*derecho al juez natural*), meaning that the state must offer a particular justification to remove a case from the civilian court in favour of a military one.[78] More broadly, this view reflects a conviction that, in a democratic state, the constitutional role of the armed forces must be limited to national security.[79] Save for a few armed opposition groups, the

[75] P. J. Rowe, 'How Well Do International Human Rights Bodies Understand Military Courts?' in A. Duxbury and M. Groves (eds), *Military justice in the modern age* (Cambridge, Cambridge University Press, 2016), at 26 (reserving states include France, Azerbaijan, Czech Republic, Slovakia, Spain, Armenia, Moldova, Portugal, Russia, Spain).

[76] See, e.g., African Commission of Human and Peoples' Rights, *Civil Liberties Association v Nigeria*, Comm. No. 218/98 (2001) § 44 ("a military tribunal per se is not offensive to the rights in the Charter nor does it imply an unfair or unjust process", although in that case, the Commission does conclude that the court fails to meet the requirement of the African Convention); Rowe, *supra* note 75, at 33–35.

[77] D. Murray, *Human Rights Obligations of Non-State Armed Groups* (Hart Publishing, 2016), at 210–214.

[78] Ch. Steiner and M.-Ch. Fuchs (eds), *Comentario Convención Americana Sobre Derechos Humanos* (2nd edn., Konrad Adenauer Stiftung, 2019), at 274; Bucherer, *supra* note 74, at 115–133.

[79] *Mustafa v Bulgaria*, ECtHR, Judgment, Appl. No 1230/17, 28 November 2019, para 35 ("[La Cour] rappelle la place particulière qu'occupe l'armée dans l'organisation constitutionnelle des États démocratiques doit être limité au domaine de la sécurité nationale, le pouvoir judiciaire relevant pour sa part, en principe, du domaine de la société civile").

rebel administration of justice will rarely involve distinct institutions devoted to civilian and military justice, a reflection of the fact that the insurgents are, more than anything else, a military organization. Even for non-state armed groups that do have judicial mechanisms for offences by members of the group that are distinct from the civilian administration of justice, such as the FARC in Colombia or the YPG in Syria, the 'civilian' arm of rebel justice remains more fully integrated into the structures of the armed group than the equivalent state-run civilian courts. It follows that the strand of decisions by human rights bodies resisting the jurisdiction of military courts over certain types of offences or certain categories of individuals cannot easily be transposed to insurgent courts.

The human rights jurisprudence insisting that military judges and prosecutors must be detached to some extent from the regular chain of command when carrying out judicial functions seems important to consider for insurgent courts.[80] Here again, the findings related to state courts-martial must be adapted, such that a demand for a military bench and bar wholly autonomous from the rest of the armed forces is surely unrealistic for non-state armed groups. To that can be added that the administration of military justice in many states still relies on decision-makers in the regular chain of command with a power to review or confirm by superior officers.[81] If, however, a rebel court is merely an emanation of the rebel leadership such that a decision in a given proceeding is predetermined by someone other than the judge, whether directly or indirectly, then such a court does not meet the requirement of independence under international law. Thus, reports that Islamic State judges have been punished or even executed for issuing decisions that did not conform to what the group's leadership thought ought to be decided corresponds to a lack of judicial independence, a regime in which fear of displeasing leaders rather than objective assessment of a case drives decision-making.[82] The Taliban model of administration of justice during its insurgency was less obviously contrary to the demands of independence. Judges were appointed by a distinct section of the central authority and operated in a manner connected

[80] See: *Findlay v United Kingdom*, ECtHR, Appl. No 22107/93, 25 Sept. 2001, §§ 74–80; Supreme Court of Canada, *R v Généreux*, (1992) 1 S.C.R. 259, 263.

[81] See generally: A. Duxbury and M. Groves (eds), *Military Justice in the Modern Age* (Cambridge University Press 2016); É. Lambert-Abdelgawad (ed.), *Juridictions militaires et tribunaux d'exception en mutation: perspectives comparées et internationales* (Archives contemporaines, 2008).

[82] Provost, *supra* note 3, at 107–118.

to the civil administration branch rather than to military operations. On the other hand, both branches were joined in the Taliban provincial military committee, which approved every decision of the courts before they were finalized. It is interesting to consider the justification of this function by the head of the Taliban military commission for the province of Laghman:

> As the head of the military commission, I am in charge of the whole province. Upon the advice of the [provincial] judicial council, I appoint all judges in the province. But as I told you, it doesn't mean that I control judges' minds. As in any organisation, there must be someone in charge, to give directions, and in this case it's me. That's all. There is no question of control that would bring me a personal benefit or anything like that.[83]

Taliban military commanders and fighters, for their part, were strictly prohibited by rule 64 of the *layeha* from becoming involved in any way in a case before the courts.[84] Thus, as regards independence, Taliban rebel justice was a model that was not so far from the structure of courts-martial used in many countries. As we have seen, the conformity with international human rights law of some aspects of such courts-martial has been contested, but the model has not been rejected outright. In *Al Hassan*, the Pre-Trial Chamber noted with apparent concern that AD/AQIM judges were armed and subject to the superior authority of the group's commander.[85] These are elements underscoring the incorporation of judges into the armed group, something that is unsurprising in this exceptional context and which does not per se signal lack of sufficient independence. The participation of the president of the Timbuktu Islamic Court in a 'crisis committee' that took strategic military decisions is more troubling, and could indicate that there was not a distance between the taking

[83] A. Baczko, 'La guerre par le droit : justice, domination et violence en Afghanistan (2001–2018)' (PhD Thesis, EHESS, 2018), at 211 (my translation).

[84] The rule reads: "64. Mujahidin commanders and individuals are not allowed to intervene in public disputes. They are not allowed to recommend anyone to a judge, or go to court with them. They cannot take sides in any disputes". See K. Clark, 'The Layeha: Calling the Taliban to Account' (Afghan Analysts Network, 2011).

[85] *Al Hassan* (Décision de la Chambre préliminaire), (n 8) §§ 426–427. The Pre-Trial Chamber incorporates these elements to its discussion of the impartiality of the rebel court, but it seems more properly understood as relevant to independence.

of military decisions and the administration of justice that is required for a court to be independent.[86]

The requirement that a court be impartial raises fewer legal complexities, even though it may set a condition of legality that will not rarely be tested in the practice of insurgent courts. As with the requirement of independence, the fact that some of the applicable provisions of international humanitarian law such as Common Article 3 predate the appearance of international human rights law should not be taken to suggest that impartiality has a different meaning in humanitarian law and human rights. The link to human rights was made explicit in the negotiations of Article 6 of Additional Protocol II.[87] As a result, despite the fact that Common Article 3 and Article 6 of Protocol II apply only to a narrow class of trials before insurgent courts, the requirement of impartiality can be understood in a consistent manner across the board for the rebel administration of justice in general. Impartiality speaks to the need for the decision-maker to avoid favouring one side over the other for reasons unrelated to the substance or procedure of the case. It bears repeating here the comment made earlier in relation to independence, to wit, the requirement of impartiality (or independence) does not imply neutrality vis-à-vis the objectives or policies of the non-state armed group to which a court belongs. As an emanation of armed groups, insurgent courts are a tool of rebel governance that is no more designed to challenge that governance than state courts are to challenge state sovereignty. Within the framework of that governance, however, international law requires that justice be administered in an impartial manner, for non-state courts as much as for state ones.

The canon of interpretation of the requirement of judicial impartiality, embraced by bodies and tribunals in international human rights as well as humanitarian law, distinguishes between the subjective and objective components of impartiality.[88] The subjective element speaks to the state of

[86] Ibid, § 424. The decision is both preliminary and heavily reacted, making it difficult to form a clear picture of the precise significance of this role.

[87] Bothe, *supra* note 58, at 745.

[88] See: *Human Rights Committee*, *supra* note 25, § 21; Knaul Report, *supra* note 53, § 44; *Findlay v UK*, *supra* note 65, § 73; *Prosecutor v Nahimana*, Appeal Judgment, (ICTR-99-52-A), 28 November 2007, §§ 47–50; Steiner and Fuchs, *supra* note 78, at 279; L. Doswald-Beck, 'Judicial Guarantees under Common Article 3' in Clapham, Gaeta and Sassòli, *supra* note 45, at 472–473; International Committee of the Red Cross, *Commentary on the Second Geneva Convention*, *supra* note 33, § 703.

mind of the decision-maker. Judges must not harbour bias, prejudice of preconceptions with respect to a case before them, so as to favour the interests of one party over the other. Neither can they have any sort of personal interest, much less involvement, in the case at bar. Subjective bias must be shown to exist in fact, as reflected in the behaviour of the judge during the proceedings, the language used and arguments relied upon in the decision, or any other concrete sign of a lack of partiality before, during, or after the proceedings.[89] The justice system must include a process whereby claims of partiality can be lodged so as to impugn a decision issued in such circumstances.[90] The objective element of impartiality refers not to the state of mind of the decision-maker but to the appearance, for a reasonable observer, that the court is or could be biased. This will typically relate to the identity, status or function of the decision-maker, and can overlap to a degree with the requirement of independence. The concern at play in relation to objective impartiality is to maintain the confidence of the parties and of the public at large in the fairness of the administration of justice. Thus, there are many decisions of human rights courts that have found that the partial or complete military composition of a court can, in some circumstances, create an appearance of partiality in addition to a lack of independence.[91] In a different setting, the fact that more than a quarter of *gacaca* judges were removed for having themselves taken part in the genocide can legitimately render suspect the entire community court structure.[92] For insurgent courts, the operation in Iraqi Kurdistan of two sets of parallel court structures, each associated with a political party that to some extent reflected a particular tribal identity, strongly suggested an appearance of partiality of the courts vis-à-vis members of the opposing party or tribe.[93] On the other hand, the Taliban's reported practice during its insurgency of continuously rotating judges and preventing them from sitting in an area to which they had connec-

[89] See IACtHR, *Duque v Colombia*, IACtHR, Sentencia (Exceptiones preliminaries, fondos, reparaciones y costas), 26 February 2016, §§ 159–166; *Kyprianou v Cyprus*, ECtHR, Appl. No. 73797/01, 15 December 2005, §§ 119, 129–133.

[90] Steiner and Fuchs, *supra* note 78, at 280.

[91] *Ergin v Turkey*, ECtHR, Appl. No. 47533/99, 4 May 2006, § 45; Knaul Report, *supra* note 53, § 45.

[92] P. Sullo, *Beyond Genocide: Transitional Justice and Gacaca Courts in Rwanda* (Springer, 2018) at 176, 184.

[93] See Provost, *supra* note 3, 376–385.

tions, in addition to a process of judicial oversight and the availability of avenues for civilians to lay a complain about a Taliban judge, are elements that conform to the requirement of impartiality.[94]

8.4 Conclusion

As the *Al Hassan* case illustrates, whether international law recognizes that non-state armed groups can lawfully establish their own regime of administration of justice in zones of armed conflict is a question the answer to which is complex and polycentric. As the previous pages have shown, it involves a combination of elements drawn from international criminal law, international humanitarian law, international human rights law, and parts of general public international law. One aspect on which no uncertainty remains is that the legality of justice practices of armed groups cannot be assessed purely on the basis of a few words in Article 8(2)(c)(iv) of the Rome Statute and the Elements of Crimes derived from Common Article 3 and Article 6 of Additional Protocol II, provisions that regulate only a fraction of what falls within the ambit of the rebel administration of justice.

To begin with, the analysis shows that an oversimplified reading of the requirement that courts must be regularly constituted must be resisted. Indeed, there is little basis to conclude that insurgent courts cannot be regularly constituted. Regular constitution can be achieved by non-state armed groups by means other than legislation, inasmuch as it corresponds to a deliberate decision by an effective authority to establish a general process to apply identified 'law' broadly defined. Justice, whether in the hands of states or armed groups, can neither be improvised nor ad hoc; it must form an integral and fixed part of a broader regime of governance. In the practice of armed groups, it can correspond to rebel legislation to create formal courts as well as to a set rebel policy to convene popular assemblies under defined conditions. Whatever the type of justice institutions and practices, and whatever form the deliberate decision of the rebel group may take, it must in all cases correspond to the requirement of regular constitution. This is so even in non-international armed conflicts that are regulated by Additional Protocol II and not merely by Common Article 3. To underscore the point, despite the fact that Article 6 of Protocol II does not mention that courts must be regularly constituted, this requirement flowing from Common Article 3 does not disappear if

[94] Ibid, at 123–140.

and when the conflict reaches the threshold of Protocol II. Common Article 3 *also* governs this narrower class of non-international armed conflicts, a fact clearly reflected in the transposition of the language of Common Article 3 into Article 8(2)(c)(iv) of the Rome Statute.

All courts must offer guarantees of independence and impartiality, whether in a non-international armed conflict of one type or another, or in an international armed conflict. The requirement of independence and impartiality, touching on the decision-making process, is distinct from the requirement of regular constitution, reflecting the establishment of the court. There is thus no basis, either statutory or conceptual, in the fusion of these elements suggested in the ICC Elements of Crimes. The effective gutting of the requirement regarding regular constitution in the Elements of Crimes amounts to a serious dilution of judicial fairness that must be resisted. Finally, the requirements of regular constitution and independence and impartiality are not different according to the type of armed conflict to which these treaty rules apply. Variations in the legal standards depends on agent, not type of conflict. For non-state armed groups, the demands of legality for insurgent courts are the same in a Common Article 3 conflict as they are in a Protocol II conflict. Conversely, the interpretation of the Geneva Conventions and Protocols do not suggest that the rebel administration of justice can only be legal in situations to which Additional Protocol II is applicable. While conditions of applicability of the Protocol such as an internal disciplinary system and territorial control are often coextensive with the type of rebel governance and institutionalization that can sustain insurgent justice, they are not systematically present. There are examples of non-international armed conflicts, such as much of the conflict in Colombia, in which the armed group does not control territory but nevertheless exerts effective authority.

How exactly a court can be regularly constituted by a non-state armed group does not necessarily mirror what states must do to establish a regularly constituted court. Likewise, the implications of the duty to provide judicial guarantees of independence and impartiality will likely be different for states and for armed groups. Both concepts historically have evolved in relation to the institutional and normative practices of states, and as such are reflections of the exercise of authority by the state. When we acknowledge that non-state actors—whether international organizations or non-state armed groups—in some circumstances may come to wield public authority, the regime regulating the exercise of that authority must be adapted to reflect the reality and capacities of these non-state actors. This is so for many human rights norms, including the requirements that courts be established by law and offer judicial guarantees of independence and impartiality. As I have aimed to sketch in this chapter, the key is to balance the meaningful and effective protection of the interests protected by these legal standards with the constraints imposed on non-state armed groups by the armed conflict.

More broadly, the attempt to translate for non-state armed groups the requirements under international law for the rebel administration of justice seeks to provide better and clearer guidance to armed groups (and states), and to capture a practice that is happening in conflict zones but that has largely escaped the scrutiny it deserves under international law. Ultimately, the aim is to incentivize non-state governance practices that bring rebel justice closer to the ideals enshrined in human rights law but that prove elusive during armed conflicts. As with all of international humanitarian law, this is the art of the possible, mixing elements that are more humanitarian to others than owe to military necessity or the stark realities of warfare. The critique of humanitarian law that it serves to legitimize (some) violence remains apt in the context of the rebel administration of justice, in that it may legitimize (some) forms of justice that remain far from what we would wish for. The alternative is to reject altogether the possibility of the rebel administration of justice or, more likely, impose conditions that will be all but impossible to meet for the vast majority of armed groups in the vast majority of conflicts. The value of a compromise approach is that it provides a foundation to differentiate insurgent justice that is justice only in name, as was broadly the case for ISIS courts that were neither regular nor independent and impartial, from that which is imperfect but not flawed in every respect, as was the case for courts run by the Taliban. This is the type of balanced and careful approach that will be required of the Trial Chamber in *Al Hassan* when it considers the nature of the AD/AQIM Islamic court. The conclusion that this or any other armed group has regularly constituted courts offering guarantees of independence and impartiality does not mean that a decision issued by such a court is fair and, accordingly, lawful. Justice administered by regularly constituted courts, state and non-state alike, may yet flounder at the implementation stage on the shoals of due process requirements. Indeed, the possibility of regularly constituted insurgent courts must imperatively and systematically be tempered by the requirements of procedural fairness.

CHAPTER 9

The Interplay Between International and National Law in Colombia's Special Jurisdiction for Peace. ICC's International Criminal Law Standards in the First Indictment by the SJP's Chamber for Acknowledgment of Truth, Responsibility and Determination of Facts and Conducts, Regarding Hostage-Taking and Other Severe Deprivations of Liberty Committed by the FARC-EP (Order 019 2021)

Walter Arévalo-Ramírez

W. Arévalo-Ramírez (✉)
Universidad del Rosario, Bogotá, Colombia
e-mail: walter.arevalo@urosario.edu.co

M. Faix, O. Svaček (eds.), *ICC Jurisprudence and the Development of International Humanitarian Law*, Global Issues,
https://doi.org/10.1007/978-3-031-45994-8_9

9.1 Introduction

Numerous scholars have praised the 2016 peace deal between the Colombian government of President Juan Manuel Santos and the Revolutionary Armed Forces of Colombia—People's Army (FARC-EP) as a significant milestone in the area of conflict resolution.[1] It has been praised for its creative and extensive provisions to address the underlying causes of the violence, it is considered comparatively more complex and comprehensive that any other recent peace agreement, and it was successful in bringing a political solution to one of the longest-running armed conflicts in the world.[2]

Among its many innovations is the Comprehensive System of Truth, Justice, Reparation and Guarantees of Non-Repetition (Comprehensive System), a transitional justice framework that includes a series of judicial and non-judicial mechanisms and measures aimed at satisfying the rights of victims. The Comprehensive System's judicial component, the Special Jurisdiction for Peace (SJP), has been of particular interest to national and international observers. Tasked with prosecuting those responsible for grave violations of human rights and international humanitarian law (IHL) committed in the context of Colombia's protracted internal armed conflict, the SJP faces the enormous challenge of delivering justice in cases that encompass large numbers of perpetrators, victims and crimes.

One of the many reasons so much attention has been paid to the SJP is that it constitutes a national accountability mechanism for serious crimes committed during the armed conflict that was conceived by the implicated parties themselves as part of a negotiated settlement, thereby avoiding the fallacies of retaliatory or 'victors' justice'. At the same time, its design was significantly influenced and shaped by international standards and obligations to investigate, prosecute and punish serious human rights violations: Colombia ratified the Rome Statute of the International Criminal Court (ICC) in 2002 and has been under preliminary examination of this body since 2004, making it the longest-running examination currently before

[1] Y. Romana-Rivas, 'Legal Pluralism, Transitional Justice, and Ethnic Justice Systems: The Story of How Colombia is Building a Transitional Justice System Observant of Legal Pluralism.', 2.1 *McGill GLSA Research Series* (2022), at 24.

[2] M. Yankson-Mensah, and M. Moreno Mantilla, 'Understanding the Dilemma of Constitutional Advice in Transitional Societies: A Comparative Analysis of Ghana and Colombia', in J. de Poorter, G. van der Schyff, M. Stremler and M. De Visser (eds), *European Yearbook of Constitutional Law* (The Hague: T.M.C. Asser Press, 2022), 129–154.

the ICC. As such, the peace talks between the FARC and the Santos government were the first in the world to take place under ICC examination, which has led to a 'constructive response or engagement with Colombia where justice and peace seem to be working in harmony'.[3] Indeed, the Office of the Prosecutor (OTP) has closely monitored the peace process and its implementation by actively engaging with domestic stakeholders to promote compliance with international obligations, while at the same time affording 'a great deal of discretion […] to Colombia in designing and implementing its local accountability mechanisms'.[4]

In light of the above, this chapter explores the interaction between national and international legal standards in the implementation of the SJP and in its first indictment rendered in January 2021. It begins by providing a brief description of some of the SJP's key features that are illustrative of this interaction. Subsequently, the authors will refer to three elements of the SJP's normative framework that challenge international legal standards and—depending on their implementation—might provide grounds for an ICC intervention in Colombia: restorative sanctions, the differentiated treatment for members of the armed forces and command responsibility. Finally, the first indictment of the SJP (Order 019) will be considered to demonstrate how its judges have drawn on international jurisprudence in attributing criminal responsibility to top leaders of the FARC-EP for war crimes and crimes against humanity. Each of these instances underlines how international jurisprudence and obligations have constructively shaped the discussion, implementation and functioning of the SJP since its creation.

9.2 Striking a Balance: The Mixed and Innovative Design of the Special Jurisdiction for Peace

Transitional justice mechanisms like the SJP have of course been widely studied, seeing as many such formulas have characterized political transitions across the globe. However, there are at least two peculiarities that set

[3] R. Teitel, 'Transitional justice and the peace process in Colombia' in C. Bernal Pulido, G. Barbosa Castillo and A. R. Ciro Gómez (eds), *Justicia Transicional. Retos teóricos. Vol I* (Bogotá: Universidad Externado de Colombia, 2016) 247–281, at 268.

[4] M. Aksenova, 'The ICC Involvement in Colombia: Walking the Fine line Between Peace and Justice', in M. Bergsmo and C. Stahn (eds), *Quality Control in Preliminary Examination: Volume 1* (Brussels: Torkel Opsahl Academic EPublisher, 2018) 257–282, at 257.

the Colombian case apart from many other experiences of this sort. On the one hand, Colombia, unlike many other countries in the region, has not experienced the fall of an authoritarian regime and a transition from dictatorship to democracy. Instead, it faces the challenge of transitioning to a sustainable peace following an over five decade long internal armed conflict that produced millions of victims and implicated various armed groups and actors responsible for massive human rights violations. On the other hand, the consolidation of international criminal law (ICL) and human rights standards has resulted in more clearly defined parameters for formulating and implementing transitional justice policies at the domestic level. As such, it is inadmissible nowadays to postpone justice under the (false) pretense of prioritizing peace and reconciliation, a fact that could not be ignored by the negotiating parties in the peace process held in Havana, Cuba. Today, universal principles pertaining to human rights and conflict resolution stress that justice and peace are in no way mutually exclusive and, instead, reinforce each other.[5]

Having said that, the adoption of transitional justice mechanisms inevitably leads to a certain 'flexibilization' of rights and obligations in practice. This flexibilization appears to create a paradox regarding the case in question: while the SJP was created under ICC scrutiny, it is also the product of negotiations between two parties that sought to end an internal armed conflict. This necessarily implied that both actors had to make concessions that stretch certain criteria and standards ascribed to the retributive and more traditional justice paradigm.

One key and innovative feature of the SJP that illustrates this flexibility is its mixed approach to sanctions. As a result of the justice-and-peace balance that was struck at the negotiating table, the SJP may impose both restorative and retributive sanctions, depending on the degree of responsibility acknowledged by the perpetrator. Those who fully acknowledge responsibility at an early stage in the proceedings will be eligible for a restorative sanction, a five- to eight-year sentence which amounts to an effective restriction of rights and liberties but does not include imprisonment. These sentences are coupled with community projects aimed at repairing the damage caused to victims and the social fabric more broadly as well as reintegrating the offender into society. Those who acknowledge

[5] United Nations, '*Guidance Note of the Secretary General. United Nations Approach to Transitional Justice*', March 2010, available online at https://www.un.org/ruleoflaw/files/TJ_Guidance_Note_March_2010FINAL.pdf, at 4.

responsibility late in the process or not at all will be subject to an adversarial proceeding and may be sentenced to a prison term of five to eight years or fifteen to twenty, respectively.

A related feature and guiding principle of the SJP is the centrality of the rights of victims. This principle provides for avenues and mechanisms for the participation of victims in the proceedings undertaken by the SJP, including an individual and collective victim accreditation system, standing to participate as victim in the recognition procedures, the determinations of fact procedures, and all the other chambers, to request precautionary measures and to request social, economic and psychological assistance and security measures. As such, it also manifests itself in the restorative nature of the sanctions that privilege the clarification of truth and reparations of victims over the severe punishment of perpetrators. In this respect, the SJP is 'fundamentally different from international criminal tribunals and courts established thus far' which have mainly 'relied on retributive grounds, where victims' participation and right to redress were minor'.[6]

The SJP has a unique an immense jurisdictional scope: it covers grave violations of human rights and IHL committed by ex-combatants of the FARC-EP, state agents and civilian third parties (The SJP rules allow state agents who are not members of the armed forces and civilians that participated in different manners in the armed conflict including financing armed groups,[7] in the context of the Colombian armed conflict may submit to the SJP that deals with a conflict which lasted over half a century and produced over nine million victims.[8]

The volume of cases and their underlying complexities make it impossible to investigate, prosecute and punish each single perpetrator on a

[6] S. Levy 'Can Colombia's Special Jurisdiction for Peace be considered slow? A preliminary comparative study of trials for international crimes', *Justice in Conflict*, 3 March 2021, available at https://justiceinconflict.org/2021/03/03/can-colombias-special-jurisdiction-for--peace-be-considered-slow-a-preliminary-comparative-study-of-trials-for-international--crimes/. Also see: W. Arévalo-Ramírez, T. Bonilla-Matiz, 'Responsabilidad internacional del Estado por hechos internacionalmente ilícitos, obligaciones internacionales emanadas del Sistema Interamericano de Derechos Humanos y procesos de justicia transicional: entre el cumplimiento y la colisión', *Reflexiones sobre el Sistema Interamericano de Derechos Humanos*. Universidad del Rosario, (2020), 1–52.

[7] See Law 1957 of 2019, article 63, paragraph 4, available online at http://www.secretariasenado.gov.co/senado/basedoc/ley_1957_2019.html.

[8] Colombia's Victims Unit registers 9.146.456 victims of the armed conflict, available online at https://www.unidadvictimas.gov.co/es/registro-unico-de-victimas-ruv/37394.

case-by-case basis. To address this logistical challenge, the SJP has adopted a selection and prioritization methodology modeled after international guidelines for prosecutorial strategies[9] in the aftermath of gross human rights violations. This essentially allows the SJP to classify and organize its cases, focus its investigation efforts on those most responsible for the most serious and representative crimes and thereby unveil the broader macro criminal patterns and the context in which they occurred.

It should be highlighted that the SJP is a national tribunal entrusted with prosecuting international crimes, not an international or hybrid entity. Although the parties to the negotiations originally intended for an institutional design to incorporate foreign judges, this suggestion was subsequently changed only to allow amicus.[10] Notwithstanding this change, the normative framework that regulates the SJP provides for a broad spectrum of applicable sources of law, which include the Colombian criminal code, international human rights law, IHL and ICL.[11] By its very nature as a transitional justice mechanism, the SJP investigates crimes that have already been committed and, in the particular case of the Colombian conflict, may have occurred many decades ago. This raises the question of how the SJP is to apply the multiple sources of law provided for in its statutes, without violating the principle of *nullum crimen sine lege* (principle of legality). A more in-depth analysis of this issue would exceed the scope of this chapter, but it is worth mentioning that it has already been addressed by the SJP in its first indictment handed down in January 2021.

Each of the features mentioned above is illustrative of the interaction between national and international legal standards that characterizes the Colombian transitional justice context, and specifically, the SJP. As many

[9] Special Jurisdiction for Peace, *Criterios y Metodología de Priorización en la Sala de Reconocimiento de Verdad, de Responsabilidad y de Determinación de Hechos y Conductas*, June 2018, available online at https://www.jep.gov.co/Documents/CriteriosYMetodologiaDePriorizacion.pdf.

[10] In a vote held on October 2, 2016, the Colombian people narrowly rejected an earlier draft of the peace deal. As a result, the participants to the negotiations changed a number of its clauses, including the inclusion of foreign judges in the SJP. The SJP is now made up exclusively of Colombian judges and a roster of a limited number of international *amicus curiae* who upon request of the SJP may issue expert opinions on a given case or question.

[11] Legislative Act 01 of 2017, transitory article 5, subparagraph 6 states that the SJP shall base its decisions and the classification of crimes on the 'Colombian criminal code and/or international norms pertaining to human rights, international humanitarian law or international criminal law', available online at http://www.secretariasenado.gov.co/senado/basedoc/acto_legislativo_01_2017.html.

authors have pointed out, this interaction has gone through different stages and considerably evolved over the years in particular as regards the OTP and its work in Colombia: What was once perceived as a 'looming threat', most notably during negotiations to demobilize right-wing paramilitary groups in 2005[12] has gradually transitioned into 'positive complementarity', whereby the ICC offers support, expertise and outreach to the domestic actors.[13] As the following section will show, this ultimately proved 'beneficial for the advancement of the international criminal justice principles and shaping the transitional justice landscape in Colombia'.[14]

9.3 International Criminal Law Standards and the Implementation of the Special Jurisdiction for Peace

Restorative Sanctions and the Interest of Justice

The institutional design of the SJP, including some of the features mentioned in the previous section, have been subject to heated political and legal debates in Colombia. One of these debates has revolved around the sanction regime adopted by the SJP. The admissibility of restorative sanctions for serious human rights violations is a contested issue that continues to be unsettled.[15]

Some researchers have argued that the Rome Statute maintains some (intentional) ambiguity with relation to the standards for alternative sanctions.[16] Article 17(1)(a) and (b) states that a matter is inadmissible to the ICC if it is 'investigated or prosecuted by a State'; however, it is unclear if these investigations must result in a punishment that includes a sentence

[12] R. Urueña, 'Notes and Comments. Prosecutorial Politics: The ICC's Influence in Colombian Peace Processes, 2003–2017', 111(9) *The American Journal of International Law* (2017) 104–125, at 104.

[13] Aksenova, *supra* note 4, at 264.

[14] *Ibid*, at 267.

[15] K. Clamp, 'Restorative justice as a contested response to conflict and the challenge of the transitional justice context: an introduction', in K. Clamp (ed), *Restorative Justice in Transitional Settings* (London and New York: Routledge, Taylor & Francis Group, 2018), 1–15.

[16] C. Stahn, 'Complementarity, Amnesties and Alternative Forms of Justice: Some Interpretive Guidelines for the International Criminal Court', 3 *Journal of International Criminal Justice* (2005) 695–720.

including privation of liberty. The effectiveness of the ICC's oversight may not directly relate to the penalties meted out, but rather to the fairness and utility of the processes.

Certain authors have also focused the attention in Rome Statute article 53(1)(c), which states that the prosecutor must consider whether to initiate an investigation and whether there are substantial reasons to believe that an investigation would not serve the interests of justice, taking into account the seriousness of the crime and the interests of the victims. If one considers that retribution is the fundamental goal of punishment and that any consequence imposed must be appropriate to the seriousness of the crime in question, then the legality of restorative punishments for international crimes is particularly debatable.[17]

The International Criminal Court (ICC) has actually held in its case law that the goal of its own punishments is deterrence.[18] Given that Article 77 of the Rome Statute, which does not expressly provide non-custodial punishments for crimes against humanity and war crimes, might be viewed as being violated by the SJP's sanctions regime, the question of whether the ICC might intervene has, of course, been raised.

The traditional justice paradigm is, however, inevitably tested and ultimately stretched in situations like those in Colombia, where society must deal with the legacy of egregious human rights violations as well as the need to move towards a stable peace. However, this stretching must still be consistent with the state's obligations under international law. Since its own sentencing mechanism is not intended to serve as a model for state parties to imitate, the ICC may thus determine whether intervening in such situations would serve the interests of justice.[19]

It is interesting to see how the OTP's attitude on the SJP's proposed restorative punishment for international crimes has changed over time. Initial concern[20] about these measures has given place to more reasonable positions that reflect the latitude allowed to national practitioners in creating procedures for transitional justice: The ICC prosecutor, Fatou

[17] Aksenova, *supra* note 4, at 257.

[18] Sentence. *Situation in the Democratic Republic of the Congo in the Case of the Prosecutor v. Germain Katanga* (ICC-01/04-01/07-3484-tENG), Trial Chamber II, 23 May 2014, § 43.

[19] Aksenova, *supra* note 4, at 278–279.

[20] Office of the Prosecutor, International Criminal Court, *Report on Preliminary Examination Activities* (2015), 12 November 2015, available online at https://www.icc-cpi.int/iccdocs/otp/OTP-PE-rep-2015-Eng.pdf, at 39.

Bensouda, expressed her approval to the terms of the peace agreement in a 2016 statement regarding the conclusion of the peace negotiations between the Colombian government and the FARC-EP highlighting the fact that it 'excludes amnesties and pardons for crimes against humanity and war crimes under the Rome Statute'[21] and the urgency of developing and implementing accountability mechanisms, and made no specific mention to sentencings involving privation of liberty.

The OTP addressed the subject of restorative punishments and clarified its opinions on their inclusion in an *amicus curia* that it sent to Colombia's Constitutional Court in October 2017. According to Bensouda, criminal penalties may be administered in a variety of ways as long as they achieve the correct goals of punishment, including deterrence, retribution, rehabilitation and restoration. The effectiveness of such sentences, in the prosecutor's opinion, 'will depend on the nature and scope of the measures that, taken together, would constitute a sanction and whether, in the particular circumstances of a case, they adequately serve sentencing objectives and provide redress for the victims'.[22]

Whether or not the sanction regime adopted by the local system ultimately satisfies the international standards is a question that will need to wait until they are executed. Meanwhile, the interplay between national stakeholders in Colombia and the OTP regarding this matter is instructive of the evolving 'institutional dynamics of complementarity',[23] and with it, on the ways in which national discretion and international standards can interact and positively influence each other. As Urueña notes, by the end of the peace negotiations which incidentally culminated with the transitional justice portion of the agreement, 'the OTP was transformed by Colombia as much as Colombia was transformed by the OTP'.[24]

[21] ICC Press Release, 'Statement of ICC Prosecutor, Fatou Bensouda, on the conclusion of the peace negotiations between the Government of Colombia and the Revolutionary Armed Forces of Colombia—People's Army', 1 September 2016, available online at https://www.icc-cpi.int/Pages/item.aspx?name=160901-otp-stat-colombia.

[22] *Escrito de Amicus Curiae de la Fiscal de la Corte Penal Internacional sobre la Jurisdicción Especial para la Paz ante la Corte Constitucional de la República de Colombia*, 18 October 2017, available online at https://www.icc-cpi.int/itemsDocuments/2017-10-18-icc-otp--amicus-curiae-colombia-spa.pdf.

[23] Urueña, *supra* note 12, at 104.

[24] *Ibid.*

Proposals and Amendments to Exclude or Affect the Prosecution of Armed Forces

The SJP has jurisdiction over FARC-EP members, third parties, and State agents, including military personnel. The latter was not a foregone conclusion and was a point of contention at the negotiation table. In reality, the SJP is Colombia's first transitional justice system with authority over the armed forces.[25] This is primarily due to the government's historical assertion that the military is an institutional body, a legitimate entity whose activities are considered to be lawful and thus cannot be compared with those of the guerrilla. As a result, a distinct chapter for State agents was included to the SJP's legislative structure.

This distinct approach translates into a number of provisions that are different from those that are applied to FARC-EP members. The exclusion of ICL as an acceptable source of law for the prosecution of state agents is the most pertinent for the purposes of this chapter (as seen in Legislative Act 01 of 2017, transitory article 22). This might have significant effects on how these players are held accountable, both in terms of how the crimes they are ultimately accused of are typified and, in terms of how their command responsibility is categorized.

Political groups that have vehemently opposed the FARC-EP peace deal worked hard to expand on this differential treatment and change the SJP's legislative structure to incorporate whole distinct judicial systems for the armed forces. One such instance was the proposal made to Congress to include a provision to the SJP Rules of Procedure Law that would have suspended the investigation of military personnel in the SJP for an eighteen-month period while the law establishing the differential treatment regime was being passed. Additionally, the right-wing ruling party, Centro Democrático, was the driving force behind a proposal to either create a separate Chamber for military personnel or appoint fourteen additional magistrates to just look into offences committed by the armed forces. Both ideas were opposed by a number of parties and challenged in the constitutional court,[26] and eventually proved ineffective, in large part

[25] R. Uprimny Yepes, 'La Fuerza Pública en la Jurisdicción Especial para la Paz en Colombia: ¿Un tratamiento especial o preferencial?' Translated as Working Paper, 2020, available online at: https://www.dejusticia.org/wp-content/uploads/2020/04/Santamar%C3%ADa-G%C3%BCiza-Uprimny_-Fuerza-P%C3%BAblica-en-la-JEP_Espa%C3%B1ol.pdf

[26] Constitutional Court of Colombia, Sentence C-112/19, 13 March 2019.

because it was believed that the state's duty to prosecute, and punish international crimes was violated by these legislative proposals.[27]

The OTP has frequently pointed to shortcomings in the investigations of the military in Colombia, specifically with regards to its involvement in the killings of civilians passed off as FARC combatants to boost statistics (commonly known as 'false positives'). Consequently, it came as no surprise when the OTP expressed serious concerns about reforms such as those described above in its 2018 preliminary examination report.[28]

The revisions proposed by the peace deal's detractors are a reflection of the profound divisions between Colombia's political players over the transitional justice system and the conflicts these arrangements cause with international legal norms. Questions remain about how this differential treatment will work in reality, especially in light of the SJP's impending prosecution of military personnel for their involvement in the 'false positives' instances, even though the specific difficulties discussed here have been resolved for the time being. This decision will likely set an important precedent on the jurisdiction's prosecutorial approach in crimes involving the military, and undoubtedly influence the ICC's assessment of the situation in Colombia.

Substantial Differences in Command Responsibility in FARC and Military Authorities

Before the peace accord, Colombian law ignored the idea of command responsibility and prosecuted military officers under various theories of accountability, ranging from commission by omission or through the notion of organized apparatus of power.[29] Another hotly contested topic

[27] See Legislative Projects (Colombia), 2017, available online at: https://www.comisionprimerasenado.com/proyectos-de-acto-legislativo/26-por-la-cual-se-adiciona-el-acto-legislativo-01-de-2017-y-se-dictan-otras-disposiciones-crea-sala-especial-dentro-del-tribunal-para-la-paz-para-miembros-de-la-fuerza-publica

[28] See: 'this matter and any other legislative initiative that could result in delays in bringing perpetrators to account, restrict the scope and thoroughness of investigations into complex crimes and, overall, call into question the genuineness of the proceedings, are of great interest to the Office to the extent it may impact on the admissibility of potential cases pertaining to state agents'., Office of the Prosecutor, International Criminal Court, *Report on Preliminary Examination Activities (2018)*, 5 December 2018, available online at: https://www.icc-cpi.int/itemsDocuments/181205-rep-otp-PE-ENG.pdf), at 42.

[29] H. Olasolo and J. Canosa Cantor, 'La Responsabilidad del Superior en el Acuerdo de Paz en Colombia a la luz del Derecho Internacional', 13(25) *Política criminal* (2018) 444–500, at 464.

that caused concern at the ICC was the inclusion of command responsibility in the peace accord and the SJP's legal structure. First, the norm applied to the armed forces does not address ICL in any way as a result of the justification for the differentiated treatment described in the previous section.

After the 2016 peace deal vote, references to Article 28 of the Rome Statute were included, but the administration unilaterally removed them immediately before the new version of the agreement was made public. It appears that this was done in response to army generals' complaints. The phrase 'international law' was used instead of references to the ICC Statute when referring to the command responsibility that applies to FARC commanders.[30] Article 28 of the Rome Statute is clear that any superior who had knowledge that his subordinates were committing a crime and failed to take action to prevent it is subject to criminal responsibility; however, the Colombian norm includes a much narrower interpretation and requires that the crimes in question be committed within the area of the superior's control and had material capacities to intervene, among other additions.[31]

In this sense, the proposed national standard would be narrower than the international criminal law current approach, since it would focus on formal assigned responsibilities and exclude material command, it would exclude the presumed knowledge that superiors have of the overall operations of their subordinates and would give a geographical sense to the notion of supervision and knowledge of the activities of troops under the command of the superior.

[30] J. Pappier, 'The "Command Responsibility" Controversy in Colombia', EJIL: *Talk! Blog of the European Journal of International Law*, 15 March 2017, available at: The 'Command Responsibility' Controversy in Colombia—EJIL: Talk! (ejiltalk.org).

[31] Legislative Act 01 of 2017, *supra* note 11, transitory article 24. (Translated by the author; *'TRANSITIONAL ARTICLE 24. Command Responsibility. To determine command responsibility, the Special Jurisdiction for Peace will apply, in the case of members of the Public Armed Forces, the Colombian Criminal Code, International Humanitarian Law as a subsidiary special law, and the operational rules of the Public Armed Forces in relation to IHL as long as they are not contrary to other national legal regulations. The determination of the command responsibility may not be based exclusively on the rank, hierarchy or scope of jurisdiction. The responsibility of the members of the Public Armed Forces for the acts of their subordinates must be based on the effective control of the respective conduct, on the knowledge based on the information available to them before, during, or after the performance of the respective conduct, as well as in the means at its disposal to prevent the punishable conduct from being committed or continued to be committed, as long as the factual conditions allow it, and if it has occurred, in their duty to promote the appropriate investigations.'*)

This definition, according to the OTP of the ICC, deviates from international customary law, which states that 'the superior's duty and responsibility to prevent or punish the crimes of their subordinates does not arise from his or her de jure authority, but instead from his or her material abilities',[32] in a clear-cut statement. The Colombian norm of command responsibility was also criticized in its 2017 report.[33]

Unsurprisingly, numerous national and international analysts and stakeholders questioned the terminology, calling on the Colombian Constitutional Court to reverse it. In the end, the Court upheld its constitutionality, contending that while domestic legislation does not exactly mirror command responsibility as defined by the Rome Statute, this does not result in the decriminalization of serious crimes or undermine the state's responsibility to look into, prosecute and punish those most accountable. The Constitutional Court emphasized the SJP's discretion in applying the normative framework in a way that balances national and international standards, ensures that major transgressions are not left unpunished, and determines liability.[34]

It is interesting to note that the SJP judges have referred to the conditions for effective control outlined in Trial Chamber III's 2016 ruling and its understanding of command responsibility, despite Jean-Pierre Bemba Gombo being exonerated by the ICC's Appeal Chamber in 2018. According to article 28 of the Rome Statute, Bemba was responsible for war crimes and crimes against humanity committed in the Central African Republic by members of the Mouvement de libération du Congo. The judges draw attention to the fact that the Appeal's Chamber considered these requirements and state expressly in the SJP's initial indictment that the FARC-organizational EP's structure reflected the requirements

[32] Office of the Prosecutor, International Criminal Court, *Report on Preliminary Examinations Activities 2017*, 4 December 2017.

[33] See: '*a tribunal applying [it], could find itself powerless to enforce customary international law against superiors with de facto but not de jure powers, if it could only accept as proof of the requisite degree of command a formal appointment. This would mean that persons with the material ability to prevent or punish the crimes of subordinates, and who knowingly failed to do so, could escape liability. This would significantly undermine application of the principle of responsible command and could bring into question whether those proceedings were vitiated by an inability or unwillingness to carry them out genuinely.*', in Office of the Prosecutor, International Criminal Court, *Report on Preliminary Examinations Activities 2017*, 4 December 2017.

[34] Constitutional Court of Colombia, Sentence C-080/18, 15 August 2018, available online at https://www.corteconstitucional.gov.co/relatoria/2018/c-080-18.htm.

specified in *Bemba*.[35] As mentioned in the previous section, what remains to be seen then is how the SJP addresses command responsibility in its upcoming indictments of members of the military,[36] especially given the peculiarities pertaining to the differentiated treatment they are subject to. Although the SJP recently published Order 033 of 2021, which revealed that an estimated 6402 civilians were killed by the army between 2002 and 2008 and passed off as combat kills, macro case 03 (extrajudicial killings, also known as 'false positives') had not yet resulted in an indictment as of the time of writing.

9.4 Contribution of International Jurisprudence to Order 019 of 2021

The SJP officially began operations in March 2018. It has since then held 135 hearings; received 380 reports filed by victims' and civil society organizations and the state; and opened seven macro cases that encompass approximately 61,823 crimes committed in the framework of the internal armed conflict.[37] These macro cases reflect the most notorious patterns of conduct identified thus far as well as those regions most affected by the armed conflict.[38]

In addition, the SJP's Chamber for Acknowledgment of Truth, Responsibility and Determination of Facts and Conduct (Chamber) recently handed down its first indictment pertaining to macro case 01 known as hostage-taking and other severe deprivations of liberty committed by the FARC-EP (Order 019). In it, the Chamber charged eight former guerrilla commanders with war crimes and crimes against humanity related to the rebel group's infamous hostage-taking policy.

[35] Chamber for Acknowledgment of Truth, Responsibility and Determination of Facts and Conduct, Special Jurisdiction for Peace, Order (*Auto*) 019 of 26 January 2021, available online at https://www.jep.gov.co/Sala-de-Prensa/Documents/CASO%2001%20TOMA%20DE%20REHENES/Auto%20No.%2019%20de%202021.pdf?csf=1&e=16bYs0, § 797.

[36] The press release and Order can be consulted online at: https://www.jep.gov.co/Sala-de-Prensa/Paginas/La-JEP-hace-p%C3%BAblica-la-estrategia-de-priorizaci%C3%B3n-dentro-del-Caso-03,-conocido-como-el-de-falsos-positivos.aspx (last visited 19 June 2022).

[37] Figures available online at https://www.jep.gov.co/jepcifras/JEP%20en%20cifras%20-%20mayo%2028%20de%202021.pdf (last visited 19 June 2021).

[38] Details on the seven macro cases are available online at: https://www.jep.gov.co/especiales1/macrocasos/index.html.

The indictment numbered 019 of 20221 is a 300-page legal piece that reveals how this national jurisdiction used international precedents to support its allegations. Both the procedural aspects of the indictment—which particularly address the standard of proof—and the more substantive section, which deals with the FARC-alleged EP's activities and crimes, make reference to the case law of international and hybrid courts. Notably, the SJP chose to apply the ICL directly in categorizing the offences, a choice with significant ramifications for a national court whose legislation is unclear about the simultaneous use of national and international sources of law.[39]

Stages of the Procedure before the SJP, Mbarushimana and the Issue of the Standard of Proof

Order 019 begins by outlining the competence of the Chamber and the aspects related to the procedural stage in which it is issued: the SJP's legislative framework stipulates that the Chamber must notify and summon the parties appearing in court if it determines that it has 'substantial grounds to suspect' that the conduct was done and that the defendant took part in it.[40] In this regard, the Chamber emphasizes that different areas of law have different requirements of proof, with criminal law settings subject to the highest level (beyond any reasonable doubt). It goes on to say that these requirements could differ based on where a criminal case is in the procedural chain. For instance, as a case progresses and its legal implications grow, the Colombian criminal law envisages certain requirements that become tighter.

The Chamber cites the *Mbarushimana* case from ICC docket to support this argument. In doing so, the SJP draws attention to the fact that the confirmation of accusations phase of an ICC process does not seek to

[39] Chamber for Acknowledgment of Truth, Responsibility and Determination of Facts and Conduct, Special Jurisdiction for Peace, Order (*Auto*) 019 of 26 January 2021.

[40] *Ibid*, §§ 82–94.

satisfy the highest standard of proof (unlike the sentencing stage). The SJP justices directly cite paragraph 74 of the Mbarushimana case in Order 019.[41]

The SJP's decision to use this standard at this procedural step is clever because it does not necessarily serve the same function as the pre-trial phase at the ICC. While one seeks to dialogically engage victims and perpetrators in a proceeding and contribute to the clarification of truth and restoration, the former seeks to filter out cases before going to trial. Applying a lesser bar at this point, the SJP contends, is reasonable because the information only serves to provide an unbiased determination that the offenses were in fact committed. As a reflection of the SJP's restorative and dialogic ideals, this objective presentation of the facts must always be augmented by many testimonials and narratives provided by offenders and victims. The accused will then have the chance to admit to the accusations made against them, and the victims will have the chance to speak up and offer more proof. Regardless of the differences between the pre-trial phase at the ICC and the dialogic phase of the SJP, its judges consciously drew on ICC practice to bolster its use of the lower standard of proof. These references to international law in the initial and more procedural considerations of the indictment foreshadow the SJP's active engagement with it throughout the subsequent sections of Order 019.

Ntaganda, Tadić and Armed Conflict

The next section of Order 019 discusses the FARC level of organization and its operational capabilities to commit international crimes. ICC and the International Criminal Tribunal for the Former Yugoslavia (ICTY) both established two requirements in their jurisprudence: (i) the level of organization of the parties involved in the armed violence; and (ii) the intensity of the armed violence. As a result, the Chamber starts by analysing the factors that constitute the existence of an armed conflict based on

[41] See: *'The Appeals Chamber recalls that the confirmation of charges hearing is not an end in itself but rather serves the purpose of filtering out those cases and charges for which the evidence is insufficient to justify a trial. This limited purpose of the confirmation of charges proceedings is reflected in the fact that the Prosecutor must only produce sufficient evidence to establish substantial grounds to believe the person committed the crimes charged. The Pre-Trial Chamber need not be convinced beyond a reasonable doubt, and the Prosecutor need not submit more evidence than is necessary to meet the threshold of substantial grounds to believe'*, in Decision on the confirmation of charges", *Situation in the Democratic Republic of the Congo, The Prosecutor v. Callixte Mbarushimana* (ICC-01/04-01/10 OA), Appeals Chamber, 30 May 2012, § 47.

these two requirements. Regarding the first, the Chamber makes express reference to the considerations and indications that were established in the Ntaganda judgment.[42]

According to the judges of the Chamber, the FARC-EP operated as an armed organization in Colombia from 1965 to 2016 with a sizable territorial presence and even temporarily exercised control over some sparsely populated regions of the nation. In order to determine whether an armed group reaches an operational threshold to commit international crimes, it concluded that these characteristics satisfy the relevant criteria put forth by the ICC in the Ntaganda case.[43]

The Chamber assesses whether the violence committed by the FARC-EP qualifies as an armed conflict in light of the intensity criteria. The Chamber draws attention to the fact that international jurisprudence and doctrine have overwhelmingly supported the terms outlined in the Tadić case, notwithstanding the Rome Statute's lack of an official definition of 'armed conflict'. Thus, it moves on to discuss the ICTY's definition of 'protracted armed violence', which reads, 'An armed conflict exists whenever there is a resort to armed force between States or protracted armed violence between governmental authorities and organized armed groups or between such groups within a State'.[44] The Ntaganda decision and its more specific intensity guidelines were also taken into consideration once again by the Chamber and expressly cited.[45]

[42] See: *'(i) the existence of a command structure, the existence of headquarters, the issuing of political statements, and the use of official spokespersons; (ii) the military (operational) capacity of the armed group, […]; (iii) the logistical capacity of the armed group […]; (iv) the existence of an internal disciplinary system and the ability to implement IHL; and (v) the group's ability to speak with one voice.'* in Judgment, *Situation in the Democratic Republic of the Congo, The Prosecutor v. Bosco Ntaganda* (ICC-01/04-02/06-2359), Trial Chamber VI, 8 July 2019, § 704.

[43] Chamber for Acknowledgement of Truth, *supra* note 39, § 713.

[44] Decision on the Defence Motion for Interlocutory Appeal on Jurisdiction, *Prosecutor v. Dusko Tadić a/k/a "Dule"* (Tadić (IT-94-1-AR72), Appeals Chamber, 2 October 1995, § 70.

[45] See: *'(i) the seriousness and frequency of attacks and armed clashes; (ii) the spread of clashes over territory and the group's ability to control territory over a period of time; (iii) whether any ceasefire orders had been issued or ceasefires agreed to; (iv) the type and number of armed forces deployed, including any involvement of the government; (v) the type of weapons used; (vi) whether the situation had attracted the attention of the UN Security Council, or involvement of other international organisations; (vii) whether those fighting considered themselves bound by IHL; and (viii) the effects of the violence on the civilian population, including the extent to which civilians left the relevant area, the extent of destruction, and the number of persons killed.'*, in Judgment, *Situation in the Democratic Republic of the Congo, The Prosecutor v. Bosco Ntaganda* (ICC-01/04-02/06-2359), Trial Chamber VI, 8 July 2019, § 716.

The Chamber concludes that the conflict between the FARC-EP and the Colombian government fulfills the intensity standard for prolonged armed violence once more on the basis of the standards established by international law.[46]

This analysis provides crucial background information for the portions of the indictment that follow, as the Chamber goes on to spell out its accusations. In making the decision to charge the FARC-EP with hostage-taking, it refers back to the analyses previously discussed to support the claim that the guerrilla's actions happened within the context of an armed struggle and so qualify as war crimes.

As such, the Chamber highlights that the existence of an armed conflict is the only contextual element established by the Rome Statute for such crimes.[47] Therefore, the SJP is not required to examine other factors such as the existence of a plan or the widespread nature in determining their commission. By drawing on international jurisprudence on the matter, the SJP not only underpins its prosecutorial strategy, it also reinforces and strengthens its argument to indict the way it does, providing solid evidence for the requirements that elevate the violence under its study to the level of armed conflict. It does so despite (or because of) the fact that the nexus between the crime and the armed conflict is a prerequisite for the SJP to exercise its jurisdiction in the first place.

Katanga and Cumulative Charges

The judges' classification of the crimes committed by the FARC as a war crime of hostage-taking and, cumulatively, as a crime against humanity of serious deprivation of liberty, which amounts to a direct application of ICL, is one important element of Order 019. As was already established, according to the SJP's statutes, it may bring charges in accordance with 'the Colombian Criminal Code and/or international legal principles related to human rights, international humanitarian law, and international criminal law'.[48] The Constitutional Court studied the consequences of the ambiguity and came to the conclusion that the SJP, in exercising its unique competence to prosecute the offenses under its jurisdiction, must harmonize these various legal regimes and it must simultaneously protect the

[46] Chamber for Acknowledgement of Truth, *supra* note 39, § 714.

[47] *Ibid*, § 714, § 710.

[48] Legislative Act 01 of 2017, *supra* note 11.

overarching principles that guide its authority, that is, centrality of victims, legal certainty, restorative justice, amongst others.[49]

For a variety of reasons, this is not a simple undertaking. The extent to which national legal systems govern the main crimes in complete conformity with these standards—if they do so at all—is still unclear despite the recent growth of international criminal law norms. For instance, national legislation in Colombia does not expressly include crimes against humanity.

Some contend that in order to prosecute such crimes, even those done more than fifty years ago, the SJP must show that they really violated treaties or customary international law at the time they were committed.[50] This presents a challenge, though, because international customary law is still in international criminal matters which is still developing. The principal defense put up by those opposed to international principles' direct application in national prosecutions is that they lack precision.[51]

In view of the aforementioned, the topic of the direct application of ICL to prosecution of core crimes in national courts has been hotly debated and seems to still be unresolved. The SJP's Chambers are required to apply sources of international law in the prosecution and there is a consensus in international law that serious violations must be prosecuted and sanctioned. In the case of Indictment 019, the SJP considered that the indictment for war crimes and crimes against humanity complied with the principle of legality since the conducts indicted were already criminalized under Colombian law (despite differences of names). International tribunals have used broad legal principles to prosecute grave international crimes, rejecting the accused's claims that these acts were not banned by national law when they were committed.[52]

Finally, the Chamber's determination that the war crimes charged in Order 019 may possibly constitute crimes against humanity is another indication of its reliance on international law. The Chamber believed that by completing its examination of the hostage-taking war crime imputed to

[49] Chamber for Acknowledgment of Truth, *supra* note 39, § 670.

[50] A. Morales, 'The rocky road to peace: current challenges at the Special Jurisdiction for Peace in Colombia', EJIL: Talk! Blog of the European Journal of International Law, 3 May 2021, available at: The rocky road to peace: current challenges at the Special Jurisdiction for Peace in Colombia—EJIL: Talk! (ejiltalk.org).

[51] H. Olásolo, 'A note on the evolution of the principle of legality in international criminal law', *Criminal Law Forum*. Vol. 18. No. 3–4. Springer Nature BV, 2007.

[52] Chamber for Acknowledgment of Truth, Responsibility and Determination of Facts and Conduct, *supra note* 39, § 670.

the FARC-EP in Order 019, it could move on to analyse the acts as crimes against humanity, including a review of organizational policy, as done by previous tribunals (i.e. ICTY).[53] The Chamber examined whether the FARC-EP could engage in systematic behavior as part of a policy, as described by the ICC in the Kenya scenario,[54] and came to the conclusion that the FARC-EP met all of the customary organizational standards established by international criminal law.[55]

The Katanga case, in which the Trial Chamber allowed cumulative convictions, led the SJP to think that successive charges for the same act are acceptable where they are carried out under the same contextual criteria. The SJP then went on to investigate the contextual factors and came to the conclusion that the actions that were first regarded as war crimes might also be classified as systematic incarceration and other forms of deprivation of liberty under the Rome Statute and crimes against humanity.[56]

9.5 Concluding Remarks

The interplay between international and national legal standards has significantly impacted the SJP before and during its existence: the international obligations of the Colombian state and the concomitant scrutiny of the ICC played a vital role in the design of this transitional justice mechanism, both at the negotiating table and in the legislative process that led to its formal establishment. In addition, three years into its existence, it has become evident that the jurisprudence of international criminal tribunals greatly influences the decisions handed down by the SJP, despite its fully national composition.

This suggests the existence of at least two tendencies that characterize the interaction between international and national law in Colombia's transitional justice process: first, the engagement of the ICC increasingly assumed the dynamics of positive complementarity, which has constructively contributed to the creation of a mechanism that seeks to materialize

[53] *Prosecutor v. Dusko Tadić a/k/a "Dule"* (IT-94-1-T), Trial Chamber, 7 May 1997, § 654.

[54] Decision Pursuant to Article 15 of the Rome Statute on the Authorization of an Investigation into the Situation in the Republic of Kenya, Situation in the Republic of Kenya (ICC-01/09-19-Corr), Pre-Trial Chamber II, 31 March 2010, § 93.

[55] Chamber for Acknowledgment of Truth, Responsibility and Determination of Facts and Conduct, *supra* note 39.

[56] Criterios y Metodología de Priorización en la Sala de Reconocimiento de Verdad, de Responsabilidad y de Determinación de Hechos y Conductas (2018).

both justice and peace as goals that are not mutually exclusive. Second, while there are elements of the SJP that stretch the traditional justice paradigm, these have not reached the threshold for ICC intervention: national efforts to introduce reforms that are at odds with ICL have been halted thus far, while other elements such as the SJP's sanction regime highlight the discretion afforded to domestic actors in conceiving transitional justice mechanisms. As such, the interplay between national and international standards in Colombia illustrates that it is a two-way process. While international law has considerably influenced the Colombian context, the innovative nature of the SJP likewise contributes to a critical reexamination of notions like proportionality and retribution which have predominated in international responses to serious crimes.

Finally, ICC assessment of controversial aspects such as the differentiated treatment of the military and command responsibility will likely depend on the forthcoming jurisprudence of the SJP on extrajudicial killings carried out by the armed forces. However, if Order 019 is any indication of the SJP's approach to and incorporation of ICL, there appears to be little room for concern for the OTP.

CHAPTER 10

Contextualizing Ongwen at the ICC: Underlying Narratives and the Expressivist Function of Judgments

Abhaya Ganashree

10.1 Introduction

> When I think about justice, I mean that I want the truth about the events I suffered from, and like me many others in Uganda. We want the truth to be established so that we may be satisfied. I want the Court to work well … and this case to end in a just manner. I trust the Court to dispense justice for us survivors.[1]
>
> (Victim a/07041/15)

The primary purpose of any criminal trial is to ascertain whether the individual in the dock committed the crimes they are accused of. However, within the wider and more complex context of international criminal law,

[1] Transcript, *The Prosecutor v. Dominic Ongwen* (ICC-02/04-01/15-T-257-ENG), Trial Chamber, 11 March 2020, 49, lines 20–23 (hereafter Ongwen).

A. Ganashree (✉)
London School of Economics, London, UK

M. Faix, O. Svaček (eds.), *ICC Jurisprudence and the Development of International Humanitarian Law*, Global Issues,
https://doi.org/10.1007/978-3-031-45994-8_10

justice may not be quite so simply achieved. Mass atrocities, of the nature tried by the International Criminal Court (ICC), are often complex in their narratives, structure, and form, and so too are the narratives of the victims and perpetrators. Within the heightened tensions and frenzy that marks protracted conflict, the lines between 'victim' and 'perpetrator' are often blurred.[2] This ambiguous status of individuals as victims as well as perpetrators is not unique in fragile African states where many youths remain uninitiated into the polity or grow up in deterritorialised military regions.[3] While the international community is vocal about the need to protect child soldiers and to prosecute those that force children to fight in rebel forces, this dilemma of individuals occupying this dual role goes unaddressed in the field of transitional justice.[4] This chapter seeks to address this gap by using the case of *Prosecutor v Ongwen* as a case study.

Although the ICC sets out to try those who allegedly committed the crimes listed under the Rome Statute, the rhetoric of international criminal trials puts 'humanity' itself on trial. ICL has been said to give the 'conscience of mankind' an institutional shape which aims to consolidate the concept of 'juridical humanity' while punishing the enemies of mankind.[5] To delegate such judgement to any group of people is questionable.[6] To delegate such judgement to a Court situated miles away from the area of protracted conflict, both geographically and culturally, probably gives rise to far more issues than it settles.[7] However, where the 'theatrical spectacle' of international criminal trials was once denounced,[8] it is now revered for the showcasing of the multiplicity of narratives and providing a platform for different voices.[9] Allowing the events that so unfairly shaped

[2] M.A. Drumbl, 'Victims who victimise', 4(2) *London Review of International Law* (2016), at 217, 218.

[3] E. K. Baines, 'Complex political perpetrators: Reflections on Dominic Ongwen', 46 *Journal of Modern African Studies* (2009), at 163, 164.

[4] Ibid., at 163, 164.

[5] G. Simpson, The Conscience of Civilisation, and its Discontents" in P. Kastner (ed.), *International Criminal Law in Context* (1st edn., Routledge, 2018).

[6] P. Levi, *The Drowned and the Saved* (Rosenthal tr, Vintage Books, 1989), at 44–45.

[7] S. M. H. Nouwen, 'Legal Equality on Trial: Sovereigns and Individuals before the International Criminal Court', 43 *Netherlands Yearbook of International Law* (2012), at 151.

[8] H. Arendt, *Eichmann in Jerusalem: A Report on the Banality of Evil* (Penguin Books, 1994), at 4–6.

[9] L. G. Minkova, 'Expressing what? The stigmatization of the defendant and the ICC's institutional interests in the Ongwen case', 34 *Leiden Journal of International Law* (2021), at 223, 226.

the lives of those that suffered to be judicially determined at an international forum goes a long way in securing justice that victims hope for. The 'expressivist' role of the Court or the symbolic power of punishment also serves to instil and uphold the beliefs of the global community by clarifying behaviour worthy of punishment.[10] Through the narrative clarity presented in the ICC's judgment in any trial, it could be demonstrated that justice has been done with the due consideration of the interests of all parties while avoiding undue stigmatisation of individual defendants while holding them to account for their part in mass atrocities.[11]

Emerging as the poster-child for victim-perpetrators is Dominic Ongwen, a former commander of the Sinia Brigade of the Lord's Resistance Army (LRA) in Northern Uganda.[12] In December 2016, Dominic Ongwen entered the courtroom and was seated in his stand at the ICC as witnesses testified to the harm they suffered at the hands of his brigade. Dressed in a suit and tie, Ongwen watched on as the prosecution, defence, and victims' counsels recounted the events that took place in Northern Uganda between 1 July 2002 and 31 December 2005.[13] The stark differences between life in the 'bush' and in The Hague begs the question whether it is possible to adequately contextualise his experience, or indeed those of the victims, at all.

Abducted from his home at the age of nine and recruited as a child soldier, Ongwen had risen within the ranks to become the leader of the Sinia Brigade.[14] In 2015, Ongwen had at last escaped the LRA after 28 years, surrendering to the American forces.[15] In open defiance of Joseph Kony, the leader of the LRA, Ongwen gave himself over to the ICC and pleaded for the Court to consider his circumstances. Pleading

[10] Ibid.

[11] L. Douglas, *The Right Wrong Man: John Demjanjuk and the Last Great Nazi War Crimes Trial* (Princeton University Press, 2016), at 218–219; Minkova, *supra* note 9, at 223, 227.

[12] Agence France-Presse, 'Senior Lord's Resistance Army Commander Surrenders to US Troops' Guardian, 7 January 2015, available at www.theguardian.com/world/2015/jan/06/lords-resistance-army-commander-surrenders-central-african-republic (last visited 2 August 2021).

[13] Judgment, *Ongwen* (ICC-02/04-01/15), Trial Chamber, 4 February 2021, § 9.

[14] Open Society Justice Initiative, 'Briefing Paper: The Trial of Dominic Ongwen at the ICC: The Judgment', Open Society Foundations, February 2021, available at www.justiceinitiative.org/publications/the-trial-of-dominic-ongwen-at-the-icc-the-judgment (last visited 13 July 2021).

[15] France-Presse, *supra* note 12.

that both mental incapacity and duress diminished his criminal responsibility while recruiting child soldiers, and committing other crimes, his defence argued that he had little room to exercise free will.[16] After lengthy proceedings, Ongwen was convicted of 61 counts of war crimes and crimes against humanity, and it was held that he *fully intended* to commit these crimes. The grounds pleaded were taken into account as mitigating factors.[17]

In section I, this chapter will deal with the role that the ICC plays in the larger political landscape and how the perception of it shapes its narratives. Then, the statutory limitations under Article 31 of the Rome Statute and the purpose of the ICC are outlined to demonstrate the extent to which the ICC is able to take facts and circumstances into account. Against this backdrop, section II will set out the facts and circumstances surrounding the case of *Ongwen*. Focussing on the issues of mental disease or defect and duress, the narratives as presented by the prosecution, defence, and victims' counsel will be used to discuss the evidence put forth in relation to these issues. Considering these narratives, section III will deal with the reasoning in the judgment itself. It will consider how far the narrative of mental incapacity and duress went in establishing the 'truth' and contextualising Ongwen's victim-perpetrator identity. Considering the ICC's role through an 'expressivist' lens, it will conclude that although the defences were available to the defendant, their application in the judgment did little to further the protection of child soldiers as victim-perpetrators. It does not argue that Ongwen is not criminally responsible for the crimes as determined by the Trial Chamber, nor that the ICC erred in its application of the requirements of the Rome Statute. Instead, the chapter argues that the rigid legal distinctions lend themselves to equally rigid characterisation of individual actors and that a more nuanced understanding would better fulfil the Court's expressivist function. In conclusion, the chapter will argue that a more complex narrative could be presented by refraining from excessive stigmatisation, while continuing to hold the individual actors to account, and in considering the two grounds more in-depth.

[16] Enough Team, 'BREAKING: LRA Top Commander Surrenders', Enough Project, 6 January 2015, available at https://enoughproject.org/press-releases/breaking-lra-top-commander-surrenders (last visited 2 August 2021).

[17] Sentence, *Ongwen* (ICC-02/04-01/15), Trial Chamber, 6 May 2021, § 385.

10.2 The Case of Dominic Ongwen and the ICC's Role

The case of Dominic Ongwen before the ICC garnered interest from both academics as well as the global media.[18] Unlike previous cases before the Court, Ongwen's background of being abducted as a child soldier brought up important questions of the roles he played. His victim-perpetrator identity and its implications to the findings of responsibility, intent, and capacity were novel issues that had never been considered by the ICC. Considering whether the use of mental incapacity and duress have helped present the complexities of the narratives, this chapter uses *Prosecutor v. Ongwen* as a case study.

Background

Dominic Ongwen was one of five commanders of the LRA against whom an arrest warrant was issued by the ICC.[19] Abducted by the LRA, headed by Joseph Kony, at the age of nine, Ongwen rose up the ranks and was indicted for the crimes committed under his leadership of the Sinia Brigade in the early 2000s.[20] Due to the roles he played as both victim and perpetrator, the trial of Ongwen at the ICC brought up conflicting views from across the international community.

Founded by Kony, in the initial years the LRA appeared to be fighting on behalf of the Acholi people, a tribe from the borderlands between Sudan and Uganda. Their cause was to overthrow Museveni's government and to install a government on Kony's principles.[21] However, in due course a spiritual ideology and a much broader political project emerged aimed at the creation of a nation of 'pure' Acholi people and set out to

[18] Drumbl, *supra* note 2, at 217, 218; W. Nortje, 'Victim or Villain: Exploring the Possible Bases of a Defence in the *Ongwen* Case at the International Criminal Court', 17 (1) *International Criminal Law Review* (2017) -at 187; S. Omeri, 'Guilty Pleas and Plea Bargaining at the ICC: *Prosecutor* v. *Ongwen* and Beyond', 16 *International Criminal Law Review* (2016), at 480.

[19] Warrant of Arrest for Dominic Ongwen, *Situation in Uganda* (ICC-02/04), Pre-Trial Chamber II, 8 July 2004.

[20] Ongwen (Public Redacted Version of 'Corrected Version of "Defence Closing Brief" filed on 24 February 2020'), § 487; Judgment, *Ongwen*, supra note 13, §§ 28–30.

[21] K. Vlassenroot and T. Allen, *The Lord's Resistance Army: Myth and Reality* (Zed Books, 2010), at 9–10.

purge those who did not subscribe to it.[22] This endeavour led to violence against all dissidents including Acholi people who refused to join the LRA.[23]

At the age of nine, Ongwen was abducted from his home in Coorom in Northern Uganda, and recruited to the LRA as a child soldier.[24] After being abducted, Ongwen went through the *rites de passage* of the LRA where he was made to believe in Kony's supernatural powers and taught that he was beyond reproach.[25] The childhoods of those in the LRA were rife with traumatic episodes such as being asked to drink the blood of those that had tried to escape.[26] Few instances of the trauma he suffered are available, with the defence informing the Court that the rebels who kidnapped him had also murdered his mother.[27]

However, at the beginning of the relevant period, Ongwen was a battalion commander in the Sinia Brigade and rose to be brigade commander by late 2004.[28] The LRA attacked the Ugandan government on a number of occasions and enslaved, killed, and injured a large number of civilians.[29] They also used civilians as 'sexual slaves'.[30] There was evidence that Ongwen had either participated in the planning or had knowledge of several attacks against civilians and had issued commands to loot their homes

[22] Ibid, at 25; R. Doom and K. Vlassenroot, 'Kony's Message: A New Koine? The Lord's Resistance Army in Northern Uganda', 98 (390) *African Affairs* (1999), at 5, 21.

[23] I. Cable, 'Child Soldiers And Accountability: The Trial Of Dominic Ongwen', Human Rights Pulse, 21 April 2021, available at www.humanrightspulse.com/mastercontentblog/child-soldiers-and-accountability-the-trial-of-dominic-ongwen (last visited 13 July 2021); OCHA, 'LRA Regional Update DRC, CAR and South Sudan: June–August 2011', ReliefWeb, 29 September 2011, available at https://reliefweb.int/map/central-african-republic/lra-regional-update-drc-car-and-south-sudan-june-august-2011 (last visited 13 July 2021): Although the number of attacks have declined and the LRA no longer operates in Uganda, it continues to thrive in the border regions.

[24] *Ongwen* (Public Redacted Version of 'Corrected Version of "Defence Closing Brief" filed on 24 February 2020'), *supra* note 20, at §§ 28–30.

[25] Transcript, *Ongwen* (ICC- 02/04-01/15) Trial Chamber, 6 December 2016, at 3.

[26] University of Manitoba, 'VLFL "The Dilemma of Dominic Ongwen: A former child soldier." Dr. Kjell Anderson' YouTube, 21 October 2020, available online at www.youtube.com/watch?v=9KPiZr5lBI0 (last visited 4 August 2021).

[27] Third Public Redacted Version of 'Defence Brief for the Confirmation of Charges Hearing', filed on 18 January 2016, *Ongwen* (ICC-02/04-01/15-404-Conf), Trial Chamber, 25 May 2016, at 3.

[28] Judgment, *Ongwen*, *supra* note 13, §§ 134–138.

[29] Ibid, §§ 142–143.

[30] Ibid, § 143.

and to abduct civilians. During the course of the attacks, civilians were killed and raped and their homes were burned down.

Ongwen, Kony, as well as others in command of the Sinia Brigade coordinated the abduction of women and girls to serve as 'wives'. Ongwen personally oversaw several women being 'distributed' and presided over the marriages. Seven women were 'distributed' to Ongwen as his 'wives' and he raped several of them and subjected them to beatings with canes.

Ongwen also engaged in a coordinated effort to abduct children under the age of 15 to be child soldiers. He had knowledge of this effort and abducted children himself. They were then taught to use guns and were trained with the aim of being assimilated in the Sinia Brigade.

His childhood and background gave rise to defences of diminished responsibility such as duress and the protection of child soldiers at the trial. The particular spiritual ideology and rituals that underpinned the traditional and judicial structure of Acholi society also merited consideration.[31] However, the Office of the Prosecutor (OTP) itself has been amenable to the issues raised and has attempted to understand and incorporate some of the Acholi rituals and methods of accountability.[32]

However, we may view him, as victim or perpetrator, Ongwen's surrender to the American Forces saw him being brought to the ICC. With 70 counts of war crimes and crimes against humanity against him,[33] this was the longest list of charges the OTP had filed.[34] However, as the Ugandan Army has itself engaged in the commission of some serious crimes and no warrants have been issued for soldiers or government officials, the proceedings are largely being seen as having a political agenda.[35]

Ongwen's dilemma, although probably not unique,[36] brings up novel questions to be addressed at the heart of mass atrocities and the blurred lines between victim and perpetrator. It tests the limits of the protection offered to child soldiers between the binaries of impunity and

[31] Decision on the admissibility of the case under article 19(1) of the Statute, *Ongwen* (ICC-02/04-01/15), Trial Chamber, 10 March 2009, §§ 33–43.

[32] T. Allen, 'The International Criminal Court and the Invention of Traditional Justice in Northern Uganda' (2007) 3(107) *Politique Africaine*, at 147, 148.

[33] France-Presse, *supra* note 12.

[34] Judgment, *Ongwen*, *supra* note 13.

[35] Allen, *supra* note 32, at 147, 148

[36] *Annual Report of the Secretary-General on Children and Armed conflict to the Security Council*, UN Doc. A/62/609 S/2007/757, 21 December 2007.

accountability.[37] Grappling with how best to present this complex narrative at the ICC and what its role might be, this next section will deal with the political and judicial function of the Court and the limits of what it can consider and adjudicate.

The Role of the ICC and the Rome Statute

Mass atrocities present a dilemma in that crimes of such a nature are inevitably seen as being both collective and individual.[38] Individuals act, but at the same time the group expresses itself in the action.[39] The established structure and hierarchy of organised groups give rise to a type of systemic criminality in which hundreds, if not thousands, of ordinary people take part.[40] Although such structures create an environment for grave crimes to occur, it is agreed that it is important to acknowledge that the crimes were indeed committed by 'men and not abstract entities' to uphold the dignity of those that had suffered.[41]

International humanitarian law (IHL) allows for the protection of child soldiers, and customary rule 136 provides that 'children must not be recruited into armed forces or armed groups'.[42] The Rome Statute itself prohibits the recruitment of child soldiers.[43] The Rome Statute also allows for the enforcement of the customary rules and considers it a source under Article 21.

[37] C. Morini,'First Victims Then Perpetrators: Child Soldiers and International Law', 3 Anuario Colombiano de Derecho Internacional (2010), at 187, 194.

[38] A. Smeulers, 'Perpetrators of International Crimes: Towards a Typology' in A. Smeulers & R. Haveman (eds), *Supranational Criminology: towards a criminology of international crimes* (Antwerp: Intersentia, 2008).

[39] G. Simpson, 'Men and Abstract Entities: Individual Responsibility and Collective Guilt in International Criminal Law' in H. van der Wilt and A. Nollkaemper (eds), *System Criminality in International Law* (Cambridge University Press, 2020), at 71.

[40] Smeulers, *supra* note 38.

[41] Nuremberg IMT, 'Judgment and sentence', 41 *American Journal of International Law* (1947) 41, at 221.

[42] Morini, *supra* note 37; Protocol Additional to the Geneva Conventions of 12 August 1949, and Relating to the Protection of Victims of Non-International Armed Conflicts (adopted 8 June 1977, entered into force 7 December 1978) 1125 UNTS 609, at Art. 4; ICRC, Customary IHL Database, available online at https://ihl-databases.icrc.org/customary-ihl/eng/docs/home (last visited 8 August 2021), Rule 136, 137.

[43] Rome Statute of the International Criminal Court (adopted 17 July 1998, entered into force 1 July 2002), 2187 UNTS 90 (hereafter Rome Statute), at Art 8(2)(b)(xxvi), Art. 8(2)(e)(vii).

The complex and large-scale nature of the crimes as well as the state actors involved, gives the ICC a unique position in that it performs both a political and legal function. Before analysing the judgment, this section will set out the normative and statutory limits that restrict the consideration of intent and responsibility.

The Expressivist Role of the ICC and its Pragmatic Considerations

The 'theatrical spectacle' of international criminal trials showcases the complex narratives that underpin the atrocities that it seeks to condemn.[44] From the situations it chooses to take cognizance of,[45] to who the investigations are requested by,[46] the ICC's case load is said to reflect its political agenda as well as that of the international community. In view of this, although the trial itself may encompass the human reckoning of a single individual, it is perceived as being an adjudication of and for the collective.[47]

International criminal trials are 'about much more than punishing the perpetrators',[48] and are trials of history and humanity. Justification of trials in recent times have turned on the 'expressivist' power of punishment, demonstrating that ICC decisions have meaning outside of their immediate consequence punishing an individual.[49] Such justification underpins the idea that these trials act as a means of 'pre-deterrence',[50] and hails international criminal judgments as mechanisms used to condemn mass

[44] Arendt, *supra* note 8, at 4–6.

[45] K. Lohne, *Advocates of Humanity: Human Rights NGOs in International Criminal Justice* (Oxford: Oxford University Press, 2019), at 219.

[46] Allen, *supra* note 32, at 147, 148.

[47] G. Simpson, 'Men and Abstract Entities: Individual Responsibility and Collective Guilt in International Criminal Law', in van der Wilt and Nollkaemper, *supra* note 39, at 73.

[48] S.-H. Song, '7th Consultative Assembly of Parliamentarians for the International Criminal Court and the Rule of Law & World Parliamentary Conference of Human Rights, International Human Rights Day 2012. Remarks at the Opening Session', ICC-CPI, 10 December 2012, available at https://www.icc-cpi.int/iccdocs/pids/statements/121210pgacap-iccspeech.pdf, (last visited 4 August 2021), at 3.

[49] B. Sander, 'The Expressive Turn of International Criminal Justice: A Field in Search of Meaning', 32 (4) *Leiden Journal of International Law* (2019), at 851, 852.

[50] Minkova, *supra* note 9, at 223.

atrocities.[51] It is said to send 'messages' by clarifying what behaviour is seen as right or wrong.[52]

In theory, trying even a few individuals for a mass atrocity would support this communication.[53] However, it leaves the apprehended few at the risk of stigmatisation from being categorically labelled as 'enemies of mankind' regardless of the relative role they played.[54] Rigid characterisation of individuals as 'victims' or 'perpetrators' as is inherent in the Western legal tradition does not easily lend itself to any nuanced discussion of the individual's agency within larger structures.[55] An increased preoccupation with determining the accused's culpability has been said to leave little room to consider the larger structural factors such as colonialism, occupation, or capitalism.[56] Local communities have been said to be less receptive of the 'messages' that such rigid distinctions send.[57] Further, judicial reasoning has also been said to take a strategic turn, with due consideration being given to the ICC and the OTP's political agenda.[58]

Such perceptions seem to demonstrate that the most essential function of the trial proceedings and indeed the judgment itself is to achieve narrative clarity. To better reflect the wrongfulness of the act, contextualising defendants is particularly important.[59] The ICC's consideration of the

[51] Sander, *supra* note 49.

[52] K. Ambos, *Treatise on International Criminal Law. Vol. 1: Foundations and General Part* (Oxford: Oxford University Press, 2013), at 72.

[53] M. Aksenova, 'Symbolism as a Constraint on International Criminal Law', 30 *Leiden Journal of International Law* (2017), at 475, 489.

[54] L. D. A Corrias and G. M. Gordon, 'Judging in the Name of Humanity: International Criminal Tribunals and the Representation of a Global Public', 13 *Journal of International Criminal Justice* (2015), at 97; I. Tallgren, 'The Voice of the International: Who is Speaking?', *Journal of International Criminal Justice* (2015) 13, at 135, 151.

[55] Drumbl, *supra* note 2, at 217.

[56] K. M. Clarke, 'The Rule of Law Through Its Economies of Appearances: The Making of the African Warlord', 18 *Indiana Journal of Global Legal Studies* (2011), at 7.

[57] M. Tripkovic, 'Not in Our Name! Visions of Community in International Criminal Justice', in M. Aksenova, E. van Sliedregt and S. Parmentier (eds), *Breaking the Cycle of Mass Atrocities: Criminological and Socio-Legal Approaches in International Criminal Law* (2019), at 165.

[58] S. M. H. Nouwen and Wouter G. Werner, 'Doing Justice to the Political: The International Criminal Court in Uganda and Sudan', *European Journal of International Law* (2010) 21, at 941; Sander, n. 48, 859.

[59] Sloane, 'The Expressive Capacity of International Punishment: The Limits of the National Law Analogy and the Potential of International Criminal Law', *Stanford Journal of International Law* (2007) 43, at 39, 65.

mens rea requirements, the defences of diminished responsibility, and Ongwen's victim-perpetrator identity, provide an interesting avenue to consider the Court's expressivist role due to the complexities it presents.

However, the ICC's more pragmatic considerations could result in greater focus of its function to end impunity by excessively emphasising Ongwen's culpability. In order to demonstrate its significance to ending impunity, the ICC has to hold at least some perpetrators to account. However, the difficulty in apprehending accused persons restricts their ability to perform this function. It has been argued that if fewer perpetrators are tried, they necessarily have to appear to be more worthy of punishment.[60] Moreover, as the ICC is dependent on state-cooperation to apprehend accused persons, it has been argued that this could lead to focussing on available defendants without due regard being given to the complex structures that they occupy.[61]

Following the consideration of the particular requirements of the Rome Statute, this chapter considers the excessive stigmatisation of Ongwen, the lack of consideration of his past as well as the ICC's socio-political role in so far as it impacts the judicial consideration.

Mens Rea *in the Rome Statute*

The ICC can hold individuals responsible for crimes under the Statute if, among other things, the requisite *mens rea* standard is met. To this end, the process of contextualising the narratives and heeding the broader interplays of structure and agency needs to adhere to definitions of intent and responsibility under Articles 30 and 25.[62]

It is essential to ascertain intent as there can be no criminal responsibility unless *mens rea* is proved under the Rome Statute.[63] Article 30 sets out both 'intent and knowledge' as necessary material elements of the offence, and lower forms such as 'recklessness' or *dolus eventualis* were kept out of the general rule.[64] The underlying premise here is that in order to 'intend'

[60] Minkova, *supra* note 9, at 223, 232.

[61] Ibid., at 223, 232.

[62] Rome Statute, *supra* note 43, at Art. 30, Art. 25.

[63] *Report of the Preparatory Committee on the Establishment of an International Criminal Court, Volume II,* UN Doc. A/51/22, 13 September 1996, at 92–93.

[64] D. Piragoff and D. Robinson, 'Article 30: Mental Element' in O. Triffterer (ed.) *Commentary on the Rome Statute of the International Criminal Court—Observer's Notes, Article by Article* (CH Beck Hart Nomos, 2nd edn., 2008), at 850.

a conduct, a person must 'mean' to engage in the act with the knowledge of the circumstances.

The modes of liability by which a person shall be 'criminally responsible and liable for punishment for a crime within the jurisdiction of the Court' are outlined in Article 25(3).[65] These various offences must be committed with intent and knowledge in order for the person to have individual criminal responsibility.[66] Article 30 also precisely applies to material elements. The accused is required to have known the *factual* elements of the offence, such as the fact that the victim was a civilian. Interpreting Article 30, the Pre-trial Chamber I ruled that the cumulative reference to 'intent' and 'knowledge' requires the existence of a volitional element of the part of the accused, and that the volitional element encompasses the three degrees of *dolus*: intent in the strict sense, oblique intent, and recklessness as to consequence.[67] If the same legal finding were to apply, to prove that Ongwen intended to commit the crimes he was charged with, it would be essential to prove that he exercised a choice and intended to act in that manner with the full knowledge of what that would result in or where he could reasonably foresee this result.

In so far as the systemic nature of the criminality affects the individual's volitional and cognitive capacities, it can only result in diminished responsibility within the confines of exclusionary grounds listed under Article 31.[68] For the circumstances of the present case, the defences of mental disease or defect under Article 31(1)(a) and duress under Article 31(1)(d) are important. As stated above, the main body of this chapter will ask the question of how far the narrative which focussed on these grounds went in contextualising Ongwen's actions.

According to Article 31(1)(a) of the ICC Statute, if a person suffers from a mental disease preventing them from 'appreciat[ing] the unlawfulness or nature' of their conduct, or their 'capacity to control the conduct to conform to the requirements of the law' has been destroyed, they shall not be held criminally responsible. A finding of a mental disease or defect

[65] Rome Statute, *supra* note 43, at Art. 25(3).

[66] M. E. Badar, 'The Mental Element in the Rome Statute of the International Criminal Court: A Commentary From a Comparative Criminal Law Perspective', *Criminal Law Forum*, (2008), at 473, 476.

[67] Decision on the confirmation of charges, *Lubanga* (ICC-01/04-01/06-803) Trial Chamber, 29 January 2007; The three degrees of *dolus* encompasses *dolus directus* of the first and second degree and *dolus eventualis*.

[68] Rome Statute, *supra* note 43, at Art. 31.

is indispensable to conclude that there is a ground excluding criminal responsibility under Article 31(1)(a) of the Statute.[69] To successfully apply this defence, the defendants need to submit themselves to psychiatric/psychological examination according to the established procedure which allows for the defence, prosecution, as well as the Court to appoint professionals.[70] With reference to the *Ongwen* trial, the defence would have had to show that a mental disease or defect had existed at the time of the crimes and that it had destroyed his capacity to control the conduct or appreciate its unlawful nature.[71] By making use of the term 'mental disease' rather than 'insanity', it appears that the State Parties intended to exclude temporary states of mind and contemplated a more persisting and substantial condition.[72] The phrase 'destroys the person's mental incapacity' has been interpreted as being 'more than merely minor' rather than as being absolute as this is not in keeping with the medical understanding of mental illness.[73]

Duress, which was also pleaded by the defence, in Article 31(1)(d) of the Statute has three elements. The first element requires that the conduct constituting the crime has been caused by duress resulting from an 'imminent threat of death or of continuing or imminent serious bodily harm against that person or another'.[74] The second element of duress in Article 31(1)(d) of the Statute is that the person acts necessarily and reasonably to avoid the threat. Finally, the third element, subjective in nature, is that the person does not intend to cause a greater harm than the one sought to be avoided.

The defence has an evidential obligation to raise the grounds for excluding criminal responsibility under Article 31(1)(a) and 31(1)(d).[75] In *Ongwen*, the decision clarified that as there was no specific provision that related to the standard of proof applicable to Article 31, the general

[69] Ibid., at Art. 31.

[70] Ibid., at Art. 55(2).

[71] Judgment, *Ongwen*, *supra* note 28, § 2454.

[72] *Report of the Preparatory Committee on the Establishment of an International Criminal Court, Volume II,* UN Doc. A/51/22, 13 September 1996.

[73] A. Eser, 'Article 31: Grounds for Excluding Criminal Responsibility' in O. Triffterer, *supra* note 64, at 875.

[74] Rome Statute, *supra* note 43, at Art. 31(1)(d).

[75] Decision on Defence Request for the Chamber to Issue an Immediate Ruling Confirming the Burden and Standard of Proof Applicable to Articles 31(1)(a) and (d) of the Rome Statute, *Ongwen* (ICC-02/04-01/15), Trial Chamber, 5 April 2019, § 15.

provisions of 'beyond reasonable doubt' would apply.[76] With reference to Article 31(1)(a), the final decision on a finding of mental disease or defect would rest with the Trial Chamber and it deemed the evidence presented during the trial to be sufficient.[77]

Applying these legal concepts to Ongwen's complex narrative, this next section will deal with Ongwen's cognitive and volitional capacities within the structures he occupied through the materials presented in court.

10.3 Presenting Ongwen's Narrative to the Court

> 'The rebel responded "If you are all civilians come out of the ditch." I was the first one to come out of the ditch. They took me out first ... The neighbour and the people I listed earlier were all taken out. The neighbour was killed instantly. My brother was also killed.'[78]
>
> (Witness P-280)

The protracted violence perpetrated by the LRA, and the immeasurable trauma suffered by survivors does not easily lend itself to measured and calm dialogue. Using the juridical space of the ICC,[79] the direct conflict between parties is converted to 'judicially regulated debate' between the legal actors emerging as the prosecution, defence, and victims. Presenting their narratives and counter-narratives, the stage is set to transport the judges into the bushes.

It is the question of Ongwen's intention and volitional and cognitive capacities that this section seeks to analyse. In the course of the proceedings, it was not in dispute that his abduction and subsequent experience within the LRA as a child are relevant to sentencing.[80] Expert evidence on the matter concerning mental disease and evidence of factual circumstances affecting duress will be considered in so far as they impact the narratives run by the parties. Using the rubric of the grounds of mental disease and duress, this section will deal with the broad case of prosecution and defence through the analysis of their briefs, expert reports, witness testimony, and closing statements.

[76] Judgment, *Ongwen*, *supra* note 28, §§ 85–93.

[77] Ibid, § 2456.

[78] Transcript, *Ongwen*, *supra* note 25, at 3.

[79] P. Bourdieu, 'The Force of Law: Towards a Sociology of the Juridical Field', 38 *Hastings Law Journal* (1987), at 226.

[80] Rome Statute, *supra* note 43, Art. 78(1).

Mental Disease or Defect

As set out in section I, for a claim of mental disease or defect to succeed, a finding of mental disease at the time of the crime needs to be made by experts. It should be evidenced that it destroyed the person's *cognitive* and *volitional* capacities.[81] Due to the novelty of this defence before the Court, and the confusion surrounding the burden of proof, the power in handling it largely rested with the Chamber itself. However, the statute allows for both the defence and the prosecution to consult experts in presenting their case to the Court.[82]

The defence submitted that Ongwen suffered from 'severe depressive illness, post-traumatic stress disorder (PTSD) [,] and dissociative disorder as well as severe suicidal ideation and high risk of committing suicide', and from 'dissociative amnesia and symptoms of obsessive-compulsive disorder'.[83] Given the uncertainty regarding the burden of proof, this section will follow the narrative of the evidence presented as it appears in the judgment.

The prosecution presented three experts: Dr. Abbo, Professor Mezey, and Professor Weierstall-Pust.[84] It is important to note here that these experts did not conduct a clinical interview of the defendant who had refused to speak to anyone except for the defence and court-appointed experts.[85] The evidence of the prosecution's experts relies on written and video evidence.[86] The validity of experts' views have been questioned by critics as they went on to present findings of Ongwen's developmental stages without ever having questioned him.[87]

Moreover, references to his time in the bush after his abduction have largely not accounted for the difference between what was usual in that environment compared to what is usual according to the Court's understanding. Professor Weierstall-Pust's reference to his abduction and time in the LRA as a single event fails to apprehend the severity and longevity

[81] Rome Statute, *supra* note 43, Art. 31(1)(a).

[82] Rome Statute, *supra* note 43, Art. 55(2).

[83] Judgment, *Ongwen*, *supra* note 28, § 2450.

[84] Ibid, § 870.

[85] Ibid, § 2464.

[86] Ibid, §§ 2464–2469.

[87] Ibid, § 2480; M. Fortuna, 'The "Mental Disorder" Defence in Prosecutor v. Ongwen', Blog of Groningen Journal of International Law, 16 February 2021 available at https://grojil.org/2021/02/16/the-mental-disorder-defence-in-prosecutor-v-ongwen/ (last visited 8 August 2021).

of his experience. In her evidence on PTSD, Professor Mezey states that symptoms of such a disorder would be severe and intrusive in a manner that would stop the individual from carrying out everyday functions without reference to the factors to life in the bush.[88] Although Dr. Abbo makes reference to ecological factors, her evidence makes assumptions about his moral development at early stages of his life.[89] All three experts testified that *from the information they had been given*, Ongwen cannot be said to have suffered from any such mental disease or defect at the time of the violence.[90]

The defence for its case presented two experts: Professor Ovuga and Dr. Akena. Their reports were based on clinical interviews of the defendant and four of his closest associates.[91] From this, the experts conclude that Ongwen suffered from severe depressive illness, PTSD, and dissociative disorder.[92] In their opinion, such mental disease destroyed his capacity such that he could not be held criminally liable. They based a majority of their findings on clinical interviews and relied on DSM-IV.

However, they presented these symptoms as being intermittent. For example, in the Second Report, the experts concluded that his feelings of sadness had been persistent for years and then went on to describe certain clinical interviews with him being happy and cheerful.[93] They later went on to explain that this behaviour was to 'mask his symptoms' and was known as 'reaction formation' to cope with difficult circumstances.[94] Explaining the lack of corroboration, Ovuga explained that '[in Uganda] we explain our psychological distress in terms of the effects of spirits, ancestral spirits.'[95]

In the closing statements, the defence counsel suggested that Ongwen exists in an arrested stage of development, and continually referred to him

[88] Transcript of Evidence of Witness P-0446, *Ongwen* (ICC-02/04-01/15), Trial Chamber, 21, lines 9–19.

[89] Judgment, n. 9, § 2481.

[90] Professor Mezey Report UGA-OTP-0280-0786, *Ongwen* (ICC-02/04-01/15), Trial Chamber, 0811-0812; Judgment, n. 9, §§ 2483, 2489.

[91] Professor Ovuga and Dr. Akena's First Report UGA-D-26-0015-0004, *Ongwen* (ICC-02/04-01/15), Trial Chamber, §§ 0004-5, 0020-23.

[92] Professor Ovuga and Dr. Akena's First Report, *Ongwen, supra* note 91, § 0017.

[93] Professor Ovuga and Dr. Akena's Second Report UGA-D26-0015-0948, *Ongwen* (ICC-02/04-01/15), Trial Chamber, 0951, 0961-62.

[94] Transcript, *Ongwen, supra* note 28, at 13.

[95] Ibid, at 15.

as 'that boy'.[96] Earlier the defence counsel had also argued that only the defence experts had taken a holistic approach and considered the LRA coercion. These circumstances alongside the disorder left him with no free will.[97] For its part, the prosecution argued that 'destroyed' in Article 31(1)(a) should be interpreted as being 'impossible to piece together'.[98] Making use of Ongwen's clinical interview, they suggest that these instances of having a moral compass show that his capacity had not been 'destroyed',[99] pointing to evidence of child soldiers who were able to escape making elaborate plans. This, alongside the transcripts of telephone calls with a witness following his arrest, during which he plotted to have his wives visit him and boasted about being the most clever man in Acholi, demonstrate that Ongwen was both charming and 'a schemer', and disprove of the defence's narrative that he had retained a childish mentality.[100] Moreover, there were no accounts of any abnormal behaviour described as possession to substantiate the defence experts claim.[101] The victims' counsel emphasised that the mere existence of emotional or psychological difficulties did not absolve Ongwen of legal responsibility as it was not sufficiently demonstrated that his cognitive and volitional capabilities were destroyed.[102]

Both the prosecution's narrative as well as the defence's counter-narrative offer a simplistic view of mental defect or disease. Where the prosecution's account is entirely dismissive of the circumstances within which these actions were performed and the effect they would have had on him psychologically, the defence's account infantilised him and failed to address the prosecution's counter-narrative while proving that his cognitive and volitional abilities were destroyed. Before considering the Chamber's view, a similar analysis of the narratives around duress will be conducted.

[96] Ibid, 12 March 2020.

[97] Defence Closing Brief, n. 1 Public Redacted Version of 'Corrected Version of "Defence Closing Brief" filed on 24 February 2020', *Ongwen* (ICC-02/04-01/15), Trial Chamber, 13 March 2020, § 529.

[98] Transcript, *Ongwen* (ICC-02/04-01/15), Trial Chamber, 10 March 2020, at 53.

[99] Ibid, at 54.

[100] Ibid, at 56.

[101] Ibid, at 61.

[102] Ibid, at 45.

Duress

Presented at the ICC at the start of the trial proceedings, Ongwen asked if they 'believed [his] life had been ruined'.[103] The defence argued that the structure of the LRA deprived him of the unrestricted exercise of his free will as he was under 'continuing threat of imminent death and serious bodily harm from Kony and his controlling military apparatus'.[104] They argued that the imminent threat was maintained through a combination of 'strict disciplinary rules', 'tight supervision of commanders', and 'assertion of spiritual powers'.[105] On the other hand, the prosecution argued that there was no evidence presented to the Chamber that the conduct was caused by such threat.[106] The burden of proof to raise and prove a ground of exclusion of criminal responsibility lay with the defence.

Although either ground would have served as complete defences, it was the defence's contention that there is a relationship between the defence of mental incapacity and duress.[107] The symptoms of both resulted in Ongwen having no free will and acting completely under duress.[108] The prosecution countered this by arguing that mental illness that satisfies the requirements of both Article 31(1)(a) and 31(1)(d) cannot co-exist. Where the former requires that mental capacity be destroyed, the latter requires the individual to act in a manner that is 'reasonable and necessary'.[109] In that regard, only if the first defence fails can the second be pursued.

Escape from the LRA was claimed to be nearly impossible as per the defence's evidence on failed attempts being punished by death. Moreover, Kony's spiritual ideology added an element of duress.[110] In response to this, the prosecution argued that if the *actus reus* of a crime had been committed under duress, one would reasonably expect the individual to take steps in the aftermath to escape the threat. Moreover, they contend that

[103] Ibid, 6 December 2016.

[104] *Ongwen (*Public Redacted Version of 'Corrected Version of "Defence Closing Brief" filed on 24 February 2020'), § 680.

[105] Ibid, §§ 681–722.

[106] Public Redacted Version of "Prosecution Closing Brief", *Ongwen* (ICC-02/04-01/15-1719-Red), Trial Chamber, 24 February 2020, § 472.

[107] Transcript, *Ongwen*, *supra* note 28, at 62.

[108] Public Redacted Version of 'Corrected Version of "Defence Closing Brief" filed on 24 February 2020', *Ongwen* (ICC-02/04-01/15), Trial Chamber, 13 March 2020, § 529.

[109] Transcript, *Ongwen*, *supra* note 28, at 62.

[110] Ibid, at 43.

there were many opportunities for Ongwen to escape following the example of many LRA members. Witness D-134 testified that 'LRA fighters would escape every day'.[111] Further, intercept evidence suggested that although Kony and Otti were frustrated by escapees, it did not move them to violence.[112] Moreover, ignoring the threat and crime-specific nature of the elements, the defence's case was scattered and broad in its claim of duress. It also made no mention of the specific factors that formed a part of each crime.[113]

However, the victims' counsel argued that Ongwen's recruitment as a child soldier did not constitute a ground for exclusion of criminal responsibility. They found that this argument was disrespectful of the sufferings of victims.[114] They also submitted that these crimes corresponded to acts that Ongwen chose to commit as an adult, after rising through the ranks of the LRA.[115] Ongwen's persistent instigation of attacks negated duress.[116] In their view, the 'exceptional magnitude' of the crimes of which Ongwen was convicted and the presence of several aggravating circumstances 'neutralise any limited impact that the defence is portraying as mitigating factors'.[117]

Having considered the narratives run by all the parties with regard to the issues of mental defect and duress, this next section will analyse the judgment and consider how far it considered the narratives of Ongwen and other parties.

10.4 Justice for the Victim-Perpetrator Duality

Speaking at the time of his surrender to the US Armed Forces, Ongwen, almost symbolically dubbed the 'White Ant' by the LRA, said:

> Each of us sin in words, deeds, and thoughts. Each of us sin in different ways. If I committed a crime through war, I am sorry. In my mind, I thought

[111] Ibid, at 60.

[112] Ibid, at 61.

[113] Ibid, at 65.

[114] Ibid, at 43.

[115] Victim's Joint Submission on Sentencing, *Ongwen* (ICC-02/04-01/15), Trial Chamber, 1 April 2021, § 88.

[116] Transcript, *Ongwen*, *supra* note 28, 11 March 2020, at 45.

[117] Victim's Joint Submission on Sentencing, *Ongwen* (ICC-02/04-01/15), Trial Chamber, 1 April 2021, § 82.

> war was the best thing … I have become like a lice, which you remove from your hair or waist and kill without any resistance.[118]

The duality of roles played by Ongwen in this story was something that captured the attention of the global community much before he ever set foot in Court.[119] This section will discuss how far the judgment delved into this duality and considered how it affected those involved. Although multiple actors within the Court put forth their understanding of the narrative, such as the psychiatrists, defence, and prosecution counsels, it is ultimately the judge and the judgment with whom the power of the narrative rests.

Considering the Chamber's analysis of the two grounds for diminished criminal responsibility, this section will analyse if these novel arguments have furthered the narrative. Critically assessing whether the complexities of narrative, structure, and agency were addressed, it will analyse if the judgment furthered the protection of victim-perpetrators such as child soldiers.

Destruction of Mental Capacity

The first key element of the defence's case was whether a finding of mental disease and a destruction of cognitive and volitional capacities could be made. This section will analyse the judgment in so far as it deals with this ground and assess whether the judicial reasoning succeeds in providing a more considered approach of the circumstances. The broader clinical and psychological issues are outside the scope of this chapter. This section will focus on the judgment's assessment of key points of contention between the prosecution and defence.

In assessing the expert reports, the Chamber reiterated its limitations under the Statute and stated that 'an assessment of mental health cannot be made in the abstract'.[120] To this end, the Chamber looked to accounts of visible manifestations of the symptoms of his mental diseases seemingly based on the report of Professor Mezey.[121] Despite objections from the

[118] News Correspondent, 'Dominic speaks out on why he quit the LRA', Daily Monitor, 18 January 2015, available at https://www.monitor.co.ug/uganda/news/national/ongwen-speaks-out-on-why-he-quit-lra-1597490, (last visited 9 August 2021).

[119] Drumbl, *supra* note 2, at 217.

[120] Judgment, *Ongwen*, *supra* note 13, § 2497.

[121] Ibid, § 2498.

defence about the cultural relativism on how these symptoms would have been viewed as spiritual possession by the LRA, the Chamber found that no such evidence was available as there were no accounts of any abnormality in his behaviour.[122]

Moreover, the extensive planning required to successfully carry out complex operations was found to be 'incompatible with a mental disorder'.[123] The testimony of his wives was considered by the Chamber but was held to be outside of the period corresponding to the charges.[124] However, testimony of LRA members was considered despite defence arguing that they were unreliable on this issue as they were victims themselves. The Chamber relied on witness testimony from LRA members as many had been able to give detailed and credible testimonies of their time in the bush.[125] This qualified treatment of both the defence's arguments as well as the evidence has invited the inference that the Chamber qualified the applicable rules only with reference to the evidence supportive of the defence's counter-narrative.[126]

In so far as the defence experts held that his capacity was destroyed such that he would not be criminally liable, the Chamber found this finding to be beyond the scope of their roles.[127] The Chamber also highlighted methodological issues they had with the evidence. It found that there was a loss of objectivity as the experts also served as treating physicians to Ongwen.[128] The Chamber sided with the prosecution in finding that the defence experts failed to apply scientifically validated methods and tools, such as using the DSM-IV instead of the DSM-V and not using structured rating scales.[129] The Chamber also dismissed the report's findings as being very general and 'not clearly anchored on the relevant period'.[130] Contradictions in the experts' witness testimony and their reports pertaining to issues such as Ongwen 'masking his symptoms', which further

[122] Ibid, § 2501.

[123] Ibid, § 2521.

[124] Transcript of Evidence of Witness P-0142, *Ongwen* (ICC-02/04-01/15), Trial Chamber, 16, lines 2–22; Judgment, *Ongwen, supra* note 13, § 2519.

[125] Judgment, *Ongwen, supra* note 28, § 2504; Judgment, *Ongwen, supra* note 13, § 2519.

[126] J. Koleski, 'Narratives of (In)Justice: Faulty Historical Narratives and Bias in the Case of The Prosecutor v. Dominic Ongwen At the International Criminal Court' (Thesis on file at Kent State University, Ohio), at 44.

[127] Judgment, *Ongwen, supra* note 13, § 2524.

[128] Ibid, § 2531.

[129] Ibid, §§ 2532–2533.

[130] Ibid, § 2569.

affected the credibility of the defence experts.[131] The possibility that Ongwen could have 'faked' his symptoms and the defence experts' lack of engagement with the specific crimes committed or with the evidence at trial were factors in the Chamber's decision not to rely on the defence experts' testimony.[132]

The prosecution's evidence suffered from various drawbacks such as a lack of any direct interaction with the accused and failing to consider the conditions of life in the bush. Further, some of the prosecution's evidence also relied on the testimony of his wives taken before the relevant period.[133] Failing to identify and explore these drawbacks in the prosecution's evidence, the Chamber found the expert reports to be 'pertinent', 'impressive', and 'entirely convincing'.[134]

Although the defence experts' evidence suffered from serious drawbacks, a lack of consideration of the drawbacks in the prosecution's expert reports failed to provide a clear narrative of the evidence available. A clear statement by the court for its reliance on certain evidence and addressing the counter-arguments put forth by the defence would have gone a long way in establishing a clear narrative in the judgment and clarifying the court's stance on the larger question of child soldiers being tried as perpetrators for crimes committed as adults.

Interplay of Structure and Agency

Interpreting the three elements of duress as under Article 31(1)(d) and outlined in section I, the Chamber took a literal approach. It stated that 'merely abstract danger or simply an elevated probability that a dangerous situation might occur' would not satisfy the requirement. The other two elements, namely that the person acts reasonably to avoid the threat and does not intend to cause greater harm than that avoided, were not addressed by the Chamber as it held that the first element had not been met.[135]

Grappling with the defence's narrative, the Chamber found that although the mechanisms that the LRA used to ensure obedience were

[131] Ibid, § 2537.
[132] Ibid, §§ 2556–2576.
[133] Ibid, § 2519.
[134] Ibid, §§ 2478, 2485, 2496.
[135] Rome Statute, *supra* note 43, at Art. 31(1)(d); Judgment, *Ongwen*, *supra* note 13, § 2585.

brutal, they were differently employed against low-ranking soldiers and commanders.[136] Although it recognised the structured and hierarchical nature of the LRA, it found that the organisation was not completely under the control of Kony and required the cooperation of commanders.[137] Further, it denied the relevance of his having been a child soldier under Article 31(1)(d) as it did not pertain to the time of the charges.[138] To solidify its position, the Chamber utilises part of witness P-0231's testimony wherein a few instances of Ongwen's insubordination are outlined.[139] Larger parts of the testimony that bore witness to the targeting of commanders who disobeyed and the killing of those who did not follow Kony's commands were downplayed.[140] This was characterised as being unreliable in the face of the prosecution's abundant evidence to the contrary.[141] Interestingly, the Chamber did not make reference to ICTY jurisprudence on child soldiers or duress.[142] Such difference in the narrative of structure and agency in the judgment has been interpreted as showcasing the Chamber's 'prosecutorial impulse'.[143]

The Chamber compared Ongwen's position in the hierarchy with that of other commanders that had been killed by Kony, such as Odonga and Lagony. It concluded that their case was decidedly different as they wanted to challenge Kony's power for the leadership.[144] However, the evidence of witness D-0032 contradicts the finding and states that they were executed for wanting to defect.[145] It also found that Ongwen's rank would have made it easier to leave, and the fact that he did not is further evidence that

[136] Judgment, *Ongwen, supra* note 13, § 2590.

[137] Ibid, § 2590.

[138] Ibid, § 2592.

[139] Transcript of Evidence of P-0231, *Ongwen* (ICC-02/04-01/15-T-123-Red2-ENG), Trial Chamber, 2 November 2017, 84 lines 8–9.

[140] Ibid., at 83, lines 23–25.

[141] Judgment, *Ongwen, supra* note 13, § 2601.

[142] Judgment, *The Prosecutor v. Dražen Erdemovć* (IT-96-22), Trial Chamber, 28 November 1996; Sentencing Judgment, *The Prosecutor v. Issa Hassan Sesay, Morris Kallon and Augustine Gbao* (SCSL-04-15-T), Trial Chamber, 8 April 2009, § 220.

[143] M. A. Drumbl, 'Shifting Narratives: Ongwen and Lubanga on the Effects of Child Soldiering', Justice Conflict, 20 April 2016, available at https://justiceinconflict.org/2016/04/20/shifting-narratives-ongwen-and-lubanga-on-the-effects-of-child-soldiering/ (last visited 8 August 2021).

[144] Judgment, *Ongwen, supra* note 13, § 2609.

[145] Transcript of Evidence of D-0032, *Ongwen* (ICC-02/04-01/15-T-199-Red-ENG), Trial Chamber, 19 February 2019, 31, lines 9–12.

he was not under duress.[146] This was substantiated with examples of others in similar positions who had managed to escape during the period pertaining to the charges.[147] Although this evidence is substantiated and reliable, it ignores the numerous examples of those killed for attempting to defect.[148]

Discussing the duress due to Kony's spiritual powers and its influence over him due to his victim-perpetrator identity, the Chamber found that while this belief was stronger in the abductees, it subsided on long-term soldiers.[149] It also found that the relationship between Ongwen and Kony was positive. Ignoring evidence of Kony's threat to Ongwen's life, the Court focussed on the evidence that the former praised the latter for his hard work.[150] Finally, in its finding concerning sexual offences committed by Ongwen in private, it found the prosecution's argument that he could have chosen not to commit these crimes when in private to be persuasive. The Chamber's finding in this regard turns on the fact that crimes of such nature are considered aggravating factors and a higher threshold would accordingly apply.

Ultimately, the Chamber found that 'Ongwen's personal background [by no means] overshadows his culpable conduct and the suffering of the victims'.[151] It found that the circumstances surrounding his abduction were relevant among other factors and should be considered while sentencing. However, they agreed with the victims that he *fully intended* as an adult to commit the crimes.[152] Although giving additional weight to his personal circumstances might be construed as depriving the victims of their dignity, the lack of discussion of or weight being given to his circumstances as well as failing to address the defence's arguments has hampered narrative clarity. This final section of the chapter argues that a fulfilment of the broader expressivist function calls for the presentation of a more complex narrative to the world. Using Ongwen as a case study, this section envisages how the Chamber might have done this.

[146] Judgment, *Ongwen, supra* note 13, § 2619.
[147] Ibid, §§ 2623–2628.
[148] Ibid, § 917.
[149] Ibid, § 2645.
[150] Ibid, §§ 2660–2663.
[151] Sentence, *Ongwen*, *supra* note 17, § 389; Partially Dissenting Opinion of Judge Raul C. Pangalangan, *Ongwen*, (ICC-02/04-01/15-1819-Anx 06-05-2021), Trial Chamber, 6 May 2021, § 16.
[152] Sentence, *Ongwen*, *supra* note 17, § 385.

Presenting a Complex Narrative to the World

The reality of conflicts is hard to capture in any courtroom, let alone one so removed from the culture and ideology of the scene of the crime. To better capture this reality, it is important to more centrally connect the LRA and its structure to how this dictates the actions of the members. Although limited by the Statute, such analysis would have helped achieve the larger expressivist function of pre-deterrence and clarifying what is acceptable conduct. Moreover, viewing perpetrators as being 'intrinsically evil people' has been seen to be both inaccurate as well as problematic. Pinpointing the type of behaviour which deserves the label of 'enemies of humankind' would go further in contextualising and not stigmatizing the accused while providing clarity on the conduct actually being condemned by the global community. Arguing for a presentation of a more complex narrative to the world, this section will deal with this in two parts: presenting a more nuanced understanding of 'victims' and 'perpetrators' and giving more judicial consideration to the questions of mental disease and duress.

A simple black-and-white discourse as presented in the judgment allows the ICC to legitimise its own power as the 'saviour'.[153] This power exists at various levels and was clearly showcased in Pre-Trial Chamber's (PTC) decision on the confirmation of charges.[154] The PTC dismissed both his background as a child soldier and any defence of duress and was reluctant to consider that it would have in any way diminished his responsibility. Although this could be attributed to a concern of opening up the floodgates to such defences, the ICC is perceived as using the trial to fulfil its duty to end impunity and hold perpetrators to account.[155] The Court's intervention was also seen as being unhelpful by aid workers, particularly to the interests of abducted children.[156] It is important for judgements to give a voice to individuals trapped within a discourse and to clarify the structures that control and create the binaries of victim and perpetrator.[157] Such is the case of a child soldier, further oppressed and stigmatised as a

[153] Simpson, "Anti-death League" (2018) Queen Margaret University, at 1, 12.

[154] Decision on Confirmation of Charges, *Ongwen* (ICC-02/04-01/15), Pre-Trial Chamber, 23 March 2016, §§ 150–156.

[155] Allen, *supra* note 32, at 147, 151.

[156] Ibid, at 147, 151.

[157] M. Foucault, *Discipline and Punish: The Birth of the Prison* (Sheridan tr, Vintage Books, 2nd edn., 1995), at 505.

result of the judgment. Although such an approach would not lead the Court to a decidedly different finding on Ongwen's criminal responsibility, it would go a long way in recognising its own power in controlling the narrative.

The expressivist function of the ICC, as outlined in section I, makes the consideration of both moral and criminal guilt increasingly relevant to the role it plays in the larger political arena. The highly complex nature of the problem being dealt with by the Court is reflected in the myriad of emotions it invokes in the victims of the LRA and Ongwen. Deeply aware of the collective nature of the crime, some of the victims themselves identify Ongwen as a victim of the LRA and Kony and that a refusal to accept the wives he was given would have gotten him killed.[158] The recognition of these existing narratives, separate to the individual case of Ongwen, within the written judgment would lead to a diffusion in the binaries of power and in the contextualising of victim-perpetrators such as child soldiers. Although international criminal law hinges on the idea of individual criminal responsibility, clarifying and edifying the existing narratives in a complex and protracted conflict would help with the development of international humanitarian law. This might also help child soldiers and others to engage with local courts and reintegrate into their local communities.[159]

Second, a greater degree of consideration should have been given to the defences of mental disease and duress. Although this would not change the ultimate finding, it would demonstrate a more nuanced understanding of the situation in Northern Uganda which local communities would be more receptive to.[160]

Further, the Statute does not specifically mention the jurisprudence of other international criminal tribunals as applicable law;[161] however, in practice, the Court has made substantial reference to the jurisprudence of the ICTY and the ICTR. Viewing the substantial legal findings of these tribunals as 'highly persuasive', the ICC relied on them heavily in

[158] J. Atingo, 'Watching the ICC Judgement of LRA commander Dominic Ongwen with Ugandan victims of enforced marriage', Africa at LSE, 17 February 2021, available at https://blogs.lse.ac.uk/africaatlse/2021/02/17/watching-icc-judgement-lra-commander-dominic-ongwen-uganda-victims-rape-marriage/ (last visited 8 August 2021).

[159] Baines, *supra* note at 163, at 185.

[160] Minkova, *supra* note 9, at 223, 224.

[161] Rome Statute, *supra* note 43, Art. 21.

Lubanga.[162] The judgment itself does not heed earlier jurisprudence on child soldiers in its discussion of duress, dismissing this fact as irrelevant. However, ICL jurisprudence recognises the need for their protection. In *Lubanga*, the ICC held that there was a clear linkage between a child soldier's past and present. It was seen as an ongoing process and not as a single event.[163] In Ongwen, however, the linkage between the accused's past as a child soldier and his present as a former child soldier was seen as discontinuous and contingent on circumstances by the PTC. Referring to the SCSL's judgement in *Sesay*, the Chamber could have qualified its reasoning. Sesay's recruitment into the Revolutionary United Front at the age of 19 was said not to mitigate the crimes which he later committed in that it 'consider[ed] he could well have chosen another path'.[164] Using this to uphold its expressivist function, the Chamber could have reasoned that the age of recruitment is immaterial based on the gravity of the crimes, the length of Ongwen's service, and the rank to which he rose.

Similarly, the Chamber makes no reference to the only other international criminal trial that considered the defence of mental incapacity on grounds of PTSD: *Celibići*.[165] As in *Ongwen*, five psychiatrists examined Landzo, one of the defendants, and while four concluded that he suffered from some impairment, the other did not. Here, the ICTY interpreted the ground as requiring that his ability to control his actions should be 'substantially impaired'. Although the finding of PTSD failed, the Chamber accepted that he suffered from a personality disorder which did not, however, impair his ability to control his actions.[166] Although the case is significantly different owing to the difference in the ICTY and ICC Statutes, it would have assisted the Chamber in examining the methodology and practices of presenting psychiatric evidence.

[162] A. Z. Borda, 'Precedent in International Criminal Courts and Tribunals', 2(2) *Cambridge Journal of International Comparative Law* (2013), at 287, 304.

[163] Decision on Sentence pursuant to Article 76 of the Statute, *Lubanga* (ICC-01/04-01/06-2901), Trial Chamber, 13 July 2012, §§ 39–42.

[164] Sentencing Judgment, *Prosecutor v. Issa Hassan Sesay, Morris Kallon, Augustine Gbao* (SCSL-04-15-T), Trial Chamber, 8 April 2009, § 220.

[165] Judgment, *Zejnil Delalić, Zdravko Mucić also know as "Pavo", Hazim Delić and Essad Landžo also known as "Zenga"*, (IT-96-21), Trial Chamber,16 November 1998.

[166] Ibid.

10.5 Conclusion

The purpose of international criminal trials is varied and stretches from its judicial function to a broader expressivist sense. Although seemingly a day of reckoning for one individual, the trial takes on different shapes underscoring the political and moral impact. However, in trying to establish a dominant narrative each party tells a complex story which comes together in the judgment. Analysing this through the trial proceedings and judgment of *Ongwen*, this chapter asked the question of how far the novel narrative of mental disease and duress went in contextualising the accused and his circumstances.

Setting out the background of *Ongwen* and his victim-perpetrator identity in section I, the chapter identified the issues identified by the defence in contextualising Ongwen: mental incapacity and duress. It then went on to explore the role of the ICC and its political/moral and judicial function. Although limited by its statutory requirements, the ICC has a larger claim to control over the narrative as ICL is increasingly being viewed through the lens of strategic expressivism or communicative power. Setting out the statutory requirements as under Article 31(1)(a) and 31(1)(d), the chapter identified the elements to be satisfied by the narratives put forth.

Using the rubric of these requirements, section II carefully analysed the narratives of the prosecution, defence, and to a certain extent the victims. Making use of expert evidence, testimony, briefs, and closing statements, the narratives asserted by each party is analysed in so far as it concerns the grounds of mental incapacity or duress. Following the debate within the juridical space, it makes a preliminary assessment of the drawbacks and counter-arguments.

The Chamber has final control over the narrative, and through the written judgment demonstrates its power in choosing to consider and weigh evidence as it sees fit. Analysing the judicial reasoning for both identified grounds, the paper infers a certain prosecutorial impulse. From downplaying the existence of any 'links' to his past as a child soldier to failing to consider the social and historical circumstances in full, the Court has failed to appreciate Ongwen's unique position within ICL as a victim-perpetrator. By controlling the narrative thus, the ICC emphasises its role in holding perpetrators to account and highlights its pragmatic considerations. It concludes by demonstrating that contextualising the suffering could have been better achieved through presenting a more nuanced understanding of the evidence available as well as a more in-depth consideration of the grounds identified.

An approach that does not consider the context at length not only fails to deter such atrocities in the future because it asserts that they could not be carried out by 'ordinary' human beings, but it also fails victims and perpetrators by not showcasing their narrative. The interplay of these complex narratives and the myriad emotions it brings up will be the only 'truth' and justice these victims of mass atrocities will ever know, and presenting this with narrative clarity will go a long way in the development of international humanitarian law.

GPSR Compliance
The European Union's (EU) General Product Safety Regulation (GPSR) is a set of rules that requires consumer products to be safe and our obligations to ensure this.

If you have any concerns about our products, you can contact us on

ProductSafety@springernature.com

In case Publisher is established outside the EU, the EU authorized representative is:

Springer Nature Customer Service Center GmbH
Europaplatz 3
69115 Heidelberg, Germany

www.ingramcontent.com/pod-product-compliance
Ingram Content Group UK Ltd.
Pitfield, Milton Keynes, MK11 3LW, UK
UKHW020835290926
15470UKWH00004B/1350

9783031459931